Teach
Yourself
C

in 24 Hours

Teach Yourself

C

in 24 Hours

Tony Zhang

SAMS
PUBLISHING

201 West 103rd Street
Indianapolis, Indiana 46290

To Ellen, my lovely wife, for her love and inspiration.
—Tony Zhang

Copyright © 1997 by Sams Publishing

FIRST EDITION

International Standard Book Number: 0-672-31068-6

Library of Congress Catalog Card Number: 97-65466

2000   99   98   4   3

Interpretation of the printing code: the rightmost double-digit number is the year of the book's printing; the rightmost single-digit, the number of the book's printing. For example, a printing code of 97-1 shows that the first printing of the book occurred in 1997.

Composed in AGaramond and MCPdigital by Macmillan Computer Publishing

Printed in the United States of America

President, Sams Publishing   Richard K. Swadley
Publishing Manager   Greg Wiegand
Director of Editorial Services   Cindy Morrow
Managing Editor   Kitty Wilson Jarrett
Director of Marketing   Kelli Spencer
Product Marketing Manager   Wendy Gilbride
Assistant Marketing Managers   Jen Pock, Rachel Wolfe

Acquisitions Editor
Sharon Cox

Development Editor
Fran Hatton

Software Development Specialist
Brad Myers

Production Editors
Mary Ann Abramson
Kitty Wilson Jarrett

Copy Editor
Kimberly K. Hannel

Indexer
Benjamin Slen

Technical Reviewer
Karen Hay

Editorial Coordinators
Mandi Rouell
Katie Wise

Technical Edit Coordinator
Lynette Quinn

Editorial Assistants
Carol Ackerman
Andi Richter
Rhonda Tinch-Mize

Cover Designer
Tim Amrhein

Book Designer
Gary Adair

Copy Writer
David Reichwein

Production Team Supervisors
Brad Chinn
Charlotte Clapp

Production
Georgiana Briggs
Cyndi Davis
Sonja Hart
Mary Ellen Stephenson

Overview

Contents

Acknowledgments

Several years ago, my friend Joey Burton, who was then my supervisor at Kinley Corporation, asked me why many computer programming books were written in a way that set a deep learning curve and scared a lot of beginners away from learning programming languages. Joey, thank you for the question that became the motivation for me to write a computer book for beginners. Today I can proudly say that there is at least one book available for people who want to learn C, but have no previous programming experience.

It's said that editors and authors are friends. I couldn't agree more. Sharon Cox and Fran Hatton at Sams Publishing are my friends, and they have given me a lot of encouragement and help in every phase of the book's creation.

I'd also like to thank my other friends, Mary Ann Abramson, Kitty Wilson Jarrett, Kim Hannel, Karen Hay, and the other members of the editorial team at Sams. It would not have been possible to finish the book without their hard work. The readers of this book are very lucky to have this team, who is committed to producing high-quality books.

I greatly appreciate the love and support of my wife, Ellen, who has inspired me to look at the high-tech world from a different perspective. It's always a great joy to discuss issues of philosophy and literature with her. I wish I could sit in her class at Temple University.

My parents, whom I can *never* thank enough, gave me not only love and affection, but also the opportunity to receive the best education I could ever have when I was in China.

About the Author

Tony Zhang is a software engineer with more than 15 years of computer programming experience. Besides application-level programming experience in GUI, client/server, database, and networking, Tony has enhanced his system-level programming skills for X86 microprocessors and advanced digital signal/image processors through his involvement on various projects. With a masters degree in physics, he has published dozens of research papers on solid-state lasers, light-scattering calculations, and computer programming.

Tony and his wife, Ellen, are currently working on a book that combines two fields: computer science and philosophy. Among his broad interests are painting and photography, the two things that Tony enjoys most.

You can reach Tony through Sams Publishing, or by e-mailing him at `tt-zhang@ti.com`.

Tell Us What You Think!

As a reader, you are the most important critic and commentator of our books. We value your opinion and want to know what we're doing right, what we could do better, what areas you'd like to see us publish in, and any other words of wisdom you're willing to pass our way. You can help us make strong books that meet your needs and give you the computer guidance you require.

Do you have access to CompuServe or the World Wide Web? Then check out our CompuServe forum by typing **GO SAMS** at any prompt. If you prefer the World Wide Web, check out our site at http://www.mcp.com.

 NOTE

> If you have a technical question about this book, call the technical support line at 317-581-4669.

As the team leader of the group that created this book, I welcome your comments. You can fax, e-mail, or write me directly to let me know what you did or didn't like about this book—as well as what we can do to make our books stronger. Here's the information:

Fax: 317-581-4669

E-mail: programming_mgr@sams.mcp.com

Mail: Greg Wiegand
         Comments Department
         Sams Publishing
         201 W. 103rd Street
         Indianapolis, IN 46290

Introduction

If one learns from others but does not think, one will be bewildered;
if one thinks but does not learn from others, one will be in peril.

—*Confucius*

Written in a plain and clear format, this book is designed to help you learn the C programming language as quickly as possible.

Unlike most other C books, this book offers many sample programs and exercises with clear explanations and answers, which makes the concepts of the C language easier to be understood. After reading this book, you'll be able to write C programs on your own.

Teach Yourself C in 24 Hours lays a solid groundwork for you in C programming. You will profit from this when you start to apply C programs to real problems or move on to learn other programming languages, such as Perl, C++, and Java.

Who Should Read This Book?

If this is your initial introduction to C, this book is written for you. In fact, in writing this book I assume that my reader has no previous programming experience. Of course, it's always a big plus if you have some knowledge of computers.

Special Features of This Book

This book contains the following special elements that make it simpler and clearer for you to digest the rudimentary features and concepts of C as they are introduced:

- [ ] Syntax boxes
- [ ] Notes
- [ ] Warnings
- [ ] Tips

Syntax boxes explain some of the more complicated features of C, such as control structures. Each syntax box consists of a formal definition of the feature followed by an explanation. Here is an example of a syntax box:

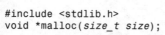

The syntax for the `malloc()` function is

```
#include <stdlib.h>
void *malloc(size_t size);
```

Here, `size` specifies the number of bytes of storage to allocate. The header file, `stdlib.h`, has to be included before the `malloc()` function can be called. Because the `malloc()` function returns a `void` pointer, its type is automatically converted to the type of pointer on the left side of an assignment operator.

(You'll learn more about the `malloc()` function later in the book.)

Notes are explanations of interesting properties of a particular C program feature. Let's have a look at the following example of a note:

NOTE

> In left-justified output, the value being displayed appears at the left end of the value field. In right-justified output, the value being displayed appears at the right end of the value field.

Warnings alert you to programming pitfalls you should avoid. Here is a typical warning:

TIP

> Never use the reserved keywords in C, or names of the C library functions as variable names in your program.

Tips are hints on how to write better C programs. The following is an example of a tip:

WARNING

> Using global variables increases your program's complexity, which in turn makes your program hard to maintain or debug. Generally, you're not advised to declare and use global variables unless they're absolutely necessary.

Programming Examples

As mentioned earlier, this book contains many useful programming examples with explanations. These examples are meant to show you how to use different data types and functions provided in C.

Each example has a listing of the C program; the output generated from that listing will follow. The example also offers an analysis of how the program works. Special icons are used to point out each part of the example: Type, Input/Output, and Analysis.

In the example shown in Listing IN.1, there are some special typographic conventions. The input you enter is shown in bold monospace type, and the output generated by the executable program of Listing IN.1 is shown in plain monospace type. The system prompt (`c:\app>` in the examples in this book) is also shown so that you know when a command is to be entered on the command line.

TYPE **Listing IN.1 Read in a character entered by the user.**

```
1:   /* INL01.c: Read input by calling getc() */
2:   #include <stdio.h>
3:
4:   main()
5:   {
6:       int ch;
7:
8:       printf("Please type in one character:\n");
9:       ch = getc(stdin);
10:      printf("The character you just entered is: %c\n", ch);
11:      return 0;
12: }
```

The following output is displayed after the executable file INL01.exe is created and run. The user enters the H character.

```
C:\app> INL01
Please type in one character:
H
The character you just entered is: H
C:\app>
```

In line 2 of Listing IN.1, the header file stdio.h is included for both the getc() and printf() functions used in the program. Lines 4–12 give the name and body of the main() function.

In line 6, an integer variable ch is declared, which is assigned to the return value from the getc() function later in line 9. Line 8 prints out a message that asks the user to enter one character from the keyboard. The printf() function in line 8 uses the default standard output stdout to display messages on the screen.

In line 9, the standard input stdin is passed to the getc() function, which indicates that the file stream is from the keyboard. After the user types in a character, the getc() function returns the numeric value (that is, an integer) of the character. Note that in line 9 the numeric value is assigned to the integer variable ch.

In line 10, the character entered is displayed on the screen with the help of printf(). Note that the character format specifier %c is used within the printf() function in line 10.

Q&A and Workshop

Each hour (that is, each chapter) ends with a Q&A section that contains answers to common questions relating to the lesson of the chapter. Following the Q&A section, there is a Workshop that consists of quiz questions and programming exercises. The answers to these quiz questions and sample solutions for the exercises are presented in Appendix E, "Answers to Quiz Questions and Exercises."

To help you solidify your understanding of each lesson, you are encouraged to try to answer the quiz questions and finish the exercises provided in the workshop.

Conventions Used in This Book

This book uses special typefaces to help you differentiate between C code and regular English, and to identify important concepts.

☐ Actual C code is typeset in a special monospace font. You'll see this font used in listings, Input/Ouput examples, and code snippets. In the explanation of C features, commands, filenames, statements, variables, and any text you see on the screen are also typeset in this font.

☐ Command input and anything that you are supposed to enter appear in a **bold monospace** font. You'll see this mainly in the Input/Output sections of examples.

☐ Placeholders in syntax descriptions appear in an *italic monospace* font. Replace the placeholder with the actual filename, parameter, or whatever element it represents.

☐ *Italics* highlight technical terms when they appear for the first time in the text and are sometimes used to emphasize important points.

What You'll Learn in 24 Hours

Teach Yourself C in 24 Hours consists of five parts. In Part I, "The Basics of C," you'll learn the basics of the C language. Here is an overview of what you're going to learn:

Hour 1, "Getting Started," introduces you to the C language, the ANSI standard, and the basic software and hardware requirements for C programming.

Hour 2, "Writing Your First C Program," demonstrates the entire procedure of writing, compiling, linking, and running a C program.

Hour 3, "The Essentials of C Programs," teaches you several important concepts, such as constants, variables, expressions, and statements. The anatomy of a function is introduced in this hour as well.

Hour 4, "Data Types and Names in C," lists all reserved C keywords. Four data types, char, int, float, and double, are introduced in detail. Also, the rules of naming a variable are explained.

Hour 5, "Reading from and Writing to Standard I/O," teaches you to receive input from the keyboard, and print output on the screen with the help of a set of C functions, such as getc(), getchar(), putc(), putchar(), and printf().

Part II, "Operators and Control-Flow Statements," emphasizes operators and control-flow statements in C. The following is an overview of what you'll learn:

Hour 6, "Manipulating Data with Operators," teaches you how to use arithmetic assignment operators, the unary minus operator, increment/decrement operators, relational operators, and the cast operator.

Hour 7, "Doing the Same Thing Over and Over," introduces looping (that is, iteration) with the for, while, or do-while statements.

Hour 8, "More Operators," tells you about more operators, such as logical operators, bitwise operators, the sizeof operator, and the ?: operator, which are frequently used in C.

Hour 9, "Playing with Data Modifiers and Math Functions," describes how to use data modifiers to enable or disable the sign bit, or change the size of a data type. Also, several mathematical functions provided by C are introduced.

Hour 10, "Getting Controls," introduces all the control-flow statements used in C. They are the `if`, `if-else`, `switch`, `break`, `continue`, and `goto` statements.

Pointers and arrays are discussed in Part III of this book, "Pointers and Arrays." The following is an overview of what you'll learn:

Hour 11, "An Introduction to Pointers," teaches you how to reference variables with pointers. Concepts such as left value and right value are also introduced.

Hour 12, "Storing Similar Data Items," explains how to declare and initialize arrays. The relationship between the array and the pointer in C is also discussed.

Hour 13, "Manipulating Strings," focuses on reading and writing strings. Several C library functions, such as `strlen()`, `strcpy()`, `gets()`, `puts()`, and `scanf()` are introduced to manipulate strings.

Hour 14, "Scope and Storage Classes in C," introduces block scope, function scope, program scope, and file scope. In addition, storage class specifiers or modifiers, such as `auto`, `static`, `register`, `extern`, `const`, and `volatile` are explained.

Part IV of this book, "Functions and Dynamic Memory Allocation," focuses on functions and dynamic memory allocations in C. The following is an overview of what you'll learn:

Hour 15, "Functions in C," describes the function declaration and definition in C. The function prototyping is explained, along with the function return type specification.

Hour 16, "Applying Pointers," teaches you how to perform pointer arithmetic operations, access elements in arrays with pointers, and how to pass pointers to functions.

Hour 17, "Allocating Memory," explains the concept of allocating memory dynamically. C functions, such as `malloc()`, `calloc()`, `realloc()`, and `free()`, are introduced with regard to the dynamic memory allocation.

Hour 18, "More Data Types and Functions," introduces the `enum` data type and the use of `typedef`. Function recursion and command-line arguments to the `main()` function are also taught in this hour.

Part V, "Structure, Union, File I/O, and More," discusses structures, unions, and disk file I/O in C. The following is an overview of what you'll learn:

Hour 19, "Collecting Data Items of Different Types," introduces the `structure` data type. You learn to access structure members, and pass structures to functions with the help of pointers. Nested and forward-referencing structures are also discussed in this hour.

Hour 20, "Unions: Another Way to Collect Dissimilar Data," describes the `union` data type, and the difference between `union` and `structure`. The applications of unions are demonstrated in several examples.

Hour 21, "Disk File Input and Output: Part I," explains the concepts of the file and the stream in C. The basics of disk file input and output are introduced in this first part. The following C functions, along with several examples are introduced in this hour: `fopen()`, `fclose()`, `fgetc()`, `fputc()`, `fgets()`, `fputs()`, `fread()`, `fwrite()`, and `feof()`.

Hour 22, "Disk File Input and Output: Part II," is the second part of disk file I/O, in which `fseek()`, `ftell()`, and `rewind()` are introduced to show how they can help you get random access to disk files. In addition, the `fscanf()`, `fprintf()`, and `freopen()` functions are taught and invoked in sample programs.

Hour 23, "The C Preprocessor," describes the role played by the C preprocessor. You can learn the preprocessor directives, such as `#define`, `#undef`, `#ifdef`, `#endif`, `#ifndef`, `#if`, `#elis`, and `#else` through the examples given in this hour.

Hour 24, "What You Can Do Now," summarizes the important concepts and features introduced in this book. In addition, programming style, modular programming, and debugging are explained briefly. A list of recommended C books is provided for further reading.

Publishing Notice

Due to paper and printing constraints, the appendixes for this book have been provided on the CD-ROM rather than in the back of the book as you would expect. When you see a reference to any of the appendixes as you're reading—including the appendix containing the answers for the book's quizzes and exercises—please consult the CD-ROM for them.

Now you're ready to start the journey of learning the C language. Have fun reading this book!

Tony Zhang
Plano, Texas
May 1997

PART
I

The Basics of C

Hour

Hour 1

Getting Started

A journey of a thousand miles is started by taking the first step.

—Chinese proverb

High thoughts must have high language.

—Aristophanes

Welcome to *Teach Yourself C in 24 Hours*. In this first lesson you'll learn the following:

- ☐ What C is
- ☐ Why you need to learn C
- ☐ The ANSI standard
- ☐ Hardware and software required in order to run the C program

What Is C?

C is a programming language. The C language was first developed in 1972 by Dennis Ritchie at AT&T Bell Labs. Ritchie called his newly developed language *C* simply because there was a *B* programming language already. (As a matter of fact, the B language led to the development of C.)

C is a high-level programming language. In fact, C is one of the most popular general-purpose programming languages.

In the computer world, the further a programming language is from the computer architecture, the higher the language's level. You can imagine that the lowest-level languages are machine languages that computers understand directly. The high-level programming languages, on the other hand, are closer to our human languages. (See Figure 1.1.)

Figure 1.1.
The language spectrum.

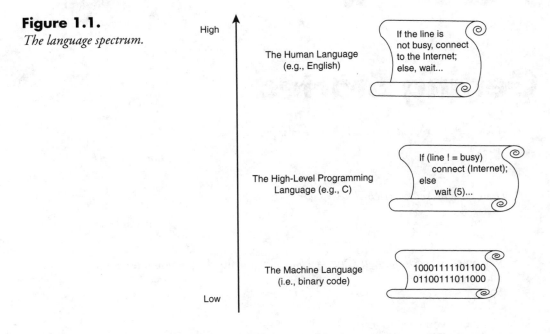

High-level programming languages, including C, have the following advantages:

☐ *Readability:* Programs are easy to read.

☐ *Maintainability:* Programs are easy to maintain.

☐ *Portability:* Programs are easy to port across different computer platforms.

1

The C language's readability and maintainability benefit directly from its relative closeness to human languages, especially English.

Each high-level language needs a *compiler* or an *interpreter* to translate instructions written in the high-level programming language into a machine language that a computer can understand and execute. Different machines may need different compilers or interpreters for the same programming language. For instance, I use Microsoft's C compiler to compile the C programs in this book for my personal computer (PC). If I need to run the C programs on a UNIX-based workstation, I have to use another type of C compiler to compile these programs. Therefore, the portability of programs written in C is realized by re-compiling the programs with different compilers for different machines. (See Figure 1.2.)

Figure 1.2.

Porting programs written in C into different types of computers.

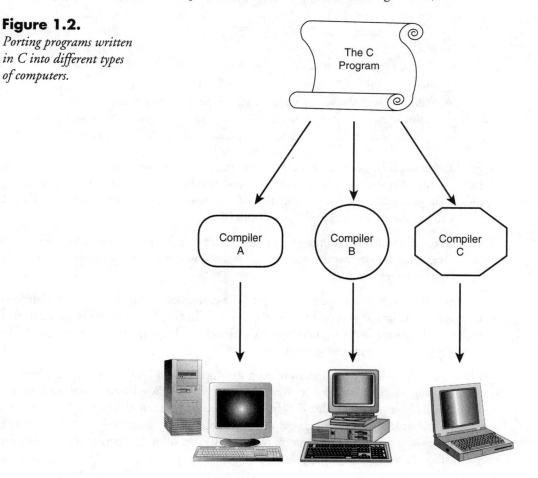

The Computer's Brain

You may know that the brain of a computer is the central processing unit (CPU). Some computers may have more than one CPU inside. A CPU has millions of transistors that make use of electronic switches. The electronic switches have only two states: off and on. (Symbolically, 0 and 1 are used to represent the two states.) Therefore, a computer can only understand instructions consisting of series of 0s and 1s. In other words, machine-readable instructions have to be in binary format.

However, a computer program written in a high-level language, such as C, Java, or Perl, is just a text file, consisting of English-like characters and words. We have to use some special programs, called *compilers* or *interpreters*, to translate such a program into a machine-readable code. That is, the text format of all instructions written in a high-level language has to be converted into the binary format. The code obtained after the translation is called *binary code*. Prior to the translation, a program in text format is called *source code*.

The smallest unit of the binary code is called a *bit* (from binary digit), which can have a value of 0 or 1. 8 bits make up one *byte*, and half a byte (4 bits) is one *nibble*.

In addition, the C language has other advantages. Programs written in C can be reused. You can save your C programs into a library file and invoke them in your next programming project simply by including the library file. More details on using libraries and invoking C library functions are covered in the rest of this book.

C is a relatively small programming language, which makes life easier for you. You don't have to remember many C keywords or commands before you start to write programs in C to solve problems in the real world.

For those who seek speed while still keeping the convenience and elegance of a high-level language, the C language is probably the best choice. In fact, C allows you to get control of computer hardware and peripherals. That's why the C language is sometimes called the lowest high-level programming language.

Many other high-level languages have been developed based on C. For instance, Perl is a popular programming language in World Wide Web (WWW) design across the Internet. Perl actually borrows a lot of features from C. If you understand C, learning Perl is a snap. Another example is the C++ language, which is simply an expanded version of C, although C++ makes object-oriented programming easier. Also, learning Java becomes much easier if you already know C.

1

NOTE

> There are two types of programming languages: *compiled* language and *interpreted* language.
>
> A compiler is needed to translate a program written in a compiled language into machine-understandable code (that is, binary code) before you can run the program on your machine. When the translation is done, the binary code can be saved into an application file. You can keep running the application file without the compiler unless the program (source code) is updated and you have to recompile it. The binary code or application file is also called *executable code* (or an *executable file*).
>
> On the other hand, a program written in an interpreted language can be run immediately after you finish writing it. But such a program always needs an interpreter to translate the high-level instructions into machine-understandable instructions (binary code) at runtime. You cannot run the program on a machine unless the right interpreter is available.
>
> You can think of the C language as a compiled language because most C language vendors make only C compilers to support programs written in C.

C and the ANSI Standard

For many years, the de facto standard for the C programming language was the K&R standard because of the book *The C Programming Language*, written by Brian Kernighan and Dennis Ritchie in 1978. However, there were many changes unofficially made to the C language that were not presented in the K&R standard.

Fearing that C might lose its portability, a group of compiler vendors and software developers petitioned the American National Standards Institute (ANSI) to build a standard for the C language in 1983. ANSI approved the application and formed the X3J11 Technical Committee to work on the C standard. By the end of 1989, the committee approved the ANSI standard for the C programming language.

The ANSI standard for C enhances the K&R standard and defines a group of commonly used C functions that are expected to be found in the ANSI C standard library. Now, all C compilers have the standard library, along with some other compiler-specific functions.

This book focuses on the C functions defined in the ANSI standard, which is supported by all compiler vendors. All programs in this book can be compiled by any compilers that support the ANSI standard. If you're interested in a specific compiler, you can learn the compiler-specific functions from the compiler's reference manual.

Assumptions About You

No previous programming experience is required for you to learn the C language from this book, although some knowledge of computers helps. Also, it's up to you to determine how quickly to go through the 24 hours of this book: You could sit up with a big pot of coffee and power through the book in a sitting or you could take an hour a day for 24 days.

Setting Up Your System

Basically, you need a computer and a C compiler in order to compile and run your own C programs or the C programs from this book. The recommended hardware and software are listed in the following sections.

Hardware

Any type of computer that has or can access a C compiler is fine. (The C compiler should support the ANSI standard.) More likely, you may have a PC on your desktop. A 286 PC with a 50MB hard drive and 1MB memory (RAM) is probably the minimum requirement to run a DOS-based C compiler. For a Windows-based C compiler, you must have a bigger hard drive and add more memory to your computer. Check your compiler vendor for more details.

Software

If you're using a UNIX-based workstation, you might already have a C compiler loaded on your machine, or at least you might be able to access a C compiler on a server machine. Check with your system administrator to find out about a C compiler that supports the ANSI standard, and set up the right path to access it. On a UNIX-based machine, you should know how to use a text editor, such as vi and emacs, to write C programs.

If you have a PC, you need to install a C compiler and a text editor on it. Most C compilers come with an editor. You can also use a text editor that is already installed on your machine.

Borland International's Turbo C and Microsoft's Quick C used to be very popular in the C compiler market. These days, C compiler vendors like to bundle C and C++ compilers together. For instance, Borland International sells Borland C++ with a C compiler. The same thing is true for Microsoft's Visual C++. Both Borland C++ and Visual C++ support the ANSI standard. Both of them provide an integrated development environment (IDE), which you can use to edit your C programs, along with other fancy features for advanced Windows programming.

Appendix D, "Some Popular Commercial C/C++ Compilers," introduces several C compilers besides Borland C++ and Microsoft's Visual C++.

You can pick up any C compiler you like, as long as the compiler supports the ANSI standard. You shouldn't have any problems installing a C compiler on your machine if you read the manuals that come with the compiler and follow the installation instructions correctly. Most C/C++ compilers provide a quick tutorial that shows you how to install the compiler and set up a development environment on your computer.

 TIP

> You can learn more about Borland C++ or Visual C++ from books such as *Teach Yourself Borland C++ 5 in 21 Days* (from Sams Publishing/Borland Press) and *Teach Yourself Visual C++ 5 in 21 Days* (also from Sams Publishing).

The Hardware and Software I Use for C Programming

I have a Pentium 100MHz PC with 32MB memory and with a 2.5GB hard drive. (32MB memory may be more than enough to run the C programs from this book, but I need a lot of memory space for Windows programming.) I have both Windows 95 and Windows NT on my machine.

In this book, all C programs are developed with Microsoft Visual C++ version 1.5. (The latest version of Visual C++ is 5.0.) The reasons I chose Visual C++ 1.5 are simple: All C programs in this book are written in ANSI C and can be compiled into DOS-based applications; Visual C++ 1.5 has a good C compiler that supports the ANSI standard, as well as a simple but friendly enough IDE. Figure 1.3 shows an example of the IDE from Visual C++ 1.5. (The later version of Visual C++ has a fancy IDE with more features added. However, many of those features are not needed for running the C programs in this book.)

I set up my development environment in such a way that all C programs in this book can be compiled and made into DOS applications. Also, I test and run the applications made from the C programs at a DOS prompt provided by Windows 95.

Figure 1.3.

An example of the IDE from Visual C++ version 1.5.

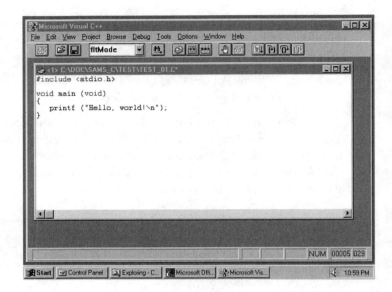

Summary

In this first lesson you've learned the following:

- ☐ C is a general-purpose programming language.
- ☐ C is a high-level language that has the advantages of readability, maintainability, and portability.
- ☐ C is a very efficient language that allows you to get control of computer hardware and peripherals.
- ☐ C is a small language that you can learn easily in a relatively short time.
- ☐ Programs written in C can be reused.
- ☐ Programs written in C must be compiled and translated into machine-readable code before the computer can execute them.
- ☐ C provides many programming languages, such as Perl, C++, and Java, with basic concepts and useful features.
- ☐ The ANSI standard for C is the standard supported by all C compiler vendors to guarantee the portability of C.
- ☐ You can use any C compilers that support the ANSI standard and compile all C programs in this book.

In the next lesson you'll learn to write your first C program.

1

Q&A

Q **What is the lowest-level language in the computer world?**

A The computer's machine language is the lowest because the machine language, made up of 0s and 1s, is the only language that the computer can understand directly.

Q **What are the advantages of high-level programming languages?**

A Readability, maintainability, and portability are the main advantages of high-level programming languages.

Q **What is C, anyway?**

A C is a general-purpose programming language. It's a high-level language that has advantages such as readability, maintainability, and portability. Also, C allows you to get down to the hardware to increase the performance speed if needed. A C compiler is needed to translate programs written in C into machine-understandable code. The portability of C is realized by recompiling the C programs with different C compilers specified for different types of computers.

Q **Can I learn C in a short time?**

A Yes. C is a small programming language. There are not many C keywords or commands to remember. Also, it's very easy to read or write in C because C is a high-level programming language that is close to human languages, especially English. You can learn C in a relatively short time.

Workshop

To help solidify your understanding of this hour's lesson, you are encouraged to answer the quiz questions provided in the Workshop before you move to the next lesson. The answers and hints to the questions are given in Appendix E, "Answers to Quiz Questions and Exercises."

Quiz

1. What are the lowest-level and highest-level languages mentioned in this book?
2. Can a computer understand a program written in C? What do you need to translate a program written in C into the machine-understandable code (that is, binary code)?
3. If needed, can a C program be reused in another C program?
4. Why do we need the ANSI standard for the C language?

Hour 2

Writing Your First C Program

Cut your own wood and it will warm you twice.

—Chinese proverb

In Hour 1, "Getting Started," you learned that C is a high-level programming language and that you need a C compiler to translate your C programs into binary code that your computer can understand and execute. In this lesson you'll learn to write your first C program and the basics of a C program, such as

☐ The #include directive

☐ Header files

☐ Comments

☐ The main() function

☐ The return statement

☐ The exit() function

☐ The newline character (\n)

☐ The void data type
☐ Translating a C program into an executable file
☐ Debugging

A Simple C Program

Let's have a look at our first C program, demonstrated in Listing 2.1. Later in this lesson you're going to write your own C program for the first time.

TYPE **Listing 2.1. A simple C program.**

```
1:  /* 02L01.c: This is my first C program */
2:  #include <stdio.h>
3:
4:  main()
5:  {
6:      printf ("Howdy, neighbor! This is my first C program.\n");
7:      return 0;
8:  }
```

This is a very simple C program, which is saved in a file called 02L01.c. Note that the name of a C program file must have an extension of .c. If you've installed a C compiler and set up the proper development environment, you should be able to compile this C program and make it into an executable file.

I set up my development environment in such a way that all C programs in this book can be compiled and made into DOS-based applications. For instance, 02L01.exe is the name of the DOS application made from 02L01.c. Note that .exe is included as the extension to the name of a DOS application program (that is, an executable file).

Also, on my machine, I save all the executable files made from the C programs in this book into a dedicated directory called c:\app. Therefore, if I type in 02L01 from a DOS prompt and press the Enter key, I can run the 02L01.exe executable file and display the message Howdy, neighbor! This is my first C program. on the screen. The following output is a copy from the screen:

OUTPUT
```
C:\app> 02L01
Howdy, neighbor! This is my first C program.
C:\app>
```

Comments

Now let's take a close look at the C program in Listing 2.1.

2

The first line contains a comment:

```
/* 02L01.C: This is my first C program */
```

You notice that this line starts with a combination of a slash and an asterisk, /*, and ends with */. In C, /* is called the *opening comment mark*, and */ is the *closing comment mark*. The C compiler ignores everything between the opening comment mark and closing comment mark. That means the comment in the first line of Listing 2.1, 02L01.C: This is my first C program, is ignored by the compiler.

The only purpose of including comments in your C program is to help you document what the program or some specific sections in the programs do. Remember, comments are written for programmers like you. For example, when you read someone's code, the comments in the code help you to understand what the code does, or at least what the code intends to do.

You don't need to worry about the size or performance speed of your C program if you add many comments into it. Adding comments into a C program does not increase the size of the binary code of the program (that is, the executable file), although the size of the program itself (that is, the source code) may become larger. Also, the performance speed of the executable file made from your C program is not affected by the comments inside your C program.

Most C compilers allow you to write a comment that crosses more than one line. For instance, you can write a comment in C like this:

```
/*
   This comment does not increase the size of
   the executable file (binary code), nor does
   it affect the performance speed.
*/
```

which is equivalent to this:

```
/* This comment does not increase the size of */
/* the executable file (binary code), nor does */
/* it affect the performance speed. */
```

NOTE

These days, there is another way to put comments into a C program. C++ started using two slashes (//) to mark the beginning of a comment line; many C compilers now use this convention as well. The comment ends at the end of the line. For instance, if I write a C program in Borland C++ or Visual C++, the following two comments are identical:

```
/*
   This comment does not increase the size of
   the executable file (binary code), nor does
   it affect the performance speed.
*/
// This comment does not increase the size of
// the executable file (binary code), nor does
// it affect the performance speed.
```

Note that this new style of using // as the beginning mark of a comment
has not been approved by ANSI. Make sure your C compiler supports //
before you use it.

One thing that needs to be pointed out is that the ANSI standard does not support *nested
comments*, that is, comments within comments. For instance, the following is not allowed by
the ANSI standard:

```
/* This is the first part of the first comment
   /* This is the second comment */
   This is the second part of the first comment */
```

 TIP

You can use the opening comment mark, /*, and closing comment mark,
*/, to help you test and fix any errors found in your C program. You can
comment out one or more C statements in your C program with /* and */
when you need to focus on other statements and watch their behaviors
closely. The C compiler will ignore the statements you comment out.

Later, you can always restore the previously commented-out statements
simply by removing the opening comment and closing comment marks. In
this way, you don't need to erase or rewrite any statements during the
testing and debugging.

The #include Directive

Let's now move to line 2 in the C program of Listing 2.1:

```
#include <stdio.h>
```

You see that this line starts with a pound sign, #, which is followed by include. In C, #include
forms a preprocessor directive that tells the C preprocessor to look for a file and place the
contents of the file in the location where the #include directive indicates.

The preprocessor is a program that does some preparations for the C compiler before your
code is compiled. More details about the C preprocessor are discussed in Hour 23, "The C
Preprocessor."

Also in this line, you see that <stdio.h> follows #include. You may guess that the file the
#include directive asks for is something called stdio.h. You are exactly right! Here, the
#include directive does ask the C preprocessor to look for and place stdio.h where the
directive is in the C program.

The name of the stdio.h file stands for *standard input-output header* file. The stdio.h file contains numerous prototypes and macros to perform input or output (I/O) for C programs. You'll see more program I/O in Hour 5, "Reading from and Writing to Standard I/O."

> **NOTE**
>
> The C programming language distinguishes between lowercase and uppercase characters. In other words, C is a *case-sensitive* language. For instance, stdio.h and STDIO.H are different filenames in C. Likewise, main() and Main() are two different function names.

Header Files

The files that are required by the #include directive, like stdio.h, are called *header files* because the #include directives are almost always placed at the head of C programs. Actually, the extension name of .h does mean "header."

Besides stdio.h, there are more header files, such as stdlib.h, string.h, math.h, and so on. Appendix A, "ANSI Standard Header Files," gives a list of all the ANSI standard header files.

Angle Brackets (< >) and Double Quotes (" ")

In the second line of Listing 2.1, there are two angle brackets, < and >, that are used to surround stdio.h. You may be wondering what the angle brackets do. In C, the angle brackets ask the C preprocessor to look for a header file in a directory other than the current one.

For instance, the current directory containing the 02L01.C file is called C:\code on my computer. Therefore, the angle brackets around <stdio.h> tell the C preprocessor to look for stdio.h in a directory other than C:\code.

If you want to let the C preprocessor look into the current directory first for a header file before it starts to look elsewhere, you can use double quotes to surround the name of the header file. For instance, when the C preprocessor sees "stdio.h", it looks in the current directory, which is C:\code on my machine, first before it goes elsewhere for the stdio.h header file.

Normally, the header files are saved in a subdirectory called include. For instance, I might install a Microsoft C compiler in the directory MSVC on my hard drive, which is labeled as the C drive. Then the path to access the header files becomes C:\MSVC\include.

The main() Function

In line 4 of Listing 2.1, you see this function:

```
main ()
```

This is a very special function in C. Every C program must have a main() function, and every C program can only have one main() function. More generic discussions about functions are given in Hour 3, "The Essentials of C Programs."

You can put the main() function wherever you want in your C program. However, the execution of your program always starts with the main() function.

In Listing 2.1, the main() function body starts in line 4 and ends in line 8. Because this is a very simple program, the main() function is the only function defined in the program. Within the main() function body, a C library function, printf(), is called in order to print out a greeting message. (See line 6.) More details about printf() are covered in Hour 5.

One more important thing about main() is that the execution of every C program ends with main(). A program ends when all the statements within the main() function have been executed.

The Newline Character (\n)

In the printf() function, one thing worth mentioning at this moment is the newline character, \n. Usually suffixed at the end of a message, the newline character tells the computer to generate a carriage-return and line-feed sequence so that anything printed out after the message will start on the next new line on the screen.

Exercise 3 in this lesson gives you a chance to use the newline character to break a one-line message into two lines.

The return Statement

All functions in C can return values. For instance, when you make a function to add two numbers, you can make such a function that returns to you the value of the addition.

The main() function itself returns a value. By default, main() returns an integer. In C, integers are decimal numbers without fraction portions.

Therefore, in line 7 of Listing 2.1, there is a statement, return 0;, that indicates that 0 is returned from the main() function and the program is terminated normally.

A nonzero value returned by the return statement tells the operating system that an error has occurred. The bigger the return value, the more severe the error.

The exit() Function

There is also a C library function, exit(), that can be used to cause a program to end. Because the exit() function is defined in a header file, stdlib.h, you have to include the header file at the beginning of your program.

Unlike main(), the exit() function itself does not return any values, but the argument to `exit()` indicates whether the program is terminated normally. A nonzero argument to the `exit()` function tells the operating system that the program has terminated abnormally.

Actually, you can replace `return 0;` in line 7 of Listing 2.1 with `exit(0);` and get a similar result after running the modified program.

Note that `return` and `exit()` can also be used in other functions. You'll see more examples in the rest of the book.

Listing 2.2 contains the program that uses `exit()` instead of `return`.

TYPE **Listing 2.2. A C program with `exit()`.**

```
1:  /* 02L02.c */
2:  #include <stdlib.h>
3:  #include <stdio.h>
4:
5:  void main()
6:  {
7:     printf ("Howdy, neighbor! This is my first C program.\n");
8:     exit(0);
9:  }
```

After compiling the program in Listing 2.2, you should be able to run the program and get the same message, `Howdy, neighbor! This is my first C program.`, printed out on the screen.

The `void` Data Type

You may notice that the `void` word has been added into the C program in Listing 2.2. `void` is a keyword for a data type in C. When a `void` is placed prior to a function name, it indicates that the function does not return a value.

As you have learned, the `exit()` function does not return any values, but, by default, the `main()` function does. Therefore, as shown in line 5 of Listing 2.2, `void` is used to modify the returning data type of `main()` and to make the `main()` function not return any value. (You'll learn more about data types in C in Hours 4, "Data Types and Names in C," and 18, "More Data Types and Functions.")

Compiling and Linking

You may already be anxious to know how an executable file is made. Let's have a look at how a C program is compiled and translated into an executable file (binary code). As shown in Figure 2.1, there are at least three steps needed to create an executable file.

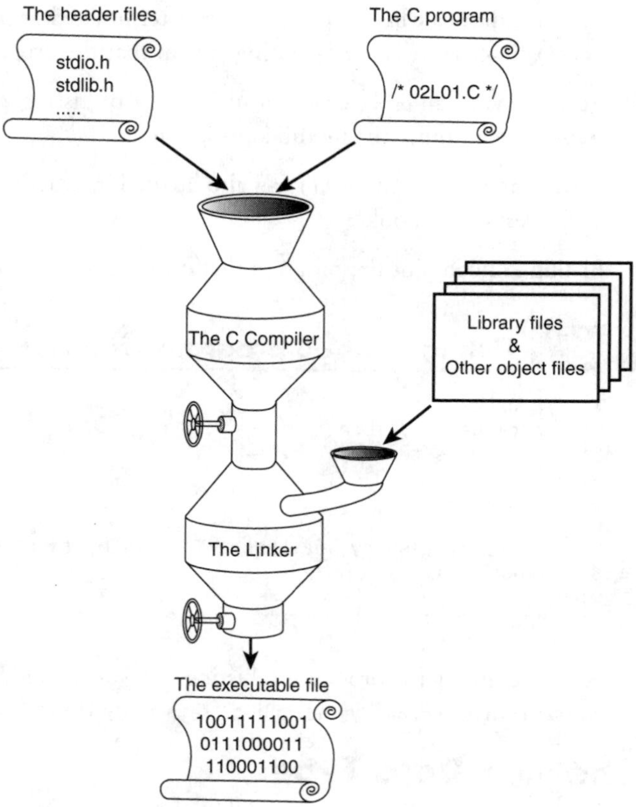

Figure 2.1.

Make an executable file by the compiler and linker.

The header files
stdio.h
stdlib.h
.....

The C program
/* 02L01.C */

The C Compiler

Library files
&
Other object files

The Linker

The executable file
10011111001
0111000011
110001100

First, a program written in C, called *source code*, is made. Then the source code is compiled by a C *compiler*, which creates a new file. The new file is an *object file*. In the UNIX operating system, the name of an object file ends with the extension .o; in the DOS operating system, the extension is .obj.

You cannot execute the object file because there is some function code missing. You have to finish the next step: linking. Linking is done by invoking a special program called a *linker*, which normally comes with the compiler package.

A linker is used to link together the object file, the ANSI standard C library, and other user-generated libraries to produce an executable file—the binary code. In this stage, the binary code of the library functions that are called in the source code is combined with the object file; the result is saved into a new file—an executable file. As you learned in the first hour of this book, the name of an executable file usually ends with the extension .exe in DOS. (.com is another extension used for a DOS executable filename.) In UNIX, it's not necessary to include such an extension to an executable filename.

2

Later, you'll learn that in many cases, there may be several object files that have to be linked together in order to make an executable program.

Note that the object file and executable file are both machine-dependent. You cannot simply move an executable file, without recompiling the source code, from the current computer platform to another one that is operated by a different operating system even though the source code of the executable file, presumably written in ANSI C, is machine independent (that is, portable).

What's Wrong with My Program?

When you finish writing a C program and start to compile it, you might get some error or warning messages. Don't panic when you see error messages. We're human beings. Everybody makes mistakes. Actually, you should appreciate that your compiler catches some errors for you before you go any further.

Usually, your compiler can help you check the grammar of your C program and make sure you've followed the C programming rules properly. For instance, if you forget to put the ending brace on the `main()` function in line 8 of Listing 2.1, you'll get an error message something like this: `syntax error : end of file found`.

Also, the linker will issue an error message if it cannot find the missing code for a needed function in the libraries. For instance, if you misspell `printf()` as `pprintf()` in the program of Listing 2.1, you'll see an error message: `'_pprintf': unresolved external` (or something similar).

All errors found by the compiler and linker must be fixed before an executable file (binary code) can be made.

Debugging Your Program

In the computer world, program errors are also called *bugs*. In many cases, your C compiler and linker do not find any errors in your program, but the result generated by running the executable file of the program is not what you expect. In order to find those "hidden" errors in your program, you may need to use a debugger.

Normally, your C compiler vendor already includes a debugger software program in the C compiler package. The debugger can execute your program one line at a time so that you can watch closely what's going on with the code in each line, or so that you can ask the debugger to stop running your program on any line. For more details about your debugger, refer to the manuals made by your C compiler vendor.

Later in this book, you'll learn that debugging is a very necessary and important step in writing software programs. (This topic is covered in Hour 24, "What You Can Do Now.")

Summary

In this lesson you've learned the following:

☐ Some header files should be included at the beginning of your C program.

☐ Header files, such as stdio.h and stdlib.h, contain the declarations for functions used in your C program; for example, the printf() and exit() functions.

☐ Comments in your C programs are needed to help you document your programs. You can put comments anywhere you like in your programs.

☐ In ANSI C, a comment starts with the opening comment mark, /*, and ends with the closing comment mark, */.

☐ Every C program should have one but only one main() function. The program execution starts and ends with the main() function.

☐ The sequence of a carriage return and a line feed is carried out when the computer sees the newline character, \n.

☐ The return statement can be used to return a value to indicate to the operating system whether an error has occurred. The exit() function terminates a program; the argument to the function indicates the error status, too.

☐ The void data type can be used to modify the type of a return value for a function. Applying void to main() tells the operating system that the main() function does not return any value after termination.

☐ Compiling and linking are consecutive steps that have to be finished before an executable file is produced.

☐ Everybody, including yourself, makes mistakes in programming. Debugging is a very important step in your program design and coding.

In the next lesson you'll learn more about the essentials of C programs.

Q&A

Q Why do you need to put comments into your programs?

A Comments help us document what a program, or a special portion of a program, does. Especially when a program becomes very complex, we need to write comments to mark different parts in the program.

Q Why is the main() function needed in your program?

A The execution of a C program starts and ends with the main() function. Without the main() function, the computer does not know where to start to run a program.

Q **What does the #include directive do?**

A The #include directive is used to include header files that contain the declarations to the functions used in your C program. In other words, the #include directive tells the C preprocessor to look into directories and find the specified header file.

Q **Why do you need a linker?**

A After compiling, some function code may still be missing in the object file of a program. A linker must then be used to link the object file to the C standard library or other user-generated libraries and include the missing function code so that an executable file can be created.

Workshop

To help solidify your understanding of this hour's lesson, you are encouraged to answer the quiz questions and finish the exercises provided in the Workshop before you move to the next lesson. The answers and hints to the questions and exercises are given in Appendix E, "Answers to Quiz Questions and Exercises."

Quiz

1. Can a C compiler see the comments within your C program?
2. What kinds of files does a C compiler actually produce?
3. Does the exit() function return a value? How about the return statement?
4. What is a header file?

Exercises

1. Is #include <stdio.h> the same as #include "stdio.h"?
2. It's time for you to write your own first program. Referring to the program in Listing 2.1, write a C program that can print out a message: It's fun to write my own program in C..
3. Update the program in Listing 2.1 by adding one more newline character into the message printed out by the printf() function. You should see two lines of the message on the screen after running the updated executable file:

```
Howdy, neighbor!
This is my first C program.
```

4. What warning or error messages will you get when you're trying to compile the following program?

```
#include <stdlib.h>
#include <stdio.h>
main()
{
    printf ("Howdy, neighbor! This is my first C program.\n");
    exit(0);
}
```

5. What error messages will you get when you're trying to compile the following program?

```
void main()
{
    printf ("Howdy, neighbor! This is my first C program.\n");
    return 0;
}
```

Hour 3

The Essentials of C Programs

The whole is equal to the sum of its parts.

—Euclid

In Hour 2, "Writing Your First C Program," you saw and wrote some simple C programs. You also learned about the basic structure of a C program. You know that a program written in C has to be compiled before it can be executed. In this lesson you'll learn more essentials within a C program, such as

☐ Constants and variables

☐ Expressions

☐ Statements

☐ Statement blocks

☐ C function types and names

☐ Arguments to functions

☐ The body of a function

☐ Function calls

The Basics of the C Program

As a building is made of bricks, a C program is made of basic elements, such as expressions, statements, statement blocks, and function blocks. These elements are discussed in the following sections. But first, you need to learn two smaller but important elements, constant and variable, which make up expressions.

Constants and Variables

As its name implies, a *constant* is a value that never changes. A *variable*, on the other hand, can be used to present different values.

You can think of a constant as a music CD-ROM; the music saved in the CD-ROM is never changed. A variable is more like an audio cassette: You can always update the contents of the cassette by simply overwriting the old songs with new ones.

You can see many examples in which constants and variables are in the same statement. For instance, consider the following:

```
i = 1;
```

where the symbol 1 is a constant because it always has the same value (1), and the symbol i is assigned the constant 1. In other words, i contains the value of 1 after the statement is executed. Later, if there is another statement,

```
i = 10;
```

after it is executed, i is assigned the value of 10. Because i can contain different values, it's called a variable in the C language.

Expressions

An *expression* is a combination of constants, variables, and operators that are used to denote computations.

For instance, the following:

```
(2 + 3) * 10
```

is an expression that adds 2 and 3 first, and then multiplies the result of the addition by 10. (The final result of the expression is 50.)

Similarly, the expression 10 * (4 + 5) yields 90. The 80/4 expression results in 20.

Here are some other examples of expressions:

Expression	Description
6	An expression of a constant.
i	An expression of a variable.
6 + i	An expression of a constant plus a variable.
exit(0)	An expression of a function call.

Arithmetic Operators

As you've seen, an expression can contain symbols such as +, *, and /. In the C language, these symbols are called *arithmetic operators*. Table 3.1 lists all the arithmetic operators and their meanings.

Table 3.1. C arithmetic operators.

Symbol	Meaning
+	Addition
-	Subtraction
*	Multiplication
/	Division
%	Remainder (or modulus)

You may already be familiar with all the arithmetic operators, except the remainder (%) operator. % is used to obtain the remainder of the first operand divided by the second operand. For instance, the expression

```
6 % 4
```

yields a value of 2 because 4 goes into 6 once with a remainder of 2.

The remainder operator, %, is also called the *modulus operator*.

Among the arithmetic operators, the multiplication, division, and remainder operators have a higher precedence than the addition and subtraction operators. For example, the expression

```
2 + 3 * 10
```

yields 32, not 50. Because of the higher precedence of the multiplication operator, 3 * 10 is calculated first, and then 2 is added into the result of the multiplication.

As you might know, you can put parentheses around an addition (or subtraction) to force the addition (or subtraction) to be performed before a multiplication, division, or modulus computation. For instance, the expression

```
(2 + 3) * 10
```

performs the addition of 2 and 3 first before it does the multiplication of 10.

You'll learn more operators of the C language in Hours 6, "Manipulating Data with Operators," and 8, "More Operators."

Statements

In the C language, a *statement* is a complete instruction, ending with a semicolon. In many cases, you can turn an expression into a statement by simply adding a semicolon at the end of the expression.

For instance, the following

```
i = 1;
```

is a statement. You may have already figured out that the statement consists of an expression of i = 1 and a semicolon (;).

Here are some other examples of statements:

```
i = (2 + 3) * 10;
i = 2 + 3 * 10;
j = 6 % 4;
k = i + j;
```

Also, in the first lesson of this book you learned statements such as

```
return 0;
exit(0);
printf ("Howdy, neighbor! This is my first C program.\n");
```

Statement Blocks

A group of statements can form a *statement block* that starts with an opening brace ({) and ends with a closing brace (}). A statement block is treated as a single statement by the C compiler.

For instance, the following

```
for(. . .) {
    s3 = s1 + s2;
    mul = s3 * c;
    remainder = sum % c;
}
```

is a statement block that starts with { and ends with }. Here for is a keyword in C that determines the statement block. The for keyword is discussed in Hour 7, "Doing the Same Thing Over and Over."

A statement block provides a way to group one or more statements together as a single statement. Many C keywords can only control one statement. If you want to put more than one statement under the control of a C keyword, you can add those statements into a statement block so that the block is considered one statement by the C keyword.

Anatomy of a C Function

Functions are the building blocks of C programs. Besides the standard C library functions, you can also use some other functions made by you or another programmer in your C program. In Hour 2 you saw the main() function, as well as two C library functions, printf() and exit(). Now, let's have a closer look at functions.

As shown in Figure 3.1, a function consists of six parts: the function type, the function name, arguments to the function, the opening brace, the function body, and the closing brace.

Figure 3.1.
The anatomy of a function in the C language.

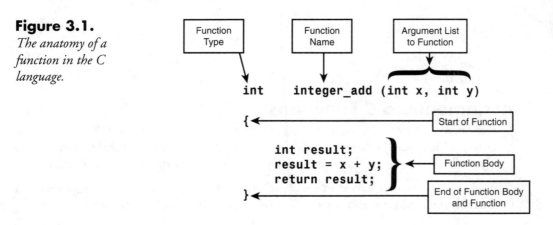

The six parts of a function are explained in the following sections.

Determining a Function's Type

The *function type* is used to signify what type of value a function is going to return after its execution. In Hour 2, for instance, you learned that the default function type of main() is integer. You also learned how to change the function type of main() to void so that the main() function does need to return any value.

In C, int is used as the keyword for the integer data type. In the next hour, you'll learn more about data types.

Giving a Function a Valid Name

A *function name* is given in such a way that it reflects what the function can do. For instance, the name of the printf() function means "print formatted data."

There are certain rules you have to follow to make a valid function name. The following are examples of illegal function names in C:

Illegal Name	The Rule
2 (digit)	A function name cannot start with a digit.
* (Asterisk)	A function name cannot start with an asterisk.
+ (Addition)	A function name cannot start with one of the arithmetic signs that are reserved C keywords.
. (dot)	A function name cannot start with ..
total-number	A function name cannot contain a minus sign.
account'97	A function name cannot contain an apostrophe.

Some samples of valid function names are as follows:

- ☐ print2copy
- ☐ total_number
- ☐ _quick_add
- ☐ Method3

Arguments to C Functions

You often need to pass a function some information before executing it. For example, in Listing 2.1 in Hour 2, a character string, `"Howdy, neighbor! This is my first C program.\n"`, is passed to the `printf()` function, and then `printf()` prints the string on the screen.

Pieces of information passed to functions are known as *arguments*. The argument of a function is placed between the parentheses that immediately follow the function name.

The number of arguments to a function is determined by the task of the function. If a function needs more than one argument, arguments passed to the function must be separated by commas; these arguments are considered an *argument list*.

If no information needs to be passed to a function, you just leave the argument field between the parentheses blank. For instance, the `main()` function in Listing 2.1 of Hour 2 has no argument, so the field between the parentheses following the function name is empty.

The Beginning and End of a Function

As you may have already figured out, braces are used to mark the beginning and end of a function. The *opening brace* (`{`) signifies the start of a function body, while the *closing brace* (`}`) marks the end of the function body.

As mentioned earlier, the braces are also used to mark the beginning and end of a statement block. You can think of it as a natural extension to use braces with functions because a function body can contain several statements.

The Function Body

The *function body* in a function is the place that contains variable declarations and C statements. The task of a function is accomplished by executing the statements inside the function body one at a time.

Listing 3.1 demonstrates a function that adds two integers specified by its argument and returns the result of the addition.

TYPE **Listing 3.1. A function that adds two integers.**

```
1:  /* This function adds two integers and returns the result */
2:  int integer_add( int x, int y )
3:  {
4:      int result;
5:      result = x + y;
6:      return result;
7:  }
```

ANALYSIS As you learned in Hour 2, line 1 of Listing 3.1 is a comment that tells the programmer what the function can do.

In line 2, you see that the `int` data type is prefixed prior to the function name. Here `int` is used as the function type, which signifies that an integer should be returned by the function. The function name shown in line 2 is `integer_add`. The argument list contains two arguments, `int x` and `int y`, in line 2, where the `int` data type specifies that the two arguments are both integers.

Line 4 contains the opening brace ({) that marks the start of the function.

The function body is in lines 4–6 in Listing 3.1. Line 4 gives the variable declaration of `result`, whose value is specified by the `int` data type as an integer. The statement in line 5 adds the two integers represented by x and y and assigns the computation result to the `result` variable. The `return` statement in line 6 then returns the computation result represented by `result`.

Last, but not least, the closing brace (}) in line 7 is used to close the function.

TIP

When you create a function in your C program, don't assign the function too much work. If a function has too much to do, it will be very difficult to write and debug. If you have a complex programming project, break it into smaller pieces. And try your best to make sure that each function has just one task to do.

Making Function Calls

Based on what you've learned so far, you can write a C program that calls the `integer_add()` function to calculate an addition and then print out the result on the screen. An example of such a program is demonstrated in Listing 3.2.

TYPE

Listing 3.2. A C program that calculates an addition and prints the result to the screen.

```
1:  /* 03L02.c: Calculate an addition and print out the result */
2:  #include <stdio.h>
3:  /* This function adds two integers and returns the result */
4:  int integer_add( int x, int y )
5:  {
6:     int result;
7:     result = x + y;
8:     return result;
9:  }
10:
11: int main()
12: {
13:    int sum;
14:
15:    sum = integer_add( 5, 12);
16:    printf("The addition of 5 and 12 is %d.\n", sum);
17:    return 0;
18: }
```

The program in Listing 3.2 is saved as a source file called `03L02.c`. After this program is compiled and linked, an executable file for `03L02.c` is created. On my machine, the executable file is named `03L02.exe`. The following is the output printed on the screen after I run the executable from a DOS prompt on my machine:

OUTPUT
```
C:\app> 03L02
The addition of 5 and 12 is 17.
C:\app>
```

ANALYSIS   Line 1 in Listing 3.2 is a comment about the program. As you learned in Hour 2, the `include` directive in line 2 includes the `stdio.h` header file because of the `printf()` function in the program.

Lines 3–9 represent the `integer_add()` function that adds two integers, as discussed in the previous section.

The `main()` function, prefixed with the `int` data type, starts in line 11. Lines 12 and 18 contain the opening brace and closing brace for the `main()` function, respectively. An integer variable, `sum`, is declared in line 13.

The statement in line 15 calls the `integer_add()` function that we examined in the previous section. Note that two integer constants, 5 and 12, are passed to the `integer_add()` function, and that the `sum` variable is assigned the result returned from the `integer_add()` function.

You first saw the C standard library function `printf()` in Hour 2. Here you may find something new added to the function in line 16. You're right. This time, there are two arguments that are passed to the `printf()` function. They are the string `"The addition of 5 and 12 is %d.\n"` and the variable `sum`.

Note that a new symbol, `%d`, is added into the first argument. The second argument is the integer variable `sum`. Because the value of `sum` is going to be printed out on the screen, you might think that the `%d` has something to do with the integer variable `sum`. You're right again. `%d` tells the computer the format in which `sum` should be printed on the screen.

More details on `%d` are covered in Hour 4, "Data Types and Names in C." The relationship between `%d` and `sum` is discussed in Hour 5, "Reading from and Writing to Standard I/O."

More importantly, you should focus on the program in Listing 3.2 and pay attention to how to call either a user-generated function or a standard C library function from the `main()` function.

Summary

In this lesson you've learned the following:

- [ ] A constant in C is a value that never changes. A variable, on the other hand, can present different values.
- [ ] A combination of constants, variables, and operators is called an expression in the C language. An expression is used to denote different computations.
- [ ] The arithmetic operators include +, -, *, /, and %.
- [ ] A statement consists of a complete expression suffixed with a semicolon.
- [ ] The C compiler treats a statement block as a single statement, although the statement block may contain more than one statement.
- [ ] The function type of a function determines the type of the return value made by the function.
- [ ] You have to follow certain rules to make a valid function name.
- [ ] An argument contains information that you want to pass to a function. An argument list contains two or more arguments that are separated by commas.

☐ The opening brace ({) and closing brace (}) are used to mark the start and end of a C function.

☐ A function body contains variable declarations and statements. Usually, a function should accomplish just one task.

In the next lesson you'll learn more about data types in the C language.

Q&A

Q What is the difference between a constant and a variable?

A The major difference is that the value of a constant cannot be changed, while the value of a variable can. You can assign different values to a variable whenever it's necessary in your C program.

Q Why do you need a statement block?

A Many C keywords can only control one statement. A statement block provides a way to put more than one statement together and put the statement block under the control of a C keyword. Then, the statement block is treated as a single statement.

Q Which arithmetic operators have a higher precedence?

A Among the five arithmetic operators, the multiplication, division, and remainder operators have a higher precedence than the addition and subtraction operators.

Q How many parts does a function normally have?

A A function normally has six parts: the function type, the function name, the arguments, the opening brace, the function body, and the closing brace.

Workshop

To help solidify your understanding of this hour's lesson, you are encouraged to answer the quiz questions and finish the exercises provided in the Workshop before you move to the next lesson. The answers and hints to the questions and exercises are given in Appendix E, "Answers to Quiz Questions and Exercises."

Quiz

1. In the C language, is 74 a constant? How about 571?
2. Is x = 570 + 1 an expression? How about x = 12 + y?

3

3. Are the following function names valid?

```
2methods

m2_algorithm

*start_function

Room_Size

.End_Exe

_turbo_add
```

4. Is 2 + 5 * 2 equal to (2 + 5) * 2?

5. Does 7 % 2 produce the same result as 4 % 3?

Exercises

1. Given two statements, x = 3; and y = 5 + x;, how can you build a statement block with the two statements?

2. What is wrong with the following function?

```c
int 3integer_add( int x, int y, int z)
{
   int sum;
   sum = x + y + z;
   return sum;
}
```

3. What is wrong with the following function?

```c
int integer_add( int x, int y, int z)
{
   int sum;
   sum = x + y + z
   return sum;
}
```

4. Write a C function that can multiply two integers and return the calculated result.

5. Write a C program that calls the C function you just wrote in exercise 4 to calculate the multiplication of 3 times 5 and then print out the return value from the function on the screen.

Hour 4

Data Types and Names in C

What's in a name? That which we call a rose
By any other name would smell as sweet.

—*W. Shakespeare*

You learned how to make a valid name for a C function in Hour 3, "The Essentials of C Programs." Now, you're going to learn more about naming a variable and the C keywords reserved by the C compiler in this hour.

Also in this hour you're going to learn about the four data types of the C language in detail:

☐ `char` data type
☐ `int` data type
☐ `float` data type
☐ `double` data type

C Keywords

The C language reserves certain words that have special meanings to the language. Those reserved words are sometimes called *C keywords*. You should not use the C keywords as variable, constant, or function names in your program. The following are the 32 reserved C keywords:

Keyword	Description
auto	Storage class specifier
break	Statement
case	Statement
char	Type specifier
const	Storage class modifier
continue	Statement
default	Label
do	Statement
double	Type specifier
else	Statement
enum	Type specifier
extern	Storage class specifier
float	Type specifier
for	Statement
goto	Statement
if	Statement
int	Type specifier
long	Type specifier
register	Storage class specifier
return	Statement
short	Type specifier
signed	Type specifier
sizeof	Operator
static	Storage class specifier
struct	Type specifier
switch	Statement
typedef	Statement
union	Type specifier
unsigned	Type specifier
void	Type specifier
volatile	Storage class modifier
while	Statement

Don't worry if you can't remember all the C keywords the first time through. In the rest of the book, you'll become more familiar with them and start to use many of the keywords through examples and exercises.

Note that all C keywords are written in lowercase letters. As I've mentioned, C is a case-sensitive language. Therefore, int, as shown in the list here, is considered as a C keyword, but INT is not.

The char **Data Type**

An object of the char data type represents a single character of the character set used by your computer. For example, A is a character, and so is a. But 7 is a number.

But a computer can only store numeric code. Therefore, characters such as A, a, B, b, and so on all have a unique numeric code that is used by computers to represent the characters. Usually, a character takes 8 bits (that is, 1 byte) to store its numeric code.

For many computers, the ASCII codes are the *de facto* standard codes to represent a character set. (ASCII, just for your information, stands for American Standard Code for Information Interchange.) The original ASCII character set has only 128 characters because it uses the lower 7 bits that can represent 2^7 (that is, 128) characters.

On IBM-compatible PCs, however, the character set is extended to contain a total of 256 (that is, 2^8) characters. Appendix C, "ASCII Character Set," gives a list of the 256 characters.

Character Variables

A variable that can represent different characters is called a *character variable*.

You can set the data type of a variable to char by using the following declaration format:

```
char    variablename;
```

where *variablename* is the place where you put the name of a variable.

If you have more than one variable to declare, you can either use the following format:

```
char    variablename1;
char    variablename2;
char    variablename3;
```

or this one:

```
char    variablename1, variablename2, variablename3;
```

Character Constants

A character enclosed in single quotes (') is called a *character constant*. For instance, 'A', 'a', 'B', and 'b' are all character constants that have their unique numeric values in the ASCII character set.

You can remember to use the single quote ('), instead of the double quote ("), in character constants because a character constant represents a single character. You'll see later in the book that the double quote is used to indicate a string of characters.

From the ASCII character set listed in Appendix C, you will find that the unique numeric (decimal) values of 'A', 'a', 'B', and 'b' are 65, 97, 66, and 98, respectively. Therefore, given x as a character variable, for instance, the following two assignment statements are equivalent:

```
x = 'A';
x = 65;
```

So are the following two statements:

```
x = 'a';
x = 97;
```

Later in this hour, you'll see a program (in Listing 4.2) that converts numeric values back to the corresponding characters.

The Escape Character (\)

Actually, you first saw the escape character (\) in Hour 2, "Writing Your First C Program," when you learned to use the newline character (\n) to break a message into two pieces. In the C language, the backslash (\) is called the *escape character*; it tells the computer that a special character follows.

For instance, when the computer sees \ in the newline character \n, it knows that the next character, n, causes a sequence of a carriage return and a line feed.

Besides the newline character, several other special characters exist in the C language, such as the following:

Character	Description
\b	The backspace character; moves the cursor to the left one character.
\f	The form-feed character; goes to the top of a new page.
\r	The return character; returns to the beginning of the current line.
\t	The tab character; advances to the next tab stop.

4

Printing Out Characters

You already know that the printf() function, defined in the C header file stdio.h, can be used to print out messages on the screen. In this section, you're going to learn to use the character format specifier, %c, which indicates to the printf() function that the argument to be printed is a character. Let's first have a look at the program in Listing 4.1, which prints out characters on the screen.

TYPE   **Listing 4.1. Printing out characters on the screen.**

```
1:  /* 04L01.c: Printing out characters */
2:  #include <stdio.h>
3:
4:  main()
5:  {
6:     char c1;
7:     char c2;
8:
9:     c1 = 'A';
10:    c2 = 'a';
11:    printf("Convert the value of c1 to character: %c.\n", c1);
12:    printf("Convert the value of c2 to character: %c.\n", c2);
13:    return 0;
14: }
```

After the executable file of 04L01.c in Listing 4.1 is created, you can run it to see what will be printed out on the screen. On my machine, the executable file is named as 04L01.exe. The following is the output printed on the screen after I run the executable from a DOS prompt:

OUTPUT
```
C:\app> 04L01
Convert the value of c1 to character: A.
Convert the value of c2 to character: a.
C:\app>
```

ANALYSIS   As you know, line 2 includes the header file, stdio.h, for the printf() function. Lines 5–14 make up the main() function body.

Lines 6 and 7 declare two character variables, c1 and c2, while lines 9 and 10 assign c1 and c2 with the character constants 'A' and 'a', respectively.

Note that the %c format specifier is used in the printf() function in lines 11 and 12, which tells the computer that the contents contained by c1 and c2 should be printed as characters. When the two statements in lines 11 and 12 are executed, two characters are formatted and output to the screen, based on the numeric values contained by c1 and c2, respectively.

Now look at the program shown in Listing 4.2. This time, %c is used to convert the numeric values back to the corresponding characters.

4

TYPE **Listing 4.2. Converting numeric values back to characters.**

```
1:  /* 04L02.c: Converting numeric values back to characters */
2:  #include <stdio.h>
3:
4:  main()
5:  {
6:     char c1;
7:     char c2;
8:
9:     c1 = 65;
10:    c2 = 97;
11:    printf("The character that has the numeric value of 65 is: %c.\n", c1);
12:    printf("The character that has the numeric value of 97 is: %c.\n", c2);
13:    return 0;
14: }
```

The following is the output printed on the screen after I run the executable file, `04L02.exe`, from a DOS prompt:

OUTPUT
```
C:\app> 04L02
The character that has the numeric value of 65 is: A.
The character that has the numeric value of 97 is: a.
C:\app>
```

ANALYSIS The program in Listing 4.2 is similar to the one in Listing 4.1 except for the two statements in lines 9 and 10. Note that in lines 9 and 10 of Listing 4.2, the character variables c1 and c2 are assigned 65 and 97, respectively.

As you know, 65 is the numeric value (decimal) of the A character in the ASCII character set; 97 is the numeric value of a. In lines 11 and 12, the %c format specifier converts the numeric values, 65 and 97, into the A and a, respectively. The A and a characters are then printed out on the screen.

The int Data Type

You saw the integer data type in Hour 3. The int keyword is used to specify the type of a variable as an integer. Integer numbers are also called *whole numbers*, which have no fractional part or decimal point. Therefore, the result of an integer division is truncated, simply because any fraction part is ignored.

Depending on the operating system and the C compiler you're using, the length of an integer varies. On most UNIX workstations, for example, an integer is 32 bits long, which means that the range of an integer is from 2147483647 (that is, $2^{31}-1$) to -2147483648. The range of a 16-bit integer is from 32767 (that is, $2^{15}-1$) to -32768.

4

The C compiler I'm using for this book is Visual C++ 1.5, which only provides the 16-bit integer, while a 32-bit version of Visual C++, such as Visual C++ 4.0 or Visual C++ 5.0, supports the 32-bit integer.

Declaring Integer Variables

You also saw the declaration of an integer in Hour 3. The following shows the basic declaration format:

```
int   variablename;
```

Similar to the character declaration, if you have more than one variable to declare, you can use either the format like this

```
int   variablename1;
int   variablename2;
int   variablename3;
```

or like this:

```
int   variablename1, variablename2, variablename3;
```

Here *variablename1, variablename2,* and *variablename3* indicate the places where you put the names of int variables.

Showing the Numeric Values of Characters

Like the character format specifier (%c) that is used to format a single character, %d, called the *integer format specifier*, is used to format an integer. You might recall that in line 16 of Listing 3.2, %d is used in the printf() function to format the second argument of the function to an integer.

In this section you're going to study a program, shown in Listing 4.3, that can print out the numeric values of characters by using the integer format specifier %d with printf().

TYPE **Listing 4.3. Showing the numeric values of characters.**

```
1:   /* 04L03.c: Showing the numeric values of characters */
2:   #include <stdio.h>
3:
4:   main()
5:   {
6:      char c1;
7:      char c2;
8:
9:      c1 = 'A';
10:     c2 = 'a';
11:     printf("The numeric value of A is: %d.\n", c1);
12:     printf("The numeric value of a is: %d.\n", c2);
13:     return 0;
14: }
```

4

I get the following output on the screen after running the executable file, `04L03.exe`:

OUTPUT
```
C:\app> 04L03
The numeric value of A is: 65.
The numeric value of a is: 97.
C:\app>
```

ANALYSIS You may find that the program in Listing 4.3 is quite similar to the one in Listing 4.1. As a matter of fact, I simply copied the source code from Listing 4.1 to Listing 4.3 and made changes in lines 11 and 12. The major change I made was to replace the character format specifier (`%c`) with the integer format specifier (`%d`).

The two statements in lines 11 and 12 format the two character variables (`c1` and `c2`) by using the integer format specifier `%d`, and then print out two messages showing the numeric values `65` and `97` that represent, respectively, the characters A and a in the ASCII character set.

The `float` Data Type

The *floating-point number* is another data type in the C language. Unlike an integer number, a floating-point number contains a decimal point. For instance, 7.01 is a floating-point number; so are 5.71 and -3.14. A floating-point number is also called a *real number*.

A floating-point number is specified by the `float` keyword in the C language. Floating-point numbers can be suffixed with f or F to specify `float`. A floating-point number without a suffix is `double` by default. The `double` data type is introduced later in this lesson.

Like an integer number, a floating-point number has a limited range. The ANSI standard requires that the range be at least plus or minus $1.0*10^{37}$. Normally, a floating-point number is represented by taking 32 bits. Therefore, a floating-point number in C is of at least six digits of precision. That is, for a floating-point number, there are at least six digits (or decimal places) on the right side of the decimal point.

Not like an integer division from which the result is truncated and the fraction part is discarded, a floating-point division produces another floating-point number. A floating-point division is carried out if both the divisor and the dividend, or one of them, are floating-point numbers.

For instance, `571.2` / `10.0` produces another floating-point number, `57.12`. So do `571.2` / `10` and `5712` / `10.0`.

Declaring Floating-Point Variables

The following shows the declaration format for a floating-point variable:

```
float    variablename;
```

Similar to the character or integer declaration, if you have more than one variable to declare, you can either use the format like this:

```
float   variablename1;
float   variablename2;
float   variablename3;
```

or like the following one:

```
float   variablename1, variablename2, variablename3;
```

The Floating-Point Format Specifier (%f)

Also, in C, you can use the *floating-point format specifier* (%f) to format your output. Listing 4.4 gives an example showing how to use the format specifier %f with the printf() function.

TYPE

Listing 4.4. Printing out results of integer and floating-point divisions.

```
 1:  /* 04L04.c: Integer vs. floating-point divisions */
 2:  #include <stdio.h>
 3:
 4:  main()
 5:  {
 6:      int int_num1, int_num2, int_num3;   /* Declare integer variables */
 7:      float flt_num1, flt_num2, flt_num3; /* Declare floating-point variables */
 8:
 9:      int_num1 = 32 / 10;     /* Both divisor and dividend are integers */
10:      flt_num1 = 32 / 10;
11:      int_num2 = 32.0 / 10;   /* The divisor is an integer */
12:      flt_num2 = 32.0 / 10;
13:      int_num3 = 32 / 10.0;   /* The dividend is an integer */
14:      flt_num3 = 32 / 10.0;
15:
16:      printf("The integer divis. of 32/10 is: %d\n", int_num1);
17:      printf("The floating-point divis. of 32/10 is: %f\n", flt_num1);
18:      printf("The integer divis. of 32.0/10 is: %d\n", int_num2);
19:      printf("The floating-point divis. of 32.0/10 is: %f\n", flt_num2);
20:      printf("The integer divis. of 32/10.0 is: %d\n", int_num3);
21:      printf("The floating-point divis. of 32/10.0 is: %f\n", flt_num3);
22:      return 0;
23:  }
```

The following output is a copy from the screen after the executable file, 04L04.exe, is run on my machine (I did get several warning messages about type conversions while I was compiling the program in Listing 4.4, but I ignored them all because I'd like to create an executable file and show you the differences between the int data type and the float data type.):

```
C:\app> 04L04
The integer divis. of 32/10 is: 3
The floating-point divis. of 32/10 is: 3.000000
The integer divis. of 32.0/10 is: 3
The floating-point divis. of 32.0/10 is: 3.200000
The integer divis. of 32/10.0 is: 3
The floating-point divis. of 32/10.0 is: 3.200000
C:\app>
```

ANALYSIS   Inside the main() function, the two statements in lines 6 and 7 declare three integer variables, int_num1, int_num2, and int_num3, and three floating-point variables, flt_num1, flt_num2, and flt_num3.

Lines 9 and 10 assign the result of 32/10 to int_num1 and flt_num1, respectively; 32.0 / 10 to int_num2 and flt_num2 in lines 11 and 12, and 32 / 10.0 to int_num3 and flt_num3 in lines 13 and 14.

Then, lines 16–21 print out the values contained by the three int variables and the three floating-point variables. Note that, %d is used for the integer variables, and the floating-point specifier (%f) is used for formatting the floating-point variables in the printf() function.

Because the truncation occurs in the integer division of 32 / 10, flt_num1 contains 3.000000, not 3.200000, which you can see from the second line of the output. However, flt_num2 and flt_num3 are assigned 3.200000, because both 32.0 / 10 and 32 / 10.0 are considered as the floating-point division.

But int_num2 and int_num3, as integer variables, discard respectively the fraction parts of the floating-point divisions of 32.0 / 10 and 32 / 10.0. Therefore, you just see the integer 3 in both the third and fifth lines of the output.

The double **Data Type**

In the C language, a floating-point number can also be represented by another data type, called the double data type. In other words, you can specify a variable by the double keyword, and assign the variable a floating-point number.

The difference between a double data type and a float data type is that the former normally uses twice as many bits as the latter. Therefore, a double floating-point number is of at least 10 digits of precision, although the ANSI standard does not specify it for the double data type.

In Hour 8, "More Operators," you'll learn to use the sizeof operator to obtain the length of a data type, such as char, int, float, or double, specified on your computer system.

Using Scientific Notation

The C language uses *scientific notation* to help you write lengthy floating-point numbers.

In scientific notation, a number can be represented by the combination of the *mantissa* and the *exponent*. The format of the notation is that the mantissa is followed by the exponent, which is prefixed by e or E. Here are two examples:

[mantissa]e[exponent],

and

[mantissa]E[exponent].

For instance, 5000 can be represented by 5e3 in scientific notation. Likewise, -300 can be represented by -3e2, and 0.0025 by 2.5e-3.

Correspondingly, the format specifier, %e or %E, is used to format a floating-point number in scientific notation. The usage of %e or %E in the printf() function is the same as %f.

Naming a Variable

You've learned how to make a valid function name. In this section, let's focus on naming variables. Function names and variable names are both *identifiers* in C.

The following are all the characters you can use to make a valid variable name:

- [ ] Characters A through Z and a through z.
- [ ] Digit characters 0 through 9, which can be used in any position except the first of a variable name.
- [ ] The underscore character (_).

For instance, stop_sign, Loop3, and _pause are all valid variable names.

Now, let's see what you cannot use in variable naming:

- [ ] A variable name cannot contain any C arithmetic signs.
- [ ] A variable name cannot contain any dots (.).
- [ ] A variable name cannot contain any apostrophes (').
- [ ] A variable name cannot contain any other special symbols such as *, @, #, ?, and so on.

Some invalid variable names, for example, are, 4flags, sum-result, method*4, and what_size?.

WARNING

Never use the C keywords reserved in the C language, or the names of the standard C library functions, as variable names in your C program.

Summary

In this lesson you've learned about the following:

- [ ] The C keywords reserved in the C language
- [ ] The char data type and the %c format specifier
- [ ] The int data type and the %d format specifier
- [ ] The float data type and the %f format specifier
- [ ] Floating-point numbers can be suffixed with f or F to specify float. A floating-point number without suffix is double by default.
- [ ] The possible ranges of the char, int, and float data types
- [ ] The double data type
- [ ] Scientific notation and the %e and %E format specifiers
- [ ] The rules you have to follow to make a valid variable name

In the next lesson you'll learn more about the printf() function and other functions to deal with input and output.

Q&A

Q Why do characters have their unique numeric values?

A Characters are stored in computers in the form of bits. The combinations of bits can be used to represent different numeric values. A character has to have a unique numeric value in order to distinguish itself. Many computer systems support the ASCII character set, which contains a set of unique numeric values for up to 256 characters.

Q How can you declare two character variables?

A There are two ways to do the declaration. The first one is

```
...char variable-name1, variable-name2;
```

The second one is

```
char   variable-name1;
char   variable-name2;
```

4

Q What are %c, %d, and %f?

A These are format specifiers. %c is used to obtain the character format; %d is for the integer format; %f is for the floating-point format. %c, %d, and %f are often used with C functions such as printf().

Q What are the main differences between the int data type (integer) and the float data type (floating-point)?

A First, an integer does not contain any fraction parts, but a floating-point number does. A floating-point number must have a decimal point. In C, the float data type takes more bits than the int data type. In other words, the float data type has a larger range of numeric values than the int data type.

Also, the integer division truncates the fraction part. For instance, the integer division of 16/10 produces a result of 1, not 1.6.

Workshop

To help solidify your understanding of this hour's lesson, you are encouraged to answer the quiz questions and finish the exercises provided in the Workshop before you move to the next lesson. The answers and hints to the questions and exercises are given in Appendix E, "Answers to Quiz Questions and Exercises."

Quiz

1. Are the integer divisions of 134/100 and 17/10 equal?

2. Is the result of 3000 + 1.0 a floating-point number? How about 3000/1.0?

3. How can you represent the following numbers in scientific notation?

   ☐ 3500

   ☐ 0.0035

   ☐ -0.0035

4. Are the following variable names valid?

   ☐ 7th_calculation

   ☐ Tom's_method

   ☐ _index

   ☐ Label_1

Exercises

1. Write a program that prints out the numeric values of characters Z and z.

2. Given two numeric values, 72 and 104, write a program to print out the corresponding two characters.

3. For a 16-bit integer variable, can you assign the variable with an integer value of 32768?

4. Given the declaration double dbl_num = 123.456;, write a program that prints out the value of dbl_num in both floating-point and scientific notation formats.

5. Write a program that can print out the numeric value of the newline character (\n). (Hint: assign '\n' to a character variable.)

4

Hour 5

Reading from and Writing to Standard I/O

I/O, I/O, it's off to work we go…

—The Seven Dwarfs (sort of)

In the last lesson you learned how to print out characters, integers, and floating-point numbers to the screen by calling the `printf()` function. In this lesson you're going to learn more about `printf()`, as well as about the following functions, which are necessary to receive the input from the user or print the output to the screen:

- ☐ The `getc()` function
- ☐ The `putc()` function
- ☐ The `getchar()` function
- ☐ The `putchar()` function

Before we jump into these new functions, let's first get an idea about the standard input and output in C.

The Standard Input and Output (I/O)

A file contains related characters and numbers. Because all characters and numbers are represented in bits on computers, the C language treats a file as a series of bytes. (8 bits make up 1 byte.) A series of bytes is also called a *stream*. In fact, the C language treats all file streams equally, although some of the file streams may come from a disk or tape drive, from a terminal, or even from a printer.

Additionally, in C, there are three file streams that are pre-opened for you:

- stdin—The standard input for reading.
- stdout—The standard output for writing.
- stderr—The standard error for writing error messages.

Usually, the standard input (stdin) file stream links to your keyboard, while the standard output (stdout) and the standard error (stderr) file streams point to your terminal screen. Also, many operating systems allow you to redirect these files' streams.

In fact, you've already used stdout. When you executed the printf() function in the last lesson, you were in fact sending the output to the default file stream, stdout, which points to your screen.

You'll learn more on stdin and stdout in the following sections.

> **NOTE**
> The C language provides many functions to manipulate file reading and writing (I/O). The header file stdio.h contains the declarations for those functions. Therefore, always include the header file stdio.h in your C program before doing anything with the file I/O.

Getting the Input from the User

In these days, typing from keyboard is still the de facto standard way to input information into computers. The C language has several functions to direct the computer to read the input from the user (typically through the keyboard.) In this lesson the getc() and getchar() functions are introduced.

Using the `getc()` Function

The `getc()` function reads the next character from a file stream, and returns the character as an integer.

The syntax for the `getc()` function is

```
#include <stdio.h>
int getc(FILE *stream);
```

Here `FILE *stream` declares a file stream (that is, a variable). The function returns the numeric value of the character read. If an end-of-file or error occurs, the function returns `EOF`.

At this moment, don't worry about the `FILE` structure. More details about it are introduced in Hours 21, "Disk File Input and Output: Part I," and 22, "Disk File Input and Output: Part II." In this section, the standard input `stdin` is used as the file stream specified by `FILE *stream`.

NOTE

> Defined in the header file `stdio.h`, `EOF` is a constant. `EOF` stands for *end-of-file*. Usually, the value of `EOF` is `-1`. But keep using `EOF`, instead of `-1`, if you need an end-of-file indicator, in case a compiler uses a different value.

Listing 5.1 shows an example that reads a character typed in by the user from the keyboard and then displays the character on the screen.

TYPE   **Listing 5.1. Reading in a character entered by the user.**

```
1:   /* 05L01.c: Reading input by calling getc() */
2:   #include <stdio.h>
3:
4:   main()
5:   {
6:       int ch;
7:
8:       printf("Please type in one character:\n");
9:       ch = getc( stdin );
10:      printf("The character you just entered is: %c\n", ch);
11:      return 0;
12:  }
```

5

The following is the output displayed on the screen after I run the executable file, `05L01.exe`, enter the character `H`, and press the Enter key:

```
C:\app> 05L01
Please type in one character:
H
The character you just entered is: H
C:\app>
```

ANALYSIS   You see in line 2 of Listing 5.1 that the header file `stdio.h` is included for both the `getc()` and `printf()` functions used in the program. Lines 4–12 give the name and body of the `main()` function.

In line 6, an integer variable, `ch`, is declared; it is assigned the return value from the `getc()` function later in line 9. Line 8 prints out a piece of message that asks the user to enter one character from the keyboard. As I mentioned earlier in this lesson, the `printf()` function in line 8 uses the default standard output `stdout` to display messages on the screen.

In line 9, the standard input `stdin` is passed to the `getc()` function, which indicates that the file stream is from the keyboard. After the user types in a character, the `getc()` function returns the numeric value (that is, an integer) of the character. You see that, in line 9, the numeric value is assigned to the integer variable `ch`.

Then, in line 10, the character entered by the user is displayed on the screen with the help of `printf()`. Note that the character format specifier (`%c`) is used within the `printf()` function in line 10. (Exercise 1 in this lesson asks you to use `%d` in a program to print out the numeric value of a character entered by the user.)

Using the `getchar()` Function

The C language provides another function, `getchar()`, to perform a similar operation to `getc()`. More precisely, the `getchar()` function is equivalent to `getc(stdin)`.

The syntax for the `getchar()` function is

```
#include <stdio.h>
int getchar(void);
```

Here `void` indicates that no argument is needed for calling the function. The function returns the numeric value of the character read. If an end-of-file or error occurs, the function returns `EOF`.

The program in Listing 5.2 demonstrates how to use the `getchar()` function to read the input from the user.

TYPE **Listing 5.2. Reading in a character by calling** `getchar()`.

```
1:  /* 05L02.c: Reading input by calling getchar() */
2:  #include <stdio.h>
3:
4:  main()
5:  {
6:      int ch1, ch2;
7:
8:      printf("Please type in two characters together:\n");
9:      ch1 = getc( stdin );
10:     ch2 = getchar( );
11:     printf("The first character you just entered is: %c\n", ch1);
12:     printf("The second character you just entered is: %c\n", ch2);
13:     return 0;
14: }
```

After running the executable file, `05L02.exe`, and entering two characters (H and i) together without spaces, I press the Enter key and the following output is displayed on the screen:

OUTPUT
```
C:\app> 05L02
Please type in two characters together:
Hi
The first character you just entered is: H
The second character you just entered is: i
C:\app>
```

ANALYSIS The program in Listing 5.2 is quite similar to the one in Listing 5.1, except that the former reads in two characters.

The statement in line 6 declares two integers, `ch1` and `ch2`. Line 8 displays a message asking the user to enter two characters together.

Then, the `getc()` and `getchar()` functions are called in lines 9 and 10, respectively, to read in two characters entered by the user. Note that in line 10, nothing is passed to the `getchar()` function. This is because, as mentioned earlier, `getchar()` has its default file stream—`stdin`. You can replace the `getchar()` function in line 10 with `getc(stdin)`, because `getc(stdin)` is equivalent to `getchar()`.

Lines 11 and 12 send two characters (kept by `ch1` and `ch2`, respectively) to the screen.

Printing the Output on the Screen

Besides `getc()` and `getchar()` for reading, the C language also provides two functions, `putc()` and `putchar()`, for writing. The following two sections introduce these functions.

Using the `putc()` Function

The `putc()` function writes a character to the specified file stream, which, in our case, is the standard output pointing to your screen.

The syntax for the `putc()` function is

```
#include <stdio.h>
int putc(int c, FILE *stream);
```

Here the first argument, `int c`, indicates that the output is a character saved in an integer variable c; the second argument, `FILE *stream`, specifies a file stream. If successful, `putc()` returns the character written; otherwise, it returns EOF.

In this lesson the standard output `stdout` is used to be the specified file stream in `putc()`.

The `putc()` function is used in Listing 5.3 to put the character A on the screen.

Listing 5.3. Putting a character on the screen.

```
1:  /* 05L03.c: Outputting a character with putc() */
2:  #include <stdio.h>
3:
4:  main()
5:  {
6:      int ch;
7:
8:      ch = 65;    /* the numeric value of A */
9:      printf("The character that has numeric value of 65 is:\n");
10:     putc(ch, stdout);
11:     return 0;
12: }
```

The following is what I get from my machine:

```
C:\app> 05L03
The character that has numeric value of 65 is:
A
C:\app>
```

As mentioned, the header file `stdio.h`, containing the declaration of `putc()`, is included in line 2.

The integer variable, ch, declared in line 6, is assigned the numeric value of 65 in line 8. You may remember that 65 is the numeric value of character A.

Line 9 displays a message to remind the user of the numeric value of the character that is going to be put on the screen. Then, the `putc()` function in line 10 puts character A on the screen. Note that the first argument to the `putc()` function is the integer variable (ch) that contains 65, and the second argument is the standard output file stream, `stdout`.

Another Function for Writing: `putchar()`

Like `putc()`, `putchar()` can also be used to put a character on the screen. The only difference between the two functions is that `putchar()` needs only one argument to contain the character. You don't need to specify the file stream, because the standard output (`stdout`) is the default file stream to `putchar()`.

SYNTAX

The syntax for the `putchar()` function is

```
#include <stdio.h>
int putchar(int c);
```

▲ Here `int c` is the argument that contains the numeric value of a character. The function returns `EOF` if an error occurs; otherwise, it returns the character that has been written.

An example of using `putchar()` is demonstrated in Listing 5.4.

TYPE **Listing 5.4. Outputting characters with `putchar()`.**

```
 1:  /* 05L04.c: Outputting characters with putchar() */
 2:  #include <stdio.h>
 3:
 4:  main()
 5:  {
 6:     putchar(65);
 7:        putchar(10);
 8:           putchar(66);
 9:              putchar(10);
10:           putchar(67);
11:        putchar(10);
12:     return 0;
13: }
```

After running the executable file, `05L04.exe`, I get the following output:

OUTPUT
```
C:\app> 05L04
A
B
C
C:\app>
```

ANALYSIS The way to write the program in Listing 5.4 is a little bit different. There is no variable declared in the program. Rather, integers are passed to `putchar()` directly, as shown in lines 6–11.

As you might have figured out, `65`, `66`, and `67` are, respectively, the numeric values of characters A, B, and C. From exercise 5 of Hour 4, "Data Types and Names in C," or from Appendix C, "ASCII Character Set," you can find out that `10` is the numeric value of the newline character (`\n`).

Therefore, respectively, lines 6 and 7 put character A on the screen and cause the computer to start at the beginning of the next line. Likewise, line 8 puts B on the screen, and line 9 starts a new line. Then, line 10 puts C on the screen, and line 11 starts another new line. Accordingly, A, B, and C, are put at the beginnings of three consecutive lines, as shown in the output section.

Revisiting the `printf()` Function

The `printf()` function is the first C library function you used in this book to print out messages on the screen. `printf()` is a very important function in C, so it's worth it to spend more time on it.

The syntax for the `printf()` function is

```
#include <stdio.h>
int printf(const char *format-string, ...);
```

Here `const char *format-string` is the first argument that contains the format specifier(s); `...` indicates the expression section that contains the expression(s) to be formatted according to the format specifiers. The number of expressions is determined by the number of the format specifiers inside the first argument. The function returns the numbers of expressions formatted if it succeeds. It returns a negative value if an error occurs.

`const char *` is explained later in this book. For the time being, consider the first argument to the `printf()` function as a series of characters surrounded with double quotes with some format specifiers inside. For instance, you can pass `"The sum of two integers %d + %d is: %d.\n"` to the function as the first argument, if needed.

Figure 5.1 shows the relationship between the format string and expressions. Note that the format specifiers and the expressions are matched in order from left to right.

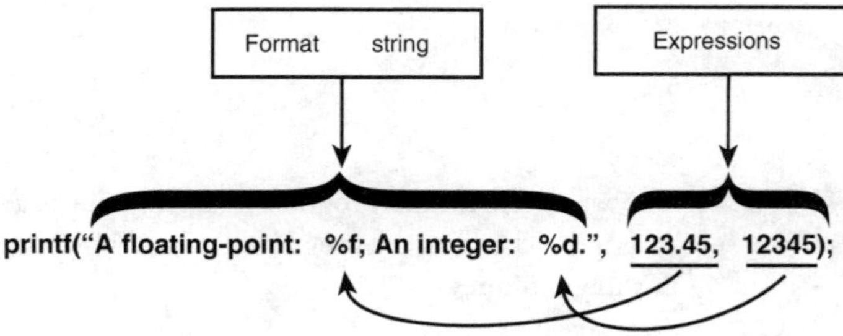

Figure 5.1.
The relation between the format string and the expressions in `printf()`.

```
printf("A floating-point: %f; An integer: %d.", 123.45, 12345);
```

Please remember that you should use exactly the same number of expressions as the number of format specifiers within the format string.

The following are all the format specifiers that can be used in printf():

%c	The character format specifier.
%d	The integer format specifier.
%i	The integer format specifier (same as %d).
%f	The floating-point format specifier.
%e	The scientific notation format specifier (note the lowercase e).
%E	The scientific notation format specifier (note the uppercase E).
%g	Uses %f or %e, whichever result is shorter.
%G	Uses %f or %E, whichever result is shorter.
%o	The unsigned octal format specifier.
%s	The string format specifier.
%u	The unsigned integer format specifier.
%x	The unsigned hexadecimal format specifier (note the lowercase x).
%X	The unsigned hexadecimal format specifier (note the uppercase X).
%p	Displays the corresponding argument that is a pointer.
%n	Records the number of characters written so far.
%%	Outputs a percent sign (%).

Among the format specifiers in this list, %c, %d, %f, %e, and %E have been introduced so far. Several others are explained later in this book. The next section shows you how to convert decimal numbers to hexadecimal numbers by using %x or %X.

Converting to Hex Numbers

The difference between a decimal number and a hexadecimal number is that the hexadecimal is a base-16 numbering system. A hexadecimal number can be represented by four bits. (2^4 is equal to 16, which means four bits can produce 16 unique numbers.) Hexadecimal is often written as hex for short.

The hexadecimal numbers 0 through 9 use the same numeric symbols founded in the decimal numbers 0 through 9. uppercase A, B, C, D, E, and F are used to represent, respectively, the hexadecimal numbers 10 through 15. (Similarly, in lowercase, a, b, c, d, e, and f are used to represent these hex numbers.)

Listing 5.5 provides an example of converting decimal numbers to hex numbers by using `%x` or `%X` in the `printf()` function.

TYPE **Listing 5.5. Converting to hex numbers.**

```
 1:   /* 05L05.c: Converting to hex numbers */
 2:   #include <stdio.h>
 3:
 4:   main()
 5:   {
 6:       printf("Hex(uppercase)    Hex(lowercase)    Decimal\n");
 7:       printf("%X                %x                %d\n", 0, 0, 0);
 8:       printf("%X                %x                %d\n", 1, 1, 1);
 9:       printf("%X                %x                %d\n", 2, 2, 2);
10:       printf("%X                %x                %d\n", 3, 3, 3);
11:       printf("%X                %x                %d\n", 4, 4, 4);
12:       printf("%X                %x                %d\n", 5, 5, 5);
13:       printf("%X                %x                %d\n", 6, 6, 6);
14:       printf("%X                %x                %d\n", 7, 7, 7);
15:       printf("%X                %x                %d\n", 8, 8, 8);
16:       printf("%X                %x                %d\n", 9, 9, 9);
17:       printf("%X                %x                %d\n", 10, 10, 10);
18:       printf("%X                %x                %d\n", 11, 11, 11);
19:       printf("%X                %x                %d\n", 12, 12, 12);
20:       printf("%X                %x                %d\n", 13, 13, 13);
21:       printf("%X                %x                %d\n", 14, 14, 14);
22:       printf("%X                %x                %d\n", 15, 15, 15);
23:       return 0;
24:   }
```

The following output is obtained by running the executable file, `05L05.exe`, on my machine:

OUTPUT

```
C:\app> 05L05
Hex(uppercase)    Hex(lowercase)    Decimal
0                 0                 0
1                 1                 1
2                 2                 2
3                 3                 3
4                 4                 4
5                 5                 5
6                 6                 6
7                 7                 7
8                 8                 8
9                 9                 9
A                 a                 10
B                 b                 11
C                 c                 12
D                 d                 13
E                 e                 14
F                 f                 15
C:\app>
```

5

ANALYSIS Don't panic when you see so many `printf()` functions being used in Listing 5.5. In fact, the program in Listing 5.5 is very simple. The program has just one function body from lines 5–23.

The `printf()` function in line 6 prints out a headline that contains three fields: `Hex(uppercase)`, `Hex(lowercase)`, and `Decimal`.

Then, lines 7–22 print out the hex and decimal numbers 0 through 15. Sixteen `printf()` functions are called to accomplish the job. Each of the `printf()` functions has a format string as the first argument followed by three integers as three expressions. Note that the hex format specifiers `%X` and `%x` are used within the format string in each of the `printf()` functions to convert the corresponding expressions to the hex format (both uppercase and lowercase).

In reality, nobody would write a program like the one in Listing 5.5. Instead, a loop can be used to call the `printf()` function repeatedly. Looping (or iteration) is introduced in Hour 7, "Doing the Same Thing Over and Over."

Adding the Minimum Field Width

The C language allows you to add an integer between the percent sign (`%`) and the letter in a format specifier. The integer is called the *minimum field width specifier* because it specifies the minimum field width and ensures that the output reaches the minimum width. For example, in `%10f`, `10` is a minimum field width specifier that ensures that the output is at least 10 character spaces wide.

The example in Listing 5.6 shows how to use the minimum field width specifier.

TYPE **Listing 5.6. Specifying the minimum field width.**

```
1:   /* 05L06.c: Specifying minimum field width */
2:   #include <stdio.h>
3:
4:   main()
5:   {
6:      int num1, num2;
7:
8:      num1 = 12;
9:      num2 = 12345;
10:     printf("%d\n", num1);
11:     printf("%d\n", num2);
12:     printf("%5d\n", num1);
13:     printf("%05d\n", num1);
14:     printf("%2d\n", num2);
15:     return 0;
16: }
```

5

The following is the result I obtain by running the executable file `05L06.exe`:

OUTPUT
```
C:\app> 05L06
12
12345
   12
00012
12345
C:\app>
```

ANALYSIS In Listing 5.6, two integer variables, num1 and num2, are declared in line 6, and assigned 12 and 12345, respectively, in lines 8 and 9.

Without using any minimum field width specifiers, lines 10 and 11 print out the two integers by calling the printf() function. You can see in the output section that the output made by the statements in line 10 is 12, which takes two character spaces, while the output, 12345, from line 11 takes five character spaces.

In line 12, a minimum field width, 5, is specified by %5d. The output from line 12 therefore takes five character spaces, with three blank spaces plus two character spaces of 12. (See the third output line in the output section.)

The %05d in printf(), shown in line 13, indicates that the minimum field width is 5, and zeros are used to pad the spaces. Therefore, you see the output made by the execution of the statement in line 13 is

`00012`

The %2d in line 14 sets the minimum field width to 2, but you still see the full-size output of 12345 from line 14. This means that when the minimum field width is shorter than the width of the output, the latter is taken, and the output is still printed in full.

Aligning Output

As you might have noticed in the previous section, all output is right-justified. In other words, by default, all output is placed on the right edge of the field, as long as the field width is longer than the width of the output.

You can change this and force output to be left-justified. To do so, you need to prefix the minimum field specifier with the minus sign (-). For example, %-12d specifies the minimum field width as 12, and justifies the output from the left edge of the field.

Listing 5.7 gives an example of aligning output by left- or right-justification.

TYPE **Listing 5.7. Left- or right-justified output.**

```
1:  /* 05L07.c: Aligning output */
2:  #include <stdio.h>
3:
```

5

```
4:   main()
5:   {
6:       int num1, num2, num3, num4, num5;
7:
8:       num1 = 1;
9:       num2 = 12;
10:      num3 = 123;
11:      num4 = 1234;
12:      num5 = 12345;
13:      printf("%8d  %-8d\n", num1, num1);
14:      printf("%8d  %-8d\n", num2, num2);
15:      printf("%8d  %-8d\n", num3, num3);
16:      printf("%8d  %-8d\n", num4, num4);
17:      printf("%8d  %-8d\n", num5, num5);
18:      return 0;
19: }
```

I get the following output displayed on the screen after I run the executable 05L07.exe from a DOS prompt on my machine:

OUTPUT

```
C:\app> 05L07
       1  1
      12  12
     123  123
    1234  1234
   12345  12345
C:\app>
```

ANALYSIS In Listing 5.7, there are five integer variables, num1, num2, num3, num4, and num5, that are declared in line 6 and are assigned values in lines 8–12.

These values represented by the five integer variables are then printed out by the printf() functions in lines 13–17. Note that all the printf() functions have the same first argument: "%8d %-8d\n". Here the first format specifier, %8d, aligns the output at the right edge of the field, and the second specifier, %-8d, does the alignment by justifying the output from the left edge of the field.

After the execution of the statements in lines 13–17, the alignment is accomplished and the output is put on the screen like this:

```
       1  1
      12  12
     123  123
    1234  1234
   12345  12345
```

Using the Precision Specifier

You can put a period (.) and an integer right after the minimum field width specifier. The combination of the period (.) and the integer makes up a *precision specifier*. The precision specifier is another important specifier you can use to determine the number of decimal places for floating-point numbers, or to specify the maximum field width (or length) for integers or strings. (Strings in C are introduced in Hour 13, "Manipulating Strings.")

For instance, with %10.3f, the minimum field width length is specified as 10 characters long, and the number of decimal places is set to 3. (Remember, the default number of decimal places is 6.) For integers, %3.8d indicates that the minimum field width is 3, and the maximum field width is 8.

Listing 5.8 gives an example of left- or right-justifying output by using precision specifiers.

TYPE | **Listing 5.8. Using precision specifiers.**

```
1:  /* 05L08.c: Using precision specifiers */
2:  #include <stdio.h>
3:
4:  main()
5:  {
6:     int int_num;
7:     double flt_num;
8:
9:     int_num = 123;
10:    flt_num = 123.456789;
11:    printf("Default integer format:    %d\n", int_num);
12:    printf("With precision specifier:  %2.8d\n", int_num);
13:    printf("Default float format:      %f\n", flt_num);
14:    printf("With precision specifier:  %-10.2f\n", flt_num);
15:    return 0;
16: }
```

After running the executable file 05L08.exe on my machine, I get the following output on the screen:

OUTPUT
```
C:\app> 05L08
Default integer format:    123
With precision specifier:  00000123
Default float format:      123.456789
With precision specifier:  123.46
C:\app>
```

ANALYSIS The program in Listing 5.8 declares one integer variable, int_num, in line 6, and one floating-point number, flt_num, in line 7. Lines 9 and 10 assign 123 and 123.456789 to int_num and flt_num, respectively.

In line 11, the default integer format is specified for the integer variable, int_num, while the statement in line 12 specifies the integer format with a precision specifier that indicates that the maximum field width is 8 characters long. Therefore, you see that five zeros are padded prior to the integer 123 in the second line of the output.

For the floating-point variable, flt_num, line 13 prints out the floating-point value in the default format, and line 14 reduces the decimal places to two by putting the precision specifier .2 within the format specifier %-10.2f. Note here that the left-justification is also specified by the minus sign (-) in the floating-point format specifier.

The floating-point number 123.46 in the fourth line of the output is produced by the statement in line 14 with the precision specifier for two decimal places. Therefore, 123.456789 rounded to two decimal places becomes 123.46.

Summary

In this lesson you've learned the following:

- ☐ The C language treats a file as a series of bytes.
- ☐ stdin, stdout, and stderr are three file streams that are pre-opened for you to use.
- ☐ The C library functions getc() and getchar() can be used to read in one character from the standard input.
- ☐ The C library functions putc() and putchar() can be used to write one character to the standard output.
- ☐ %x or %X can be used to convert decimal numbers to hex numbers.
- ☐ A minimum field width can be specified and ensured by adding an integer into a format specifier.
- ☐ An output can be aligned at either the left or right edge of the output field.
- ☐ A precision specifier can be used to specify the decimal place number for floating-point numbers, or the maximum field width for integers or strings.

In the next lesson you'll learn about some important operators in C.

Q&A

Q What are stdin, stdout, and stderr?

A In C, a file is treated as a series of bytes that is called file stream. stdin, stdout, and stderr are all pre-opened file streams. stdin is the standard input for reading; stdout is the standard output for writing; stderr is the standard error for outputting error messages.

Q How much is the hex number 32?

A Hexadecimal, or hex for short, is a base-16 numerical system. Therefore, 32 (hex) is equal to $3*16^1+2*16^0$, or 50 in decimal.

5

Q Are getc(stdin) and getchar() equivalent?

A Because the getchar() function reads from the file stream stdin by default, getc(stdin) and getchar() are equivalent.

Q In the function printf("The integer %d is the same as the hex %x", 12, 12), what is the relationship between the format specifiers and the expressions?

A The two format specifiers, %d and %x, specify the formats of numeric values contained in the expression section. Here the first numeric value of 12 is going to be printed out in integer format, while the second 12 (in the expression section) will be displayed in the hex format. Generally speaking, the number of format specifiers in the format section should match the number of expressions in the expression section.

Workshop

To help solidify your understanding of this hour's lesson, you are encouraged to answer the quiz questions and finish the exercises provided in the Workshop before you move to the next lesson. The answers and hints to the questions and exercises are given in Appendix E, "Answers to Quiz Questions and Exercises."

Quiz

1. Can you align your output at the left edge, rather than the right edge, of the output field?
2. What is the difference between putc() and putchar()?
3. What does getchar() return?
4. Within %10.3f, which part is the minimum field width specifier, and which one is the precision specifier?

Exercises

1. Write a program to put the characters B, y, and e together on the screen.
2. Display the two numbers 123 and 123.456 and align them at the left edge of the field.
3. Given three integers—15, 150, and 1500—write a program that prints the integers on the screen in the hex format.
4. Write a program that uses getchar() and putchar() to read in a character entered by the user and write the character to the screen.

5. If you compile the following C program, what warning or error messages will you get?

```
main()
{
    int ch;
    ch = getchar();
    putchar(ch);
    return 0;
}
```

5

PART

II

Operators and Control-Flow Statements

Hour

Hour 6

Manipulating Data with Operators

"The question is," said Humpty Dumpty, "which is to be master—that's all."

—*L. Carroll*

You can think of operators as verbs in C that let you manipulate data. In fact, you've learned some operators, such as + (addition), - (subtraction), * (multiplication), / (division), and % (remainder), in Hour 3, "The Essentials of C Programs." The C language has a rich set of operators. In this hour, you'll learn about more operators, such as

- ☐ Arithmetic assignment operators
- ☐ Unary minus operators
- ☐ Increment and decrement operators
- ☐ Relational operators
- ☐ Cast operator

Arithmetic Assignment Operators

Before jumping into the arithmetic assignment operators, you first need to learn more about the assignment operator.

The Assignment Operator (=)

In the C language, the = operator is called an *assignment operator*, which you've seen and used for several hours.

The general statement form to use an assignment operator is

```
left-hand-operand = right-hand-operand;
```

Here the statement causes the value of the `right-hand-operand` to be assigned (or written) to the memory location of the `left-hand-operand`. Additionally, the assignment statement itself returns the same value that is assigned to the `left-hand-operand`.

For example, the a = 5; statement writes the value of the right-hand operand (5) into the memory location of the integer variable a (which is the left-hand operand in this case).

Similarly, the b = a = 5; statement assigns 5 to the integer variable a first, and then to the integer variable b. After the execution of the statement, both a and b contain the value of 5.

WARNING

> Don't confuse the assignment operator (=) with the relational operator, == (called the *equal-to operator*). The == operator is introduced later in this hour.

Combining Arithmetic Operators with =

Consider this example: Given two integer variables, x and y, how do you assign the sum of x and y to another integer variable, z?

By using the assignment operator (=) and the addition operator (+), you get the following statement:

```
z = x + y;
```

As you can see, it's pretty simple. Now, consider the same example again. This time, instead of assigning the result to the third variable, z, let's write the sum back to the integer variable, x:

```
x = x + y;
```

Here, on the right side of the assignment operator (=), the addition of x and y is executed; on the left side of =, the previous value saved by x is replaced with the result of the addition from the right side.

6

The C language gives you a new operator, +=, to do the addition and the assignment together. Therefore, you can rewrite the x = x + y; statement to

```
x += y;
```

The combinations of the assignment operator (=) with the arithmetic operators, +, -, *, /, and %, give you another type of operators—*arithmetic assignment operators*:

Operator	Description
+=	Addition assignment operator
-=	Subtraction assignment operator
*=	Multiplication assignment operator
/=	Division assignment operator
%=	Remainder assignment operator

The following shows the equivalence of statements:

x += y; is equivalent to x = x + y;

x -= y; is equivalent to x = x - y;

x *= y; is equivalent to x = x * y;

x /= y; is equivalent to x = x / y;

x %= y; is equivalent to x = x % y;

Note that the statement

```
z = z * x + y;
```

is not equivalent to the statement

```
z *= x + y;
```

because

```
z *= x + y
```

is indeed the same as

```
z = z * (x + y);
```

Listing 6.1 gives an example of using some of the arithmetic assignment operators.

TYPE **Listing 6.1. Using arithmetic assignment operators.**

```
1:  /* 06L01.c: Using arithmetic assignment operators */
2:  #include <stdio.h>
3:
```

continues

Listing 6.1. continued

```
4:   main()
5:   {
6:       int x, y, z;
7:
8:       x = 1;   /* initialize x */
9:       y = 3;   /* initialize y */
10:      z = 10;  /* initialize z */
11:      printf("Given x = %d, y = %d, and z = %d,\n", x, y, z);
12:
13:      x = x + y;
14:      printf("x = x + y  assigns %d to x;\n", x);
15:
16:      x = 1;  /* reset x */
17:      x += y;
18:      printf("x += y  assigns %d to x;\n", x);
19:
20:      x = 1;  /* reset x */
21:      z = z * x + y;
22:      printf("z = z * x + y  assigns %d to z;\n", z);
23:
24:      z = 10;  /* reset z */
25:      z = z * (x + y);
26:      printf("z = z * (x + y) assigns %d to z;\n", z);
27:
28:      z = 10;  /* reset z */
29:      z *= x + y;
30:      printf("z *= x + y assigns %d to z.\n", z);
31:
32:      return 0;
33: }
```

After this program is compiled and linked, an executable file is created. On my machine, this executable file is named as 06L01.exe. The following is the output printed on the screen after I run the executable from a DOS prompt:

OUTPUT
```
C:\app> 06L01
Given x = 1, y = 3, and z = 10,
x = x + y  assigns 4 to x;
x += y  assigns 4 to x;
z = z * x + y  assigns 13 to z;
z = z * (x + y) assigns 40 to z;
z *= x + y assigns 40 to z.
C:\app>
```

ANALYSIS Line 2 in Listing 6.1 includes the header file stdio.h by using the include directive in C. The stdio.h header file is needed for the printf() function used in the main() function body in lines 4–33.

Lines 8–10 initialize three integer variables, x, y, and z, which are declared in line 6. Line 11 then prints out the initial values assigned to x, y, and z.

The statement in line 13 uses the one addition operator and one assignment operator to add the values contained by x and y, and then assigns the result to x. Line 14 displays the result on the screen.

Similarly, lines 17 and 18 do the same addition and display the result again, after the variable x is reset in line 16. This time, the arithmetic assignment operator, +=, is used. Also, line 16 in Listing 6.1 resets the value of x to 1, before the addition.

The value of x is reset again in line 20. Line 21 performs a multiplication and an addition and saves the result to the integer variable z; that is, z = z * x + y;. The printf() function in line 22 displays the result, 13, on the screen. Again, the x = 1; statement in line 20 resets the integer variable, x.

Lines 24–30 display two results from two computations. The two results are actually the same (that is, 40), because the two computations in lines 25 and 29 are equivalent. The only difference between the two statements in lines 25 and 29 is that the arithmetic assignment operator, *=, is used in line 29.

Getting Negations of Numeric Numbers

If you want to change the sign of a numeric number, you can put the minus operator (-) right before the number. For instance, given an integer of 7, you can get its negation by changing the sign of the integer like this: -7. Here, - is the minus operator.

Precisely, - is called the *unary minus operator* in C. This is because the operator takes only one operand. The type of the operand can be any integer or floating-point number.

You can apply the unary minus operator to an integer or a floating-point variable as well. For example, given x = 1.234, -x equals -1.234. Or, given x = -1.234, -x equals 1.234.

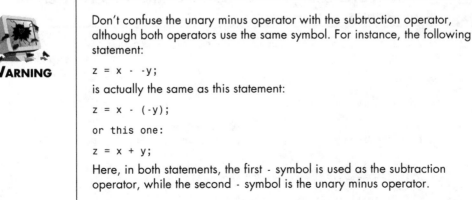

WARNING

Don't confuse the unary minus operator with the subtraction operator, although both operators use the same symbol. For instance, the following statement:

```
z = x - -y;
```

is actually the same as this statement:

```
z = x - (-y);
```

or this one:

```
z = x + y;
```

Here, in both statements, the first - symbol is used as the subtraction operator, while the second - symbol is the unary minus operator.

6

Incrementing or Decrementing by One

The increment and decrement operators are very handy to use when you want to add or subtract 1 from a variable. The symbol for the increment operator is ++. The decrement operator is --.

For instance, you can rewrite the statement x = x + 1; as ++x;, or you can replace x = x 1; with --x;.

Actually, there are two versions of the increment operator and of the decrement operator. In the ++x; statement, the increment operator is called the *pre-increment operator*, because the operator adds 1 to x first and then gets the value of x. Likewise, in the --x; statement, the *pre-decrement operator* first subtracts 1 from x and then gets the value of x.

If you have an expression like x++, you're using the *post-increment operator*. Similarly, in x--, the decrement operator is called the *post-decrement operator*.

For example, in the y = x++; statement, y is assigned the original value of x, not the one after x is increased by 1. In other words, the post-increment operator makes a copy of the original value of x and stores the copy in a temporary location. Then, x is increased by 1. However, instead of the modified value of x, the copy of the unmodified value of x is returned and assigned to y.

The post-decrement operator has a similar story. This operator returns a copy of the original value of a variable, rather than the current value of the variable (which has been decreased by 1).

The program in Listing 6.2 shows the differences between the two versions of increment operators and decrement operators.

TYPE

Listing 6.2. Using pre- or post-increment and decrement operators.

```
1:   /* 06L02.c: pre- or post-increment(decrement) operators */
2:   #include <stdio.h>
3:
4:   main()
5:   {
6:      int w, x, y, z, result;
7:
8:      w = x = y = z = 1;   /* initialize x and y */
9:      printf("Given w = %d, x = %d, y = %d, and z = %d,\n", w, x, y, z);
10:
11:     result = ++w;
12:     printf("++w gives: %d\n", result);
13:     result = x++;
14:     printf("x++ gives: %d\n", result);
15:     result = --y;
16:     printf("--y gives: %d\n", result);
```

6

```
17:     result = z--;
18:     printf("z-- gives: %d\n", result);
19:     return 0;
20: }
```

The following result is obtained by running the executable file 06L02.exe:

OUTPUT
```
C:\app> 06L02
Given w = 1, x = 1, y = 1, and z = 1,
++w gives: 2
x++ gives: 1
--y gives: 0
z-- gives: 1
C:\app>
```

ANALYSIS Inside the main() function, line 8 in Listing 6.2 assigns 1 to each of the integer variables, w, x, y, and z. The printf() function in line 9 displays the values contained by the four integer variables.

Then, the statement in line 11 is executed and the result of the pre-increment of w is given to the integer variable result. In line 12, the value of result, which is 2, is printed out to the screen.

Lines 13 and 14 get the post-increment of x and print out the result. As you know, the result is obtained before the value of x is increased. Therefore, you see the numeric value 1 from the result of x++ on the screen.

The pre-decrement operator in line 15 causes the value of y to be reduced by 1 before the value is assigned to the integer variable result. Therefore, you see 0 as the result of --y shown on the screen.

In line 17, however, the post-decrement operator has no effect on the assignment because the original value of z is given to the integer variable result before z is decreased by 1. Line 18 thus prints out 1, which is the original value of z.

Greater Than or Less Than?

There are six types of relationships between two expressions: equal to, not equal to, greater than, less than, greater than or equal to, and less than or equal to. Accordingly, the C language provides six relational operators:

Operator	Description
==	Equal to
!=	Not equal to
>	Greater than

continues

Operator	Description
<	Less than
>=	Greater than or equal to
<=	Less than or equal to

All the relational operators have lower precedence than the arithmetic operators. Therefore, all arithmetic operations are carried out before any comparison is made. You should use parentheses to enclose operations of operators that have to be performed first.

Among the six operators, the >, <, >=, and <= operators have higher precedence than the == and != operators.

For example, the expression

```
x * y < z + 3
```

is interpreted as

```
(x * y) < (z + 3)
```

Another important thing is that all relational expressions produce a result of either 0 or 1. In other words, a relational expression returns 1 if the specified relationship holds. Otherwise, 0 is returned.

Given x = 3 and y = 5, for instance, the relational expression x < y gives a result of 1.

Listing 6.3 shows more examples of using relational operators.

TYPE   **Listing 6.3. Results produced by relational expressions.**

```
1:  /* 06L03.c: Using relational operators */
2:  #include <stdio.h>
3:
4:  main()
5:  {
6:     int x, y;
7:     double z;
8:
9:     x = 7;
10:    y = 25;
11:    z = 24.46;
12:    printf("Given x = %d, y = %d, and z = %.2f,\n", x, y, z);
13:    printf("x >= y   produces: %d\n", x >= y);
14:    printf("x == y   produces: %d\n", x == y);
15:    printf("x < z    produces: %d\n", x < z);
16:    printf("y > z    produces: %d\n", y > z);
17:    printf("x != y - 18   produces: %d\n", x != y - 18);
18:    printf("x + y != z    produces: %d\n", x + y != z);
19:    return 0;
20: }
```

6

After the executable 06L03.exe is executed from a DOS prompt, the following output is displayed on the screen:

OUTPUT

```
C:\app> 06L03
Given x = 7, y = 25, and z = 24.46,
x >= y   produces: 0
x == y   produces: 0
x < z    produces: 1
y > z    produces: 1
x != y - 18  produces: 0
x + y != z   produces: 1
C:\app>
```

ANALYSIS There are two integer variables, x and y, and one floating-point variable z, declared in lines 6 and 7, respectively.

Lines 9–11 initialize the three variables. Line 12 prints out the values assigned to the variables.

Because the value of x is 7 and the value of y is 25, y is greater than x. Therefore, line 13 prints out 0, which is returned from the relational expression, x >= y.

Likewise, in line 14, the relational expression x == y returns 0.

Lines 15 and 16, however, print out the result of 1, returned from either x < z or y > z.

The statement in line 17 displays 0, which is the result of the relational expression x != y - -18. In line 18, the expression x + y != z produces 1, which is output on the screen.

WARNING

Be careful when you compare two values for equality. Because of the truncation, or rounding up, some relational expressions, which are algebraically true, may return 0 instead of 1. For example, look at the following relational expression:

1 / 2 + 1 / 2 == 1

this is algebraically true and is supposed to return 1.

The expression, however, returns 0, which means that the equal-to relationship does not hold. This is because the truncation of the integer division—that is, 1 / 2—produces 0, not 0.5.

Another example is 1.0 / 3.0, which produces 0.33333.... This is a number with an infinite number of decimal places. But the computer can only hold a limited number of decimal places. Therefore, the expression

1.0 / 3.0 + 1.0 / 3.0 + 1.0 / 3.0 == 1.0

might not return 1 on some computers, although the expression is theoretically true.

6

Playing with the Cast Operator

In C, you can convert one data type to a different one by prefixing the cast operator to the operand.

The general form of the cast operator is

`(data-type)x`

Here `data-type` specifies the data type you want to convert to. `x` is a variable (or, expression) that contains the value of the current data type. You have to include the parentheses (and) to make up a cast operator.

For example, the `(float)5` expression converts the integer 5 to a floating-point number, 5.0.

The program in Listing 6.4 shows another example of using the cast operator.

TYPE   **Listing 6.4. Using the cast operator.**

```
1:  /* 06L04.c: Using the cast operator */
2:  #include <stdio.h>
3:
4:  main()
5:  {
6:     int x, y;
7:
8:     x = 7;
9:     y = 5;
10:    printf("Given x = %d, y = %d\n", x, y);
11:    printf("x / y produces: %d\n",  x / y);
12:    printf("(float)x / y produces: %f\n",  (float)x / y);
13:    return 0;
14: }
```

The following output is obtained by running the executable `06L04.exe` from a DOS prompt:

```
C:\app> 06L04
Given x = 7, y = 5
x / y produces: 1
(float)x / y produces: 1.400000
C:\app>
```

In Listing 6.4, there are two integer variables, x and y, declared in line 6, and initialized in lines 8 and 9, respectively. Line 10 then displays the values contained by the integer variables x and y.

The statement in line 11 prints out the integer division of x/y. Because the fractional part is truncated, the result of the integer division is 1.

However, in line 12, the cast operator (float) converts the value of x to a floating-point value. Therefore, the (float)x/y expression becomes a floating-point division that returns a floating-point number. That's why you see the floating-point number 1.400000 shown on the screen after the statement in line 12 is executed.

Summary

In this lesson you've learned about the following:

- [ ] The assignment operator (=), which has two operands on each side. The value of the right-side operand is assigned to the operand on the left side.

- [ ] The arithmetic assignment operators, +=, -=, *=, /=, and %=, which are the combinations of the arithmetic operators with the assignment operator.

- [ ] The unary minus operator (-), which returns the negation of a numeric value.

- [ ] The two versions of the increment operator, ++. You know that in ++x, the ++ operator is called the pre-increment operator; and in x++, ++ is the post-increment operator.

- [ ] The two versions of decrement operator, --. You have learned that, for example, in --x, the -- operator is the pre-decrement operator, while in x--, -- is called the post-decrement operator.

- [ ] The six relational operators in C: == (equal to), != (not equal to), > (greater than), < (less than), >= (greater than or equal to), and <= (less than or equal to).

- [ ] How to change the type of data by prefixing a cast operator to the data.

In the next lesson you'll learn about loops in the C language.

Q&A

Q What is the difference between the pre-increment operator and the post-increment operator?

A The pre-increment operator increases the operand's value by 1 first, and then returns the modified value. On the other hand, the post-increment operator stores a copy of the operand value in a temporary location and then increases the operand value by 1. However, the copy of the unmodified operand value is returned in the expression. For instance, given x = 1, the ++x expression returns 2, while the x++ expression returns 1.

6

Q Is the unary minus operator (-) the same as the subtraction operator (-)?

A No, they are not the same, although the two operators share the same symbol. The unary minus operator is used to change the sign of a value. In other words, the unary minus operator returns the negation of the value. The subtraction operator is an arithmetic operator that performs subtraction between its two operands.

Q Which one has a higher precedence, a relational operator or an arithmetic operator?

A An arithmetic operator has a higher precedence than a relational operator. For instance, the x * y + z > x + y expression is interpreted as ((x * y) + z) > (x + y).

Q What does a relational expression return?

A A relational expression returns either 0 or 1. If the relationship indicated by a relational operator in an expression is true, the expression returns 1; otherwise, the expression returns 0.

Workshop

To help solidify your understanding of this hour's lesson, you are encouraged to answer the quiz questions and finish the exercises provided in the Workshop before you move to the next lesson. The answers and hints to the questions and exercises are given in Appendix E, "Answers to Quiz Questions and Exercises."

Quiz

1. What is the difference between the = operator and the == operator?
2. In the x + - y - - z expression, which operator is the subtraction operator, and which one is the unary minus operator?
3. Given x = 15 and y = 4, what do the x / y and (float)x / y expressions return, respectively?
4. Is the y *= x + 5 expression equivalent to the y = y * x + 5 expression?

Exercises

1. Given x = 1 and y = 3, write a program to print out the results of these expressions: x += y, x += -y, x -= y, x -= -y, x *= y, and x *= -y.
2. Given x = 3 and y = 6, what is the value of z after the expression

   z = x * y == 18 is executed?

3. Write a program that initializes the integer variable x with 1 and outputs results with the following two statements:

```
printf("x++ produces:    %d\n", x++);
printf("Now x contains: %d\n", x);
```

4. Rewrite the program you wrote in exercise 3. This time, include the following two statements:

```
printf("x = x++ produces: %d\n", x = x++);
printf("Now x contains:    %d\n", x);
```

What do you get after running the executable of the program? Can you explain why you get such a result?

5. The following program is supposed to compare the two variables, x and y, for equality. What's wrong with the program? (Hint: Run the program to see what it prints out.)

```
#include <stdio.h>

main()
{
   int x, y;

   x = y = 0;
   printf("The comparison result is: %d\n",  x = y);
   return 0;
}
```

6

Hour **7**

Doing the Same Thing Over and Over

Heaven and earth:
Unheard sutra chanting
Repeated…

—Zen saying

In the previous lessons, you've learned the basics of the C program, several important C functions, standard I/O, and some useful operators. In this lesson you'll learn a very important feature of the C language—looping. Looping, also called *iteration*, is used in programming to perform the same set of statements over and over until certain specified conditions are met.

Three statements in C are designed for looping:

☐ The `for` statement

☐ The `while` statement

☐ The `do-while` statement

The following sections explore these statements.

Looping Under the for Statement

The general form of the for statement is

```
for (expression1; expression2; expression3) {
   statement1;
   statement2;
   .
   .
   .
}
```

You see from this example that the for statement uses three expressions (*expression1*, *expression2*, and *expression3*) that are separated by semicolons.

Several statements, such as *statement1* and *statement2*, are placed within the braces ({ and }). All the statements and the braces form a statement block that is treated as a single statement. (You learned about this in Hour 3, "The Essentials of C Programs.")

In the preceding for statement format, the beginning brace ({) is put on the same line of the for keyword. You can place the beginning brace on a separate line beneath the for keyword.

The for statement first evaluates *expression1*, which usually initializes one or more variables. In other words, *expression1* is only evaluated once when the for statement is first encountered.

The second expression, *expression2*, is the conditional part that is evaluated right after the evaluation of *expression1* and then is evaluated after each successful looping by the for statement. If *expression2* returns a nonzero value, the statements within the braces are executed. Usually, the nonzero value is 1. If *expression2* returns 0, the looping is stopped and the execution of the for statement is finished.

The third expression in the for statement, *expression3*, is not evaluated when the for statement is first encountered. However, *expression3* is evaluated after each looping and before the statement goes back to test *expression2* again.

In Hour 5, "Reading from and Writing to Standard I/O," you saw an example (in Listing 5.5) that converts the decimal numbers 0 through 15 into hex numbers. Back then, conversions made for each number had to be written in a separate statement. Now, with the for statement, we can rewrite the program in Listing 5.5 in a very efficient way. Listing 7.1 shows the rewritten version of the program.

Listing 7.1. Converting 0 through 15 to hex numbers.

```
1:   /* 07L01.c: Converting 0 through 15 to hex numbers */
2:   #include <stdio.h>
3:
4:   main()
5:   {
6:      int i;
7:
8:      printf("Hex(uppercase)   Hex(lowercase)   Decimal\n");
9:      for (i=0; i<16; i++){
10:        printf("%X               %x                %d\n", i, i, i);
11:     }
12:     return 0;
13: }
```

After creating the executable file 07L01.exe and running it by typing in 07L01 from a DOS prompt, I obtain the same output as the one from 05L05.exe:

OUTPUT
```
C:\app> 07L01
Hex(uppercase)   Hex(lowercase)   Decimal
0                0                0
1                1                1
2                2                2
3                3                3
4                4                4
5                5                5
6                6                6
7                7                7
8                8                8
9                9                9
A                a                10
B                b                11
C                c                12
D                d                13
E                e                14
F                f                15
C:\app>
```

ANALYSIS   Now, let's have a look at the code in Listing 7.1. As you know, line 2 includes the header file stdio.h for the printf() function used later in the program.

Inside the body of the main() function, the statement in line 6 declares an integer variable, i. Line 8 displays the headline of the output on the screen.

Lines 9–11 contain the for statement. Note that the first expression in the for statement is i=0, which is an assignment expression that initializes the integer variable i to 0.

7

The second expression in the for statement is i<16, which is a relational expression. This expression returns 1 as long as the relation indicated by the less-than operator (<) holds. As mentioned earlier, the second expression is evaluated by the for statement each time after a successful looping. If the value of i is less than 16, which means the relational expression remains true, the for statement will start another loop. Otherwise, it will stop looping and exit.

The third expression in the for statement is i++ in this case. This expression is evaluated and the integer variable i is increased by 1 each time after the statement inside the body of the for statement is executed. Here it doesn't make a big difference whether the post-increment operator (i++) or the pre-increment operator (++i) is used in the third expression.

In other words, when the for loop is first encountered, i is set to 0, the expression

```
i<16
```

is evaluated and found to be true, and therefore the statements within the body of the for loop are executed. Following execution of the for loop, the third expression i++ is executed incrementing i to 1, and i<16 is again evaluated and found to be true, thus the body of the loop is executed again. The looping lasts until the conditional expression i<16 is no longer true.

There is only one statement inside the for statement body, as you can see in line 10. The statement contains the printf() function, which is used to display the hex numbers (both uppercase and lowercase) converted from the decimal values by using the format specifiers, %X and %x.

Here the decimal value is provided by the integer variable i. As explained, i contains the initial value of 0 right before and during the first looping. After each looping, i is increased by 1 because of the third expression, i++, in the for statement. The last value provided by i is 15. When i reaches 16, the relation indicated by the second expression, i<16, is no longer true. Therefore, the looping is stopped and the execution of the for statement is completed.

Then, the statement in line 12 returns 0 to indicate a normal termination of the program, and finally, the main() function ends and returns the control back to the operating system.

As you see, with the for statement, you can write a very concise program. In fact, the program in Listing 7.1 is more than 10 lines shorter than the one in Listing 5.5, although the two programs can do exactly the same thing.

Actually, you can make the program in Listing 7.1 even shorter. In the for statement, you can discard the braces ({ and }) if there is only one statement inside the statement block.

The Null Statement

As you may notice, the `for` statement does not end with a semicolon. The `for` statement has within it either a statement block that ends with the closing brace (}) or a single statement that ends with a semicolon. The following `for` statement contains a single statement:

```
for (i=0; i<8; i++)
    sum += i;
```

Now consider a statement such as this:

```
for (i=0; i<8; i++);
```

Here the `for` statement is followed by a semicolon immediately.

In the C language, there is a special statement called the *null statement*. A null statement contains nothing but a semicolon. In other words, a null statement is a statement with no expression.

Therefore, when you review the statement `for (i=0; i<8; i++);`, you can see that it is actually a `for` statement with a null statement. In other words, you can rewrite it as

```
for (i=0; i<8; i++)
    ;
```

Because the null statement has no expression, the `for` statement actually does nothing but loop. You'll see some examples of using the null statement with the `for` statement later in the book.

WARNING

Because the null statement is perfectly legal in C, you should pay attention to placing semicolons in your `for` statements. For example, suppose you intended to write a `for` loop like this:

```
for (i=0; i<8; i++)
    sum += i;
```

If you accidentally put a semicolon at the end of the `for` statement like this, however,

```
for (i=0; i<8; i++);
    sum += i;
```

your C compiler will still accept it, but the results from the two `for` statements will be quite different. (See exercise 1 in this lesson for an example.)

7

Adding More Expressions into for

The C language allows you to put more expressions into the three expression fields in the for statement. Expressions in a single expression field are separated by commas.

For instance, the following form is valid in C:

```
for (i=0, j=10; i<10, j>0; i++, j--){
   /* statement block */
}
```

Here, in the first expression field, the two integer variables, i and j, are initialized, respectively, with 0 and 10 when the for statement is first encountered. Then, in the second field, the two relational expressions, i<10 and j>0, are evaluated and tested. If one of the relational expressions returns 0, the looping is stopped. After each iteration and the statements in the statement block are executed successfully, i is increased by 1, j is reduced by 1 in the third expression field, and the expressions i<10 and j>0 are evaluated to determine whether to do one more looping.

Now, let's look at a real program. Listing 7.2 shows an example of using multiple expressions in the for statement.

TYPE

Listing 7.2. Adding multiple expressions to the for statement.

```
1:  /* 07L02.c: Multiple expressions */
2:  #include <stdio.h>
3:
4:  main()
5:  {
6:     int i, j;
7:
8:     for (i=0, j=8; i<8; i++, j--)
9:        printf("%d  +  %d  =  %d\n", i, j, i+j);
10:    return 0;
11: }
```

I get the following output displayed on the screen after running the executable, 07L02.exe:

OUTPUT

```
C:\app> 07L02
0  +  8  =  8
1  +  7  =  8
2  +  6  =  8
3  +  5  =  8
4  +  4  =  8
5  +  3  =  8
6  +  2  =  8
7  +  1  =  8
C:\app>
```

7

ANALYSIS   In Listing 7.2, line 6 declares two integer variables, i and j, which are used in a for loop.

In line 8, i is initialized with 0 and j is set to 8 in the first expression field of the for statement. The second expression field contains a condition, i<8, which tells the computer to keep looping as long as the value of i is less than 8.

Each time, after the statement controlled by for in line 8 is executed, the third expression field is evaluated, and i is increased by 1 while j is reduced by 1. Because there is only one statement inside the for loop, no braces ({ and }) are used to form a statement block.

The statement in line 9 displays the addition of i and j on the screen during the looping, which outputs eight results during the looping by adding the values of the two variables, i and j.

Adding multiple expressions into the for statement is a very convenient way to manipulate more than one variable in a loop. To learn more about using multiple expressions in a for loop, look at the example in Listing 7.3.

Listing 7.3. Another example of using multiple expressions in the for statement.

TYPE

```
1:  /* 07L03.c: Another example of multiple expressions */
2:  #include <stdio.h>
3:
4:  main()
5:  {
6:      int i, j;
7:
8:      for (i=0, j=1; i<8; i++, j++)
9:          printf("%d  -  %d  =  %d\n", j, i, j - i);
10:     return 0;
11: }
```

The following output is displayed on the screen after the executable 07L03.exe is run on my machine:

OUTPUT
```
C:\app> 07L03
1  -  0  =  1
2  -  1  =  1
3  -  2  =  1
4  -  3  =  1
5  -  4  =  1
6  -  5  =  1
7  -  6  =  1
8  -  7  =  1
C:\app>
```

ANALYSIS   In Listing 7.3, two integer variables, i and j, are declared in line 6.

Note that in line 8, there are two assignment expressions, i=0 and j=1, in the first expression field of the for statement. These two assignment expressions initialize the i and j integer variables, respectively.

There is one relational expression, i<8, in the second field, which is the condition that has to be met before the looping can be carried out. Because i starts at 0 and is incremented by 1 after each loop, there are a total of eight loops that will be performed by the for statement.

The third expression field contains two expressions, i++ and j++, that increase the two integer variables by 1 each time after the statement in line 9 is executed.

The printf() function in line 9 displays the subtraction of the two integer variables, j and i, within the for loop. Because there is only one statement in the statement block, the braces ({ and }) are discarded.

Playing with an Infinite Loop

If you have a for statement like this,

```
for ( ; ; ){
  /* statement block */
}
```

you encounter an infinite loop. Note that in this for statement, there are no expressions in the three expression fields. The statements inside the statement block will be executed over and over without stopping.

You use the infinite loop if you don't know the exact number of loops you need. However, you have to set up some other conditions with the loop to test and determine whether and when you want to break the infinite loop.

The program in Listing 7.4 demonstrates an example that takes the characters entered by the user, and puts them on the screen. The for loop in the program keeps looping until the user enters the character x.

TYPE   **Listing 7.4. Adding conditions to a for loop.**

```
1:  /* 07L04.c: Conditional loop */
2:  #include <stdio.h>
3:
4:  main()
5:  {
6:      int c;
7:
```

7

```
8:      printf("Enter a character:\n(enter x to exit)\n");
9:      for ( c=' '; c != 'x'; ) {
10:        c = getc(stdin);
11:        putchar(c);
12:     }
13:     printf("\nOut of the for loop. Bye!\n");
14:     return 0;
15: }
```

After running the executable, 07L04.exe, I enter characters, such as H, i, and the \n character (I have to press the Enter key each time after I enter a character), which are all displayed back on the screen. Finally, I enter x to exit from the infinite for loop. (Note that in the following copy from the screen, the characters that I entered are in bold.)

OUTPUT

```
C:\app> 07L04
Enter a character:
(enter x to exit)
H
H
i
i
x
x
Out of the for loop. Bye!
C:\app>
```

ANALYSIS In Listing 7.4, there is only one integer variable, c, declared in line 6. The printf() function in line 8 displays the message Enter a character: on one line on the screen, and another message, (enter x to exit), on another line because there is a newline character (\n) added in the middle of the format string in the printf() function.

In line 9, the integer variable c is initialized with the numeric value of the space character. Then, a condition is evaluated in the second expression field of the for statement like this: c != 'x', which means that the condition is met if c does not contain the numeric value of x; otherwise, the condition is not met.

If the condition is met, the two statements in lines 10 and 11 will be executed over and over. The looping can last forever until the user enters the character x. Then, the statement in line 13 prints out a good-bye message right after the looping is terminated.

The while Loop

The while statement is also used for looping. Unlike the situation with the for statement, there is only one expression field in the while statement.

7

The general form of the while statement is

```
while (expression) {
    statement1;
    statement2;
      .
      .
      .
}
```

Here *expression* is the field of the expression in the while statement. The expression is evaluated first. If the expression returns a nonzero value (normally 1), the looping continues; that is, the statements inside the statement block are executed. After the execution, the expression is evaluated again. The statements are then executed one more time if the expression still returns nonzero value. The process is repeated over and over until the expression returns 0.

You see that a statement block, surround by the braces { and }, follows the while keyword and the expression field. Of course, if there is only one statement in the statement block, the braces can be discarded.

Now, let's look at an example of using the while statement. The program in Listing 7.5 is a modified version of the one in Listing 7.4, but this one uses the while statement.

TYPE **Listing 7.5. Using a while loop.**

```
1:   /* 07L05.c: Using a while loop */
2:   #include <stdio.h>
3:
4:   main()
5:   {
6:      int c;
7:
8:      c = ' ';
9:      printf("Enter a character:\n(enter x to exit)\n");
10:     while (c != 'x') {
11:        c = getc(stdin);
12:        putchar(c);
13:     }
14:     printf("\nOut of the while loop. Bye!\n");
15:     return 0;
16: }
```

The executable 07L05.exe can do a similar job as the executable 07L04.exe. The following is a copy from the screen:

OUTPUT
```
C:\app> 07L05
Enter a character:
(enter x to exit)
H
H
i
i
x
x
Out of the while loop. Bye!
C:\app>
```

ANALYSIS
You see that the output from the execution of the program in Listing 7.5 is similar to the one from Listing 7.4, except the while statement is used in lines 10–13 of Listing 7.5.

The char variable c is initialized with a space character in line 8. Unlike the for statement in Listing 7.4, the while statement does not set c before the looping.

In line 10, the relational expression c != 'x' is tested. If the expression returns 1, which means the relation still holds, the statements in lines 11 and 12 are executed. The looping continues as long as the expression returns 1. If, however, the user enters the character x, which makes the relational expression return 0, the looping stops.

The Infinite while Loop

You can also make a while loop infinite by putting 1 in the expression field, like this:

```
while (1) {
   statement1;
   statement2;
      .
      .
      .
}
```

Because the expression always returns 1, the statements inside the statement block will be executed over and over—that is, the while loop will continue forever. Of course, you can set certain conditions inside the while loop to break the infinite loop as soon as the conditions are met.

The C language provides some statements, such as if and break statements, that you can use to set conditions and break the infinite while loop if needed. Details on the if and break statements are covered in Hour 10, "Getting Controls."

7

The do-while **Loop**

You may note that in the for and while statements, the expressions are set at the top of the loop. However, in this section, you're going to see another statement used for looping, do-while, which puts the expressions at the bottom of the loop. In this way, the statements controlled by the do-while statement are executed at least once before the expression is tested. Note that statements in a for or while loop are not executed at all if the condition expression does not hold in the for or while statement.

The general form for the do-while statement is

```
do {
   statement1;
   statement2;
      .
      .
      .
} while (expression);
```

Here expression is the field for the expression that is evaluated in order to determine whether the statements inside the statement block are to be executed one more time. If the expression returns a nonzero value, the do-while loop continues; otherwise, the looping stops.

Note that the do-while statement ends with a semicolon, which is an important distinction from the if and while statements.

The program in Listing 7.6 displays the characters A through G by using a do-while loop to repeat the printing and adding.

TYPE   **Listing 7.6. Using a do-while loop.**

```
1:   /* 07L06.c: Using a do-while loop */
2:   #include <stdio.h>
3:
4:   main()
5:   {
6:      int i;
7:
8:      i = 65;
9:      do {
10:        printf("The numeric value of %c is %d.\n", i, i);
11:        i++;
12:     } while (i<72);
13:     return 0;
14: }
```

7

After running the executable 07L06.exe of Listing 7.6, I have the characters A through G, along with their numeric values, shown on the screen as follows:

OUTPUT

```
C:\app> 07L06
The numeric value of A is 65.
The numeric value of B is 66.
The numeric value of C is 67.
The numeric value of D is 68.
The numeric value of E is 69.
The numeric value of F is 70.
The numeric value of G is 71.
C:\app>
```

ANALYSIS

The statement in line 8 of Listing 7.6 initializes the integer variable i with 65. The integer variable is declared in line 6.

Lines 9–12 contain the do-while loop. The expression i<72 is at the bottom of the loop in line 12. When the loop first starts, the two statements in lines 10 and 11 are executed before the expression is evaluated. Because the integer variable i contains the initial value of 65, the printf() function in line 10 displays the numeric value as well as the corresponding character A on the screen.

After the integer variable i is increased by 1 in line 11, the program control reaches the bottom of the do-while loop. Then the expression i<72 is evaluated. If the relationship in the expression still holds, the program control jumps up to the top of the do-while loop, and then the process is repeated. When the expression returns 0 after i is increased to 72, the do-while loop is terminated immediately.

Using Nested Loops

You can put a loop inside another one to make *nested loops*. The computer will run the inner loop first before it resumes the looping for the outer loop.

Listing 7.7 is an example of how nested loops work.

TYPE   **Listing 7.7. Using nested loops.**

```
1:  /* 07L07.c: Demonstrating nested loops */
2:  #include <stdio.h>
3:
4:  main()
5:  {
6:      int i, j;
7:
```

continues

Listing 7.7. continued

```
8:     for (i=1; i<=3; i++) {    /* outer loop */
9:        printf("The start of iteration %d of the outer loop.\n", i);
10:        for (j=1; j<=4; j++)  /* inner loop */
11:           printf("   Iteration %d of the inner loop.\n", j);
12:        printf("The end of iteration %d of the outer loop.\n", i);
13:     }
14:     return 0;
15: }
```

The following result is obtained by running the executable file 07L07.exe:

OUTPUT
```
C:\app> 07L07
The start of iteration 1 of the outer loop.
    Iteration 1 of the inner loop.
    Iteration 2 of the inner loop.
    Iteration 3 of the inner loop.
    Iteration 4 of the inner loop.
The end of iteration 1 of the outer loop.
The start of iteration 2 of the outer loop.
    Iteration 1 of the inner loop.
    Iteration 2 of the inner loop.
    Iteration 3 of the inner loop.
    Iteration 4 of the inner loop.
The end of iteration 2 of the outer loop.
The start of iteration 3 of the outer loop.
    Iteration 1 of the inner loop.
    Iteration 2 of the inner loop.
    Iteration 3 of the inner loop.
    Iteration 4 of the inner loop.
The end of iteration 3 of the outer loop.
C:\app>
```

ANALYSIS In Listing 7.7, two for loops are nested together. The outer for loop starts in line 8 and ends in line 13, while the inner for loop starts in line 10 and ends in line 11.

The inner loop controls one statement that prints out the iteration number according to the numeric value of the integer variable j. As you see in line 10, j is initialized with 1, and is increased by 1 after each looping (that is, iteration). The execution of the inner loop stops when the value of j is greater than 4.

Besides the inner loop, the outer loop has two statements in lines 9 and 12, respectively. The printf() function in line 9 displays a message showing the beginning of an iteration from the outer loop. An ending message is sent out in line 12 to show the end of the iteration from the outer loop.

From the output, you can see that the inner loop is finished before the outer loop starts another iteration. When the outer loop begins another iteration, the inner loop is encountered and run again. The output from the program in Listing 7.7 clearly shows the execution orders of the inner and outer loops.

WARNING

Don't confuse the two relational operators (< and <=) and misuse them in the expressions of loops.

For instance, the following

```
for (j=1; j<10; j++){
    /* statement block */
}
```

means that if j is less than 10, keep looping. Thus, the total number of iterations is 9. However, in the following example,

```
for (j=1; j<=10; j++){
    /* statement block */
}
```

the total number of iterations is 10 because the relational expression j<=10 is evaluated in this case. Note that the expression returns 1 as long as j is less than or equal to 10.

Therefore, you see the difference between the operators < and <= causes the looping in the first example to be one iteration shorter than the looping in the second example.

Summary

In this lesson you've learned the following:

☐ Looping can be used to perform the same set of statements over and over until specified conditions are met.

☐ Looping makes your program concise.

☐ There are three statements, for, while, and do-while, that are used for looping in C.

☐ There are three expression fields in the for statement. The second field contains the expression used as the specified condition(s).

☐ The for statement does not end with a semicolon.

☐ The empty for(; ;) statement can be used to form an infinite loop.

7

☐ Multiple expressions, separated by commas, can be used in the `for` statement.

☐ There is only one expression field in the `while` statement, and the expression is used as the specified condition.

☐ The `while` statement does not end with a semicolon.

☐ The `while (1)` statement can create an infinite loop.

☐ The `do-while` statement places its expression at the bottom of the loop.

☐ The `do-while` statement does end with a semicolon.

☐ The inner loop must finish first before the outer loop resumes its iteration in nested loops.

In the next lesson you'll learn about more operators used in the C language.

Q&A

Q How does a `for` loop work?

A There are three expression fields in the `for` statement. The first field contains an initializer that is evaluated first and only once before the iteration. The second field keeps the conditional expression that must be tested before the statements controlled by the `for` statement are executed. If the conditional expression returns a nonzero value, which means the specified condition is met, one iteration of the `for` loop is carried out. After each iteration, the expression in the third field is evaluated, and then the expression in the second field is reevaluated. The process (that is, looping) is repeated until the conditional expression returns 0.

Q What is the difference between the `while` and `do-while` statements?

A The main difference is that in the `while` statement, the conditional expression is evaluated at the top of the loop, while in the `do-while` statement, the conditional expression is evaluated at the bottom of the loop. Therefore, the statements controlled by the `do-while` statement are executed at least once.

Q Can the `while` statement end with a semicolon?

A By definition, the `while` statement does not end with a semicolon. However, it's legal in C to put a semicolon right after the `while` statement like this: `while(expression);`, which means there is a null statement controlled by the `while` statement. Remember that the result will be quite different from what you expect if you accidentally put a semicolon at the end of the `while` statement.

Q If two loops are nested together, which one must finish first, the inner loop or the outer loop?

A The inner loop must finish first. Then the outer loop will start another iteration if the specified condition is still met.

Workshop

To help you solidify your understanding of this hour's lesson, you are encouraged to try to answer the quiz questions and finish the exercises provided in the Workshop before you move to the next lesson. The answers and hints to the questions and exercises are given in Appendix E, "Answers to Quizzes and Exercises."

Quiz

1. Do the following two `for` loops have the same number of iterations?

```
for (j=0; j<8; j++);
for (k=1; k<=8; k++);
```

2. Is the following `for` loop

```
for (j=65; j<72; j++) printf("%c", j);
```

   equivalent to the following `while` loop?

```
int k = 65;
while (k<72)
    printf("%c", k);
    k++;
}
```

3. Can the following `while` loop print out anything?

```
int k = 100;
while (k<100){
    printf("%c", k);
    k++;
}
```

4. Can the following `do-while` loop print out anything?

```
int k = 100;
do {
    printf("%c", k);
    k++;
} while (k<100);
```

Exercises

1. What is the difference between the following two pieces of code?

```
for (i=0, j=1; i<8; i++, j++)
    printf("%d  +  %d  =  %d\n", i, j, i+j);

for (i=0, j=1; i<8; i++, j++);
    printf("%d  +  %d  =  %d\n", i, j, i+j);
```

2. Write a program that contains the two pieces of code shown in exercise 1, and then execute the program. What are you going to see on the screen?

3. Rewrite the program in Listing 7.4. This time, you want the for statement to keep looping until the user enters the character K.

4. Rewrite the program in Listing 7.6 by replacing the do-while loop with a for loop.

5. Rewrite the program in Listing 7.7. This time, use a while loop as the outer loop and a do-while loop as the inner loop.

Hour 8

More Operators

Civilization advances by extending the number of important operations we can perform without thinking about them.

—*A. N. Whitehead*

In Hour 6, "Manipulating Data with Operators," you learned about some important operators in C, such as the arithmetic assignment operators, the unary minus operator, the increment and decrement operators, and the relational operators. In this lesson you'll learn about more operators, including

- ☐ The sizeof operator
- ☐ Logical operators
- ☐ Bit-manipulation operators
- ☐ The conditional operator

Measuring Data Sizes

You may remember in Hour 4, "Data Types and Names in C," I mentioned that each data type has its own size. Depending on the operating system and the C compiler you're using, the size of a data type varies. For example, on most UNIX workstations, an integer is 32 bits long, while most C compilers only support 16-bit integers on a DOS-based machine.

So, how do you know the size of a data type on your machine? The answer is that you can measure the data type size by using the sizeof operator provided by C.

The general form of the sizeof operator is

```
sizeof (expression)
```

Here *expression* is the data type or variable whose size is measured by the sizeof operator. The value of the size is returned, in units of bytes, by the sizeof operator. For instance, if an integer is 16 bits long, the value returned by the sizeof operator will be 2 (bytes). (Note that 8 bits are equal to 1 byte.)

The parentheses are optional in the general form of the operator. If the expression is not a C keyword for a data type, the parentheses can be discarded.

For instance, the following statement

```
size = sizeof(int);
```

measures the size of the int data type and returns the number of bytes required by the data type to an int variable size.

The program in Listing 8.1 finds the sizes of the char, int, float, and double data types on my machine.

TYPE   **Listing 8.1. Using the sizeof operator.**

```
1:   /* 08L01.c: Using the sizeof operator */
2:   #include <stdio.h>
3:
4:   main()
5:   {
6:       char   ch = ' ';
7:       int    int_num = 0;
8:       float  flt_num = 0.0f;
9:       double dbl_num = 0.0;
10:
11:      printf("The size of char is: %d-byte\n", sizeof(char));
12:        printf("The size of ch is: %d-byte\n", sizeof ch );
13:          printf("The size of int is: %d-byte\n", sizeof(int));
14:            printf("The size of int_num is: %d-byte\n", sizeof int_num);
15:              printf("The size of float is: %d-byte\n", sizeof(float));
```

8

```
16:          printf("The size of flt_num is: %d-byte\n", sizeof flt_num);
17:        printf("The size of double is: %d-byte\n", sizeof(double));
18:      printf("The size of dbl_num is: %d-byte\n", sizeof(dbl_num);
19:    return 0;
20: }
```

After this program is compiled and linked, an executable file, 08L01.exe, is created. The following is the output printed on the screen after the executable is run from a DOS prompt on my machine:

OUTPUT
```
C:\app> 08L01
The size of char is: 1-byte
The size of ch is: 1-byte
The size of int is: 2-byte
The size of int_num is: 2-byte
The size of float is: 4-byte
The size of flt_num is: 4-byte
The size of double is: 8-byte
The size of dbl_num is: 8-byte
C:\app>
```

ANALYSIS Line 2 in Listing 8.1 includes the header file stdio.h for the printf() function used in the statements inside the main() function body. Lines 6–9 declare a char variable (ch), an int variable (int_num), a float variable (flt_num), and a double variable (dbl_num), respectively. Also, these four variables are initialized. Note that in line 8, the initial value to flt_num is suffixed with f to specify float. (As you learned in Hour 4, you can use f or F to specify the float type for a floating-point number.)

Lines 11 and 12 display the size of the char data type, as well as the char variable ch. Note that the sizeof operator is used in both line 11 and line 12 to obtain the number of bytes the char data type or the variable ch can have. Because the variable ch is not a keyword in C, the parentheses are discarded for the sizeof operator in line 12.

The first two lines in the output are printed out by executing the two statements in line 11 and 12, respectively. From the output, you see that the size of the char data type is 1 byte long, which is the same as the size of the variable ch. This is not surprising because the variable ch is declared as the char variable.

Likewise, lines 13 and 14 print out the sizes of the int data type and the int variable int_num by using the sizeof operator. You see that the size of each is 2 bytes.

Also, by using the sizeof operator, lines 15–18 give the sizes of the float data type, the float variable flt_num, the double data type, and the double variable dbl_num, respectively. The results in the output section show that the float data type and the variable flt_num have the same size (4 bytes). The double data type and the variable dbl_num are both 8 bytes long.

From the output you see that char uses 1 byte, while an int uses 2 bytes. Accordingly, while variables of type char have been used to store integers, they cannot store integers of the same range as a variable of type int can.

Everything Is Logical

Now, it's time for you to learn about a new set of operators: logical operators.

There are three logical operators in the C language:

&&   The logical AND operator

¦¦   The logical OR operator

!   The logical negation operator

The logical AND operator (&&) evaluates the truth or falseness of pairs of expressions. If both expressions are true, the logical AND operator returns 1. Otherwise, the operator returns 0.

However, the logical OR operator (¦¦) returns 1 if at least one of the expressions is true. The ¦¦ operator returns 0 if both expressions are false.

Only one operand (or expression) can be taken by the logical negation operator (!). If the operand is true, the ! operator returns 0; otherwise, the operator returns 1.

NOTE

> In C, if an expression or operator returns a nonzero value, the expression returns TRUE. If an expression or operator returns 0, the expression returns FALSE. In other words, TRUE can be used to represent any nonzero value returned by an expression or operator; FALSE is equivalent to 0.

The following three sections contain examples that show you how to use the three logical operators.

The Logical AND Operator (&&)

A general format of using the logical AND operator is:

exp1 && *exp2*

where *exp1* and *exp2* are two expressions evaluated by the AND operator.

We can have a table that shows the return values of the AND operator under the following conditions when *exp1* and *exp2* return 1 or 0, respectively. See Table 8.1, which can be called the *truth table* of the AND operator.

8

Table 8.1. The values returned by the AND operator.

exp1	exp2	Value Returned by &&
1	1	1
1	0	0
0	1	0
0	0	0

Listing 8.2 is an example of using the logical AND operator (&&).

TYPE | **Listing 8.2. Using the logical AND operator (&&).**

```
1:   /* 08L02.c: Using the logical AND operator */
2:   #include <stdio.h>
3:
4:   main()
5:   {
6:      int   num;
7:
8:      num = 0;
9:      printf("The AND operator returns: %d\n",
10:            (num%2 == 0) && (num%3 == 0));
11:     num = 2;
12:     printf("The AND operator returns: %d\n",
13:            (num%2 == 0) && (num%3 == 0));
14:     num = 3;
15:     printf("The AND operator returns: %d\n",
16:            (num%2 == 0) && (num%3 == 0));
17:     num = 6;
18:     printf("The AND operator returns: %d\n",
19:            (num%2 == 0) && (num%3 == 0));
20:
21:     return 0;
22: }
```

After this program is compiled and linked, an executable file, 08L02.exe, is created. The following is the output printed on the screen after the executable is run from a DOS prompt on my machine:

OUTPUT
```
C:\app> 08L02
The AND operator returns: 1
The AND operator returns: 0
The AND operator returns: 0
The AND operator returns: 1
C:\app>
```

ANALYSIS In Listing 8.2, an integer variable, num, is declared in line 6 and initialized for the first time in line 8. Lines 9 and 10 print out the value returned by the logical AND operator in the following expression:

```
(num%2 == 0) && (num%3 == 0)
```

Here you see two relational expressions, num%2 == 0 and num%3 == 0. In Hour 3, "The Essentials of C Programs," you learned that the arithmetic operator % can be used to obtain the remainder after its first operand is divided by the second operand. Therefore, num%2 yields the remainder of num divided by 2. The relational expression num%2 == 0 returns 1 (TRUE) if the remainder is equal to 0—that is, the value of num can be divided evenly by 2. Likewise, if the value of num can be divided by 3, the relational expression num%3 == 0 returns 1 as well. Then, according to the truth table of the && operator (see Table 8.1), we know that the combination of the logical AND operator (&&) and the two relational expressions yields 1 if the two relational expressions both return 1; otherwise, it yields 0.

In our case, when num is initialized to 0 in line 8, both 0%2 and 0%3 yield remainders of 0 so that the two relational expressions return TRUE. Therefore, the logical AND operator returns 1.

However, when num is assigned with the value of 2 or 3 as shown in lines 11 and 14, the logical AND operator in line 13 or line 16 returns 0. The reason is that 2 or 3 cannot be divided by both 2 and 3.

Line 17 then assigns num the value of 6. Because 6 is a multiple of both 2 and 3, the logical AND operator in line 19 returns 1, which is printed out by the printf() function in lines 18 and 19.

From the program in Listing 8.2, you see several single statements spanning into multiple lines. The output from the program in Listing 8.2 shows the values returned by the AND operator when num is assigned with different values.

The Logical OR Operator (¦ ¦)

As mentioned earlier, the logical OR operator returns 1 if at least one of the expressions is true. The ¦ ¦ operator returns 0 if both expressions are false.

A general format of using the logical OR operator is:

```
exp1 ¦¦ exp2
```

where *exp1* and *exp2* are two expressions evaluated by the OR operator.

Table 8.2 shows the truth table of the OR operator.

Table 8.2. The values returned by the OR operator.

exp1	exp2	Value Returned by ||
1	1	1
1	0	1
0	1	1
0	0	0

The program in Listing 8.3 shows how to use the logical OR operator (¦¦).

TYPE **Listing 8.3. Using the logical OR operator (¦¦).**

```
1:  /* 08L03.c: Using the logical OR operator */
2:  #include <stdio.h>
3:
4:  main()
5:  {
6:     int   num;
7:
8:     printf("Enter a single digit that can be divided\nby both 2 and 3:\n");
9:     for (num = 1; (num%2 != 0) ¦¦ (num%3 != 0); )
10:       num = getchar() - 48;
11:    printf("You got such a number: %d\n", num);
12:    return 0;
13: }
```

The following is the output printed on the screen after the executable, 08L03.exe, is run from a DOS prompt on my machine. The numbers in bold font are what I entered. (The Enter key is pressed after each number is entered.) In the range of 0–9, 0 and 6 are the only two numbers that can be divided evenly by both 2 and 3:

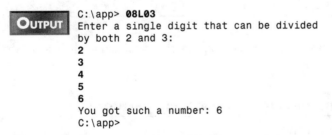

```
C:\app> 08L03
Enter a single digit that can be divided
by both 2 and 3:
2
3
4
5
6
You got such a number: 6
C:\app>
```

ANALYSIS In Listing 8.3, an integer variable, num, is declared in line 6. Line 8 of Listing 8.3 prints out a headline asking the user to enter a single digit. Note that there is a newline character (\n) in the middle of the headline message in the printf() function to break the message into two lines.

In line 9, the integer variable num is initialized in the first expression field of the for statement. The reason to initialize num with 1 is that 1 is such a number that cannot be divided by either 2 nor 3. Thus, the for loop is guaranteed to be executed at least once.

The key part of the program in Listing 8.3 is the logical expression in the for statement:

```
(num%2 != 0) ¦¦ (num%3 != 0)
```

Here the relational expressions num%2 != 0 and num%3 != 0 are evaluated. According to the truth table of the ¦¦ operator (see Table 8.2), we know that if one of the relational expression returns TRUE, i.e., the value of num cannot be divided completely by either 2 or 3. Then the logical expression returns 1, which allows the for loop to continue.

The for loop stops only if the user enters a digit that can be divided by both 2 and 3. In other words, when both the relational expressions return FALSE, the logical OR operator yields 0, which causes the termination of the for loop.

You can rewrite the program in Listing 8.3 with the if statement, too.

The Logical Negation Operator (!)

A general format of using the logical OR operator is:

```
!expression
```

where expression is an expression operated by the negation operator.

The truth table of the negation operator is shown in Table 8.3.

Table 8.3. The values returned by the ! operator.

expression	Value Returned by !
1	0
0	1

Now, let's take a look at the example, shown in Listing 8.4, that demonstrates how to use the logical negation operator (!).

TYPE   **Listing 8.4. Using the logical negation operator (!).**

```
1:  /* 08L04.c: Using the logical negation operator */
2:  #include <stdio.h>
3:
4:  main()
5:  {
6:     int   num;
7:
```

8

```
8:       num = 7;
9:       printf("Given num = 7\n");
10:      printf("!(num < 7)  returns: %d\n", !(num < 7));
11:      printf("!(num > 7)  returns: %d\n", !(num > 7));
12:      printf("!(num == 7) returns: %d\n", !(num == 7));
13:      return 0;
14: }
```

The following result is obtained by running the executable file 08L04.exe:

```
C:\app> 08L04
Given num = 7
!(num < 7)  returns: 1
!(num > 7)  returns: 1
!(num == 7) returns: 0
C:\app>
```

ANALYSIS In line 8, note that an integer variable, num, is initialized with 7, which is then displayed by the printf() function in line 9.

In line 10, the relational expression num < 7 returns FALSE (that is, 0), because the value of num is not less than 7. However, by using the logical negation operator, !(num < 7) yields 1. (Refer to the truth table of the ! operator shown in Table 8.3.)

Similarly, the logical expression !(num > 7) returns 1 in line 11.

Because num has the value of 7, the relational expression num == 7 is true; however, the logical expression !(num == 7) in line 12 returns 0 due to the logical negation operator (!).

Manipulating Bits

In previous hours, you learned that computer data and files are made of bits (or bytes). There is even an operator in C—the sizeof operator—that can be used to measure the number of bytes for data types.

In this section, you'll learn about a set of operators that enable you to access and manipulate specific bits.

There are six bit-manipulation operators in the C language:

Operator	Description
&	The bitwise AND operator
¦	The bitwise OR operator
^	The bitwise exclusive OR (XOR) operator
~	The bitwise complement operator
>>	The right-shift operator
<<	The left-shift operator

The following two sections give explanations and examples of the bit-manipulation operators.

TIP

It's easy to convert a decimal number into a hex or a binary. Each digit in a hex number consists of four bits. A bit represents a digit in a binary number. Table 8.4 shows the hex numbers (0–F) and their corresponding binary and decimal representations.

Table 8.4. Numbers expressed in different formats.

Hex	Binary	Decimal
0	0000	0
1	0001	1
2	0010	2
3	0011	3
4	0100	4
5	0101	5
6	0110	6
7	0111	7
8	1000	8
9	1001	9
A	1010	10
B	1011	11
C	1100	12
D	1101	13
E	1110	14
F	1111	15

Let's see how to convert a decimal number into a binary, or vice versa. As we know, that binary is a 2-based numbering system. Each digit in a binary number is called a bit and can be 1 or 0. If the position of a bit in a binary number is n, then the bit can have a value of 2 to the power of n. The position of a bit in a binary number is counted from the right of the binary number.

The most-right bit is at the position of zero. Thus, given a binary number 1000, we can calculate its decimal value like this:

$$1000 \rightarrow 1 * 2^3 + 0 * 2^2 + 0 * 2^1 + 0 * 2^0 \rightarrow 2^3 \rightarrow 8 \text{ (decimal)}$$

That is, the decimal vale of the binary number 1000 is 8.

If we want to convert a decimal number, for example 10, to its binary counterpart, we have the following process:

$$10 \rightarrow 2^3 + 2^1 \rightarrow 1 * 2^3 + 0 * 2^2 + 1 * 2^1 + 0 * 2^0 \rightarrow 1010 \text{ (binary)}$$

Likewise, you can convert the rest of the decimal numbers in Table 8.4 to their binary counterparts, or vice versa.

Using Bitwise Operators

The general forms of the bitwise operators are as follows:

```
x & y
x ¦ y
x ^ y
~x
```

Here x and y are operands.

The & operator compares each bit of x to the corresponding bit in y. If both bits are 1, 1 is placed at the same position of the bit in the result. If one of the bits, or two of them, is 0, 0 is placed in the result.

For instance, the expression with two binary operands, 01 & 11, returns 01.

The ¦ operator, however, places 1 in the result if either operand is 1. For example, the expression 01 ¦ 11 returns 11.

The ^ operator places 1 in the result if either operand, but not both, is 1. Therefore, the expression 01 ^ 11 returns 10.

Finally, the ~ operator takes just one operand. This operator reverses each bit in the operand. For instance, ~01 returns 10.

Table 8.5 shows more examples of using the bitwise operators in decimal, hex, and binary formats (in the left three columns). The corresponding results, in binary, hex, and decimal formats, are listed in the right three columns. The hex numbers are prefixed with 0x.

Table 8.5. Examples of using bitwise operators.

| | Expressions | | | Results | |
Decimal	Hex	Binary	Decimal	Hex	Binary
12 & 10	0x0C & 0x0A	1100 & 1010	8	0x08	1000
12 ¦ 10	0x0C ¦ 0x0A	1100 ¦ 1010	14	0x0E	1110
12 ^ 10	0x0C ^ 0x0A	1100 ^ 1010	6	0x06	0110
~12	~0x000C	~0000000000001100	65523	FFF3	1111111111110011

Note that the complementary value of 12 is 65523, because the unsigned integer data type (16-bit) has the maximum number 65535. In other words, 65,523 is the result of subtracting 12 from 65,535. (The unsigned data modifier is introduced in Hour 9, "Playing with Data Modifiers and Math Functions.")

The program in Listing 8.5 demonstrates the usage of the bitwise operators.

TYPE **Listing 8.5. Using bitwise operators.**

```
1:  /* 08L05.c: Using bitwise operators */
2:  #include <stdio.h>
3:
4:  main()
5:  {
6:     int   x, y, z;
7:
8:     x = 4321;
9:     y = 5678;
10:    printf("Given x = %u, i.e., 0X%04X\n", x, x);
11:    printf("      y = %u, i.e., 0X%04X\n", y, y);
12:    z = x & y;
13:    printf("x & y  returns: %6u, i.e., 0X%04X\n", z, z);
14:    z = x ¦ y;
15:    printf("x ¦ y  returns: %6u, i.e., 0X%04X\n", z, z);
16:    z = x ^ y;
17:    printf("x ^ y  returns: %6u, i.e., 0X%04X\n", z, z);
18:    printf("  ~x   returns: %6u, i.e., 0X%04X\n", ~x, ~x);
19:    return 0;
20: }
```

After the executable, 08L05.exe, is created and run from a DOS prompt, the following output is shown on the screen:

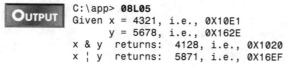

```
C:\app> 08L05
Given x = 4321, i.e., 0X10E1
        y = 5678, i.e., 0X162E
    x & y  returns:  4128, i.e., 0X1020
    x ¦ y  returns:  5871, i.e., 0X16EF
```

8

```
x ^ y  returns:  1743, i.e., 0X06CF
  ~x   returns: 61214, i.e., 0XEF1E
C:\app>
```

ANALYSIS In Listing 8.5, three integer variables, x, y, and z, are declared in line 6. Lines 8 and 9 set x and y to 4321 and 5678, respectively. Lines 10 and 11 then print out the values of x and y in both decimal and hex formats. The hex numbers are prefixed with 0x.

The statement in line 12 assigns the result of the operation made by the bitwise AND operator (&) with the variables x and y. Then, line 13 displays the result in both decimal and hex formats.

Lines 14 and 15 perform the operation specified by the bitwise operator (¦) and print out the result in both decimal and hex formats. Similarly, lines 16 and 17 give the result of the operation made by the bitwise XOR operator (^).

Last, the statement in line 18 prints out the complementary value of x by using the bitwise complement operator (~). The result is displayed on the screen in both decimal and hex formats.

Note that the unsigned integer format specifier with a minimum field width of 6, %6u, and the uppercase hex format specifier with the minimum width of 4, %04X, are used in the printf() function. The unsigned integer data type (that is, the non-negative integer data type) is chosen so that the complementary value of an integer can be shown and understood easily. More details on the unsigned data modifier are introduced in Hour 9.

WARNING

> Don't confuse the bitwise operators & and ¦ with the logical operators && and ¦¦. For instance,
>
> (x=1) & (y=10)
>
> is a completely different expression from
>
> (x=1) && (y=10)

Using Shift Operators

There are two shift operators in C. The >> operator shifts the bits of an operand to the right; the << operator shifts the bits to the left.

The general forms of the two shift operators are

```
x >> y
x << y
```

Here *x* is an operand that is going to be shifted. *y* contains the specified number of places to shift.

For instance, the 8 >> 2 expression tells the computer to shift 2 bits of the operand 8 to the right, which returns 2 in decimal. The following:

$$8 >> 2 \rightarrow (1 * 2^3 + 0 * 2^2 + 0 * 2^1 + 0 * 2^0) >> 2$$

produces the following:

$$(0 * 2^3 + 0 * 2^2 + 1 * 2^1 + 0 * 2^0) \rightarrow 0010 \text{ (binary)} \rightarrow 2 \text{ (decimal)}.$$

Likewise, the 5 << 1 expression shifts 1 bit of the operand 5, and yields 10 in decimal.

The program in Listing 8.6 prints out more results by using the shift operators.

TYPE **Listing 8.6. Using the shift operators.**

```
1:   /* 08L06.c: Using shift operators */
2:   #include <stdio.h>
3:
4:   main()
5:   {
6:      int   x, y, z;
7:
8:      x = 255;
9:      y = 5;
10:     printf("Given x = %4d, i.e., 0X%04X\n", x, x);
11:     printf("      y = %4d, i.e., 0X%04X\n", y, y);
12:     z = x >> y;
13:     printf("x >> y  returns: %6d, i.e., 0X%04X\n", z, z);
14:     z = x << y;
15:     printf("x << y  returns: %6d, i.e., 0X%04X\n", z, z);
16:     return 0;
17: }
```

The following output is obtained by running the executable, 08L06.exe, from a DOS prompt:

OUTPUT
```
C:\app> 08L06
Given x =  255, i.e., 0X00FF
        y =    5, i.e., 0X0005
x >> y  returns:      7, i.e., 0X0007
x << y  returns:   8160, i.e., 0X1FE0
C:\app>
```

ANALYSIS Three integer variables, x, y, and z, are declared in line 6 of Listing 8.6. x is initialized with 255 in line 8; y is set to 5 in line 9. Then, lines 10 and 11 display the values of x and y on the screen.

The statement in line 12 shifts y bits of the operand x to the right, and then assigns the result to z. Line 13 prints out the result of the shifting made in line 12. The result is 7 in decimal, or 0X0007 in hex.

Lines 14 and 15 shift the operand x to the left by y bits and display the result on the screen, too. The result of the left-shifting is 8160 in decimal, or 0x1FE0 in hex.

> **TIP**
>
> The operation of the shift-right operator (>>) is equivalent to dividing by powers of 2. In other words, the following:
>
> x >> y
>
> is equivalent to the following:
>
> x / 2^y
>
> Here x is a non-negative integer.
>
> On the other hand, shifting to the left is equivalent to multiplying by powers of 2; that is,
>
> x << y
>
> is equivalent to
>
> x * 2^y

What Does x?y:z Mean?

In C, ?: is called the *conditional operator*, which is the only operator that takes three operands. The general form of the conditional operator is

x ? y : z

Here x, y, and z are three operands. Among them, x contains the test condition, and y and z represent the final value of the expression. If x returns nonzero (that is, TRUE), y is chosen; otherwise, z is the result.

For instance, the expression x > 0 ? 'T' : 'F' returns 'T' if the value of x is greater than 0. Otherwise, the expression returns 'F'.

Listing 8.7 demonstrates the usage of the conditional operator in the C language.

TYPE **Listing 8.7. Using the conditional operator.**

```
1:  /* 08L07.c: Using the ?: operator */
2:  #include <stdio.h>
3:
4:  main()
5:  {
6:     int   x;
7:
```

continues

Listing 8.7. continued

```
8:      x = sizeof(int);
9:      printf("%s\n",
10:         (x == 2) ? "The int data type has 2 bytes." : "int doesn't have 2
            ➡bytes.");
11:     printf("The maximum value of int is: %d\n",
12:         (x != 2) ? ~(1 << x * 8 - 1) : ~(1 << 15) );
13:     return 0;
14: }
```

I get the following output shown on the screen when I run the executable 08L07.exe from a DOS prompt on my machine:

OUTPUT
```
C:\app> 08L07
The int data type has 2 bytes.
The maximum value of int is: 32767
C:\app>
```

ANALYSIS In Listing 8.7, the size of the int data type is measured first in line 8, by using the sizeof operator and the number of bytes assigned to the integer variable x.

Lines 9 and 10 contain one statement, in which the conditional operator (?:) is used to test whether the number of bytes saved in x is equal to 2. (Here you see another example that a single statement can span multiple lines.) If the x == 2 expression returns nonzero (that is, TRUE), the string of The int data type has 2 bytes. is printed out by the printf() function in the statement. Otherwise, the second string, int doesn't have 2 bytes., is displayed on the screen.

In addition, the statement in lines 11 and 12 tries to find out the maximum value of the int data type on the current machine. The x != 2 expression is evaluated first in the statement. If the expression returns nonzero (that is, the byte number of the int data type is not equal to 2), the ~(<< x * 8 - 1) expression is evaluated, and the result is chosen as the return value. Here the ~(1 << x * 8 - 1) expression is a general form to calculate the maximum value of the int data type, which is equivalent to $2 ** (x * 8 - 1) - 1$. (The complement operator, ~, and the shift operator, <<, were introduced in the previous sections of this hour.)

On the other hand, if the test condition x != 2 in line 12 returns 0, which means the value of x is indeed equal to 2, the result of the ~(1 << 15) expression is chosen. Here you may have already figured out that ~(1 << 15) is equivalent to $2^{15}-1$, which is the maximum value that the 16-bit int data type can have.

The result displayed on the screen shows that the int data type on my machine is 2 bytes (or 16 bits) long, and the maximum value of the int data type is 32767.

8

Summary

In this lesson you've learned the following:

☐ The sizeof operator returns the number of bytes that a specified data type can have. You can use the operator to measure the size of a data type on your machine.

☐ The logical AND operator (&&) returns 1 only if both its two operands (that is, expressions) are TRUE. Otherwise, the operator returns 0.

☐ The logical OR operator (¦¦) returns 0 only if both its two operands are FALSE. Otherwise, the operator returns 1.

☐ The logical negation operator (!) reverses the logical value of its operand.

☐ There are six bit-manipulation operators: the bitwise AND operator (&), the bitwise OR operator (¦), the bitwise XOR operator (^), the bitwise complement operator (~), the right-shift operator (>>), and the left-shift operator (<<).

☐ The conditional operator (?:) is the only operator in C that can take three operands.

In next lesson you'll learn about the data type modifiers in the C language.

Q&A

Q Why do we need the sizeof operator?

A The sizeof operator can be used to measure the sizes of all data types defined in C. When you write a portable C program that needs to know the size of an integer variable, it's a bad idea to hard-code the size as 16 or 32. The better way to tell the program the size of the variable is to use the sizeof operator, which returns the size of the integer variable at runtime.

Q What's the difference between ¦ and ¦¦?

A ¦ is the bitwise OR operator that takes two operands. The ¦ operator compares each bit of one operand to the corresponding bit in another operand. If both bits are 0, 0 is placed at the same position of the bit in the result. Otherwise, 1 is placed in the result.

On the other hand, ¦¦, the logical OR operator, requires two operands (or expressions). The operator returns 0 (that is, FALSE) if both its operands are false. Otherwise, a nonzero value (that is, TRUE) is returned by the ¦¦ operator.

Q Why is `1 << 3` **equivalent to** `1 * 2³`**?**

A The `1 << 3` expression tells the computer to shift 3 bits of the operand `1` to the left. The binary format of the operand is `0001`. (Note that only the lowest four bits are shown here.) After being shifted 3 bits to the left, the expression returns `1000`, which is equivalent to $1 * 2^3 + 0 * 2^2 + 0 * 2^1 + 0 * 2^0$; that is, $1 * 2^3$.

Q What can the conditional operator (`?:`) **do?**

A If there are two possible answers under certain conditions, you can use the `?:` operator to pick up one of the two answers based on the result made by testing the conditions. For instance, the expression `(age > 65) ? "Retired" : "Not retired"` tells the computer that if the value of `age` is greater than `65`, the string of `Retired` should be chosen; otherwise, `Not retired` is chosen.

Workshop

To help solidify your understanding of this hour's lesson, you are encouraged to answer the quiz questions and finish the exercises provided in the Workshop before you move to the next lesson. The answers and hints to the questions and exercises are given in Appendix E, "Answers to Quiz Questions and Exercises."

Quiz

1. What do the `(x=1) && (y=10)` and `(x=1) & (y=10)` expressions return, respectively?
2. Given `x = 96`, `y = 1`, and `z = 69`, what does the expression `!y ? x == z : y` return?
3. What do the `~0011000000111001` and `~1100111111000110` expressions return?
4. Given `x=9`, what does `(x%2==0)||(x%3==0)` return? How about `(x%2==0)&&(x%3==0)`?
5. Is `8 >> 3` equivalent to $8 / 2^3$? How about `1 << 3`?

Exercises

1. Given `x = 0xEFFF` and `y = 0x1000`, what do `~x` and `~y` return, respectively, in the hex format?
2. Taking the values of `x` and `y` assigned in exercise 1, write a program that prints out the return values of `!x` and `!y` by using both the `%d` and `%u` formats in the `printf()` function.
3. Given `x = 123` and `y = 4`, write a program that displays the results of the `x << y` and `x >> y` expressions.

4. Write a program that shows the return values (in hex) of the 0xFFFF^0x8888, 0xABCD & 0x4567, and 0xDCBA ¦ 0x1234 expressions.

5. Use the ?: operator and the for statement to write a program that keeps taking the characters entered by the user until the character q is accounted. (Hint: Put the x!='q' ? 1 : 0 expression to the second field in the for statement.)

8

Hour 9

Playing with Data Modifiers and Math Functions

If at first you don't succeed, transform your data.

—Murphy's Laws of Computers

In Hour 4, "Data Types and Names in C," you learned about several data types, such as char, int, float, and double, in the C language. In this hour, you'll learn about four data modifiers that enable you to have greater control over the data. The C keywords for the four data modifiers are

☐ signed

☐ unsigned

☐ short

☐ long

You're also going to learn about several mathematical functions provided by the C language, such as

☐ The sin() function
☐ The cos() function
☐ The tan() function
☐ The pow() function
☐ The sqrt() function

Enabling or Disabling the Sign Bit

As you know, it's very easy to express a negative number in decimal. All you need to do is put a minus sign in front of the absolute value of the number. But how does the computer represent a negative number in the binary format?

Normally, one bit can be used to indicate whether the value of a number represented in the binary format is negative. This bit is called the *sign bit*. The following two sections introduce two data modifiers, signed and unsigned, that can be used to enable or disable the sign bit.

The signed Modifier

For integers, the leftmost bit can be used as the sign bit. For instance, if the int data type is 16 bits long and the rightmost bit is counted as bit 0, you can use bit 15 as a sign bit. When the sign bit is set to 1, the C compiler knows that the value represented by the data variable is negative.

There are several ways to represent a negative value of the float or double data types. The implementations of the float and double data types are beyond the scope of this book. You can refer to Kernighan and Ritchie's book *The C Programming Language* for more details on the implementations of negative values of the float or double type.

The C language provides a data modifier, signed, that can be used to indicate to the compiler that the int or char data type uses the sign bit. By default, the int data type is a signed quantity. But the ANSI standard does not require the char data type be signed; it's up to the compiler vendors. Therefore, if you want to use a signed character variable, and make sure the compiler knows it, you can declare the character variable like this:

```
signed char ch;
```

so that the compiler knows that the character variable ch is signed, which means the variable can take a value in the range of -128 (that is, -2^7) to 127 (that is, 2^7-1).

(Remember that for an unsigned character variable, the range is 0 to 255; that is, 2^8-1.)

TIP

> To represent a negative number in the binary format, you can first get its equivalent positive value's binary format. Then you perform the complement operation on the binary, and finally, add one to the complemented binary.
>
> For instance, given a negative integer -12345, how can you represent it in the binary format?
>
> First, you need to find the binary format for the positive integer 12345, which is 0011000000111001.
>
> Then, you perform the complement operation on 0011000000111001; that is, ~0011000000111001, and obtain the following:
>
> 1100111111000110
>
> And finally, adding 1 to 1100111111000110 gives you 1100111111000111, which is the binary format of the negative integer -12345.

9

The `unsigned` **Modifier**

The C language also gives you the unsigned modifier, which can be used to tell the C compiler that no sign bit is needed in the specified data type.

Like the signed modifier, the unsigned modifier is meaningful only to the int and char data types.

For instance, the declaration

```
unsigned int x;
```

tells the C compiler that the integer variable x can only assume positive values from 0 to 65535 (that is, $2^{16}-1$), if the int data type is 16 bits long.

In fact, unsigned int is equivalent to unsigned according to the ANSI standard. In other words, unsigned int x; is the same as unsigned x;.

Also, the ANSI standard allows you to indicate that a constant is of type unsigned by suffixing u or U to the constant. For instance,

```
unsigned int x, y;
x = 12345U;
y = 0xABCDu;
```

Here, the unsigned integer constants 12345U and 0xABCDu are assigned to variables x and y, respectively.

The program in Listing 9.1 is an example of using the signed and unsigned modifiers.

TYPE   **Listing 9.1. Modifying data with signed and unsigned.**

```
1:  /* 09L01.c: Using signed and unsigned modifiers */
2:  #include <stdio.h>
3:
4:  main()
5:  {
6:      signed char  ch;
7:      int          x;
8:      unsigned int y;
9:
10:     ch = 0xFF;
11:     x = 0xFFFF;
12:     y = 0xFFFFu;
13:     printf("The decimal of signed 0xFF is %d.\n", ch);
14:     printf("The decimal of signed 0xFFFF is %d.\n", x);
15:     printf("The decimal of unsigned 0xFFFFu is %u.\n", y);
16:     printf("The hex of decimal 12345 is 0x%X.\n", 12345);
17:     printf("The hex of decimal -12345 is 0x%X.\n", -12345);
18:     return 0;
19: }
```

On my machine, the executable file of the program in Listing 9.1 is named 09L01.exe. (Note that when you compile the program in Listing 9.1, you'll see a warning message regarding the assignment statement ch = 0xFF; in line 10, due to the fact that ch is declared as a signed char variable. You can ignore the warning message.)

The following is the output printed on the screen after I run the executable from a DOS prompt:

OUTPUT
```
C:\app> 09L01
The decimal of signed 0xFF is -1
The decimal of signed 0xFFFF is -1.
The decimal of unsigned 0xFFFFu is 65535.
The hex of decimal 12345 is 0x3039.
The hex of decimal -12345 is 0xCFC7.
C:\app>
```

ANALYSIS   As you see in Listing 9.1, line 6 declares a signed char variable, ch. The int variable x and the unsigned int variable y are declared in lines 7 and 8, respectively. The three variables, ch, x, and y, are initialized in lines 10–12. Note that in line 12, u is suffixed to 0xFFFF to indicate that the constant is an unsigned integer.

The statement in line 13 displays the decimal value of the signed char variable ch. The output on the screen shows that the corresponding decimal value of 0xFF is -1 for the signed char variable ch.

9

Lines 14 and 15 print out the decimal values of the int variable x (which is signed by default) and the unsigned int variable y, respectively. Note that for the variable y, the unsigned integer format specifier %u is used in the printf() function in line 15. (Actually, you might recall that %u was used to specify the unsigned int data type as the display format in the previous hour.)

Based on the output, you see that 0xFFFF is equal to -1 for the signed int data type, and 65535 for the unsigned int data type. Here, the integer data type is 16 bits long.

Lines 16 and 17 print out 0x3039 and 0xCFC7, which are the hex formats of the decimal values of 12345 and -12345, respectively. According to the method mentioned in the last section, 0xCFC7 is obtained by adding 1 to the complemented value of 0x3039.

Changing Data Sizes

Sometimes, you want to reduce the memory taken by variables, or you need to increase the storage space of certain data types. Fortunately, the C language gives you the flexibility to modify sizes of data types. The two data modifiers, short and long, are introduced in the following two sections.

The short Modifier

A data type can be modified to take less memory by using the short modifier. For instance, you can apply the short modifier to an integer variable that is 32 bits long, which might reduce the memory taken by the variable to as little as 16 bits.

You can use the short modifier like this:

```
short x;
```

or

```
unsigned short y;
```

By default, a short int data type is a signed number. Therefore, in the short x; statement, x is a signed variable of short integer.

The long Modifier

If you need more memory to keep values from a wider range, you can use the long modifier to define a data type with increased storage space.

For instance, given an integer variable x that is 16 bits long, the declaration

```
long int x;
```

increases the size of x to 32 bits. In other words, after the modification, x is capable of holding a range of values from -2147483648 (that is, -2^{31}) to 2147483647 (that is, $2^{31}-1$).

The ANSI standard allows you to indicate that a constant has type long by suffixing l or L to the constant. For instance:

```
long int x, y;
x = 1234567891;
y = 0xABCD1234L;
```

Here, the constants of the long int data type, 1234567891 and 0xABCD1234L, are assigned to variables x and y, respectively.

Also, you can declare a long integer variable simply like this:

```
long x;
```

which is equivalent to

```
long int x;
```

Listing 9.2 contains a program that can print out the numbers of bytes for different modified data types.

TYPE **Listing 9.2. Modifying data with short and long.**

```
1:  /* 09L02.c: Using short and long modifiers */
2:  #include <stdio.h>
3:
4:  main()
5:  {
6:     printf("The size of short int is: %d.\n",
7:        sizeof(short int));
8:     printf("The size of long int is: %d.\n",
9:        sizeof(long int));
10:    printf("The size of float is: %d.\n",
11:       sizeof(float));
12:    printf("The size of double is: %d.\n",
13:       sizeof(double));
14:    printf("The size of long double is: %d.\n",
15:       sizeof(long double));
16:    return 0;
17: }
```

I obtain the following output printed on the screen after I run the executable 09L02.exe from a DOS prompt:

OUTPUT

```
C:\app> 09L02
The size of short int is: 2.
The size of long int is: 4.
The size of float is: 4.
The size of double is: 8.
The size of long double is: 10.
C:\app>
```

ANALYSIS In Listing 9.2, the sizeof operator and printf() function are used to measure the sizes of the modified data types and display the results on the screen.

For instance, lines 6 and 7 obtain the size of the short int data type and print out the number of the byte, 2, on the screen. From the output, you know that the short int data type is 16 bits (that is, 2 bytes) long on my machine.

Likewise, lines 8 and 9 find the size of the long int data type is 4 bytes (that is, 32 bits) long, which is the same length as the float data type obtained in lines 10 and 11.

Lines 12 and 13 obtain the size of the double data type, which is 8 bytes (that is, 64 bits) on my machine. Then, after being modified by the long modifier, the size of the double data type is increased to 10 bytes (that is, 80 bits), which is printed out by the printf() function in lines 14 and 15.

Adding h, l, or L to Format Specifiers

You can add h into the integer format specifier (like this: %hd, %hi, or %hu) to specify that the corresponding number is a short int or unsigned short int.

On the other hand, using %ld or %Ld specifies that the corresponding datum is long int. %lu or %Lu is then used for the long unsigned int data.

The program in Listing 9.3 shows the usage of %hd, %lu, and %ld.

TYPE **Listing 9.3. Using %hd, %ld, and %lu.**

```
 1:  /* 09L03.c: Using %hd, %ld, and %lu specifiers */
 2:  #include <stdio.h>
 3:
 4:  main()
 5:  {
 6:     short int        x;
 7:     unsigned int     y;
 8:     long int         s;
 9:     unsigned long int t;
10:
11:     x = 0xFFFF;
12:     y = 0xFFFFU;
```

continues

Listing 9.3. continued

```
13:     s = 0xFFFFFFFFl;
14:     t = 0xFFFFFFFFL;
15:     printf("The short int of 0xFFFF is %hd.\n", x);
16:     printf("The unsigned int of 0xFFFF is %u.\n", y);
17:     printf("The long int of 0xFFFFFFFF is %ld.\n", s);
18:     printf("The unsigned long int of 0xFFFFFFFF is %lu.\n", t);
19:     return 0;
20: }
```

After the executable `09L03.exe` is created and run from a DOS prompt, the following output is shown on the screen:

OUTPUT
```
C:\app> 09L03
The short int of 0xFFFF is -1.
The unsigned int of 0xFFFF is 65535.
The long int of 0xFFFFFFFF is -1.
The unsigned long int of 0xFFFFFFFF is 4294967295
C:\app>
```

ANALYSIS There are four data types declared in Listing 9.3: the `short int` variable x, the `unsigned int` variable y, the `long int` variable s, and the `unsigned long int` variable t. The four variables are initialized in lines 6–9.

To display the decimal values of x, y, s, and t, the format specifiers %hd, %u, %ld, and %lu are used, respectively, in lines 15–18 to convert the corresponding hex numbers to decimal numbers. The output from the program in Listing 9.3 shows that values contained by x, y, s, and t have been correctly displayed on the screen.

Mathematical Functions in C

Basically, the math functions provided by the C language can be classified into three groups:

☐ Trigonometric and hyperbolic functions, such as `acos()`, `cos()`, and `cosh()`.

☐ Exponential and logarithmic functions, such as `exp()`, `pow()`, and `log10()`.

☐ Miscellaneous math functions, such as `ceil()`, `fabs()`, and `floor()`.

You have to include the header file `math.h` in your C program before you can use any math functions defined in the header file. Appendix B, "ANSI C Library Functions," lists all the math functions available in C.

The following two sections introduce several math functions and tell you how to use them in your programs.

Calling `sin()`, `cos()`, and `tan()`

You should appreciate that C gives you a set of functions to deal with trigonometric or hyperbolic calculations, if you think those calculations are very tough.

For instance, given an angle x in radians, the `sin(x)` expression returns the sine of the angle.

The following formula can be used to convert the value of an angle in degrees into the value in radians:

`radians = degree * (3.141593 / 180.0).`

Here, `3.141593` is the approximate value of pi. If needed, you can use more decimal digits from pi.

Now, let's have a look at the syntax of the `sin()`, `cos()`, and `tan()` functions.

SYNTAX

The syntax for the `sin()` function is

```
#include <math.h>
double sin(double x);
```

Here, the `double` variable x contains the value of an angle in radians. The `sin()` function returns the sine of x in the `double` data type.

SYNTAX

The syntax for the `cos()` function is

```
#include <math.h>
double cos(double x);
```

Here, the `double` variable x contains the value of an angle in radians. The `cos()` function returns the cosine of x in the `double` data type.

SYNTAX

The syntax for the `tan()` function is

```
#include <math.h>
double tan(double x);
```

Here, the `double` variable x contains the value of an angle in radians. The `tan()` function returns the tangent of x in the `double` data type.

Listing 9.4 demonstrates how to use the `sin()`, `cos()`, and `tan()` functions.

TYPE

Listing 9.4. Calculating trigonometric values with `sin()`, `cos()`, and `tan()`.

```
1:  /* 09L04.c: Using sin(), cos(), and tan() functions */
2:  #include <stdio.h>
3:  #include <math.h>
4:
```

continues

Listing 9.4. continued

```
5:  main()
6:  {
7:      double x;
8:
9:      x = 45.0;                    /* 45 degree */
10:     x *= 3.141593 / 180.0;       /* convert to radians */
11:     printf("The sine of 45 is:    %f.\n", sin(x));
12:     printf("The cosine of 45 is:  %f.\n", cos(x));
13:     printf("The tangent of 45 is: %f.\n", tan(x));
14:     return 0;
15: }
```

The following output is displayed on the screen when the executable 09L04.exe is executed:

```
C:\app> 09L04
The sine of 45 is:    0.707107.
The cosine of 45 is:  0.707107.
The tangent of 45 is: 1.000000.
C:\app>
```

Note that the header file math.h is included in line 3, which is required by the C math functions.

The double variable x in Listing 9.4 is initialized with 45.0 in line 9. Here, 45.0 is the value of the angle in degrees, which is converted into the corresponding radians in line 10.

Then, the statement in line 11 calculates the sine of x by calling the sin() function and prints out the result on the screen. Similarly, line 12 obtains the cosine of x and shows it on the screen as well. Because x contains the value of a 45-degree angle, it's not surprising to see that both the sine and cosine values are the same, about 0.707107.

Line 13 gives the tangent value of x by using the tan() function. As you might know, the tangent of x is equal to the sine of x divided by the cosine of x. Because the sine of a 45-degree angle is the same as the cosine of a 45-degree angle, the tangent of a 45-degree angle is equal to 1. The result (in the floating-point format) of 1.000000, in the third line of the listing's output, proves it.

You can declare a constant PI initialized to 3.141593, and another constant initialized to 180.0. Or, simply declare a single constant initialized to the result of 3.141593/180.0. In Hour 23, "The C Preprocessor," you'll learn to use the C preprocessor #define directive to do so.

Calling pow() and sqrt()

The pow() and sqrt() functions are two other useful math functions in C.

SYNTAX

The syntax for the `pow()` function is

```
#include <math.h>
double pow(double x, double y);
```

Here, the value of the `double` variable x is raised to the power of y. The `pow()` function returns the result in the `double` data type.

SYNTAX

The syntax for the `sqrt()` function is

```
#include <math.h>
double sqrt(double x);
```

Here, the `sqrt()` function returns the non-negative square root of x in the `double` data type. The function returns an error if x is negative.

In fact, if you set up the second argument in the `pow()` function to `0.5`, and x contains a non-negative value, the two expressions, `pow(x, 0.5)` and `sqrt(x)`, are equivalent.

Now, take a look at how to call the `pow()` and `sqrt()` functions in the program shown in Listing 9.5.

TYPE **Listing 9.5. Applying the `pow()` and `sqrt()` functions.**

```
 1:   /* 09L05.c: Using pow() and sqrt() functions */
 2:   #include <stdio.h>
 3:   #include <math.h>
 4:
 5:   main()
 6:   {
 7:       double x, y, z;
 8:
 9:       x = 64.0;
10:       y = 3.0;
11:       z = 0.5;
12:       printf("pow(64.0, 3.0) returns: %7.0f\n", pow(x, y));
13:       printf("sqrt(64.0) returns:    %2.0f\n", sqrt(x));
14:       printf("pow(64.0, 0.5) returns: %2.0f\n", pow(x, z));
15:       return 0;
16:   }
```

The following output is displayed on the screen after the executable `09L05.exe` is executed:

OUTPUT
```
C:\app> 09L05
pow(64.0, 3.0) returns: 262144
sqrt(64.0) returns:    8
pow(64.0, 0.5) returns: 8
C:\app>
```

ANALYSIS   The three double variables in Listing 9.5, x, y, and z, are initialized with 64.0, 3.0, and 0.5, respectively, in lines 9–11.

The pow() function in line 12 takes x and y and then calculates the value of x raised to the power of y. Because the fractional part is all decimal digits of 0s, the format specifier %7.0f is used in the printf() function to convert only the non-fractional part of the value. The result is shown on the screen as 262144.

In line 13, the non-negative square root of x is calculated by calling the sqrt() function. As in line 12, the format specifier %2.0f is used in line 13 to convert the non-fractional part of the value returned from the sqrt() function, because the fractional part consists of decimal digits of 0s. As you see in the output, the non-negative square root of x is 8.

As I mentioned earlier, the pow(x, 0.5) expression is equivalent to the sqrt(x) expression. Thus, it's no surprise to see that pow(x, z) in the statement of line 14 produces the same result as sqrt(x) does in line 13.

NOTE

All floating-point calculations, including both the float and double data types, are done in double-precision arithmetic. That is, a float data variable must be converted to a double in order to carry on the calculation. After the calculation, the double has to be converted back to a float before the result can be assigned to the float variable. Therefore, a float calculation may take more time.

The main reason that C supports the float data type is to save memory space, because the double data type takes twice as much memory space for storage as the float data type does.

Summary

In this lesson you've learned the following:

- [ ] The signed modifier can be used to enable the sign bit for the char and int data types.
- [ ] All int variables in C are signed by default.
- [ ] The unsigned modifier can be used to disable the sign bit for the char and int data types.
- [ ] The memory space taken by a data variable can be reduced or increased by using the short, or long, data modifier respectively.

☐ There is a set of C library functions, such as `sin()`, `cos()`, and `tan()`, that can be used to perform trigonometric or hyperbolic computations.

☐ There is another group of math functions in C—for example, `pow()`—that can perform exponential and logarithmic calculation.

☐ The `sqrt()` function returns a non-negative square root. The expression `sqrt(x)` is equivalent to the `pow(x, 0.5)` expression, if `x` has a non-negative value.

☐ The header file `math.h` must be included in your C program if you call some math functions defined in the header file.

In the next lesson you'll learn several very important control flow statements in C.

Q&A

Q Which bit can be used as the sign bit in an integer?

A The leftmost bit can be used as the sign bit for an integer. For instance, assume the `int` data type is 16 bits long. If you count the bit position from right to left, and the first bit counted is bit 0, then bit 15 is the leftmost bit that can be used as the sign bit.

Q What can the `%lu` format specifier do?

A The `%lu` format specifier can be used to convert the corresponding datum to the `unsigned long int` data type. In addition, the `%lu` format specifier is equivalent to `%Lu`.

Q When do I use `short` and `long`?

A If you need to save memory space, and you know the value of an integer data variable stays within a smaller range, you can try to use the `short` modifier to tell the C compiler to reduce the default memory space assigned to the variable, for instance, from 32 bits to 16 bits.

On the other hand, if a variable has to hold a number that is beyond the current range of a data type, you can use the `long` modifier to increase the storage space of the variable in order to hold the number.

Q Does the `sin()` function take a value in degrees or in radians?

A Like other trigonometric math functions in C, the `sin()` function takes a value in radians. If you have an angle in degrees, you have to convert it into the form of radians. The formula is:

```
radians = degree * (3.141593 / 180.0).
```

Workshop

To help solidify your understanding of this hour's lesson, you are encouraged to answer the quiz questions and finish the exercises provided in the Workshop before you move to the next lesson. The answers and hints to the questions and exercises are given in Appendix E, "Answers to Quiz Questions and Exercises."

Quiz

1. Given an int variable x and an unsigned int variable y, as well as x = 0x8765 and y = 0x8765, is x equal to y?

2. Given that the int data type is 16 bits long, what is the hex format of the decimal number -23456?

3. Which format specifier, %ld or %lu, should be used to specify an unsigned long int variable?

4. What is the name of the header file you have to include if you're calling some C math functions from your C program?

Exercises

1. Given the following statements,

   ```
   int x;
   unsigned int y;
   x = 0xAB78;
   y = 0xAB78;
   ```

   write a program to display the decimal values of x and y on the screen.

2. Write a program to measure the sizes of short int, long int, and long double on your machine.

3. Give the binary representations of the following:

   □ 512

   □ -1

   □ 128

   □ -128

4. Write a program to display the decimal value given in quiz question 2 in the hex format. Does the result from the program match your answer to that question?

5. Given an angle of 30 degrees, write a program to calculate its sine and tangent values.

6. Write a program to calculate the non-negative square root of 0x19A1.

Hour 10

Getting Controls

It is harder to command than to obey.

—*F. Nietzsche*

In Hour 7, "Doing the Same Thing Over and Over," you learned to use the for, while, and do-while statements to do the same things over and over. These three statements can be grouped into the *looping* category that is a part of the control flow statements in C.

In this lesson you'll learn about the statements that belong to another group of control flow statements—*conditional branching* (or *jumping*), such as

- [ ] The if statement
- [ ] The if-else statement
- [ ] The switch statement
- [ ] The break statement
- [ ] The continue statement
- [ ] The goto statement

Always Saying "if..."

If life were a straight line, it would be very boring. The same thing is true for programming. It would be too dull if the statements in your program could only be executed in the order in which they appear.

In fact, an important task of a program is to instruct the computer to *branch* (that is, jump) to different portions of the code and work on different jobs whenever the specified conditions are met.

However, in most cases, you don't know in advance what will come next. What you do know is that something is bound to happen if certain conditions are met. Therefore, you can just write down tasks and conditions in the program. The decisions of when to perform the tasks are made by the conditional branching statements.

In C, the if statement is the most popular conditional branching statement; it can be used to evaluate the conditions as well as to make the decision whether the block of code controlled by the statement is going to be executed.

The general form of the if statement is

```
if (expression) {
    statement1;
    statement2;
      .
      .
      .
}
```

Here *expression* is the conditional criterion. If *expression* is logical TRUE (that is, nonzero), the statements inside the braces ({ and }), such as *statement1* and *statement2*, are executed. If *expression* is logical FALSE (zero), then the statements are skipped.

Note that the braces ({ and }) form a block of statements that is under the control of the if statement. If there is only one statement inside the block, the braces can be ignored. The parentheses ((and)), however, must always be used to enclose the conditional expression.

For instance, the following expression

```
if (x > 0)
  printf("The square root of x is: %f\n", sqrt(x));
```

tells the computer that if the value of x is greater than zero (that is, positive), it should calculate the square root of x by calling the sqrt() function, and then print out the result. Here the conditional criterion is the relational expression x > 0, which returns 1 for true and 0 for false.

Listing 10.1 gives you another example of using the if statement.

10

10

TYPE **Listing 10.1. Using the if statement in decision making.**

```
1:  /* 10L01.c  Using the if statement */
2:  #include <stdio.h>
3:
4:  main()
5:  {
6:     int i;
7:
8:     printf("Integers that can be divided by both 2 and 3\n");
9:     printf("(within the range of 0 to 100):\n");
10:    for (i=0; i<=100; i++){
11:       if ((i%2 == 0) && (i%3 == 0))
12:          printf("   %d\n", i);
13:    }
14:    return 0;
15: }
```

After 10L01.exe, the executable of the program in Listing 10.1, is created and run from a DOS prompt, the following output is printed on the screen:

OUTPUT
```
C:\app> 10L01
Integers that can be divided by both 2 and 3
(within the range of 0 to 100):
   0
   6
   12
   18
   24
   30
   36
   42
   48
   54
   60
   66
   72
   78
   84
   90
   96
C:\app>
```

ANALYSIS As you see in Listing 10.1, line 6 declares an integer variable, i. Lines 8 and 9 print out two headlines. Starting in line 10, the for statement keeps looping 101 times.

Within the for loop, the if statement in lines 11 and 12 evaluates the logical expression (i%2 == 0) && (i%3 == 0). If the expression returns 1 (that is, the value of i can be divided by both 2 and 3 completely), the value of i is displayed on the screen by calling the printf() function in line 12. Otherwise, the statement in line 12 is skipped.

Note that the braces ({ and }) are discarded in the if statement because there is only one statement under the control of the statement.

The result shown on the screen gives all integers within the range of 0 to 100 that can be divided by both 2 and 3.

The if-else Statement

In the if statement, when the conditional expression is logical TRUE, the computer will jump to the statements controlled by the if statement and execute them right away. If the expression is false, the computer will ignore those statements controlled by the if statement.

From time to time, you will want the computer to execute some other specified statements when the conditional expression of the if statement is logical FALSE. By doing so, you can use another conditional branching statement in C—the if-else statement.

As an expansion of the if statement, the if-else statement has the following form:

```
if (expression) {
    statement1;
    statement2;
    .
    .
    .
}
else {
    statement_A;
    statement_B;
    .
    .
    .
}
```

Here if expression is logical TRUE, the statements controlled by if, including statement1 and statement2, are executed. The statements, such as statement_A and statement_B, inside the statement block and following the else keyword are executed if expression is not logical TRUE.

The program in Listing 10.2 shows how to use the if-else statement.

Listing 10.2. Using the if-else statement.

```
 1:  /* 10L02.c  Using the if-else statement */
 2:  #include <stdio.h>
 3:
 4:  main()
 5:  {
 6:      int i;
 7:
 8:      printf("Even Number   Odd Number\n");
 9:      for (i=0; i<10; i++)
10:          if (i%2 == 0)
```

TYPE

10

```
11:            printf("%d", i);
12:        else
13:            printf("%14d\n", i);
14:
15:    return 0;
16: }
```

The following result is obtained by running the executable file 10L02.exe:

```
C:\app>10L02
Even Number   Odd Number
        0              1
        2              3
        4              5
        6              7
        8              9
C:\app>
```

OUTPUT

Line 6 of Listing 10.2 declares an integer variable, i. The printf() function in line 8 displays a headline on the screen.

ANALYSIS The integer variable i is initialized in the first expression field of the for statement in line 9. Controlled by the for statement, the if-else statement in lines 10–13 is executed 10 times. According to the if-else statement, the printf() function in line 11 prints out even numbers if the relational expression i%2 == 0 in line 10 returns 1 (that is, TRUE). If the relational expression returns 0 (that is, FALSE), the printf() function controlled by the else keyword in line 12 outputs odd numbers to the standard output.

Because the if-else statement is treated as a single statement, the braces { and } are not needed to form a block of statement in the for statement. Likewise, there are no braces used in the if-else statement because the if and else keywords each control a single statement, respectively, in lines 11 and 13.

Note that the minimum width of 14 is specified in the printf() function in line 13, so the output of the odd numbers is listed to the right side of the even numbers, as you can see in the output section. Because the program in Listing 10.2 checks numbers in a range of 0 to 9, the output shows that 0, 2, 4, 6, and 8 are even numbers, and 1, 3, 5, 7, and 9 are odd ones.

Nested if Statements

As you saw in the previous sections, one if statement enables a program to make one decision. In many cases, a program has to make a series of decisions. To enable it to do so, you can use nested if statements.

Listing 10.3 demonstrates the usage of nested if statements.

Listing 10.3. Using nested `if` statements.

```
 1:  /* 10L03.c  Using nested if statements */
 2:  #include <stdio.h>
 3:
 4:  main()
 5:  {
 6:      int i;
 7:
 8:      for (i=-5; i<=5; i++){
 9:         if (i > 0)
10:            if (i%2 == 0)
11:                printf("%d is an even number.\n", i);
12:            else
13:                printf("%d is an odd number.\n", i);
14:         else if (i == 0)
15:            printf("The number is zero.\n");
16:         else
17:            printf("Negative number: %d\n", i);
18:      }
19:      return 0;
20: }
```

After running the executable file `10L03.exe`, I obtain the following output:

```
C:\app>10L03
Negative number: -5
Negative number: -4
Negative number: -3
Negative number: -2
Negative number: -1
The number is zero.
1 is an odd number.
2 is an even number.
3 is an odd number.
4 is an even number.
5 is an odd number.
C:\app>
```

Listing 10.3 contains a `for` loop, starting in line 8 and ending in line 18. According to the expressions of the `for` statement in line 8, any tasks controlled by the `for` statement are executed up to 11 times.

First, a decision has to be made based on the return value of the relational expression `i > 0` in the `if` statement of line 9. The `i > 0` expression is used to test whether the value of `i` is positive or negative (including zero.) If the return value is `1`, the computer jumps to the second (that is, nested) `if` statement in line 10.

Note that line 10 contains another relational expression, `i%2 == 0`, which tests whether the integer variable `i` is even or odd. Therefore, the second decision of displaying even numbers

10

or odd numbers has to be made according to the return value of the second relational expression, i%2 == 0. The printf() function in line 11 prints out an even number if the return value is 1. Otherwise, the statement in line 13 is executed, and an odd number is shown on the screen.

The computer branches to line 14 if the i > 0 expression returns 0; that is, if the value of i is not greater than 0. In line 14, another if statement is nested within an else phrase, and the relational expression i == 0 is evaluated. If i == 0 is true, which means i contains the value of zero, the string of The number is zero. is displayed on the screen. Otherwise, the value of i is negative, according to the value returned by the i > 0 expression. The statement in line 17 then outputs the negative number to the standard output.

As you can see in the example, the value of i is within the range of 5 to -5. Thus, -5, -4, -3, -2, and -1 are printed out as negative numbers. In addition, the odd numbers 1, 3, and 5, as well as the even numbers 2 and 4, are also printed out.

The switch Statement

In the last section, you saw that nested if statements are used when there is more than one decision to be made. The nested if statements will become very complex if there are many decisions that need to be made, however. Sometimes, the programmer will have problems following the complex if statements.

Fortunately there is another statement in C, the switch statement, that you can use to make unlimited decisions or choices based on the value of a conditional expression and specified cases.

The general form of the switch statement is

```
switch (expression) {
   case expression1:
       statement1;
   case expression2:
       statement2;
   .
   .
   .
   default:
       statement-default;
}
```

Here the conditional expression, expression, is evaluated first. If the return value of expression is equal to the constant expression expression1, the statement statement1 is executed. If the value of expression is the same as the value of expression2, statement2 is executed. If, however, the value of expression is not equal to any values of the constant expressions labeled by the case keyword, the statement (*statement-default*) following the default keyword is executed.

You have to use the case keyword to label each case. The default keyword is recommended to be used for the default case. Note that no constant expressions are identical in the switch statement.

The program in Listing 10.4 gives you an example of using the switch statement. The program also demonstrates an important feature of the switch statement.

Listing 10.4. Using the switch statement.

```
 1:  /* 10L04.c  Using the switch statement */
 2:  #include <stdio.h>
 3:
 4:  main()
 5:  {
 6:     int day;
 7:
 8:     printf("Please enter a single digit for a day\n");
 9:     printf("(within the range of 1 to 3):\n");
10:     day = getchar();
11:     switch (day){
12:        case '1':
13:            printf("Day 1\n");
14:        case '2':
15:            printf("Day 2\n");
16:        case '3':
17:            printf("Day 3\n");
18:        default:
19:            ;
20:     }
21:     return 0;
22: }
```

TYPE

If I run the executable file 10L04.exe and enter 3, I obtain the following output:

```
C:\app>10L04
Please enter a single digit for a day
       (within the range of 1 to 3):
3
Day 3
C:\app>
```

OUTPUT

As you can see in line 6, an int variable, day, is declared; it is assigned the input entered by the user in line 10.

ANALYSIS

In line 11, the value of the integer variable day is evaluated in the switch statement. If the value is equal to one of the values of the constant expressions, the computer starts to execute statements from there. The constant expressions are labeled by prefixing case in front of them.

For instance, I entered 3 and then pressed the Enter key. The numeric value of 3 is assigned to day in line 10. Then, after finding a case in which the value of the constant expression matches the value contained by day, the computer jumps to line 17 to execute the printf() function and display Day 3 on the screen.

Note that under the default label in Listing 10.4, there is an empty (that is, null) statement ending with semicolon (;) in line 19. The computer does nothing with the empty statement.

However, if I enter 1 from my keyboard and then press the Enter key, I get the following output:

OUTPUT

```
C:\app>10L04
Please enter a single digit for a day
     (within the range of 1 to 3):
     1
Day 1
Day 2
Day 3
C:\app>
```

From the output, you can see that the statement controlled by the selected case, case 1, and the statements controlled by the rest of the cases are executed, because Day 1, Day 2, and Day 3 are displayed on the screen. Likewise, if I enter 2 from my keyboard, I have Day2 and Day3 shown on the screen.

This is an important feature of the switch statement: The computer continues to execute the statements following the selected case until the end of the switch statement.

You're going to learn how to exit from the switch construct in the next section.

The break **Statement**

You can add a break statement at the end of the statement list following every case label, if you want to exit the switch construct after the statements within a selected case are executed.

The program in Listing 10.5 does a similar job as the one in Listing 10.4, but this time, the break statement is used.

Listing 10.5. Adding the break **statement.**

```
TYPE    1:  /* 10L05.c  Adding the break statement */
        2:  #include <stdio.h>
        3:
        4:  main()
        5:  {
        6:      int day;
        7:
        8:      printf("Please enter a single digit for a day\n");
        9:      printf("(within the range of 1 to 7):\n");
       10:      day = getchar();
       11:      switch (day){
       12:         case '1':
       13:             printf("Day 1 is Sunday.\n");
       14:             break;
       15:         case '2':
       16:             printf("Day 2 is Monday.\n");
       17:             break;
       18:         case '3':
       19:             printf("Day 3 is Tuesday.\n");
       20:             break;
       21:         case '4':
       22:             printf("Day 4 is Wednesday.\n");
       23:             break;
       24:         case '5':
       25:             printf("Day 5 is Thursday.\n");
       26:             break;
       27:         case '6':
       28:             printf("Day 6 is Friday.\n");
       29:             break;
       30:         case '7':
       31:             printf("Day 7 is Saturday.\n");
       32:             break;
       33:         default:
       34:             printf("The digit is not within the range of 1 to 7.\n");
       35:             break;
       36:      }
       37:      return 0;
       38: }
```

With the help from the break statement, I can run the executable file 10L05.exe and only obtain the output of the selected case:

```
C:\app>10L05
Please enter a single digit for a day
        (within the range of 1 to 7):
OUTPUT  1
        Day 1 is Sunday.
        C:\app>
```

ANALYSIS

This program has seven case labels followed by the constant expressions of '1', '2', '3', '4', '5', '6', and '7', respectively. (See lines 12, 15, 18, 21, 24, 27, and 30.)

In each case, there is a statement followed by a break statement. As mentioned, the break statements help to exit the switch construct after the statement in a selected case is executed.

For example, after the int variable day is assigned the value of 1 and evaluated in the switch statement, the case with '1' is selected, and the statement in line 13 is executed. Then, the break statement in line 14 is executed, which breaks the control of the switch statement and returns the control to the next statement outside the switch construct. In Listing 10.5, the next statement is the return statement in line 37, which ends the main function.

The printf() function in line 13 outputs a string of Day 1 is Sunday. on the screen.

Note that in a switch statement, braces are not needed to group the statements within an individual case into a statement block.

Breaking an Infinite Loop

You can also use the break statement to break an infinite loop. As you saw in Hour 7, the following for and while loops are all infinite loops:

```
for (;;){
   statement1;
   statement2;
      .
      .
      .
}

while (1){
   statement1;
   statement2;
      .
      .
      .
}
```

The program in Listing 10.6 shows an example of using the break statement in an infinite while loop.

TYPE   Listing 10.6. Breaking an infinite loop.

```
1:   /* 10L06.c: Breaking an infinite loop */
2:   #include <stdio.h>
3:
4:   main()
5:   {
6:      int c;
7:
```

continues

Listing 10.6. continued

```
8:      printf("Enter a character:\n(enter x to exit)\n");
9:      while (1) {
10:        c = getc(stdin);
11:        if (c == 'x')
12:           break;
13:     }
14:     printf("Break the infinite while loop. Bye!\n");
15:     return 0;
16: }
```

The following is the result I got after running the executable file (`10L06.exe`) on my machine:

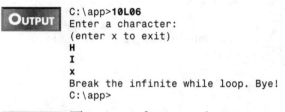

```
C:\app>10L06
Enter a character:
(enter x to exit)
H
I
x
Break the infinite while loop. Bye!
C:\app>
```

ANALYSIS   There is an infinite `while` loop in Listing 10.6, which starts in line 9 and ends in line 13. Within the infinite loop, the characters the user entered are assigned, one at a time, to the integer variable c. (See line 10.)

The relational expression `c == 'x'` in the `if` statement (see line 11) is evaluated each time during the looping. If the expression returns `0` (that is, the user does not enter the letter x), the looping continues. Otherwise, the `break` statement in line 12 is executed, which causes the computer to jump out of the infinite loop and start executing the next statement, which is shown in line 14.

You can see in the sample output, the `while` loop continues until I have entered the letter x, which causes the infinite loop to be broken and a piece of message, `Break the infinite while loop. Bye!`, to be displayed on the screen.

The `continue` **Statement**

Instead of breaking a loop, there are times when you want to stay in a loop but skip over some statements within the loop. To do this, you can use the `continue` statement provided by C. The `continue` statement causes execution to jump to the top of the loop immediately. You should be aware that using the `continue` statement, as well as the `break` statement, may make your program hard to debug.

For example, Listing 10.7 demonstrates how to use the continue statement in a loop doing sums.

TYPE **Listing 10.7. Using the continue statement.**

```
1:  /* 10L07.c: Using the continue statement */
2:  #include <stdio.h>
3:
4:  main()
5:  {
6:     int i, sum;
7:
8:     sum = 0;
9:     for (i=1; i<8; i++){
10:        if ((i==3) || (i==5))
11:           continue;
12:        sum += i;
13:     }
14:     printf("The sum of 1, 2, 4, 6, and 7 is: %d\n", sum);
15:     return 0;
16: }
```

After the executable file 10L07.exe is run from a DOS prompt, the output is shown on the screen:

OUTPUT
```
C:\app>10L07
The sum of 1, 2, 4, 6, and 7 is: 20
C:\app>
```

ANALYSIS In Listing 10.7, we want to calculate the sum of the integer values of 1, 2, 4, 6, and 7. Because the integers are almost consecutive, a for loop is built in lines 9–13. The statement in line 12 sums all consecutive integers from 1 to 7 (except for 3 and 5, which aren't in the listing and are skipped in the for loop).

By doing so, the expression (i==3) || (i==5) is evaluated in the if statement of line 10. If the expression returns 1 (that is, the value of i is equal to either 3 or 5), the continue statement in line 11 is executed, which causes the sum operation in line 12 to be skipped, and another iteration to be started at the beginning of the for loop. In this way, we obtain the sum of the integer values of 1, 2, 4, 6, and 7, but skip 3 and 5, automatically by using one for loop.

After the for loop, the value of sum, 20, is displayed on the screen by the printf() function in the statement of line 14.

The goto **Statement**

I feel that this book would not be not complete without mentioning the goto statement, although I do not recommend that you use the goto statement unless it's absolutely necessary. The main reason that the goto statement is discouraged is because its usage may make the C program unreliable and hard to debug.

The following is the general form of the goto statement:

```
labelname:
   statement1;
   statement2;
   .
   .
   .
   goto  labelname;
```

Here *labelname* is a label name that tells the goto statement where to jump. You have to place *labelname* in two places: One is at the place where the goto statement is going to jump (note that a colon must follow the label name), and the other is the place following the goto keyword. You have to follow the same rules to make a label name as you name a variable or function.

Also, the place for the goto statement to jump to can appear either before or after the statement.

Summary

In this lesson you've learned the following:

- ☐ An important task of a program is to instruct the computer to jump to a different portion of the code according to the specified branch conditions.
- ☐ The if statement is a very important statement for conditional branching in C.
- ☐ The if statement can be nested for making a series of decisions in your program.
- ☐ The if-else statement is an expansion of the if statement.
- ☐ The switch statement helps you to keep your program more readable when there are more than just a couple decisions to be made in your code.
- ☐ The case and default keywords, followed by a colon (:) and an integral value, are used in the switch statement as labels.
- ☐ The break statement can be used to exit the switch construct or a loop (usually, an infinite loop).

☐ The continue statement is used to let you stay within a loop while skipping over some statements.

☐ The goto statement enables the computer to jump to some other spot in your computer. Using this statement is not recommended because it may cause your program to be unreliable and hard to debug.

In the next lesson you'll learn about a very important concept—pointers.

Q&A

Q How many expressions are there in the if statement?

A The if statement takes only one expression to hold the conditional criteria. When the expression is true (that is, the conditions are met), the statements controlled by the if statement are executed. Otherwise, the next statement following the if statement block is executed.

Q Why is the if-else statement an expansion of the if statement?

A When the conditional expression in the if statement is false, the program control flow is returned back to the original track. However, when the conditional expression in the if-else statement is false, the program control flow branches to the statement block under the else keyword and returns to its original track after the statements controlled by else are executed. In other words, the if statement allows a single statement block to be executed or skipped entirely, whereas the if-else statement executes one of the two statement blocks under the control of the if-else statement.

Q Why do you normally need to add the break statement into the switch statement?

A When one of the cases within the switch statement is selected, the program control will branch to the case and execute all statements within the selected case and the rest of the cases that follow it. Therefore, you might get more results than you expected. To tell the computer to execute only the statements inside a selected case, you can put a break statement at the end of the case so that the program control flow will exit the switch construct after the statements within the case are executed.

Q What can the continue statement do inside a loop?

A When the continue statement inside a loop is executed, the program control is branched back to the beginning of the loop so that another iteration can be started. Inside the loop, any statements following the continue statement will be skipped over each time if the continue statement is executed.

10

Workshop

To help solidify your understanding of this hour's lesson, you are encouraged to answer the quiz questions and finish the exercises provided in the Workshop before you move to the next lesson. The answers and hints to the questions and exercises are given in Appendix E, "Answers to Quiz Questions and Exercises."

Quiz

1. Given x = 0, will the arithmetic operations inside the following if statement be performed?

   ```
   if (x != 0)
      y = 123 / x + 456;
   ```

2. Given x = 4, y = 2, and operator = '-', what is the final value of x after the following switch statement is executed?

   ```
   switch (operator){
      case '+':  x += y;
      case '-':  x -= y;
      case '*':  x *= y;
      case '/':  x /= y;
      default:   break;
   }
   ```

3. Similarly to in question 2, using x = 4, y = 2, and operator = '-', what is the final value of x after the following switch statement is executed?

   ```
   switch (operator){
      case '+':  x += y; break;
      case '-':  x -= y; break;
      case '*':  x *= y; break;
      case '/':  x /= y; break;
      default:   break;
   }
   ```

4. What is the value of the integer variable x after the following code is executed?

   ```
   x = 1;
   for (i=2; i<10; i++){
      if (i%3 == 0)
         continue;
      x += i;
   }
   ```

Exercises

1. Rewrite the program in Listing 10.1. This time, use the logical expression i%6 == 0 in the if statement.

2. Rewrite the program in Listing 10.1 by using nested if statements.

3. Write a program to read characters from the standard I/O. If the characters are A, B, and C, display their numeric values on the screen. (The switch statement is required.)

4. Write a program that keeps reading characters from the standard input until the character q is entered.

5. Rewrite the program in Listing 10.7. This time, instead of skipping 3 and 5, skip the integer that can be divided evenly by both 2 and 3.

10

PART

III

Pointers and Arrays

Hour

Hour 11

An Introduction to Pointers

The duties of the Pointer were to point out, by calling their names, those in the congregation who should take note of some point made in the sermon.

—H. B. Otis, Simple Truth

You've learned about many important C data types, operators, functions, and loops in the last 10 hours. In this lesson you'll learn about one of the most important and powerful features in C: pointers. The topics covered in this hour are

- ☐ Pointer variables
- ☐ Memory addresses
- ☐ The concept of indirection
- ☐ Declaring a pointer
- ☐ The address-of operator
- ☐ The dereference operator

What Is a Pointer?

A *pointer* is a variable whose value is used to point to another variable.

From this definition, you know two things: first, that a pointer is a variable, so you can assign different values to a pointer variable, and second, that the value contained by a pointer must be an address that indicates the location of another variable in the memory. That's why a pointer is also called an *address variable*.

Address (Left Value) Versus Content (Right Value)

As you might know, the memory inside your computer is used to hold the binary code of your program, which consists of statements and data, as well as the binary code of the operating system on your machine.

Each memory location must have a unique address so that the computer can read from or write to the memory location without any confusion. This is similar to the concept that each house in a city must have a unique address.

When a variable is declared, a piece of unused memory will be reserved for the variable, and the unique address to the memory will be associated with the name of the variable. The address associated with the variable name is usually called the *left value* of the variable.

Then, when the variable is assigned a value, the value is stored into the reserved memory location as the content. The content is also called the *right value* of the variable.

For instance, after the integer variable x is declared and assigned to a value like this:

```
int x;
x = 7;
```

the variable x now has two values:

> Left value: 1000
>
> Right value: 7

Here the left value, 1000, is the address of the memory location reserved for x. The right value, 7, is the content stored in the memory location. Note that depending on computers and operating systems, the right value of x can be different from one machine to another.

You can imagine that the variable x is the mailbox in front of your house, which has the address (normally the street number) 1000. The right value, 7, can be thought as a letter delivered to the mailbox.

11

Note that when your C program is being compiled and a value is being assigned to a variable, the C compiler has to check the left value of the variable. If the compiler cannot find the left value, it will issue an error message saying that the variable is undefined in your program. That's why, in C, you have to declare a variable before you can use it. (Imagine a postal worker complaining that he or she cannot drop the letters addressed to you because you haven't built a mailbox yet.)

By using a variable's left value, the C compiler can easily locate the appropriate memory storage reserved for a variable, and then read or write the right value of the variable.

The Address-of Operator (&)

The C language even provides you with an operator, &, in case you want to know the left value of a variable. This operator is called the *address-of operator* because it can return the address (that is, the left value) of a variable.

The following code, for example,

```
long int x, y;
y = &x;
```

assigns the address of the long integer variable x to another variable, y.

Listing 11.1 gives another example of obtaining addresses (that is, left values) of variables.

TYPE   **Listing 11.1. Obtaining the left values of variables.**

```
1:  /* 11L01.c: Obtaining addresses */
2:  #include <stdio.h>
3:
4:  main()
5:  {
6:     char  c;
7:     int   x;
8:     float y;
9:
10:    printf("c: address=0x%p, content=%c\n", &c, c);
11:    printf("x: address=0x%p, content=%d\n", &x, x);
12:    printf("y: address=0x%p, content=%5.2f\n", &y, y);
13:    c = 'A';
14:    x = 7;
15:    y = 123.45;
16:    printf("c: address=0x%p, content=%c\n", &c, c);
17:    printf("x: address=0x%p, content=%d\n", &x, x);
18:    printf("y: address=0x%p, content=%5.2f\n", &y, y);
19:    return 0;
20: }
```

After the executable (11L01.exe) of this program is created and run from a DOS prompt, the following output is displayed on the screen (note that you might get a different result, depending on your computer and operating system):

OUTPUT

```
C:\app> 11L01
c: address=0x1AF4, content=@
x: address=0x1AF2, content=-32557
y: address=0x1AF6, content=0.00
c: address=0x1AF4, content=A
x: address=0x1AF2, content=7
y: address=0x1AF6, content=123.45
C:\app>
```

ANALYSIS

As you can see in Listing 11.1, there are three variables, c, x, and y, declared in lines 6–8, respectively.

The statement in line 10 displays the address (that is, the left value) and the content (that is, the right value) of the character variable c on the screen. Here the &c expression returns the address of c.

Note that the format specifier %p is used in the printf() function of line 10 for displaying the address returned from &c.

Likewise, lines 11 and 12 print out the addresses of x and y, as well as the contents of x and y.

From the first part of the output, you see that the addresses (in hex format) of c, x, and y are 0x1AF4, 0x1AF2, and 0x1AF6. Because these three variables have not been initialized yet, the contents contained in their memory locations are what is left there from the last memory writing.

However, after the initializations that are carried on in lines 13–15, the memory slots reserved for the three variables have the contents of the initial values. Lines 16–18 display the addresses and contents of c, x, and y after the initialization.

You can see in the second part of the output, the contents of c, x, and y are now 'A', 7, and 123.45, respectively, with the same memory addresses.

NOTE

The format specifier %p used in the printf() function is supported by the ANSI standard. If, somehow, your compiler does not support %p, you can try to use %u or %lu in the printf() function to convert and print out a left value (that is, an address).

Also, the addresses printed out by the examples in this lesson are obtained by running the examples on my machine. The values may be different from what you can get by running the examples on your machine. This is because the address of a variable may vary from one type of computer to another.

11

Declaring Pointers

As mentioned at the beginning of this lesson, a pointer is a variable, which means that a pointer has a left value and a right value as well. However, both the left and right values are addresses. The left value of a pointer is used to refer to the pointer itself, whereas the right value of a pointer, which is the content of the pointer, is the address of another variable.

The general form of a pointer declaration is

```
data-type  *pointer-name;
```

Here `data-type` specifies the type of data to which the pointer points. `pointer-name` is the name of the pointer variable, which can be any valid variable name in C.

Note that right before the pointer name is an asterisk (`*`), which indicates that the variable is a pointer. When the compiler sees the asterisk in the declaration, it makes a note in its symbol table so that the variable can be used as a pointer.

The following shows different types of pointers:

```
char *ptr_c;    /* declare a pointer to a character */

int  *ptr_int;  /* declare a pointer to an integer */

float *ptr_flt; /* declare a pointer to a floating-point */
```

The program in Listing 11.2 demonstrates how to declare pointers and assign values to them.

TYPE **Listing 11.2. Declaring and assigning values to pointers.**

```
1:  /* 11L02.c: Declaring and assigning values to pointers */
2:  #include <stdio.h>
3:
4:  main()
5:  {
6:      char  c, *ptr_c;
7:      int   x, *ptr_x;
8:      float y, *ptr_y;
9:
10:     c = 'A';
11:     x = 7;
12:     y = 123.45;
13:     printf("c: address=0x%p, content=%c\n", &c, c);
14:     printf("x: address=0x%p, content=%d\n", &x, x);
15:     printf("y: address=0x%p, content=%5.2f\n", &y, y);
16:     ptr_c = &c;
17:         printf("ptr_c: address=0x%p, content=0x%p\n", &ptr_c, ptr_c);
18:         printf("*ptr_c => %c\n", *ptr_c);
19:     ptr_x = &x;
20:         printf("ptr_x: address=0x%p, content=0x%p\n", &ptr_x, ptr_x);
21:         printf("*ptr_x => %d\n", *ptr_x);
```

continues

11

Listing 11.2. continued

```
22:    ptr_y = &y;
23:        printf("ptr_y: address=0x%p, content=0x%p\n", &ptr_y, ptr_y);
24:        printf("*ptr_y => %5.2f\n", *ptr_y);
25:    return 0;
26: }
```

I get the following output displayed on the screen after running the executable `11L02.exe` from a DOS prompt on my machine:

```
C:\app> 11L02
c: address=0x1B38, content=A
x: address=0x1B36, content=7
y: address=0x1B32, content=123.45
ptr_c: address=0x1B30, content=0x1B38
*ptr_c => A
ptr_x: address=0x1B2E, content=0x1B36
*ptr_x => 7
ptr_y: address=0x1B2C, content=0x1B32
*ptr_y => 123.45
C:\app>
```

In Listing 11.2, there are three variables, c, x, and y, and three pointer variables, ptr_c, ptr_x, and ptr_y, declared in lines 6–8, respectively.

The statements in lines 10–12 initialize the three variables c, x, and y. Then, lines 13–15 print out the addresses as well as the contents of the three variables.

In line 16, the left value of the character variable c is assigned to the pointer variable ptr_c. The output made by the statement in line 17 shows that the pointer variable ptr_c contains the address of c. In other words, the content (that is, the right value) of ptr_c is the address (that is, the left value) of c.

Then in line 18, the value referred to by the pointer *ptr_c is printed out. The output proves that the pointer *ptr_c does point to the memory location of c.

Line 19 assigns the left value of the integer x to the integer pointer variable ptr_x. The statements in lines 20 and 21 print out the left value and right value of the pointer variable ptr_x, as well as the value referred to by the pointer *ptr_x.

Similarly, the left value of the float variable y is assigned to the float pointer variable ptr_y in line 22. To prove that ptr_y contains the address of y, and *ptr_y gives the content held by y, lines 23 and 24 print out the right values of ptr_y and *ptr_y, respectively.

The statements in lines 16, 19, and 22 show you how to assign the value of a variable to another—in an indirect way. In other words, the left value of a variable can be assigned to another variable so that the latter can be used as a pointer variable to obtain the right value of the former. In this case, the variable name and the pointer refer to the same memory location. Accordingly, if either the variable name or the pointer is used in an expression to change the contents of the memory location, the contents of the memory location has changed for the other.

To help you understand the indirection of assigning values, Figure 11.1 demonstrates the memory image of the relationships between c and ptr_c, x and ptr_x, and y and ptr_y, based on the output obtained on my machine.

Figure 11.1.
The memory image of variables and their pointers.

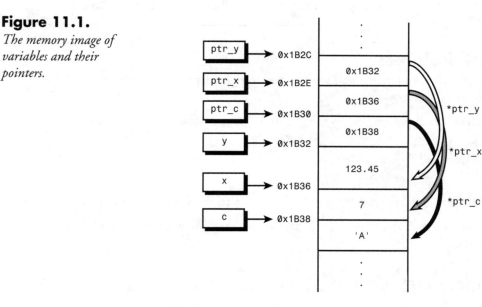

The Dereference Operator (*)

You've seen the asterisk (*) in the declaration of a pointer. In C, the asterisk is called the *dereference operator* when it is used as a unary operator. (Sometimes, it's also called the *indirection operator.*) The value of a variable can be referenced by the combination of the * operator and its operand, which contains the address of the variable.

For instance, in the program shown in Listing 11.2, after the address of the character variable c is assigned to the pointer variable ptr_c, the expression *ptr_c refers to the value contained by c. Therefore, you can use the *ptr_c expression, instead of calling the variable c directly, to obtain the value of c.

Likewise, given an integer variable x and x = 1234, you can declare an integer pointer variable, ptr_x, for instance, and assign the left value (address) of x to ptr_x—that is, ptr_x = &x. Then, the expression *ptr_x returns 1234, which is the right value (content) of x.

Warning

Don't confuse the dereference operator with the multiplication operator, although they share the same symbol, *.

The *dereference operator* is a unary operator, which takes only one operand. The operand contains the address (that is, left value) of a variable.

On the other hand, the *multiplication operator* is a binary operator that requires two operands to perform the operation of multiplication.

Null Pointers

A pointer is said to be a *null pointer* when its right value is 0. Remember, a null pointer can never point to valid data.

To set a null pointer, simply assign 0 to the pointer variable. For example:

```
char *ptr_c;
int  *ptr_int;

ptr_c = ptr_int = 0;
```

Here ptr_c and ptr_int become null pointers after the integer value of 0 is assigned to them.

You'll see applications of null pointers used in control-flow statements and arrays later in this book.

Updating Variables via Pointers

As you learned in the previous section, as long as you link up a variable to a pointer variable, you can obtain the value of the variable by using the pointer variable. In other words, you can read the value by pointing to the memory location of the variable and using the dereferencing operator.

This section shows you that you can write a new value to the memory location of a variable using a pointer that contains the left value of the variable. Listing 11.3 gives an example.

TYPE **Listing 11.3. Changing variable values via pointers.**

```
1:   /* 11L03.c: Changing values via pointers */
2:   #include <stdio.h>
3:
4:   main()
5:   {
6:      char  c,  *ptr_c;
7:
8:      c = 'A';
9:      printf("c: address=0x%p, content=%c\n", &c, c);
```

11

```
10:    ptr_c = &c;
11:        printf("ptr_c: address=0x%p, content=0x%p\n", &ptr_c, ptr_c);
12:        printf("*ptr_c => %c\n", *ptr_c);
13:    *ptr_c = 'B';
14:        printf("ptr_c: address=0x%p, content=0x%p\n", &ptr_c, ptr_c);
15:        printf("*ptr_c => %c\n", *ptr_c);
16:    printf("c: address=0x%p, content=%c\n", &c, c);
17:    return 0;
18: }
```

After running the executable 11L03.exe from a DOS prompt on my machine, I get the following output displayed on the screen:

OUTPUT

```
C:\app> 11L03
c: address=0x1828, content=A
ptr_c: address=0x1826, content=0x1828
*ptr_c => A
ptr_c: address=0x1826, content=0x1828
*ptr_c => B
c: address=0x1828, content=B
C:\app>
```

ANALYSIS A char variable, c, and a char pointer variable, ptr_c, are declared in line 6 of Listing 11.3.

The variable c is initialized with 'A' in line 8, which is printed out, along with the address of the variable, by the printf() function in line 9.

Then, in line 10, the pointer variable ptr_c is assigned the left value (address) of c. It's not surprising to see the output printed out by the statements in lines 11 and 12, where the right value of ptr_c is the left value of c, and the pointer *ptr_c points to the right value of c.

In line 13 the expression *ptr_c = 'B' asks the computer to write 'B' to the location pointed to by the pointer *ptr_c. The output printed by the statement in line 15 proves that the content of the memory location pointed to by *ptr_c is updated. The statement in line 14 prints out the left and right values of the pointer variable ptr_c and shows that these values remain the same.

As you know, *ptr_c points to where the character variable c resides. Therefore, the expression *ptr_c = 'B' actually updates the content (that is, the right value) of the variable c to 'B'. To prove this, the statement in line 16 displays the left and right values of c on the screen. Sure enough, the output shows that the right value of c has been changed.

Pointing to the Same Thing

A memory location can be pointed to by more than one pointer. For example, given that c = 'A' and that ptr_c1 and ptr_c2 are two character pointer variables, ptr_c1 = &c and ptr_c2 = &c set the two pointer variables to point to the same location in the memory.

The program in Listing 11.4 shows another example of pointing to the same thing with several pointers.

TYPE

Listing 11.4. Pointing to the same thing with more than one pointer.

```
1:  /* 11L04.c: Pointing to the same thing */
2:  #include <stdio.h>
3:
4:  main()
5:  {
6:     int x;
7:     int *ptr_1, *ptr_2, *ptr_3;
8:
9:     x = 1234;
10:    printf("x: address=0x%p, content=%d\n", &x, x);
11:    ptr_1 = &x;
12:    printf("ptr_1: address=0x%p, content=0x%p\n", &ptr_1, ptr_1);
13:       printf("*ptr_1 => %d\n", *ptr_1);
14:    ptr_2 = &x;
15:    printf("ptr_2: address=0x%p, content=0x%p\n", &ptr_2, ptr_2);
16:       printf("*ptr_2 => %d\n", *ptr_2);
17:    ptr_3 = ptr_1;
18:    printf("ptr_3: address=0x%p, content=0x%p\n", &ptr_3, ptr_3);
19:       printf("*ptr_3 => %d\n", *ptr_3);
20:    return 0;
21: }
```

The following output is displayed on the screen by running the executable 11L04.exe from a DOS prompt on my machine (note that you might get different address values if you run the program on your machine):

OUTPUT

```
C:\app> 11L04
x: address=0x1838, content=1234
ptr_1: address=0x1834, content=0x1838
*ptr_1 => 1234
ptr_2: address=0x1836, content=0x1838
*ptr_2 => 1234
ptr_3: address=0x1832, content=0x1838
*ptr_3 => 1234
C:\app>
```

ANALYSIS   As shown in Listing 11.4, line 6 declares an integer variable, x, and line 7 declares three integer pointer variables, ptr_1, ptr_2, and ptr_3.

The statement in line 10 prints out the left and right values of x. On my machine, the left value (address) of x is 0x1838. The right value (content) of x is 1234, which is the initial value assigned to x in line 9.

Line 11 assigns the left value of x to the pointer variable ptr_1 so that ptr_1 can be used to refer to the right value of x. To make sure that the pointer variable ptr_1 now contains the address of x, line 12 prints out the right value of ptr_1, along with its left value. The output shows that ptr_1 does hold the address of x, 0x1838. Then, line 13 prints out the value 1234, which is referred to by the *ptr_1 expression. Note that the asterisk * in the expression is the dereference operator.

In line 14, the *ptr_2 = &x expression assigns the left value of x to another pointer variable, ptr_2; that is, the pointer variable ptr_2 is now linked with the address of x. The statement in line 16 displays the integer 1234 on the screen by using the dereference operator * and its operand, ptr_2. In other words, the memory location of x is referred to by the second pointer *ptr_2.

In line 17, the pointer variable ptr_3 is assigned with the right value of ptr_1. Because ptr_1 now holds the address of x, the expression ptr_3 = ptr_1 is equivalent to ptr_3 = &x. Then, from the output made by the statements in lines 18 and 19, you see the integer 1234 again on the screen. This time the integer is referred to by the third pointer, *ptr_3.

Summary

In this lesson you've learned the following:

- ☐ A pointer is a variable whose value is used to point to another variable.
- ☐ A variable declared in C has two values: the left value and the right value.
- ☐ The left value of a variable is the address; the right value is the content of the variable.
- ☐ The address-of operator (&) can be used to obtain the left value (address) of a variable.
- ☐ The asterisk (*) in a pointer declaration tells the compiler that the variable is a pointer variable.
- ☐ The dereference operator (*) is a unary operator; as such, it requires only one operand.
- ☐ The *ptr_name expression returns the value pointed to by the pointer variable ptr_name, where ptr_name can be any valid variable name in C.
- ☐ If the right value of a pointer variable is 0, the pointer is a null pointer. A null pointer cannot point to valid data.
- ☐ You can update the value of a variable referred by a pointer variable.
- ☐ Several pointers can point to the same location of a variable in the memory.

In the next lesson you'll learn about an aggregate type—an array, which is closely related to pointers in C.

Q&A

Q What are the left and right values?

A The left value refers to the address of a variable, and the right value refers to the content stored in the memory location of a variable. There are two ways to get the right value of a variable: use the variable name directly, or use the left value of the variable to refer to where the right value resides. The second way is also called the indirect way.

Q How can you obtain the address of a variable?

A By using the address-of operator, &. For instance, given an integer variable x, the &x expression returns the address of x. To print out the address of x, you can use the %p format specifier in the printf() function.

Q What is the concept of indirection in terms of using pointers?

A Before this hour, the only way you knew for reading from or writing to a variable was to invoke the variable directly. For instance, if you wanted to write a decimal, 16, to an integer variable x, you could call the statement x = 16;.

As you learned in this hour, C allows you to access a variable in another way—using pointers. Therefore, to write 16 to x, you can first declare an integer pointer (ptr) and assign the left value (address) of x to ptr—that is, ptr = &x;. Then, instead of executing the statement x = 16;, you can use another statement:

```
*ptr = 16;
```

Here the pointer *ptr refers to the memory location reserved by x, and the content stored in the memory location is updated to 16 after the statement is executed. So, you see, making use of pointers to access the memory locations of variables is a way of indirection.

Q Can a null pointer point to valid data?

A No. A null pointer cannot point to valid data. This is so because the value contained by a null pointer is 0. You'll see examples of using null pointers in arrays, strings, or memory allocation later in the book.

11

Workshop

To help solidify your understanding of this hour's lesson, you are encouraged to answer the quiz questions and finish the exercises provided in the Workshop before you move to the next lesson. The answers and hints to the questions and exercises are given in Appendix E, "Answers to Quiz Questions and Exercises."

Quiz

1. How can you obtain the left value of a character variable `ch`?

2. In the following expressions, does the asterisk (*) act as a dereference operator or as a multiplication operator?

   ☐ `*ptr`

   ☐ `x * y`

   ☐ `y *= x + 5`

   ☐ `*y *= *x + 5`

3. Given that `x = 10`, the address of `x` is `0x1A38`, and `ptr_int = &x`, what will `ptr_int` and `*ptr_int` return, respectively?

4. Given that `x = 123`, and `ptr_int = &x` after the execution of `*ptr_int = 456`, what does `x` contain?

Exercises

1. Given three integer variables, `x = 512`, `y = 1024`, and `z = 2048`, write a program to print out their left values as well as their right values.

2. Write a program to update the value of the `double` variable `flt_num` from `123.45` to `543.21` by using a `double` pointer.

3. Given a character variable `ch` and `ch = 'A'`, write a program to update the value of `ch` to decimal `66` by using a pointer.

4. Given that `x=5` and `y=6`, write a program to calculate the multiplication of the two integers and print out the result, which is saved in `x`, all in the way of indirection (that is, using pointers).

11

Hour 12

Storing Similar Data Items

Gather up the fragments that remain, that nothing be lost.

—*John 6:12*

In last hour's lesson you learned about pointers and the concept of indirection. In this lesson you'll learn about arrays, which are collections of similar data items and are closely related to pointers. The main topics covered in this lesson are

- ☐ Single-dimension arrays
- ☐ Indexing arrays
- ☐ Pointers and arrays
- ☐ Character arrays
- ☐ Multidimensional arrays
- ☐ Unsized arrays

What Is an Array?

You now know how to declare a variable with a specified data type, such as char, int, float, or double. In many cases, you have to declare a set of variables that have the same data type. Instead of declaring them individually, C allows you to declare a set of variables of the same data type collectively as an array.

An *array* is a collection of variables that are of the same data type. Each item in an array is called an *element*. All elements in an array are referenced by the name of the array and are stored in a set of consecutive memory slots.

Declaring Arrays

The following is the general form to declare an array:

```
data-type   Array-Name[Array-Size];
```

Here data-type is the type specifier that indicates what data type the declared array will be. Array-Name is the name of the declared array. Array-Size defines how many elements the array can contain. Note that the brackets ([and]) are required in declaring an array. The bracket pair ([and]) is also called the *array subscript operator*.

For example, an array of integers is declared in the following statement,

```
int array_int[8];
```

where int specifies the data type of the array whose name is array_int. The size of the array is 8, which means that the array can store eight elements (that is, integers in this case).

In C, you have to declare an array explicitly, as you do for other variables, before you can use it.

Indexing Arrays

After you declare an array, you can access each of the elements in the array separately.

For instance, the following declaration declares an array of characters:

```
char day[7];
```

You can access the elements in the array of day one after another.

The important thing to remember is that all arrays in C are indexed starting at 0. In other words, the index to the first element in an array is 0, not 1. Therefore, the first element in the array of day is day[0]. Because there are 7 elements in the day array, the last element is day[6], not day[7].

The seven elements of the array have the following expressions: day[0], day[1], day[2], day[3], day[4], day[5], and day[6].

Because these expressions reference the elements in the array, they are sometimes called *array element references*.

Initializing Arrays

With the help of the array element references, you can initialize each element in an array.

For instance, you can initialize the first element in the array of day, which was declared in the last section, like this:

day[0] = 'S';

Here the numeric value of S is assigned to the first element of day, day[0].

Likewise, the statement day[1] = 'M'; assigns 'M' to the second element, day[1], in the array.

The second way to initialize an array is to initialize all elements in the array together. For instance, the following statement initializes an integer array, arInteger:

int arInteger[5] = {100, 8, 3, 365, 16};

Here the integers inside the braces ({ and }) are assigned to the corresponding elements of the array arInteger. That is, 100 is given to the first element (arInteger[0]), 8 to the second element (arInteger[1]), 3 to the third (arInteger[2]), and so on.

Listing 12.1 gives another example of initializing arrays.

TYPE | **Listing 12.1. Initializing an array.**

```
1:   /* 12L01.c: Initializing an array */
2:   #include <stdio.h>
3:
4:   main()
5:   {
6:      int i;
7:      int list_int[10];
8:
9:      for (i=0; i<10; i++){
10:        list_int[i] = i + 1;
11:        printf( "list_int[%d] is initialized with %d.\n", i, list_int[i]);
12:     }
13:     return 0;
14: }
```

12

The following output is displayed on the screen after the executable (12L01.exe) of the program in Listing 12.1 is created and run from a DOS prompt:

OUTPUT
```
C:\app>12L01
list_int[0] is initialized with 1.
list_int[1] is initialized with 2.
list_int[2] is initialized with 3.
list_int[3] is initialized with 4.
list_int[4] is initialized with 5.
list_int[5] is initialized with 6.
list_int[6] is initialized with 7.
list_int[7] is initialized with 8.
list_int[8] is initialized with 9.
list_int[9] is initialized with 10.
C:\app>
```

ANALYSIS As you can see in Listing 12.1, there is an integer array, called list_int, which is declared in line 7. The array list_int can contain 10 elements.

Lines 9–12 make up a for loop that iterates 10 times. The statement in line 10 initializes list_int[i], the *i*th element of the array list_int, with the value returned from the i + 1 expression.

Line 11 then prints out the name of the element, list_int[i], and the value assigned to the element.

The Size of an Array

As mentioned earlier in this lesson, an array consists of consecutive memory locations. Given an array, like this:

```
data-type  Array-Name[Array-Size];
```

you can then calculate the total bytes of the array by the following expression:

```
sizeof(data-type) * Array-Size
```

Here *data-type* is the data type of the array; *Array-Size* specifies the total number of elements the array can take. The result returned by the expression is the total number of bytes the array takes.

Another way to calculate the total bytes of an array is simpler; it uses the following expression:

```
sizeof(Array-Name)
```

Here *Array-Name* is the name of the array.

The program in Listing 12.2 shows how to calculate the memory space taken by an array.

12

TYPE **Listing 12.2. Calculating the size of an array.**

```
1:   /* 12L02.c: Total bytes of an array */
2:   #include <stdio.h>
3:
4:   main()
5:   {
6:      int total_byte;
7:      int list_int[10];
8:
9:      total_byte = sizeof (int) * 10;
10:     printf( "The size of int is %d-byte long.\n", sizeof (int));
11:     printf( "The array of 10 ints has total %d bytes.\n", total_byte);
12:     printf( "The address of the first element: 0x%x\n", &list_int[0]);
13:     printf( "The address of the last element:  0x%x\n", &list_int[9]);
14:     return 0;
15: }
```

After running the executable 12L02.exe, I have the following output printed on my screen:

OUTPUT
```
C:\app>12L02
The size of int is 2-byte long.
The array of 10 ints has total 20 bytes
The address of the first element: 0x1806
The address of the last element:  0x%1818
C:\app>
```

ANALYSIS Note that you might get different address values when you run the program in Listing 12.2 on your machine. However, the difference between the address of the first element and the address of the last element should be the same as the one obtained from the output on my machine.

In Listing 12.2, there is an integer array, list_int, which is declared in line 7. The total memory space taken by the array is the result of multiplying the size of int and the total number of elements in the array. As declared in this example, there are a total of 10 elements in the array list_int.

The statement in line 10 prints out the size of int on my machine. You can see from the output that each integer element in the array takes 2 bytes. Therefore, the total memory space (in bytes) taken by the array is 10 * 2. In other words, the statement in line 9 assigns the value of 20, returned by the sizeof (int) * 10 expression, to the integer variable total_byte. Line 11 then displays the value contained by the total_byte variable on the screen.

To prove that the array does take the consecutive memory space of 20 bytes, the address of the first element in the array is printed out by the statement in line 12. Note that the ampersand (&), which was introduced as the address-of operator in Hour 11, "An Introduction to Pointers," is used in line 12 to obtain the address of the first element, list_int[0], in the array. Here the address of the first element is the start address of the array. From the output, you can see that the address of the list_int[0] element is 0x1806 on my machine.

12

Then, the &list_int[9] expression in line 13 returns the address of the last element in the array, which is 0x1818 on my machine. Thus, the distance between the last element and the first element is 0x1818–0x1806, or 18 bytes long.

As mentioned earlier in the book, hexadecimal is a 16-based numbering system. We know that 0x1818 minus 0x1806 produces 0x0012 (that is, 0x12). Then 0x12 in hexadecimal is equal to 1*16 + 2 that yields 18 in decimal.

Because each element takes 2 bytes, the total number of bytes taken by the array list_int is indeed 20 bytes. You can calculate it another way: The distance between the last element and the first element is 18 bytes. The total number of bytes taken by the array should be counted from the very first byte in the first element to the last byte in the last element. Therefore, the total number bytes taken by the array is equal to 18 plus 2, that is 20 bytes.

Figure 12.1 shows you the memory space taken by the array list_int.

Figure 12.1.

The memory space taken by the array list_int.

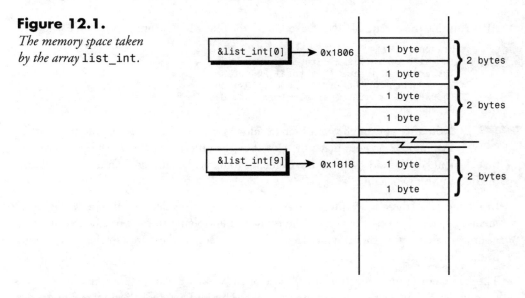

Arrays and Pointers

As I mentioned earlier in this hour, pointers and arrays have a close relationship in C. In fact, you can make a pointer that refers to the first element of an array by simply assigning the array name to the pointer variable. If an array is referenced by a pointer, the elements in the array can be accessed with the help of the pointer.

For instance, the following statements declare a pointer and an array, and assign the address of the first element to the pointer variable:

```
char  *ptr_c;
char  list_c[10];
ptr_c = list_c;
```

Because the address of the first element in the array list_c is the beginning address of the array, the pointer variable ptr_c is actually now referencing the array via the beginning address.

Listing 12.3 demonstrates how to reference an array with a pointer.

TYPE **Listing 12.3. Referencing an array with a pointer.**

```
1:  /* 12L03.c: Referencing an array with a pointer */
2:  #include <stdio.h>
3:
4:  main()
5:  {
6:      int *ptr_int;
7:      int list_int[10];
8:      int i;
9:
10:     for (i=0; i<10; i++)
11:         list_int[i] = i + 1;
12:     ptr_int = list_int;
13:     printf( "The start address of the array: 0x%p\n", ptr_int);
14:     printf( "The value of the first element: %d\n", *ptr_int);
15:     ptr_int = &list_int[0];
16:     printf( "The address of the first element: 0x%p\n", ptr_int);
17:     printf( "The value of the first element: %d\n", *ptr_int);
18:     return 0;
19: }
```

After the executable 12L03.exe is run from a DOS prompt, the following output is printed on my screen:

OUTPUT
```
C:\app>12L03
The start address of the array: 0x1802
The value of the first element: 1
The address of the first element: 0x1802
The value of the first element: 1
C:\app>
```

ANALYSIS In Listing 12.3, an integer pointer variable, ptr_int, is declared in line 6. Then, an integer array, list_int, which is declared in line 7, is initialized by the list_int[i] = i + 1 expression in a for loop. (See lines 10 and 11.)

The statement in line 12 assigns the address of the first element in the array to the pointer variable ptr_int. To do so, the name of the array list_int is simply placed on the right side of the assignment operator (=) in line 12.

Line 13 displays the address assigned to the pointer variable ptr_int. The output shows that 0x1802 is the start address of the array. (You might get a different address on your machine.) The *ptr_int expression in line 14 returns the value referenced by the pointer. This value is

12

the value contained by the first element of the array, which is the initial value, 1, given in the for loop. You can see that the output from the statement in line 14 shows the value correctly.

The statement in line 15 is equivalent to the one in line 12, which assigns the address of the first element to the pointer variable. Lines 16 and 17 then print out the address and the value kept by the first element, 0x1802 and 1, respectively.

In Hour 16, "Applying Pointers," you'll learn to access an element of an array by incrementing or decrementing a pointer.

Displaying Arrays of Characters

This subsection focuses on arrays of characters. On most machines, the char data type takes one byte. Therefore, each element in a character array is one byte long. The total number of elements in a character array is the total number of bytes the array takes in the memory.

More importantly in C, a *character string* is defined as a character array whose last element is the null character (\0). Hour 13, "Manipulating Strings," introduces more details about strings.

In Listing 12.4, you see various ways to display an array of characters on the screen.

TYPE   **Listing 12.4. Printing out an array of characters.**

```
1:  /* 12L04.c: Printing out an array of characters */
2:  #include <stdio.h>
3:
4:  main()
5:  {
6:      char array_ch[7] = {'H', 'e', 'l', 'l', 'o', '!', '\0'};
7:      int i;
8:
9:      for (i=0; i<7; i++)
10:         printf("array_ch[%d] contains: %c\n", i, array_ch[i]);
11:     /*---  method I ---*/
12:     printf( "Put all elements together(Method I):\n");
13:     for (i=0; i<7; i++)
14:         printf("%c", array_ch[i]);
15:     /*---  method II ---*/
16:     printf( "\nPut all elements together(Method II):\n");
17:     printf( "%s\n", array_ch);
18:
19:     return 0;
20: }
```

The following output is a copy from my screen (I obtained these results by running the executable 12L04.exe):

```
C:\app>12L04
array_ch[0] contains: H
array_ch[1] contains: e
array_ch[2] contains: l
array_ch[3] contains: l
array_ch[4] contains: o
array_ch[5] contains: !
array_ch[6] contains:
Put all elements together(Method I):
Hello!
Put all elements together(Method II):
Hello!
C:\app>
```

As you can see from Listing 12.4, a character array, array_ch, is declared and initialized in line 6. Each element in the character array is printed out by the printf() function in a for loop shown in lines 9 and 10. There are a total of seven elements in the array; they contain the following character constants: 'H', 'e', 'l', 'l', 'o', '!', and '\0'.

There are two ways to display all characters in the array, and to treat them as a character string.

Lines 12–14 show the first way, which fetches each individual element, array_ch[i], consecutively in a loop, and prints out one character next to another by using the character format specifier %c in the printf() function in line 14.

The second way is simpler. You tell the printf() function where to find the first element to start with. Also, you need to use the string format specifier %s in the printf() function as shown in line 17. Note that the array_ch expression in line 17 contains the address of the first element in the array—that is, the start address of the array.

You may be wondering how the printf() function knows where the end of the character array is. Do you remember that the last element in the character array array_ch is a \0 character? It's this null character that marks the end of the character array. As I mentioned earlier, a character array ended with a null character is called a character string in C.

The Null Character (\0)

The null character (\0) is treated as one character in C; it is a special character that marks the end of a string. Therefore, when functions like printf() act on a character string, they process one character after another until they encounter the null character. (You'll learn more about strings in Hour 13.)

The null character (\0), which is always evaluated as FALSE, can also be used for a logical test in a control-flow statement. Listing 12.5 gives an example of using the null character in a for loop.

12

TYPE	**Listing 12.5. Stopping printing at the null character.**

```
1:  /* 12L05.c: Stopping at the null character */
2:  #include <stdio.h>
3:
4:  main()
5:  {
6:     char array_ch[15] = {'C', ' ',
7:                          'i', 's', ' ',
8:                          'p', 'o', 'w', 'e', 'r',
9:                          'f', 'u', 'l', '!', '\0'};
10:    int i;
11:    /*  array_ch[i] in logical test */
12:    for (i=0; array_ch[i] != '\0'; i++)
13:       printf("%c", array_ch[i]);
14:    return 0;
15: }
```

By running the executable 12L05.exe, I obtain the following output:

| OUTPUT | ```
C:\app>12L05
C is powerful!
C:\app>
``` |
| --- | --- |

ANALYSIS	In Listing 12.5, a character array, array_ch, is declared and initialized with the characters (including the space characters) from the string C is powerful!, in lines 6–9.

Note that the last element in the array contains the null character (\0), which is needed later in a for loop.

The for loop in lines 12 and 13 tries to print out each element in the array array_ch to show the string C is powerful! on the screen. So in the first expression field of the for statement (loop), the integer variable i, which is used as the index to the array, is initialized with 0.

Then, the expression in the second field, array_ch[i] != '\0', is evaluated. If the expression returns logical TRUE, the for loop iterates; otherwise, the loop stops. Starting at the first element in the array, the array_ch[i] expression keeps returning TRUE until the null character is encountered. Therefore, the for loop can put all characters of the array on the screen, and stop printing right after the array_ch[i] returns logical FALSE. In fact, you can simplify the array_ch[i] != '\0' expression in the second field of the for statement to array_ch[i] because '\0' is evaluated as FALSE anyway.

Multidimensional Arrays

So far, all the arrays you've seen have been one-dimensional arrays, in which the dimension sizes are placed within a pair of brackets ([and]).

12
```

In addition to one-dimensional arrays, the C language also supports multidimensional arrays. You can declare arrays with as many dimensions as your compiler allows.

The general form of declaring a *N*-dimensional array is

```
data-type  Array-Name[Array-Size1][Array-Size2]. . . [Array-SizeN];
```

where *N* can be any positive integer.

Because the two-dimensional array, which is widely used, is the simplest form of the multidimensional array, let's focus on two-dimensional arrays in this section. Anything you learn from this section can be applied to arrays of more than two dimensions, however.

For example, the following statement declares a two-dimensional integer array:

```
int  array_int[2][3];
```

Here there are two pairs of brackets that represent two dimensions with a size of 2 and 3 integer elements, respectively.

You can initialize the two-dimensional array array_int in the following way:

```
array_int[0][0] = 1;
array_int[0][1] = 2;
array_int[0][2] = 3;
array_int[1][0] = 4;
array_int[1][1] = 5;
array_int[1][2] = 6;
```

which is equivalent to the statement

```
int array_int[2][3] = {1, 2, 3, 4, 5, 6};
```

Also, you can initialize the array_int array in the following way:

```
int array_int[2][3] = {{1, 2, 3}, {4, 5, 6}};
```

Note that array_int[0][0] is the first element in the two-dimensional array array_int; array_int[0][1] is the second element in the array; array_int[0][2] is the third element; array_int[1][0] is the fourth element; array_int[1][1] is the fifth element; and array_int[1][2] is the sixth element in the array.

The program in Listing 12.6 shows a two-dimensional integer array that is initialized and printed out on the screen.

TYPE   **Listing 12.6. Printing out a two-dimensional array.**

```
1:  /* 12L06.c: Printing out a 2-D array */
2:  #include <stdio.h>
3:
4:  main()
```

continues

Listing 12.6. continued

```
5:  {
6:      int two_dim[3][5] = {1, 2, 3, 4, 5,
7:                           10, 20, 30, 40, 50,
8:                           100, 200, 300, 400, 500};
9:      int i, j;
10:
11:     for (i=0; i<3; i++){
12:        printf("\n");
13:        for (j=0; j<5; j++)
14:           printf("%6d", two_dim[i][j]);
15:     }
16:     return 0;
17: }
```

The following output is obtained by running the executable 12L06.exe:

OUTPUT
```
C:\app>12L06
     1     2     3     4     5
    10    20    30    40    50
   100   200   300   400   500
C:\app>
```

ANALYSIS   As you can see in Listing 12.6, there is a two-dimensional integer array, two_dim, declared and initialized in lines 6–8.

In lines 11–15, two for loops are nested together. The outer for loop increments the integer variable i and prints out the newline character \n in each iteration. Here the integer variable i is used as the index to the first dimension of the array, two_dim.

The inner for loop in lines 13 and 14 prints out each element, represented by the two_dim[i][j] expression, by incrementing the index to the second dimension of the array. Therefore, I obtain output like the following

```
     1     2     3     4     5
    10    20    30    40    50
   100   200   300   400   500
```

after the two nested for loops are run successfully.

Unsized Arrays

As you've seen, the size of a dimension is normally given during the declaration of an array. It means that you have to count each element in an array. It could be tedious to do so, though, especially if there are many elements in an array.

The good news is that the C compiler can actually calculate a dimension size of an array automatically if an array is declared as an *unsized array*. For example, when the compiler sees the following unsized array:

```
int  list_int[] = { 10, 20, 30, 40, 50, 60, 70, 80, 90};
```

it will create an array big enough to store all the elements.

Likewise, you can declare a multidimensional unsized array. However, you have to specify all but the leftmost (that is, the first) dimension size. For instance, the compiler can reserve enough memory space to hold all elements in the following two-dimensional unsized array:

```
char list_ch[][2] = {
         'a', 'A',
         'b', 'B',
         'c', 'C',
         'd', 'D',
         'e', 'E',
         'f', 'F',
         'g', 'G'};
```

The program in Listing 12.7 initializes a one-dimensional character unsized array and a two-dimensional unsized integer array, and then measures the memory spaces taken for storing the two arrays.

TYPE   **Listing 12.7. Initializing unsized arrays.**

```
1:   /* 12L07.c: Initializing unsized arrays */
2:   #include <stdio.h>
3:
4:   main()
5:   {
6:      char array_ch[] = {'C', ' ',
7:                          'i', 's', ' ',
8:                          'p', 'o', 'w', 'e', 'r',
9:                          'f', 'u', 'l', '!', '\0'};
10:     int list_int[][3] = {
11:             1, 1, 1,
12:             2, 2, 8,
13:             3, 9, 27,
14:             4, 16, 64,
15:             5, 25, 125,
16:             6, 36, 216,
17:             7, 49, 343};
18:
19:     printf("The size of array_ch[] is %d bytes.\n", sizeof (array_ch));
20:     printf("The size of list_int[][3] is %d bytes.\n", sizeof (list_int));
21:     return 0;
22: }
```

12

The following output is obtained by running the executable `12L07.exe`:

OUTPUT

```
C:\app>12L07
The size of array_ch[] is 15 bytes.
The size of list_int[][3] is 42 bytes.
C:\app>
```

ANALYSIS A character unsized array, `array_ch`, is declared and initialized in lines 6–9. In lines 10–17, a two-dimensional unsized integer array, `list_int`, is declared and initialized too.

The statement in line 19 measures and prints out the total memory space (in bytes) taken by the array `array_ch`. The result shows that the unsized character array is assigned 15 bytes of memory to hold all its elements after compiling. When you calculate the total number of the elements in the character array manually, you find that there are indeed 15 elements. Because each character takes one byte of memory, the character array `array_ch` takes a total of 15 bytes accordingly.

Likewise, the statement in line 20 gives the total number of bytes reserved in the memory for the unsized two-dimensional integer array `list_int`. Because there are a total of 21 integer elements in the array, and an integer takes 2 bytes, the compiler should allocate 42 bytes for the integer array `list_int`. The result printed out by the `printf()` function in line 20 proves that there are 42 bytes reserved in the memory for the two-dimensional integer array. (If the size of `int` or `char` is different on your machine, you may get different values for the sizes of the arrays in the program of Listing 12.7.)

Summary

In this lesson you've learned the following:

- [ ] An array is a collection of variables that are of the same data type.
- [ ] In C, the index to an array starts at 0.
- [ ] You can initialize each individual element of an array after the declaration of the array, or you can place all initial values into a data block surrounded by { and } during the declaration of an array.
- [ ] The memory storage taken by an array is determined by the product of the size of the data type and the dimensions of the array.
- [ ] A pointer is said to *refer to* an array when the address of the first element in the array is assigned to the pointer. The address of the first element in an array is also called the start address of the array.
- [ ] To assign the start address of an array to a pointer, you can either put the combination of the address-of operator (&) and the first element name of the array, or simply use the array name, on the right side of an assignment operator (=).

☐ A character array is considered a character string in C if the last element in the array contains a null character (\0).

☐ The null character (\0) marks the end of a string. C functions, such as printf(), will stop processing the string when the null character is encountered.

☐ C supports multidimensional arrays, too. A pair of brackets (the array subscript operator—[and]) indicates a dimension.

☐ The compiler can automatically calculate the memory space needed by an unsized array.

In the next lesson you'll learn more about strings in C.

Q&A

Q Why do you need to use arrays?

A In many cases, you need to declare a set of variables that are of the same data type. Instead of declaring each variable separately, you can declare all variables collectively in the format of an array. Each variable, as an element of the array, can be accessed either through the array element reference or through a pointer that references the array.

Q What is the minimum index in an array?

A In C, the minimum index of a one-dimensional array is 0, which marks the first element of the array. For instance, given an integer array,

```
int array_int[8];
```

the first element of the array is array_int[0].

Likewise, for a multidimensional array, the minimum index of each dimension starts at 0.

Q How do you reference an array by using a pointer?

A You can use a pointer to reference an array by assigning the start address of an array to the pointer. For example, given a pointer variable ptr_ch and a character array array_ch, you can use one of the following statements to reference the array by the pointer:

```
ptr_ch = array_ch;
```

or

```
ptr_ch = &array_ch[0];
```

Q What can the null character do?

A The null character (\0) in C can be used to mark the end of a string. For instance, the printf() function puts the next character on the screen when the null character is encountered. Also, the null character always returns FALSE in a logical test.

12

Workshop

To help solidify your understanding of this hour's lesson, you are encouraged to answer the quiz questions and finish the exercises provided in the Workshop before you move to the next lesson. The answers and hints to the questions and exercises are given in Appendix E, "Answers to Quiz Questions and Exercises."

Quiz

1. What does the following statement do?

   ```
   int array_int[4] = {12, 23, 9, 56};
   ```

2. Given an array, `int data[3]`, what's wrong with the following initialization?

   ```
   data[1] = 1;
   data[2] = 2;
   data[3] = 3;
   ```

3. How many dimensions do the following arrays have?

   □ `char array1[3][19];`

   □ `int array2[];`

   □ `float array3[][8][16];`

   □ `char array4[][80];`

4. What's wrong with the following declaration?

   ```
   char list_ch[][] = {
           'A', 'a',
           'B', 'b',
           'C', 'c',
           'D', 'd',
           'E', 'e'};
   ```

Exercises

1. Given this character array:

   ```
   char array_ch[5] = {'A', 'B', 'C', 'D', 'E'};
   ```

   write a program to display each element of the array on the screen.

2. Rewrite the program in exercise 1, but this time use a `for` loop to initialize the character array with `'a'`, `'b'`, `'c'`, `'d'`, and `'e'`, and then print out the value of each element in the array.

3. Given this two-dimensional unsized array:

   ```
   char list_ch[][2] = {
           '1', 'a',
           '2', 'b',
           '3', 'c',
           '4', 'd',
   ```

```
        '5', 'e',
        '6', 'f'};
```

write a program to measure the total bytes taken by the array, and then print out all elements of the array.

4. Rewrite the program in Listing 12.5. This time put a string of characters, I like C!, on the screen.

5. Given the following array:

```
double list_data[6] = {
        1.12345,
        2.12345,
        3.12345,
        4.12345,
        5.12345};
```

use the two equivalent ways taught in this lesson to measure the total memory space taken by the array, and then display the results on the screen.

12

Hour 13

Manipulating Strings

I have made this letter longer than usual, because I lack the time to make it short.

—B. Pascal

In the last hour's lesson you learned how to use arrays to collect variables of the same type. You also learned that a character string is actually a character array ended with a null character \0. In this lesson you'll learn more about strings and C functions that can be used to manipulate strings. The following topics are covered:

☐ Declaring a string

☐ The length of a string

☐ Copying strings

☐ Reading strings with scanf()

☐ The gets() and puts() functions

Declaring Strings

This section teaches you how to declare and initialize strings, as well as the difference between string constants and character constants. First, let's review the definition of a string.

What Is a String?

As introduced in Hour 12, "Storing Similar Data Items," a *string* is a character array terminated by a null character (\0).

For instance, a character array, `array_ch`, declared in the following statement, is considered a character string:

```
char array_ch[7] = {'H', 'e', 'l', 'l', 'o', '!', '\0'};
```

In C, the null character can be used to mark the end of a string, or to return logical FALSE. C treats \0 as one character. Each character in a string takes only 1 byte.

A series of characters enclosed in double quotes (" ") is called a *string constant*. The C compiler can automatically add a null character (\0) at the end of a string constant to indicate the end of the string.

For example, the character string "A character string." is considered a string constant; so is "Hello!".

Initializing Strings

As taught in the last lesson, a character array can be declared and initialized like this:

```
char arr_str[6] = {'H', 'e', 'l', 'l', 'o', '!'};
```

Here the array `arr_str` is treated as a character array. However, if you add a null character (\0) into the array, you can have the following statement:

```
char arr_str[7] = {'H', 'e', 'l', 'l', 'o', '!', '\0'};
```

Here the array `arr_str` is expanded to hold seven elements; the last element contains a null character. Now, the character array `arr_str` is considered a character string because of the null character that is appended to the array.

You can also initialize a character array with a string constant. For example, the following statement initializes a character array, `str`, with a string constant, "Hello!":

```
char str[7] = "Hello!";
```

The compiler can automatically append a null character (\0) to the end of the array, and treat the character array as a character string. Note that the size of the array is specified to hold up to seven elements, although the string constant has only six characters enclosed in double quotes. The extra space is reserved for the null character that the compiler will add later.

You can declare an unsized character array if you want the compiler to calculate the total number of elements in the array. For instance, the following statement

```
char str[] = "I like C.";
```

initializes an unsized character array, str, with a string constant. Later, when the compiler sees the statement, it will figure out the total memory space needed to hold the string constant plus an extra null character added by the compiler itself.

If you like, you can also declare a char pointer and then initialize the pointer with a string constant. The following statement is an example:

```
char *ptr_str = "I teach myself C.";
```

WARNING

Don't specify the size of a character array as too small. Otherwise, it cannot hold a string constant plus an extra null character. For instance, the following declaration is considered illegal:

```
char str[4] = "text";
```

Note that many C compilers will not issue a warning or an error message on this incorrect declaration. The runtime errors that could eventually arise as a result could be very difficult to debug. Therefore, it's your responsibility to make sure you specify enough space for a string.

The following statement is a correct one, because it specifies the size of the character array str that is big enough to hold the string constant plus an extra null character:

```
char str[5] = "text";
```

String Constants Versus Character Constants

As you know, a string constant is a series of characters enclosed in double quotes (" "). On the other hand, a character constant is a character enclosed in single quotes (' ').

When a character variable ch and a character array str are initialized with the same character, x, such as the following,

```
char ch = 'x';
char str[] = "x";
```

13

1 byte is reserved for the character variable ch, and two bytes are allocated for the character array str. The reason that an extra byte is needed for str is that the compiler has to append a null character to the array.

Another important thing is that a string is interpreted as a char pointer. Therefore, you can assign a character string to a pointer variable directly, like this:

```
char *ptr_str;
ptr_str = "A character string.";
```

However, you can not assign a character constant to the pointer variable, as shown in the following:

```
ptr_str = 'x';   /* It's wrong. */
```

In other words, the character constant 'x' contains a right value, and the pointer variable ptr_str expects a left value. But C requires the same kind of values on both sides of an assignment operator =.

It's legal to assign a character constant to a dereferenced char pointer like this:

```
char *ptr_str;
*ptr_str = 'x';
```

Now the values on both sides of the = operator are of the same type.

The program in Listing 13.1 demonstrates how to initialize, or assign character arrays with string constants.

TYPE   Listing 13.1. Initializing strings.

```
1:  /* 13L01.c: Initializing strings */
2:  #include <stdio.h>
3:
4:  main()
5:  {
6:      char str1[] = {'A', ' ',
7:                     's', 't', 'r', 'i', 'n', 'g', ' ',
8:                     'c', 'o', 'n', 's', 't', 'a', 'n', 't', '\0'};
9:      char str2[] = "Another string constant";
10:     char *ptr_str;
11:     int i;
12:
13:     /* print out str2 */
14:     for (i=0; str1[i]; i++)
15:         printf("%c", str1[i]);
16:     printf("\n");
17:     /* print out str2 */
18:     for (i=0; str2[i]; i++)
19:         printf("%c", str2[i]);
20:     printf("\n");
21:     /* assign a string to a pointer */
22:     ptr_str = "Assign a string to a pointer.";
23:     for (i=0; *ptr_str; i++)
24:         printf("%c", *ptr_str++);
```

13

```
25:    return 0;
26: }
```

The following output is displayed on the screen after the executable 13L01.exe of the program in Listing 13.1 is created and run from a DOS prompt:

```
C:\app>13L01
A string constant
Another string constant
Assign a string to a pointer.
C:\app>
```

ANALYSIS As you can see from Listing 13.1, there are two character arrays, str1 and str2, that are declared and initialized in lines 6–9. In the declaration of str1, a set of character constants, including a null character, is used to initialize the array. For str2, a string constant is assigned to the array in line 9. The compiler will append a null character to str2 later. Note that both str1 and str2 are declared as unsized arrays for which the compiler can automatically figure out how much memory is needed. The statement in line 10 declares a char pointer variable, ptr_str.

The for loop in lines 14 and 15 then prints out all the elements in str1. Because the last element contains a null character (\0) that is evaluated as FALSE, the str1[i] expression is used in the second field of the for statement. The str1[i] expression returns logical TRUE for each element in str1 except the last one holding the null character. After the execution of the for loop, the string A string constant is shown on the screen.

Likewise, another for loop in lines 18 and 19 displays the string constant assigned to str2 by putting every element of the array on the screen. Because the compiler appends a null character to the array, the str2[i] expression is evaluated in the for statement. The for loop stops iterating when str2[i] returns a logical FALSE. By that time, the content of the string constant, Another string constant, has already been displayed on the screen.

The statement in line 22 assigns a string constant, "Assign a string to a pointer.", to the char pointer variable ptr_str. Also, a for loop is used to print out the string constant by putting every item in the string on the screen (see lines 23 and 24). Note that the dereferenced pointer *ptr_str is used to refer to one of the characters in the string constant. When the null character appended to the string is encountered, *ptr_str returns logical FALSE, which causes the iteration of the for loop to stop. In line 24, the *ptr_str++ expression indicates that the dereferenced pointer moves to the next character of the string after the current character referred to by the pointer is fetched. In Hour 16, "Applying Pointers," you'll learn more about pointer arithmetic.

13

How Long Is a String?

Sometimes, you need to know how many bytes are taken by a string. In C, you can use a function called strlen() to measure the length of a string.

The `strlen()` Function

Let's have a look at the syntax of the `strlen()` function.

The syntax for the `strlen()` function is

```
#include <string.h>
size_t strlen(const char *s);
```

Here `s` is a `char` pointer variable. The return value from the function is the number of bytes. `size_t` is a data type defined in the `string.h` header file. The size of the data type depends on the particular computer system. Note that `string.h` has to be included in your program before you can call the `strlen()` function.

Listing 13.2 gives an example of using the `strlen()` function to measure string lengths.

TYPE   **Listing 13.2. Measuring string lengths.**

```
1:  /* 13L02.c: Measuring string length */
2:  #include <stdio.h>
3:  #include <string.h>
4:
5:  main()
6:  {
7:     char str1[] = {'A', ' ',
8:                    's', 't', 'r', 'i', 'n', 'g', ' ',
9:                    'c', 'o', 'n', 's', 't', 'a', 'n', 't', '\0'};
10:    char str2[] = "Another string constant";
11:    char *ptr_str = "Assign a string to a pointer.";
12:
13:    printf("The length of str1 is: %d bytes\n", strlen(str1));
14:    printf("The length of str2 is: %d bytes\n", strlen(str2));
15:    printf("The length of the string assigned to ptr_str is: %d bytes\n",
16:       strlen(ptr_str));
17:    return 0;
18: }
```

I get the following output by running the executable `13L02.exe` of the program in Listing 13.2 from a DOS prompt:

OUTPUT
```
C:\app>13L02
The length of str1 is: 17 bytes
The length of str2 is: 23 bytes
The length of the string assigned to ptr_str is: 29 bytes
C:\app>
```

ANALYSIS   In Listing 13.2, two `char` arrays, `str1` and `str2`, and one pointer variable, `ptr_str`, are declared and initialized in lines 7–11, respectively.

Then, the statement in line 13 obtains the length of the string constant held by `str1`, and prints out the result on the screen. From the result, you can see that the null character (`\0`) contained by the last element of `str1` is not counted by the `strlen()` function.

13

In lines 14–16, the lengths of the string constants referenced by str2 and ptr_str are measured and shown on the screen. The results indicate that the strlen() function does not count the null characters appended to the two string constants by the compiler, either.

Copying Strings with strcpy()

If you want to copy a string from one array to another, you can copy each item of the first array to the corresponding element in the second array, or you can simply call the C function strcpy() to do the job for you.

The syntax for the strcpy() function is

```
#include <string.h>
char *strcpy(char *dest, const char *src);
```

Here the content of the string *src* is copied to the array referenced by *dest*. The strcpy() function returns the value of *src* if it is successful. The header file string.h must be included in your program before the strcpy() function is called.

The program in Listing 13.3 demonstrates how to copy a string from one array to another by either calling the strcpy() function or by doing it yourself.

TYPE **Listing 13.3. Copying strings.**

```
1:  /* 13L03.c: Copying strings */
2:  #include <stdio.h>
3:  #include <string.h>
4:
5:  main()
6:  {
7:      char str1[] = "Copy a string.";
8:      char str2[15];
9:      char str3[15];
10:     int  i;
11:
12:     /* with strcpy() */
13:     strcpy(str2, str1);
14:     /* without strcpy() */
15:     for (i=0; str1[i]; i++)
16:         str3[i] = str1[i];
17:     str3[i] = '\0';
18:     /* display str2 and str3 */
19:     printf("The content of str2: %s\n", str2);
20:     printf("The content of str3: %s\n", str3);
21:     return 0;
22: }
```

After the executable 13L03.exe is created and run, the following output is shown on the screen:

OUTPUT
```
C:\app>13L03
The content of str2: Copy a string.
The content of str3: Copy a string.
C:\app>
```

ANALYSIS Three char arrays, str1, str2, and str3, are declared in Listing 13.3. In addition, str1 is initialized with a string constant, "Copy a string.", in line 7.

The statement in line 13 calls the strcpy() function to copy the content of str1 (including the null character appended by the compiler) to the array referenced by str2.

Lines 15–17 demonstrate another way to copy the content of str1 to an array referenced by str3. To do so, the for loop in lines 15 and 16 keeps copying characters of str1 to the corresponding elements in str3 one after another, until the null character (\0) appended by the compiler is encountered. When the null character is encountered, the str1[i] expression used as the condition of the for statement in line 15 returns logical FALSE, which in turn causes the loop to stop.

Because the for loop does not copy the null character from str1 to str3, the statement in line 17 appends a null character to the array referenced by str3. In C, it's very important to make sure that an array that is used to store a string has a null character as its last element.

To prove that the string constant referenced by str1 has been copied to str2 and str3 successfully, the contents held by str2 and str3 are displayed on the screen. Note that the string format specifier %s and the start addresses of str2 and str3 are invoked in the printf() function in lines 19 and 20 to print out all characters, except the null character, stored in str2 or str3. The results displayed on the screen show that str2 and str3 have the exact same content as str1.

Reading and Writing Strings

Now let's focus on how to read or write strings with the standard input and output streams—that is, stdin and stdout. In C, there are several functions you can use to deal with string reading or writing. The following subsections introduce some of the functions.

The gets() and puts() Functions

The gets() function can be used to read characters from the standard input stream.

SYNTAX

The syntax for the gets() function is

```
#include <stdio.h>
char *gets(char *s);
```

Here the characters read from the standard input stream are stored in the character array identified by s. The gets() function stops reading, and appends a null character \0 to the array, when a newline or end-of-file (EOF) is encountered. The function returns s if it concludes successfully. Otherwise, a null pointer is returned.

The puts() function can be used to write characters to the standard output stream (that is, stdout).

The syntax for the puts() function is

```
#include <stdio.h>
int puts(const char *s);
```

Here s refers to the character array that contains a string. The puts() function writes the string to the stdout. If the function is successful, it returns 0. Otherwise, a nonzero value is returned.

▲ The puts() function appends a newline character to replace the null character at the end of a character array.

Both the gets() and puts() functions require the header file stdio.h. In Listing 13.4, you can see the application of the two functions.

TYPE **Listing 13.4. Using the gets() and puts() functions.**

```
 1:  /* 13L04.c: Using gets() and puts() */
 2:  #include <stdio.h>
 3:
 4:  main()
 5:  {
 6:     char str[80];
 7:     int i, delt = 'a' - 'A';
 8:
 9:     printf("Enter a string less than 80 characters:\n");
10:     gets( str );
11:     i = 0;
12:     while (str[i]){
13:       if ((str[i] >= 'a') && (str[i] <= 'z'))
14:          str[i] -= delt;   /* convert to upper case */
15:       ++i;
16:     }
17:     printf("The entered string is (in uppercase):\n");
18:     puts( str );
19:     return 0;
20:  }
```

13

After running the executable 13L04.exe, I enter a line of characters from the keyboard and have the characters (all in uppercase) shown on the screen:

```
C:\app>13L04
Enter a string less than 80 characters:
This is a test.
The entered string is (in uppercase):
THIS IS A TEST.
C:\app>
```

The program in Listing 13.4 accepts a string of characters entered from the keyboard (that is, stdin), and then converts all lowercase characters to uppercase ones. Finally, the modified string is put back to the screen.

In line 6, a character array (str) is declared that can hold up to 80 characters. The gets() function in line 10 reads any characters the user enters from the keyboard until the user presses the Enter key, which is interpreted as a newline character. The characters read in by the gets() function are stored into the character array indicated by str. The newline character is not saved into str. Instead, a null character is appended to the array as a terminator.

The while loop in lines 12–15 has a conditional expression, str[i]. The while loop keeps iterating as long as str[i] returns logical TRUE. Within the loop, the value of each character represented by str[i] is evaluated in line 13, to find out whether the character is a lowercase character within the range of a through z. If the character is one of the lowercase characters, it is converted into uppercase by subtracting the value of an int variable, delt, from its current value in line 14. The delt variable is initialized in line 7 by the value of the 'a' - 'A' expression, which is the difference between a lowercase character and its uppercase counterpart. In other words, by subtracting the difference of 'a' and 'A' from the lower case integer value, we obtain the uppercase integer value.

Then the puts() function in line 18 outputs the string with all uppercase characters to stdout, which leads to the screen by default. A newline character is appended by the puts() function to replace the null character at the end of the string.

Using %s with the printf() Function

We've used the printf() function in many program examples in this book. As you know, many format specifiers can be used with the printf() function to specify different display formats for numbers of various types.

For instance, you can use the string format specifier, %s, with the printf() function to display a character string saved in an array on the screen. (See the example in Listing 13.3.)

In the next section, the scanf() function is introduced as a way to read values of various data types with different format specifiers, including the format specifier %s.

13

The `scanf()` Function

The `scanf()` function provides another way to read strings from the standard input stream. Moreover, this function can actually be used to read various types of input data. The formats of arguments to the `scanf()` function are quite similar to those used in the `printf()` function.

The syntax for the `scanf()` function is

```
#include <stdio.h>
int scanf(const char *format, ...);
```

Here various format specifiers can be included inside the format string referenced by the char pointer variable `format`. If the `scanf()` function concludes successfully, it returns the number of data items read from the `stdin`. If an error occurs, the `scanf()` function returns EOF (end-of-file).

Note that using the string format specifier %s causes the `scanf()` function to read characters until a space, a newline, a tab, a vertical tab, or a form feed is encountered. Characters read by the `scanf()` function are stored into an array referenced by the corresponding argument. The array should be big enough to store the input characters.

A null character is automatically appended to the array after the reading.

The program in Listing 13.5 shows how to use various format specifiers with the `scanf()` function.

Listing 13.5. Using the `scanf()` function with various format specifiers.

```
1:  /* 13L05.c: Using scanf() */
2:  #include <stdio.h>
3:
4:  main()
5:  {
6:     char str[80];
7:     int x, y;
8:     float z;
9:
10:    printf("Enter two integers separated by a space:\n");
11:    scanf("%d  %d", &x, &y);
12:    printf("Enter a floating-point number:\n");
13:    scanf("%f", &z);
14:    printf("Enter a string:\n");
15:    scanf("%s", str);
16:    printf("Here are what you've entered:\n");
17:    printf("%d  %d\n%f\n%s\n", x, y, z, str);
18:    return 0;
19: }
```

13

The following output is a sample displayed on the screen after I run the executable 13L05.exe and enter data (which appears in bold) from my keyboard:

OUTPUT
```
C:\app>13L05
Enter two integers separated by a space:
10  12345
Enter a floating-point number:
1.234567
Enter a string:
Test
Here are what you've entered:
10  12345
1.234567
Test
C:\app>
```

ANALYSIS In Listing 13.5, there are one char array (str), two int variables (x and y), and a float variable (z) declared in lines 6–8.

Then, the scanf() function in line 11 reads in two integers entered by the user and saves them into the memory locations reserved for the integer variables x and y. The statement in line 13 reads and stores a floating-point number into z. Note that the format specifiers, %d and %f, are used to specify proper formats for entered numbers in lines 11 and 13.

Line 15 reads a series of characters entered by the user with the scanf() function by using the format specifier %s, and then saves the characters, plus a null character as the terminator, into the array pointed to by str.

To prove that the scanf() function reads all the numbers and characters entered by the user, the printf() function in line 17 displays the contents saved in x, y, z, and str on the screen. Sure enough, the result shows that the scanf() does a good job.

One thing you need to be aware of is that the scanf() function doesn't actually start reading the input until the Enter key is pressed. Data entered from the keyboard is placed in an input buffer. When the Enter key is pressed, the scanf() function looks for its input in the buffer. You'll learn more about buffered input and output in Hour 21, "Disk File Input and Output: Part I."

Summary

In this lesson you've learned the following:

☐ A string is a character array with a null character as the terminator at the last element.

☐ A string constant is a series of characters enclosed by double quotes.

☐ The C compiler automatically appends a null character to the array that has been initialized by a string constant.

☐ You cannot assign a string constant to a dereferenced char pointer.

☐ The strlen() function can be used to measure the length of a string. This function does not count the null character in the last element.

☐ You can copy a string from one array to another by calling the C function strcpy().

☐ The gets() function can be used to read a series of characters. This function stops reading when the newline character or end-of-file (EOF) is encountered. A null character is attached to the array that stores the characters automatically after the reading.

☐ The puts() function sends all characters, except the null character, in a string to the stdout, and appends a newline character to the output.

☐ You can read different data items with the scanf() function by using various format specifiers.

In the next lesson you'll learn about the concepts of scope and storage in C.

Q&A

Q What is a string? How do you know its length?

A In C, a string is a character array terminated by a null character. Whenever a null character is encountered in a string, functions, such as puts() or strcpy(), will stop printing or copying the next character.

The C function strlen() can be used to measure the length of a string. If it is successful, the strlen() function returns the total number of bytes taken by the string; however, the null character in the string is not counted.

Q What are the main differences between a string constant and a character constant?

A A string constant is a series of characters enclosed by double quotes, while a character constant is a single character surrounded by single quotes. The compiler will append a null character to the array that is initialized with a string constant. Therefore, an extra byte has to be reserved for the null character. On the other hand, a character constant takes only 1 byte in the memory.

Q Does the gets() function save the newline character from the standard input stream?

A No. The gets() function keeps reading characters from the standard input stream until a newline character or end-of-file is encountered. Instead of saving the newline character, the gets() function appends a null character to the array that is referenced by the argument to the gets() function.

13

Q **What types of data can the `scanf()` function read?**

A Depending on the format specifiers indicated in the function, the `scanf()` function can read various types of data, such as a series of characters, integers, or floating-point numbers. Unlike `gets()`, `scanf()` stops reading the current input item (and moves to the next input item, if there is one) when it encounters a space, a newline, a tab, a vertical tab, or a form feed.

Workshop

To help solidify your understanding of this hour's lesson, you are encouraged to answer the quiz questions and finish the exercises provided in the Workshop before you move to the next lesson. The answers and hints to the questions and exercises are given in Appendix E, "Answers to Quiz Questions and Exercises."

Quiz

1. In the following list, which statements are legal?

   ☐ `char str1[5] = "Texas";`

   ☐ `char str2[] = "A character string";`

   ☐ `char str3[2] = "A";`

   ☐ `char str4[2] = "TX";`

2. Given a `char` pointer variable `ptr_ch`, are the following statements legal?

   ☐ `*ptr_ch = 'a';`

   ☐ `ptr_ch = "A character string";`

   ☐ `ptr_ch = 'x';`

   ☐ `*ptr_ch = "This is Quiz 2.";`

3. Can the `puts()` function print out the null character in a character array?

4. Which format specifier do you use with the `scanf()` function to read in a string, and which one do you use to read a floating-point number?

Exercises

1. Given a character array in the following statement,

   `char str1[] = "This is Exercise 1.";`

   write a program to copy the string from `str1` to another array, called `str2`.

2. Write a program to measure the length of a string by evaluating the elements in the character array one by one. To prove you get the right result, you can use the `strlen()` function to measure the same string again.

3. Rewrite the program in Listing 13.4. This time, convert all uppercase characters to their lowercase counterparts.

4. Write a program that uses the `scanf()` function to read in two integers entered by the user, adds the two integers, and then prints out the sum on the screen.

13

Hour 14

Scope and Storage Classes in C

Nobody owns anything and all anyone has is the use of his presumed possessions.

—P. Wylie

In the previous hours, you've learned how to declare variables of different data types, as well as to initialize and use those variables. It's been assumed that you can access variables from anywhere. Now, the question is: Can we declare variables that are accessible only to certain portions of a program? In this lesson you'll learn about the scope and storage classes of data in C. The main topics covered in this lesson are

- ☐ Block scope
- ☐ Function scope
- ☐ File scope
- ☐ Program scope
- ☐ The auto specifier

☐ The static specifier

☐ The register specifier

☐ The extern specifier

☐ The const modifier

☐ The volatile modifier

Hiding Data

To solve a complex problem in practice, the programmer normally breaks the problem into smaller pieces and deals with each piece of the problem by writing one or two functions (or routines). Then, all the functions are put together to form a complete program that can be used to solve the complex problem.

In the complete program, there might be variables that have to be shared by all the functions. On the other hand, the use of some other variables may be limited to only certain functions. That is, the visibility of those variables is limited, and values assigned to those variables are hidden from many functions.

Limiting the scope of variables is very useful when several programmers are working on different pieces of the same program. If they limit the scope of their variables to their pieces of code, they do not have to worry about conflicting with variables of the same name used by others in other parts of the program.

In C, you can declare a variable and indicate its visibility level by designating its scope. Thus, variables with local scope can only be accessed within the block in which they are declared.

The following sections teach you how to declare variables with different scopes.

Block Scope

In this section, a *block* refers to any sets of statements enclosed in braces ({ and }). A variable declared within a block has *block scope*. Thus, the variable is active and accessible from its declaration point to the end of the block. Sometimes, block scope is also called *local scope*.

For example, the variable i declared within the block of the following main function has block scope:

```
int main()
{
   int i;   /* block scope */
   .
   .
   .
   return 0;
}
```

14

Usually, a variable with block scope is called a *local variable*.

Nested Block Scope

You can also declare variables within a nested block. If a variable declared in the outer block shares the same name with one of the variables in the inner block, the variable within the outer block is hidden by the one within the inner block for the scope of the inner block.

Listing 14.1 gives an example of variable scopes in nested blocks.

TYPE

Listing 14.1. Printing out variables with different scope levels.

```
1:   /* 14L01.c: Scopes in nested block */
2:   #include <stdio.h>
3:
4:   main()
5:   {
6:      int i = 32;    /* block scope 1*/
7:
8:      printf("Within the outer block: i=%d\n", i);
9:
10:     {   /* the beginning of the inner block */
11:       int i, j;    /* block scope 2, int i hides the outer int i*/
12:
13:       printf("Within the inner block:\n");
14:       for (i=0, j=10; i<=10; i++, j--)
15:           printf("i=%2d, j=%2d\n", i, j);
16:     }   /* the end of the inner block */
17:     printf("Within the outer block:  i=%d\n", i);
18:     return 0;
19: }
```

The following output is displayed on the screen after the executable (14L01.exe) of the program in Listing 14.1 is created and run from a DOS prompt:

OUTPUT

```
C:\app>14L01
Within the outer block: i=32
Within the inner block:
i= 0, j=10
i= 1, j= 9
i= 2, j= 8
i= 3, j= 7
i= 4, j= 6
i= 5, j= 5
i= 6, j= 4
i= 7, j= 3
i= 8, j= 2
i= 9, j= 1
i=10, j= 0
Within the outer block: i=32
C:\app>
```

14

The purpose of the program in Listing 14.1 is to show you the different scopes of variables in nested blocks. As you can see, there are two nested blocks in Listing 14.1. The integer variable i declared in line 6 is visible within the outer block enclosed by the braces ({ and }) in lines 5 and 19. Another two integer variables, i and j, declared in line 11, are visible only within the inner block from line 10 to line 16.

Although the integer variable i within the outer block has the same name as one of the integer variables within the inner block, the two integer variables can not be accessed at the same time due to their different scopes.

To prove this, line 8 prints out the value, 32, contained by i within the outer block for the first time. Then, the for loop in lines 14 and 15 displays 10 pairs of values assigned to i and j within the inner block. At this point, there is no sign showing that the integer variable i within the outer block has any effects on the one within the inner block. When the inner block is exited, the variables within the inner block are no longer accessible.

Finally, the statement in line 17 prints out the value of i within the outer block again to find out whether the value has been changed due to the integer variable i within the inner block. The result shows that these two integer variables hide from each other, and no conflict occurs.

Function Scope

Function scope indicates that a variable is active and visible from the beginning to the end of a function.

In C, only the goto label has function scope. For example, the goto label, start, shown in the following code portion has function scope:

```
int main()
{
   int i;   /* block scope */
   .
   .
   .
   start:   /* A goto label has function scope */
   .
   .
   .
   goto  start;  /* the goto statement */
   .
   .
   .
   return 0;
}
```

Here the label start is visible from the beginning to the end of the main() function. Therefore, there should not be more than one label having the same name within the main() function.

14

Program Scope

A variable is said to have *program scope* when it is declared outside a function. For instance, look at the following code:

```
int x = 0;          /* program scope */
float y = 0.0;      /* program scope */
int main()
{
   int i;   /* block scope */
   .
   .
   .
   return 0;
}
```

Here the `int` variable x and the `float` variable y have program scope.

Variables with program scope are also called *global variables*, which are visible among different files. These files are the entire source files that make up an executable program. Note that a global variable is declared with an initializer outside a function.

The program in Listing 14.2 demonstrates the relationship between variables with program scope and variables with block scope.

TYPE

Listing 14.2. The relationship between program scope and block scope.

```
1:  /* 14L02.c: Program scope vs block scope */
2:  #include <stdio.h>
3:
4:  int x = 1234;           /* program scope */
5:  double y = 1.234567;    /* program scope */
6:
7:  void function_1()
8:  {
9:     printf("From function_1:\n  x=%d, y=%f\n", x, y);
10: }
11:
12: main()
13: {
14:    int x = 4321;    /* block scope 1*/
15:
16:    function_1();
17:    printf("Within the main block:\n  x=%d, y=%f\n", x, y);
18:    /* a nested block */
19:    {
20:       double y = 7.654321;  /* block scope 2 */
21:       function_1();
22:       printf("Within the nested block:\n  x=%d, y=%f\n", x, y);
23:    }
24:    return 0;
25: }
```

14

I have the following output shown on the screen after the executable `14L02.exe` is created and run from a DOS prompt:

OUTPUT

```
C:\app>14L02
From function_1:
   x=1234, y=1.234567
Within the main block:
   x=4321, y=1.234567
From function_1:
   x=1234, y=1.234567
Within the nested block:
   x=4321, y=7.654321
C:\app>
```

ANALYSIS
As you can see in Listing 14.2, there are two global variables, x and y, with program scope; they are declared in lines 4 and 5.

In lines 7–10, a function, called `function_1()`, is declared. (More details about function declarations and prototypes are taught in the next hour.) The `function_1()` function contains only one statement; it prints out the values held by both x and y. Because there is no variable declaration made for x or y within the function block, the values of the global variables x and y are used for the statement inside the function. To prove this, the `function_1()` function is called twice in lines 16 and 21, respectively, from two nested blocks. The output shows that the values of the two global variables x and y are passed to `printf()` enclosed in the `function_1()` function body.

Then, line 14 declares another integer variable, x, with block scope, which can replace the global variable x within the block of the `main()` function. The result made by the statement in line 17 shows that the value of x is the value of the local variable x with block scope, while the value of y is still that of the global variable y.

There is a nested block in lines 19 and 23, within which another `double` variable y, with block scope, is declared and initialized. Like the variable x within the `main()` block, this variable, y, within the nested block replaces the global variable y. The statement in line 22 puts the values of the local variables x and y on the screen.

TIP

Since a global variable is visible among different source files of a program, using global variables increases your program's complexity, which in turn makes your program hard to maintain or debug. Generally, it's not recommended that you declare and use global variables, unless it's very necessary. For instance, you can declare a global variable whose value is used but never changed by several subroutines in your program. (In Hour 23, "The C Preprocessor," you'll learn to use the `#define` directive to define constants that are used in many places in a program.)

Before I introduce file scope, let's talk about the storage class specifiers.

The Storage Class Specifiers

In C, the *storage class* of a variable refers to the combination of its spatial and temporal regions.

You've learned about scope, which specifies the spatial region of a variable. Now, let's focus on *duration*, which indicates the temporal region of a variable.

There are four specifiers and two modifiers that can be used to indicate the duration of a variable. These specifiers and modifiers are introduced in the following sections.

The `auto` Specifier

The auto specifier indicates that the memory location of a variable is temporary. In other words, a variable's reserved space in the memory can be erased or relocated when the variable is out of its scope.

Only variables with block scope can be declared with the auto specifier. The auto keyword is rarely used, however, because the duration of a variable with block scope is temporary by default.

The `static` Specifier

The static specifier, on the other hand, can be applied to variables with either block scope or program scope. When a variable within a function is declared with the static specifier, the variable has a permanent duration. In other words, the memory storage allocated for the variable is not destroyed when the scope of the variable is exited, the value of the variable is maintained outside the scope, and if execution ever returns to the scope of the variable, the last value stored in the variable is still there.

For instance, in the following code portion:

```c
int main()
{
   int i;          /* block scope and temporary duration */
   static int j;   /* block scope and permanent duration */
   .
   .
   .
   return 0;
}
```

the integer variable i has temporary duration by default. But the other integer variable, j, has permanent duration due to the storage class specifier static.

The program in Listing 14.3 shows the effect of the static specifier on variables.

14

TYPE   **Listing 14.3. Using the static specifier.**

```
1:   /* 14L03.c: Using the static specifier */
2:   #include <stdio.h>
3:   /* the add_two function */
4:   int add_two(int x, int y)
5:   {
6:      static int counter = 1;
7:
8:      printf("This is the function call of %d,\n", counter++);
9:      return (x + y);
10: }
11: /* the main function */
12: main()
13: {
14:    int i, j;
15:
16:    for (i=0, j=5; i<5; i++, j--)
17:       printf("the addition of %d and %d is %d.\n\n",
18:              i, j, add_two(i, j));
19:    return 0;
20: }
```

The following output is displayed on the screen after the executable (14L03.exe) is run from a DOS prompt:

OUTPUT
```
C:\app>14L03
This is the function call of 1,
the addition of 0 and 5 is 5.

This is the function call of 2,
the addition of 1 and 4 is 5.

This is the function call of 3,
the addition of 2 and 3 is 5.

This is the function call of 4,
the addition of 3 and 2 is 5.

This is the function call of 5,
the addition of 4 and 1 is 5.
C:\app>
```

ANALYSIS   The purpose of the program in Listing 14.3 is to call a function to add two integers and then print out the result returned by the function on the screen. The function is called several times. A counter is set to keep track of how many times the function has been called.

This function, called add_two(), is declared in lines 4–10. There are two int arguments, x and y, that are passed to the function, and the addition of the two arguments is returned in line 9. Note that there is an integer variable, counter, that is declared with the static specifier in line 6. Values stored by counter are retained because the duration of the variable is permanent. In other words, although the scope of counter is within the block of the add_two() function, the memory location of counter and value saved in the location are not changed after the add_two() function is called and the execution control is returned back to the main() function.

Therefore, the counter variable is used as a counter to keep the number of calls received by the add_two() function. In fact, the statement of the printf() function in line 8 prints out the value saved by the counter variable each time the add_two() function is called. In addition, counter is incremented by one each time after the printf() function is executed.

The for loop, declared in lines 16–18 within the main() function, calls the add_two() function five times. The values of the two integer variables, i and j, are passed to the add_two() function for the operation of addition. Then, the return value from the add_two() function is displayed on the screen by the printf() function in lines 17 and 18.

From the output, you can see that the value saved by counter is indeed incremented by one each time the add_two() function is called, and is retained after the function exits because the integer variable counter is declared with static. Note that counter is only initialized once when the add_two() function is called for the first time.

File Scope and the Hierarchy of Scopes

In the first part of this hour, I mentioned three of the four types of scopes: block scope, function scope, and program scope. It's time now to introduce the fourth scope—*file scope*.

In C, a global variable declared with the static specifier is said to have file scope. A variable with file scope is visible from its declaration point to the end of the file. Here the file refers to the program file that contains the source code. Most large programs consist of several program files.

The following portion of source code shows variables with file scope:

```
int x = 0;            /* program scope */
static int y = 0;     /* file scope */
static float z = 0.0; /* file scope */
int main()
{
   int i;   /* block scope */
   .
   .
   .
   return 0;
}
```

Here the int variable y and the float variable z both have file scope.

14

Figure 14.1 shows the hierarchy of the four scopes. As you can see, a variable with block scope is the most limited and is not visible outside the block within which the variable is declared. On the other hand, a variable with program scope is visible within all files, functions, and other blocks that make up the program.

Figure 14.1.

The hierarchy of the four scopes.

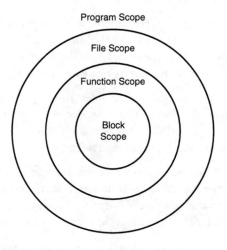

The register **Specifier**

The word *register* is borrowed from the world of computer hardware. Each computer has a certain number of registers to hold data and perform arithmetic or logical calculations. Because registers are located within the CPU (central processing unit) chip, it's much quicker to access a register than a memory location. Therefore, storing variables in registers may help to speed up your program.

The C language provides you with the register specifier. You can apply this specifier to variables when you think it's necessary to put the variables into the computer registers.

However, the register specifier only gives the compiler a suggestion. In other words, a variable specified by the register keyword is not guaranteed to be stored in a register. The compiler can ignore the suggestion if there is no register available, or if some other restrictions have to apply.

It's illegal to take the address of a variable that is declared with the register specifier because the variable is intended to be stored in a register, not in the memory.

In the following portion of code, the integer variable i is declared with the register specifier:

```
int main()
{
    /* block scope with the register specifier */
    register int i;
    . . .
    for (i=0; i<MAX_NUM; i++){
        /* some statements */
    }
    . . .
    return 0;
}
```

The declaration of i suggests that the compiler store the variable in a register. Because i is intensively used in the for loop, storing i in a register may increase the speed of the code shown here.

The extern Specifier

As stated in the section titled "Program Scope," a variable with program scope is visible through all source files that make up an executable program. A variable with program scope is also called a *global variable*.

Here is a question: How can a global variable declared in file A, for instance, be seen in file B? In other words, how does the compiler know that the variable used in file B is actually the same variable declared in file A?

The answer is: Use the extern specifier provided by the C language to allude to a global variable defined elsewhere. In this case, we declare a global variable in file A, and then declare the variable again using the extern specifier in file B.

For instance, suppose you have two global int variables, y and z, that are defined in one file, and then, in another file, you may have the following declarations:

```
int x = 0;          /* a global variable */
extern int y;       /* an allusion to a global variable y */
int main()
{
    extern int z;   /* an allusion to a global variable z */
    int i;          /* a local variable */
    .
    .
    .
    return 0;
}
```

14

As you can see, there are two integer variables, y and z, that are declared with the extern specifier, outside and inside the main() function, respectively. When the compiler sees the two declarations, it knows that the declarations are actually allusions to the global variables y and z that are defined elsewhere.

NOTE

To make your program portable across different computer platforms, you can apply the following rules in your program when you declare or allude to global variables:

☐ You can ignore the extern specifier, but include an initializer, when you declare a global variable.

☐ You should use the extern specifier (without an initializer) when you allude to a global variable defined elsewhere.

The Storage Class Modifiers

Besides the four storage class specifiers introduced in the previous sections, C also provides you with two storage class modifiers (or *qualifiers*, as they're sometimes called) that you can use to indicate to the C compiler how variables may be accessed.

The const Modifier

If you declare a variable with the const modifier, the content of the variable cannot be changed after it is initialized.

For instance, the following expression indicates to the compiler that circle_ratio is a variable whose value should not be changed:

```
const double circle_ratio = 3.141593;
```

Likewise, the value of the character array str declared in the following statement cannot be changed, either:

```
const char str[] = "A string constant";
```

Therefore, it's illegal to do something like this:

```
str[0] = 'a';   /* It's not allowed here. */
```

In addition, you can declare a pointer variable with the const modifier so that an object pointed to by the pointer cannot be changed. For example, consider the following pointer declaration with the const modifier:

```
char const *ptr_str = "A string constant";
```

After the initialization, you cannot change the content of the string pointed to by the pointer `ptr_str`. For instance, the following statement is not allowed:

```
*ptr_str = 'a';      /* It's not allowed here. */
```

However, the `ptr_str` pointer itself can be assigned a different address of a string that is declared with `char const`.

The `volatile` Modifier

Sometimes, you want to declare a variable whose value can be changed without any explicit assignment statement in your program. For instance, you might declare a global variable that contains characters entered by the user. The address of the variable is passed to a device register that accepts characters from the keyboard. However, when the C compiler optimizes your program automatically, it intends to not update the value held by the variable unless the variable is on the left side of an assignment operator (=). In other words, the value of the variable is likely not changed even though the user is typing in characters from the keyboard.

To ask the compiler to turn off certain optimizations on a variable, you can declare the variable with the `volatile` specifier. For instance, in the following code portion, a variable, `keyboard_ch`, declared with the `volatile` specifier, tells the compiler not to optimize any expressions of the variable because the value saved by the variable may be changed without execution of any explicit assignment statement:

```
void read_keyboard()
{
    volatile char keyboard_ch;  /* a volatile variable */
    .
    .
    .
}
```

Summary

In this lesson you've learned the following:

☐ A variable declared within a block has block scope. Such a variable is also called a local variable and is only visible within the block.

☐ The `goto` label has function scope, which means that it is visible through the whole block of the function within which the label is placed. No two `goto` labels share the same name within a function block.

☐ A variable declared with the `static` specifier outside a function has file scope, which means that it is visible throughout the entire source file in which the variable is declared.

14

☐ A variable declared outside a function is said to have program scope. Such a variable is also called a global variable. A global variable is visible in all source files that make up an executable program.

☐ A variable with block scope has the most limited visibility. On the other hand, a variable with program block is the most visible through all files, functions, and other blocks that make up the program.

☐ The storage class of a variable refers to the combination of its spatial and temporal regions (that is, its scope and duration.)

☐ By default, a variable with block scope has an auto duration, and its memory storage is temporary.

☐ A variable declared with the static specifier has permanent memory storage, even though the function in which the variable is declared has been called and the function scope has exited.

☐ A variable declared with the register specifier may be stored in a register to speed up the performance of a program; however, the compiler can ignore the specifier if there is no register available or if some other restrictions have to apply.

☐ You can also allude to a global variable defined elsewhere by using the extern specifier from the current source file.

☐ To make sure the value saved by a variable cannot be changed, you can declare the variable with the const modifier.

☐ If you want to let the compiler know that the value of a variable can be changed without an explicit assignment statement, declare the variable with the volatile modifier so that the compiler will turn off optimizations on expressions involving the variable.

In the next lesson you'll learn about function declarations and prototypes in C.

Q&A

Q Can a global variable be hidden by a local variable with block scope?

A Yes. If a local variable shares the same name with a global variable, the global variable can be hidden by the local variable for the scope of the block within which the local variable is defined with block scope. However, outside the block, the local variable cannot be seen, but the global variable becomes visible again.

Q Why do you need the static specifier?

A In many cases, the value of a variable is needed, even if the scope of the block, in which the variable is declared, has exited. By default, a variable with block scope has a temporary memory storage—that is, the lifetime of the variable starts when the block is executed and the variable is declared, and ends when the execution is finished. Therefore, to declare a variable with permanent duration, you have to use the static specifier to indicate to the compiler that the memory location of the variable and the value stored in the memory location should be retained after the execution of the block.

Q Does using the register specifier guarantee to improve the performance of a program?

A Not really. Declaring a variable with the register specifier only suggests to the compiler that the variable be stored in a register. But there is no guarantee that the variable *will* be stored in a register. The compiler can ignore the request based on the availability of registers or other restrictions.

Q When you declare a variable with the extern specifier, do you define the variable or allude to a global variable elsewhere?

A When a variable is declared with the extern specifier, the compiler considers the declaration of the variable as an allusion rather than a definition. The compiler will therefore look somewhere else to find a global variable to which the variable with extern alludes.

Workshop

To help solidify your understanding of this lesson, you are encouraged to answer the quiz questions and finish the exercises provided in the Workshop before you move to the next lesson. The answers and hints to the questions and exercises are given in Appendix E, "Answers to Quiz Questions and Exercises."

Quiz

1. Given the following code portion, which variables are global variables, and which ones are local variables with block scope?

```
int x = 0;
float y = 0.0;
int myFunction()
{
   int i, j;
   float y;
   . . .
   {
      int x, y;
      . . .
   }
   . . .
}
```

2. When two variables with the same name are defined, how does the compiler know which one to use?

14

3. Identify the storage class of each declaration in the following code portion:

```
int i = 0;
static int x;
extern float y;
int myFunction()
{
    int i, j;
    extern float z;
    register long s;
    static int index;
    const char str[] = "Warning message.";
    . . .
}
```

4. Given the following declaration:

```
const char ch_str[] = "The const specifier";
```

is the `ch_str[9] = '-';` statement legal?

Exercises

1. Given the following,

   ☐ An `int` variable with block scope and temporary storage

   ☐ A constant character variable with block scope

   ☐ A `float` local variable with permanent storage

   ☐ A register `int` variable

   ☐ A `char` pointer initialized with a null character

   write declarations for all of them.

2. Rewrite the program in Listing 14.2. This time, pass the `int` variable x and the `float` variable y as arguments to the `function_1()` function. What do you get on your screen after running the program?

3. Compile and run the following program. What do you get on the screen, and why?

```
#include <stdio.h>
int main()
{
    int i;

    for (i=0; i<5; i++){
        int x = 0;
        static int y = 0;
        printf("x=%d, y=%d\n", x++, y++);
    }
    return 0;
}
```

4. Rewrite the `add_two()` function in Listing 14.3 to print out the previous result of the addition, as well as the counter value.

PART

IV

Functions and Dynamic Memory Allocation

Hour

Hour 15

Functions in C

Form follows function.

—*L. H. Sullivan*

In Hour 14, "Scope and Storage Classes in C," you might have noticed that a function definition is always given first, before the function is called from a `main()` function. In fact, you can put a function definition anywhere you want, as long as you keep the function declaration at the first place before the function is called. You'll learn about many function features from the following topics covered in this lesson:

☐ Function declarations

☐ Prototyping

☐ Values returned from functions

☐ Arguments to functions

☐ Structured programming

In addition, several C library functions and macros, such as `time()`, `localtime()`, `asctime()`, `va_start()`, `va_arg()`, and `va_end()` are introduced in this hour.

Declaring Functions

As you know, you have to declare or define a variable before you can use it. This is also true for functions. In C, you have to declare or define a function before you can call it.

Declaration Versus Definition

According to the ANSI standard, the *declaration* of a variable or function specifies the interpretation and attributes of a set of identifiers. The *definition*, on the other hand, requires the C compiler to reserve storage for a variable or function named by an identifier.

A variable declaration is a definition, but a function declaration is not. A function declaration alludes to a function that is defined elsewhere and specifies what kind of value is returned by the function. A function definition defines what the function does, as well as gives the number and type of arguments passed to the function.

A function declaration is not a function definition. If a function definition is placed in your source file before the function is first called, you don't need to make the function declaration. Otherwise, the declaration of a function must be made before the function is invoked.

For example, I've used the `printf()` function in almost every sample program in this book. Each time, I had to include a header file, `stdio.h`, because the header file contains the declaration of `printf()`, which indicates to the compiler the return type and prototype of the function. The definition of the `printf()` function is placed somewhere else. In C, the definition of this function is saved in a library file that is invoked during the linking states.

Specifying Return Types

A function can be declared to return any data type, except an array or function. The `return` statement used in a function definition returns a single value whose type should match the one declared in the function declaration.

By default, the return type of a function is `int`, if no explicit data type is specified for the function. A data type specifier is placed prior to the name of a function like this:

```
data_type_specifier  function_name();
```

Here `data_type_specifier` specifies the data type that the function should return. `function_name` is the function name that should follow the rule of naming in C.

In fact, this declaration form represents the traditional function declaration form before the ANSI standard was created. After setting up the ANSI standard, the function prototype is added to the function declaration.

Using Prototypes

Before the ANSI standard was created, a function declaration only included the return type of the function. With the ANSI standard, the number and types of arguments passed to a function are allowed to be added into the function declaration. The number and types of an argument are called the *function prototype*.

The general form of a function declaration, including its prototype, is as follows:

```
data_type_specifier  function_name(
     data_type_specifier argument_name1,
     data_type_specifier argument_name2,
     data_type_specifier argument_name3,
     .
     .
     .
     data_type_specifier argument_nameN,
);
```

The purpose of using a function prototype is to help the compiler check whether the data types of arguments passed to a function match what the function expects. The compiler issues an error message if the data types do not match.

Although argument names, such as `argument_name1`, `argument_name2`, and so on, are optional, it is recommended that you include them so that the compiler can identify any mismatches of argument names.

Making Function Calls

As shown in Figure 15.1, when a function call is made, the program execution jumps to the function and finishes the task assigned to the function. Then the program execution resumes after the called function returns.

A *function call* is an expression that can be used as a single statement or within other statements.

Listing 15.1 gives an example of declaring and defining functions, as well as making function calls.

Figure 15.1.

*Program execution jumps
to an invoked function
when a function call is
made.*

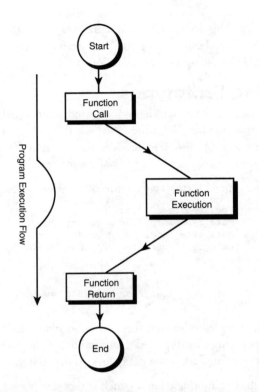

Listing 15.1. Calling functions after they are declared and defined.

TYPE

```
 1:  /* 15L01.c: Making function calls */
 2:  #include <stdio.h>
 3:
 4:  int function_1(int x, int y);
 5:  double function_2(double x, double y)
 6:  {
 7:      printf("Within function_2.\n");
 8:      return (x - y);
 9:  }
10:
11:  main()
12:  {
13:      int x1 = 80;
14:      int y1 = 10;
15:      double x2 = 100.123456;
16:      double y2 = 10.123456;
17:
18:      printf("Pass function_1  %d and %d.\n", x1, y1);
19:      printf("function_1 returns %d.\n", function_1(x1, y1));
20:      printf("Pass function_2  %f and %f.\n", x2, y2);
```

```
21:     printf("function_2 returns %f.\n", function_2(x2, y2));
22:     return 0;
23: }
24: /* function_1() definition */
25: int function_1(int x, int y)
26: {
27:     printf("Within function_1.\n");
28:     return (x + y);
29: }
```

The following output is displayed on the screen, after the executable (15L01.exe) of the program in Listing 15.1 is created and run from a DOS prompt:

OUTPUT

```
C:\app>15L01
Pass function_1  80 and 10.
Within function_1.
function_1 returns 90.
Pass function_2  100.123456. and 10.123456.
Within function_2.
function_2 returns 90.000000.
C:\app>
```

ANALYSIS   The purpose of the program in Listing 15.1 is to show you how to declare and define functions. The statement in line 4 is a function declaration with a prototype. The declaration alludes to the function_1 defined later in Listing 15.1. The return type of function_1 is int, and the function prototype includes two int variables, called x and y.

In lines 5–9, the second function, function_2, is defined before it is called. As you can see, the return type of function_2 is double, and two double variables are passed to the function. Note that the names of the two variables are also x and y. Don't worry because function_1 and function_2 share the same argument names. There is no conflict because these arguments are in different function blocks.

Then, in the main() function defined in lines 11–23, two int variables, x1 and y1, and two double variables, x2 and y2, are declared and initialized in lines 13–16, respectively. The statement in line 18 shows the values of x1 and y1 that are passed to the function_1 function. Line 19 calls function_1 and displays the return value from function_1.

Likewise, lines 20 and 21 print out the values of x2 and y2 that are passed to function_2, as well as the value returned by function_2 after the function is called and executed.

Lines 25–29 contain the definition of the function_1 function, specifying that the function can perform an addition of two integer variables (see line 28) and print out the string of Within function_1. in line 27.

Prototyping Functions

In the following subsections, we're going to study three cases regarding arguments passed to functions. The first case is a function that takes no argument; the second one is a function that takes a fixed number of arguments; the third case is a function that takes a variable number of arguments.

Functions with No Arguments

The first case is a function that takes no argument. For instance, the C library function `getchar()` does not need any arguments. It can be used in a program like this:

```
int c;
c = getchar();
```

As you can see, the second statement is left blank between the parentheses ((and)) when the function is called.

In C, the declaration of the `getchar()` function can be something like this:

```
int getchar(void);
```

Note that the keyword `void` is used in the declaration to indicate to the compiler that no argument is needed by this function. The compiler will issue an error message if somehow there is an argument passed to `getchar()` later in a program when this function is called.

Therefore, for a function with no argument, the `void` data type is used as the prototype in the function declaration.

The program in Listing 5.2 gives another example of using `void` in function declarations.

TYPE **Listing 15.2. Using `void` in function declarations.**

```
 1:  /* 15L02.c: Functions with no arguments */
 2:  #include <stdio.h>
 3:  #include <time.h>
 4:
 5:  void GetDateTime(void);
 6:
 7:  main()
 8:  {
 9:     printf("Before the GetDateTime() function is called.\n");
10:     GetDateTime();
11:     printf("After the GetDateTime() function is called.\n");
12:     return 0;
13:  }
14:  /* GetDateTime() definition */
15:  void GetDateTime(void)
16:  {
```

15

15

```
17:     time_t now;
18:
19:     printf("Within GetDateTime().\n");
20:     time(&now);
21:     printf("Current date and time is: %s\n",
22:         asctime(localtime(&now)));
23: }
```

I obtain the following output after I run the executable, 15L02.exe, of the program in Listing 15.2 from a DOS prompt:

OUTPUT
```
C:\app>15L02
Before the GetDateTime() function is called.
Within GetDateTime().
Current date and time is: Sat Apr 05 11:50:10 1997

After the GetDateTime() function is called.
C:\app>
```

ANALYSIS The purpose of the program in Listing 15.2 is to give you the current date and time on your computer by calling the function GetDateTime(), declared in line 5. Because no argument needs to be passed to the function, the void data type is used as the prototype in the declaration of GetDateTime().

Additionally, another void keyword is used in front of the name of the GetDateTime() function to indicate that this function doesn't return any value either. (See line 5.)

The statements in lines 9 and 11 print out messages respectively before and after the GetDateTime() function is called from within the main() function.

In line 10, the function is called by the statement GetDateTime();. Note that no argument should be passed to this function, because the function prototype is void.

The definition of GetDateTime() is in lines 15–23; it obtains the calendar time and converts it into a character string by calling several C library functions, such as time(), localtime(), and asctime(). Then, the character string containing the information of current date and time is printed out on the screen by the printf() function with the format specifier %s. As you can see, the output on my screen shows that at the moment the executable 15L02.exe is being executed, the date and time are

```
Sat Apr 05 11:50:10 1997
```

time(), localtime(), and asctime() are date and time functions provided by the C language. These functions are discussed in the following subsection. You might notice that the header file time.h is included at the beginning of the program in Listing 15.2 before these time functions can be used.

Using `time()`, `localtime()`, and `asctime()`

Several C functions are called *date and time functions*. The declarations of all date and time functions are included in the header file `time.h`. These functions can give three types of date and time:

☐ Calendar time

☐ Local time

☐ Daylight savings time

Here *calendar time* gives the current date and time based on the Gregorian calendar. *Local time* represents the calendar time in a specific time zone. *Daylight savings time* is the local time under the daylight savings rule.

In this section, three date and time functions—`time()`, `localtime()`, and `asctime()`—are briefly introduced.

In C, the `time()` function returns the calendar time.

The syntax for the `time()`   function is

```
#include <time.h>
time_t time(time_t *timer);
```

Here `time_t` is the arithmetic type that is used to represent time. `timer` is a pointer variable pointing to a memory storage that can hold the calendar time returned by this function. The `time()` function returns `-1` if the calendar time is not available on the computer.

The `localtime()` function returns the local time converted from the calendar time.

The syntax for the `localtime()` function is

```
#include <time.h>
struct tm *localtime(const time_t *timer);
```

Here `tm` is a structure that contains the components of the calendar time. `struct` is the keyword for structure, which is another data type in C. (The concept of structures is introduced in Hour 19, "Collecting Data Items of Different Types.") `timer` is a pointer variable pointing to a memory storage that holds the calendar time returned by the `time()` function.

To convert the date and time represented by the structure `tm`, you can call the `asctime()` function.

15

SYNTAX

The syntax for the `asctime()` function is

```
#include <time.h>
char *asctime(const struct tm *timeptr);
```

Here *timeptr* is a pointer referencing the structure *tm* returned by date and time functions like `localtime()`. The `asctime()` function converts the date and time represented by *tm* into a character string.

In Listing 15.2, the statement in line 17 declares a `time_t` variable called now. Line 20 stores the calendar time into the memory location referenced by the now variable. Note that the argument passed to the `time()` function should be the left value of a variable; therefore, the address-of operator (&) is used prior to now. Then, the expression in line 22, `asctime(localtime(&now))`, obtains the local time expression of the calendar time by calling `localtime()`, and converts the local time into a character string with help from `asctime()`. The character string of the date and time is then printed out by the `printf()` function in lines 21 and 22, which has the following format:

```
Sat Apr 05 11:50:10 1997\n\0
```

Note that there is a newline character appended right before the null character in the character string that is converted and returned by the `asctime()` function.

Functions with a Fixed Number of Arguments

You have actually seen several examples that declare and call functions with a fixed number of arguments. For instance, in Listing 15.1, the declaration of the `function_1()` function in line 4

```
int function_1(int x, int y);
```

contains the prototype of two arguments, x and y.

To declare a function with a fixed number of arguments, you need to specify the data type of each argument. Also, it's recommended to indicate the argument names so that the compiler can have a check to make sure that the argument types and names declared in a function declaration match the implementation in the function definition.

Prototyping a Variable Number of Arguments

As you may still remember, the syntax of the `printf()` function is

```
int printf(const char *format[, argument, ...]);
```

Here the ellipsis token ... (that is, three dots) represents a variable number of arguments. In other words, besides the first argument that is a character string, the printf() function can take an unspecified number of additional arguments, as many as the compiler allows. The brackets ([and]) indicate that the unspecified arguments are optional.

The following is a general form to declare a function with a variable number of arguments:

```
data_type_specifier   function_name(
     data_type_specifier argument_name1, ...
);
```

Note that the first argument name is followed by the ellipsis (...) that represents the rest of unspecified arguments.

For instance, to declare the printf() function, you can have something like this:

```
int printf(const char *format, ...);
```

Processing Variable Arguments

There are three routines, declared in the header file stdarg.h, that enable you to write functions that take a variable number of arguments. They are va_start(), va_arg(), and va_end().

Also included in stdarg.h is a data type, va_list, that defines an array type suitable for containing data items needed by va_start(), va_arg(), and va_end().

To initialize a given array that is needed by va_arg() and va_end(), you have to use the va_start() macro routine before any arguments are processed.

The syntax for the va_start() macro is

```
#include <stdarg.h>
void va_start(va_list ap, lastfix);
```

Here *ap* is the name of the array that is about to be initialized by the va_start() macro routine. *lastfix* should be the argument before the ellipsis (...) in the function declaration.

By using the va_arg() macro, you're able to deal with an expression that has the type and value of the next argument. In other words, the va_arg() macro can be used to get the next argument passed to the function.

The syntax for the va_arg() macro is

```
#include <stdarg.h>
type va_arg(va_list ap, data_type);
```

Here *ap* is the name of the array that is initialized by the va_arg() macro routine. *data_type* is the data type of the argument passed to function.

To facilitate a normal return from your function, you have to use the va_end() function in your program after all arguments have been processed.

SYNTAX

The syntax for the va_end() function is

```
#include <stdarg.h>
void va_end(va_list ap);
```

Here ap is the name of the array that is initialized by the va_end() macro routine.

Remember to include the header file, stdarg.h, in your program before you call va_start(), va_arg(), or va_end().

Listing 5.3 demonstrates how to use va_start(), va_arg(), and va_end() in a function that takes a variable number of arguments.

TYPE **Listing 15.3. Processing variable arguments.**

```
1:  /* 15L03.c: Processing variable arguments */
2:  #include <stdio.h>
3:  #include <stdarg.h>
4:
5:  double AddDouble(int x, ...);
6:
7:  main ()
8:  {
9:     double d1 = 1.5;
10:    double d2 = 2.5;
11:    double d3 = 3.5;
12:    double d4 = 4.5;
13:
14:    printf("Given an argument: %2.1f\n", d1);
15:    printf("The result returned by AddDouble() is: %2.1f\n\n",
16:       AddDouble(1, d1));
17:    printf("Given arguments: %2.1f and %2.1f\n", d1, d2);
18:    printf("The result returned by AddDouble() is: %2.1f\n\n",
19:       AddDouble(2, d1, d2));
20:    printf("Given arguments: %2.1f, %2.1f and %2.1f\n", d1, d2, d3);
21:    printf("The result returned by AddDouble() is: %2.1f\n\n",
22:       AddDouble(3, d1, d2, d3));
23:    printf("Given arguments: %2.1f, %2.1f, %2.1f, and %2.1f\n", d1, d2, d3,
➥d4);
24:    printf("The result returned by AddDouble() is: %2.1f\n",
25:       AddDouble(4, d1, d2, d3, d4));
26:    return 0;
27: }
28: /* definition of AddDouble() */
29: double AddDouble(int x, ...)
30: {
31:    va_list   arglist;
32:    int i;
33:    double result = 0.0;
34:
```

continues

Listing 15.3. continued

```
35:    printf("The number of arguments is: %d\n", x);
36:    va_start (arglist, x);
37:    for (i=0; i<x; i++)
38:       result += va_arg(arglist, double);
39:    va_end (arglist);
40:    return result;
41: }
```

The following output is displayed on the screen after the executable, 15L03.exe, is run from a DOS prompt:

OUTPUT
```
C:\app>15L03
Given an argument: 1.5
The number of arguments is: 1
The result returned by AddDouble() is: 1.5

Given arguments: 1.5 and 2.5
The number of arguments is: 2
The result returned by AddDouble() is: 4.0

Given arguments: 1.5, 2.5, and 3.5
The number of arguments is: 3
The result returned by AddDouble() is: 7.5

Given arguments: 1.5, 2.5, 3.5, and 4.5
The number of arguments is: 4
The result returned by AddDouble() is: 12.0
C:\app>
```

ANALYSIS The program in Listing 15.3 contains a function that can take a variable number of double arguments, perform the operation of addition on these arguments, and then return the result to the main() function.

The declaration in line 5 indicates to the compiler that the AddDouble() function takes a variable number of arguments. The first argument to AddDouble() is an integer variable that holds the number of the rest of the arguments passed to the function each time AddDouble() is called. In other words, the first argument indicates the number of remaining arguments to be processed.

The definition of AddDouble() is given in lines 29–41, in which a va_list array, arglist, is declared in line 31. As mentioned, the va_start() macro has to be called before the arguments are processed. Thus, line 36 invokes va_start() to initialize the array arglist. The for loop in lines 37 and 38 fetches the next double argument saved in the array arglist by calling va_arg(). Then, each argument is added into a local double variable called result.

15

The va_end() function is called in line 39 after all arguments saved in arglist have been fetched and processed. Then, the value of result is returned back to the caller of the AddDouble() function, which is the main() function in this case.

The va_end() function has to be called in a C program to end variable argument processing. Otherwise, the behavior of the program is undefined.

As you can see, within the main() function, AddDouble() is called four times, with a different number of arguments each time. These arguments passed to AddDouble() are displayed by the printf() functions in lines 14, 17, 20, and 23. Also, the four different results returned by AddDouble() are printed out on the screen.

Learning Structured Programming

Now you've learned the basics of function declaration and definition. Before we go to the next hour, let's talk a little bit about *structured programming* in program design.

Structured programming is one of the best programming methodologies. Basically, there are two types of structured programming: top-down programming and bottom-up programming.

When you start to write a program to solve a problem, one way to do it is to work on the smallest pieces of the problem. First, you define and write functions for each of the pieces. After each function is written and tested, you begin to put them together to build a program that can solve the problem. This approach is normally called *bottom-up programming*.

On the other hand, to solve a problem, you can first work out an outline and start your programming at a higher level. For instance, you can work on the main() function at the beginning, and then move to the next lower level until the lowest-level functions are written. This type of approach is called *top-down programming*.

You'll find that it's useful to combine these two types of structured programming and use them alternately in order to solve a real problem.

Summary

In this lesson you've learned the following:

- ☐ A function declaration alludes to a function that is defined elsewhere, and specifies what type of arguments and values are passed to and returned from the function as well.
- ☐ A function definition reserves the memory space and defines what the function does, as well as the number and type of arguments passed to the function.

- [ ] A function can be declared to return any data type, except an array or a function.
- [ ] The return statement used in a function definition returns a single value whose type must be matched with the one declared in the function declaration.
- [ ] A function call is an expression that can be used as a single statement or within other expressions or statements.
- [ ] The void data type is needed in the declaration of a function that takes no argument.
- [ ] To declare a function that takes a variable number of arguments, you have to specify at least the first argument, and use an ellipsis (...) to represent the rest of the arguments passed to the function.
- [ ] va_start(), va_arg(), and va_end(), all included in stdarg.h, are needed in processing a variable number of arguments passed to a function.
- [ ] time(), localtime(), and asctime() are three time functions provided by C. They can be used together to obtain a character string that contains information of local date and time based on the calendar time.

In the next lesson you'll learn more about pointers and their applications in C.

Q&A

Q What is the main difference between a function declaration and a function definition?

A The main difference between a function declaration and a function definition is that the former does not reserve any memory space, nor does it specify what a function does. A function declaration only alludes to a function definition that is placed elsewhere. It also specifies what type of arguments and values are passed to and returned from the function. A function definition, on the other hand, reserves the memory space and specifies tasks the function can complete.

Q Why do we need function prototypes?

A By declaring a function with prototypes, you specify not only the data type returned by the function, but also the types and names of arguments passed to the function. With the help of a function prototype, the compiler can automatically perform type checking on the definition of the function, which saves you time to debug the program.

Q Can a function return a pointer?

A Yes. In fact, a function can return a single value that can be any data type except an array or a function. A pointer value—that is, the address—returned by a function can refer to a character array, or a memory location that stores another type of data.

For instance, the C library function asctime() returns a character pointer that points to a character string converted from a date-time structure.

Q Can you use top-down programming and bottom-up programming together to solve a problem?

A Yes. In practice, you can find that it's actually a good idea to combine the top-down and bottom-up programming approaches to solve problems. Using the two types of structured programming can make your program easy to write and understand.

Workshop

To help solidify your understanding of this hour's lesson, you are encouraged to answer the quiz questions and finish the exercises provided in the Workshop before you move to the next lesson. The answers and hints to the questions and exercises are given in Appendix E, "Answers to Quiz Questions and Exercises."

Quiz

1. Given the following function declarations, which ones are functions with a fixed number of arguments, which ones are functions with no arguments, and which ones are functions with a variable number of arguments?

   ☐ `int function_1(int x, float y);`

   ☐ `void function_2(char *str);`

   ☐ `char *asctime(const struct tm *timeptr);`

   ☐ `int function_3(void);`

   ☐ `char function_4(char c, …);`

   ☐ `void function_5(void);`

2. Which one of the following two expressions is a function definition?

   ```
   int function_1(int x, int y);
   int function_2(int x, int y){return x+y;}
   ```

3. What is the data type returned by a function when a type specifier is omitted?

4. Of the following function declarations, which ones are illegal?

   ☐ `double function_1(int x, ...);`

   ☐ `void function_2(int x, int y, ...);`

   ☐ `char function_3(...);`

   ☐ `int function_4(int, int, int, int);`

Exercises

1. Rewrite the program in Listing 15.2. This time use the format specifier %c, instead of %s, to print out the character string of the local time on your computer.

2. Declare and define a function, called MultiTwo(), that can perform multiplication on two integer variables. Call the MultiTwo() function from the main() function and pass two integers to MultiTwo(). Then print out the result returned by the MultiTwo() function on the screen.

3. Rewrite the program in Listing 15.3. This time, make a function that takes a variable number of int arguments and performs the operation of multiplication on these arguments.

4. Rewrite the program in Listing 15.3 again. This time, print out all arguments passed to the AddDouble() function. Does va_arg() fetch each argument in the same order (that is, from left to right) of the argument list passed to AddDouble()?

Hour 16

Applying Pointers

Think twice and do once.

—Chinese proverb

In Hour 11, "An Introduction to Pointers," you learned the basics of using pointers in C. Because pointers are very useful in programming, it's worth spending another hour to learn more about them. In this lesson, the following topics are discussed:

☐ Pointer arithmetic

☐ Passing arrays to functions

☐ Passing pointers to functions

☐ Pointing to functions

Pointer Arithmetic

In C, you can move the position of a pointer by adding or subtracting integers to or from the pointer. For example, given a character pointer variable `ptr_str`, the following expression

```
ptr_str + 1
```

indicates to the compiler to move to the memory location that is one byte away from the current position of ptr_str.

Note that for pointers of different data types, the integers added to or subtracted from the pointers have different scalar sizes. In other words, adding 1 to (or subtracting 1 from) a pointer is not instructing the compiler to add (or subtract) one byte to the address, but to adjust the address so that it skips over one element of the type of the pointer. You'll see more details in the following sections.

The Scalar Size of Pointers

The general format to change the position of a pointer is

```
pointer_name + n
```

Here n is an integer whose value can be either positive or negative. pointer_name is the name of a pointer variable that has the following declaration:

```
data_type_specifier *pointer_name;
```

When the C compiler reads the pointer_name + n expression, it interprets the expression as

```
pointer_name + n * sizeof(data_type_specifier)
```

Note that the sizeof operator is used to obtain the number of bytes that a specified data type can have. Therefore, for the char pointer variable ptr_str, the ptr_str + 1 expression actually means

```
ptr_str + 1 * sizeof(char).
```

Because the size of a character is one byte long, ptr_str + 1 tells the compiler to move to the memory location that is 1 byte after the current location referenced by the pointer.

The program in Listing 16.1 shows how the scalar sizes of different data types affect the offsets added to or subtracted from pointers.

TYPE   **Listing 16.1. Moving pointers of different data types.**

```
1:  /* 16L01.c: Pointer arithmetic */
2:  #include <stdio.h>
3:
4:  main()
5:  {
6:      char *ptr_ch;
7:      int *ptr_int;
8:      double *ptr_db;
9:      /* char pointer ptr_ch */
10:     printf("Current position of ptr_ch: 0x%p\n", ptr_ch);
11:     printf("The position after ptr_ch + 1: 0x%p\n", ptr_ch + 1);
12:     printf("The position after ptr_ch + 2: 0x%p\n", ptr_ch + 2);
13:     printf("The position after ptr_ch - 1: 0x%p\n", ptr_ch - 1);
```

```
14:      printf("The position after ptr_ch - 2: 0x%p\n", ptr_ch - 2);
15:      /* int pointer ptr_int */
16:      printf("Current position of ptr_int: 0x%p\n", ptr_int);
17:      printf("The position after ptr_int + 1: 0x%p\n", ptr_int + 1);
18:      printf("The position after ptr_int + 2: 0x%p\n", ptr_int + 2);
19:      printf("The position after ptr_int - 1: 0x%p\n", ptr_int - 1);
20:      printf("The position after ptr_int - 2: 0x%p\n", ptr_int - 2);
21:      /* double pointer ptr_ch */
22:      printf("Current position of ptr_db: 0x%p\n", ptr_db);
23:      printf("The position after ptr_db + 1: 0x%p\n", ptr_db + 1);
24:      printf("The position after ptr_db + 2: 0x%p\n", ptr_db + 2);
25:      printf("The position after ptr_db - 1: 0x%p\n", ptr_db - 1);
26:      printf("The position after ptr_db - 2: 0x%p\n", ptr_db - 2);
27:
28:      return 0;
29: }
```

The following output is obtained by running the executable, 16L01.exe, of the program in Listing 16.1 on my machine. You might get a different address on your computer, but the offsets should remain the same:

OUTPUT

```
C:\app>16L01
Current position of ptr_ch: 0x000B
The position after ptr_ch + 1: 0x000C
The position after ptr_ch + 2: 0x000D
The position after ptr_ch - 1: 0x000A
The position after ptr_ch - 2: 0x0009
Current position of ptr_int: 0x028B
The position after ptr_int + 1: 0x028D
The position after ptr_int + 2: 0x028F
The position after ptr_int - 1: 0x0289
The position after ptr_int - 2: 0x0287
Current position of ptr_db: 0x0128
The position after ptr_db + 1: 0x0130
The position after ptr_db + 2: 0x0138
The position after ptr_db - 1: 0x0120
The position after ptr_db - 2: 0x0118
C:\app>
```

ANALYSIS

As you can see in Listing 16.1, there are three types of pointers—ptr_ch, ptr_int, and ptr_db—declared in lines 6–8. Among them, ptr_ch is a pointer to a character, ptr_int is a pointer to an integer, and ptr_db is a pointer to a double.

The statement in line 10 shows the memory address, 0x000B, contained by the char pointer variable ptr_ch. Lines 11 and 12 display the two addresses, 0x000C and 0x000D, when ptr_ch is added to 1 and 2, respectively. Similarly, lines 13 and 14 give 0x000A and 0x0009 when ptr_ch is moved down to lower memory addresses. Because the size of char is 1 byte, ptr_ch+1 means to move to the memory location that is 1 byte higher than the current memory location, 0x000B, referenced by the pointer ptr_ch.

Line 16 shows the memory location referenced by the int pointer variable ptr_int at 0x028B. Because the size of int is 2 bytes long, the ptr_int+1 expression simply means to move to the memory location that is 2 bytes higher than the current one pointed to by ptr_int. That's exactly what has been printed out in line 17. Likewise, line 18 shows that ptr_int+2 causes the reference to be moved to 0x028F, which is 4 bytes higher than 0x028B. The memory location of 0x0289 is referenced by the ptr_int-1 expression in line 19; 0x0287 is referenced by ptr_int-2 in line 20.

The size of the double data type is 8 bytes long. Therefore, the ptr_db+1 expression is interpreted as the memory address referenced by ptr_db plus 8 bytes—that is, 0x0128+8, which gives 0x0130 in hex format. (See the output made by the statement in line 23.)

Lines 24–26 print out the memory addresses referenced by ptr_db+2, ptr_db-1, and ptr_db-2, respectively, which prove that the compiler has taken the scalar size of double in the pointer arithmetic.

WARNING

Pointers are useful if you use them properly. On the other hand, a pointer can get you into trouble if it contains a wrong value. A common error, for instance, is to assign a right value to a pointer that actually expects a left one. Fortunately, many C compilers can find such an error and issue a warning message.

There is another common error that the compiler does not pick up for you: using uninitialized pointers. For example, the following code has a potential problem:

```
int x, ptr_int;
x = 8;
*ptr_int = x;
```

The problem is that the ptr_int pointer is not initialized; it points to some unknown memory location. Therefore, assigning a value, like 8 in this case, to an unknown memory location is dangerous. It may overwrite some important data that is already saved at the memory location, thus causing a serious problem. The solution is to make sure that a pointer is pointing at a legal and valid memory location before it is used.

You can rewrite this C code to avoid the potential problem like this:

```
int x, ptr_int;
x = 8;
ptr_int = &x;    /* initialize the pointer */
```

Pointer Subtraction

For two pointers of the same type, you can subtract one pointer value from the other. For instance, given two char pointer variables, ptr_str1 and ptr_str2, you can calculate the offset between the two memory locations pointed to by the two pointers like this:

```
ptr_str2 - ptr_str1
```

However, it's illegal in C to subtract one pointer value from another if they do not share the same data type.

Listing 16.2 gives an example of performing subtraction on an int pointer variable.

TYPE **Listing 16.2. Performing subtraction on pointers.**

```
1:   /* 16L02.c: Pointer subtraction */
2:   #include <stdio.h>
3:
4:   main()
5:   {
6:      int *ptr_int1, *ptr_int2;
7:
8:      printf("The position of ptr_int1: 0x%p\n", ptr_int1);
9:      ptr_int2 = ptr_int1 + 5;
10:     printf("The position of ptr_int2 = ptr_int1 + 5: 0x%p\n", ptr_int2);
11:     printf("The subtraction of ptr_int2 - ptr_int1: %d\n", ptr_int2 -
        ➥ptr_int1);
12:     ptr_int2 = ptr_int1 - 5;
13:     printf("The position of ptr_int2 = ptr_int1 - 5: 0x%p\n", ptr_int2);
14:     printf("The subtraction of ptr_int2 - ptr_int1: %d\n", ptr_int2 -
        ➥ptr_int1);
15:
16:     return 0;
17: }
```

After running the executable (16L02.exe) of the program in Listing 16.2 on my machine, I have the following output shown on the screen:

OUTPUT
```
C:\app>16L02
The position of ptr_int1: 0x0128
The position of ptr_int2 = ptr_int1 + 5: 0x0132
The subtraction of ptr_int2 - ptr_int1: 5
The position of ptr_int2 = ptr_int1 - 5: 0x011E
The subtraction of ptr_int2 - ptr_int1: -5
C:\app>
```

ANALYSIS   The program in Listing 16.2 declares two int pointer variables, ptr_int1 and ptr_int2, in line 6. The statement in line 8 prints out the memory position held by ptr_int1. Line 9 assigns the memory address referenced by ptr_int1+5 to ptr_int2. Then, the content of ptr_int2 is printed out in line 10.

The statement in line 11 shows the difference between the two int pointers—that is, the subtraction of ptr_int2 and ptr_int1. The result is 5.

Line 12 then assigns another memory address, referenced by the ptr_int1-5 expression, to the ptr_int2 pointer. Now, ptr_int2 points to a memory location that is 10 bytes lower than the memory location pointed to by ptr_int1 (see the output made by line 13.) The difference between ptr_int2 and ptr_int1 is obtained by the subtraction of the two pointers, which is -5 as printed out by the statement in line 14.

Pointers and Arrays

As indicated in previous lessons, pointers and arrays have a close relationship. You can access an array through a pointer that contains the start address of the array. The following subsection introduces how to access array elements through pointers.

Accessing Arrays via Pointers

Because an array name that is not followed by a subscript is interpreted as a pointer to the first element of the array, you can assign the start address of the array to a pointer of the same data type; then you can access any element in the array by adding a proper integer to the pointer. The value of the integer is the same as the subscript value of the element that you want to access.

In other words, given an array, array, and a pointer, ptr_array, if array and ptr_array are of the same data type, and ptr_array contains the start address of the array, that is

```
ptr_array = array;
```

then the expression array[n] is equivalent to the expression

```
*(ptr_array + n)
```

Here n is a subscript number in the array.

Listing 16.3 demonstrates how to access arrays and change values of array elements by using pointers.

TYPE **Listing 16.3. Accessing arrays by using pointers.**

```
1:   /* 16L03.c: Accessing arrays via pointers */
2:   #include <stdio.h>
3:
4:   main()
5:   {
6:      char str[] = "It's a string!";
7:      char *ptr_str;
8:      int list[] = {1, 2, 3, 4, 5};
9:      int *ptr_int;
10:
11:     /* access char array */
12:     ptr_str = str;
13:     printf("Before the change, str contains: %s\n", str);
14:     printf("Before the change, str[5] contains: %c\n", str[5]);
15:     *(ptr_str + 5) = 'A';
16:     printf("After the change, str[5] contains: %c\n", str[5]);
17:     printf("After the change, str contains: %s\n", str);
18:     /* access int array */
19:     ptr_int = list;
20:     printf("Before the change, list[2] contains: %d\n", list[2]);
21:     *(ptr_int + 2) = -3;
```

```
22:     printf("After the change, list[2] contains: %d\n", list[2]);
23:
24:     return 0;
25: }
```

The following output is displayed on the screen after the executable, 16L03.exe, is created and run from a DOS prompt:

OUTPUT
```
C:\app>16L03
Before the change, str contains: It's a string!
Before the change, str[5] contains: a
After the change, str[5] contains: A
After the change, str contains: It's A string!
Before the change, list[2] contains: 3
After the change, list[2] contains: -3
C:\app>
```

ANALYSIS The purpose of the program in Listing 16.3 is to access a char array, str, and an int array, list. In lines 6 and 8, str and list are declared and initialized with a string and a set of integers, respectively. A char pointer, ptr_str, and an int pointer, ptr_int, are declared in lines 7 and 9.

Line 12 assigns the start address of the str array to the ptr_str pointer. The statements in lines 13 and 14 demonstrate the content of the string saved in the str array, as well as the character contained by the str[5] element in the array before any changes are made to str.

The statement in line 15 shows that the character constant, 'A', is assigned to the element of the str array pointed to by the expression

```
*(ptr_str + 5)
```

To verify that the content of the element in str has been updated, lines 16 and 17 print out the element and the whole string, respectively. The output indicates that 'A' has replaced the original character constant, 'a'.

The start address of the int array list is assigned to the ptr_int pointer in line 19. Before I do anything with the list[2] element of the list array, I print out its value, which is 3 at this moment (see the output made by line 20). In line 21, the list[2] element is given another value, -3, through the dereferenced pointer, *(ptr_int + 2). The printf() function in line 22 prints the latest value of list[2].

Pointers and Functions

Before I talk about passing pointers to functions, let's first have a look at how to pass arrays to functions.

Passing Arrays to Functions

In practice, it's usually awkward if you pass more than five or six arguments to a function. One way to save the number of arguments passed to a function is to use arrays. You can put all variables of the same type into an array, and then pass the array as a single argument.

The program in Listing 16.4 shows how to pass an array of integers to a function.

TYPE   **Listing 16.4. Passing arrays to functions.**

```
 1:  /* 16L04.c: Passing arrays to functions */
 2:  #include <stdio.h>
 3:
 4:  int AddThree(int list[]);
 5:
 6:  main()
 7:  {
 8:      int sum, list[3];
 9:
10:      printf("Enter three integers separated by spaces:\n");
11:      scanf("%d%d%d", &list[0], &list[1], &list[2]);
12:      sum = AddThree(list);
13:      printf("The sum of the three integers is: %d\n", sum);
14:
15:      return 0;
16: }
17:
18: int AddThree(int list[])
19: {
20:      int i;
21:      int result = 0;
22:
23:      for (i=0; i<3; i++)
24:          result += list[i];
25:      return result;
26: }
```

The following output is obtained after I run the executable, 16L04.exe, and enter three integers, 10, 20, and 30, from a DOS prompt:

OUTPUT
```
C:\app>16L04
Enter three integers separated by spaces:
10  20  30
The sum of the three integers is: 60
C:\app>
```

ANALYSIS   The purpose of the program in Listing 16.4 is to obtain three integers entered by the user, and then pass the three integers as an array to a function called AddThree() to perform the operation of addition.

Line 4 gives the declaration of the AddThree() function. Note that the unsized array, list[ ], is used in the argument expression, which indicates that the argument contains the start address of the list array.

The list array and an integer variable, sum, are declared in line 8. The printf() function in line 10 displays a message asking the user to enter three integers. Then, line 11 fetches the integers entered by the user and stores them in the three memory locations of the elements in the integer array referenced by &list[0], &list[1], and &list[2], respectively.

The statement in line 12 calls the AddThree() function with the name of the array as the argument. The AddThree(list) expression is actually passing the start address of the list array to the AddThree() function.

The definition of the AddThree() function is in lines 18–26; it adds the values of all three elements in the list array and returns the sum. The result returned from the AddThree() function is assigned to the integer variable sum in line 12 and is printed out in line 13.

NOTE

> You can also specify the size of an array that is passed to a function. For instance, the following
>
> ```
> function(char str[16]);
> ```
>
> is equivalent to the following statement:
>
> ```
> function(char str[]);
> ```
>
> Remember that the compiler can figure out the size for the unsized array str[ ].
>
> For multidimensional arrays, the format of an unsized array should always be used in the declaration. (See the section titled "Passing Multidimensional Arrays as Arguments," later in this hour.)

Passing Pointers to Functions

As you know, an array name that is not followed by a subscript is interpreted as a pointer to the first element of the array. In fact, the address of the first element in an array is the start address of the array. Therefore, you can assign the start address of an array to a pointer, and then pass the pointer name, instead of the unsized array, to a function.

Listing 16.5 gives an example of passing pointers to functions, which is similar to the situation in which arrays are passed to functions.

TYPE　**Listing 16.5. Passing pointers to functions.**

```
1:  /* 16L05.c: Passing pointers to functions */
2:  #include <stdio.h>
3:
4:  void ChPrint(char *ch);
5:  int DataAdd(int *list, int max);
6:  main()
7:  {
8:      char str[] = "It's a string!";
9:      char *ptr_str;
10:     int list[5] = {1, 2, 3, 4, 5};
11:     int *ptr_int;
12:
13:     /* assign address to pointer */
14:     ptr_str = str;
15:     ChPrint(ptr_str);
16:     ChPrint(str);
17:
18:     /* assign address to pointer */
19:     ptr_int = list;
20:     printf("The sum returned by DataAdd(): %d\n",
21:             DataAdd(ptr_int, 5));
22:     printf("The sum returned by DataAdd(): %d\n",
23:             DataAdd(list, 5));
24:     return 0;
25: }
26: /* function definition */
27: void ChPrint(char *ch)
28: {
29:     printf("%s\n", ch);
30: }
31: /* function definition */
32: int DataAdd(int *list, int max)
33: {
34:     int i;
35:     int sum = 0;
36:
37:     for (i=0; i<max; i++)
38:         sum += list[i];
39:     return sum;
40: }
```

After executing the 16L05.exe program, the following output is displayed on the screen:

OUTPUT
```
C:\app>16L05
It's a string!
It's a string!
The sum returned by DataAdd(): 15
The sum returned by DataAdd(): 15
C:\app>
```

ANALYSIS　The purpose of the program in Listing 16.5 is to demonstrate how to pass an integer pointer that points to an integer array and a character pointer that references a character string to two functions that are declared in lines 4 and 5.

16

Note that expressions, such as char *ch and int *list, are used as arguments in the function declarations, which indicates to the compiler that a char pointer and an int pointer are respectively passed to the functions ChPrint() and DataAdd().

Inside the main() function body, lines 8 and 9 declare a char array (str) that is initialized with a character string, and a char pointer variable (ptr_str). Line 10 declares and initializes an int array (list) with a set of integers. An int pointer variable, ptr_int, is declared in line 11.

The start address of the str array is assigned to the ptr_str pointer by the assignment statement in line 14. Then, the ptr_str pointer is passed to the ChPrint() function as the argument in line 15. According to the definition of ChPrint() in lines 27–30, the content of the str array whose start address is passed to the function as the argument is printed out by the printf() function that is invoked inside the ChPrint() function in line 29.

In fact, you can still use the name of the str array as the argument and pass it to the ChPrint() function. Line 16 shows that the start address of the character array is passed to ChPrint() via the name of the array.

The statement in line 19 assigns the start address of the integer array list to the integer pointer ptr_int. Then, the ptr_int pointer is passed to the DataAdd() function in line 21, along with 5, which is the maximum number of the elements contained by the list array. From the definition of the DataAdd() function in lines 32–40, you can see that DataAdd() adds all the integer elements in list and returns the sum to the caller. Thereafter, the statement in lines 20 and 21 prints out the result returned from DataAdd().

The expression in line 23 also invokes the DataAdd() function, but this time, the name of the list array is used as the argument to the function. Not surprisingly, the start address of the list array is passed to the DataAdd() function successfully, and the printf() statement in lines 22 and 23 displays the right result on the screen.

Passing Multidimensional Arrays as Arguments

In Hour 12, "Storing Similar Data Items," you learned about multidimensional arrays. In this section, you're going to see how to pass multidimensional arrays to functions.

As you might have guessed, passing a multidimensional array to a function is similar to passing a one-dimensional array to a function. You can either pass the unsized format of a multidimensional array or a pointer that contains the start address of the multidimensional array to a function. Listing 16.6 is an example of these two methods.

TYPE   **Listing 16.6. Passing multidimensional arrays to functions.**

```
1:  /* 16L06.c: Passing multidimensional arrays to functions */
2:  #include <stdio.h>
3:  /* function declarations */
4:  int DataAdd1(int list[][5], int max1, int max2);
```

continues

Listing 16.6. continued

```
 5:   int DataAdd2(int *list, int max1, int max2);
 6:   /* main() function */
 7:   main()
 8:   {
 9:      int list[2][5] = {1, 2, 3, 4, 5,
10:                         5, 4, 3, 2, 1};
11:      int *ptr_int;
12:
13:      printf("The sum returned by DataAdd1(): %d\n",
14:             DataAdd1(list, 2, 5));
15:      ptr_int = &list[0][0];
16:      printf("The sum returned by DataAdd2(): %d\n",
17:             DataAdd2(ptr_int, 2, 5));
18:
19:      return 0;
20:   }
21:   /* function definition */
22:   int DataAdd1(int list[][5], int max1, int max2)
23:   {
24:      int i, j;
25:      int sum = 0;
26:
27:      for (i=0; i<max1; i++)
28:         for (j=0; j<max2; j++)
29:         sum += list[i][j];
30:      return sum;
31:   }
32:   /* function definition */
33:   int DataAdd2(int *list, int max1, int max2)
34:   {
35:      int i, j;
36:      int sum = 0;
37:
38:      for (i=0; i<max1; i++)
39:         for (j=0; j<max2; j++)
40:         sum += *(list + i*max2 + j);
41:      return sum;
42:   }
```

The following output is displayed on the screen after the executable (16L06.exe) is executed:

OUTPUT
```
C:\app>16L06
The sum returned by DataAdd1(): 30
The sum returned by DataAdd2(): 30
C:\app>
```

ANALYSIS   At the beginning of the program in Listing 16.6, I declare two functions, DataAdd1()
and DataAdd2(), in lines 4 and 5. Note that the first argument to DataAdd1() in line
4 is the unsized array of list. In fact, list is a two-dimensional integer array declared in lines
9 and 10 inside the main() function body. The other two arguments, max1 and max2, are two
dimension sizes of the list array.

16

As you can tell from the definition of DataAdd1() in lines 22–31, each element of the list array, expressed as list[i][j], is added and assigned to a local variable called sum that is returned at the end of the DataAdd1() function in line 30. Here i is from 0 to max1 - 1, and j is within the range of 0 to max2 - 1.

The DataAdd1() function is called in line 14, with the name of the list array and the two dimension sizes, 2 and 5. The result returned by DataAdd1() is printed out by the statement in lines 13 and 14. So you see, passing a multidimensional array to a function is quite similar to passing a one-dimensional array to a function.

Another way to do the job is to pass a pointer that contains the start address of a multidimensional array to a function. In this example, the DataAdd2() function is declared in line 5 with a pointer expression, int *list, as the function's first argument. The definition of DataAdd2() is given in lines 33–42.

Note that in line 40, each element in the list array is fetched by moving the pointer to point to the memory location of the element. That is, the dereferenced pointer *(list + i*max2 + j) returns the value of an element that is located at row i and column j, if you imagine that the two-dimensional array has both a horizontal and a vertical dimension. Therefore, adding i*max2 to list calculates the address of row i (that is, rows 0 through i-1 are skipped over); then adding j calculates the address of element j (that is, column j) in the current row (i). In this example, the range of the row is from 0 to 1 (that is, 2 rows total); the range of the column is from 0 to 4 (that is, 5 columns total). (See Figure 16.1.)

The result returned by the DataAdd2() function is displayed on the screen by the statement declared in lines 16 and 17.

Figure 16.1.

The two-dimensional coordinate shows the locations of the elements in the list *array.*

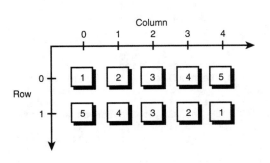

Arrays of Pointers

In many cases, it's useful to declare an array of pointers and access the contents pointed to by the array by dereferencing each pointer. For instance, the following declaration declares an int array of pointers:

```
int *ptr_int[3];
```

In other words, the variable ptr_int is a three-element array of pointers to integers. In addition, you can initialize the array of pointers. For example:

```
int x1 = 10;
int x2 = 100;
int x3 = 1000;
ptr_int[0] = &x1;
ptr_int[1] = &x2;
ptr_int[2] = &x3;
```

Listing 16.7 shows another example. Here an array of pointers is used to access arrays of strings.

TYPE **Listing 16.7. Using an array of pointers to character strings.**

```
1:  /* 16L07.c: Using an array of pointers */
2:  #include <stdio.h>
3:  /* function declarations */
4:  void StrPrint1(char **str1, int size);
5:  void StrPrint2(char *str2);
6:  /* main() function */
7:  main()
8:  {
9:     char *str[4] = {"There's music in the sighing of a reed;",
10:                    "There's music in the gushing of a rill;",
11:                    "There's music in all things if men had ears;",
12:                    "There earth is but an echo of the spheres.\n"
13:                   };
14:    int i, size = 4;
15:
16:    StrPrint1(str, size);
17:    for (i=0; i<size; i++)
18:        StrPrint2(str[i]);
19:
20:    return 0;
21: }
22: /* function definition */
23: void StrPrint1(char **str1, int size)
24: {
25:    int i;
26:    /* Print all strings in an array of pointers to strings */
27:    for (i=0; i<size; i++)
28:        printf("%s\n", str1[i]);
29: }
30: /* function definition */
31: void StrPrint2(char *str2)
32: {
33:    /* Prints one string at a time */
34:    printf("%s\n", str2);
35: }
```

A piece of a poem written by Lord Byron is printed out after the executable (16L07.exe) of the program in Listing 16.7 is created and executed:

OUTPUT

```
C:\app>16L07
There's music in the sighing of a reed;
There's music in the gushing of a rill;
There's music in all things if men had ears;
There earth is but an echo of the spheres.
There's music in the sighing of a reed;
There's music in the gushing of a rill;
There's music in all things if men had ears;
There earth is but an echo of the spheres.
C:\app>
```

ANALYSIS   Let's first have a look at the array of pointers, str, which is declared and initialized in lines 9–13 inside the main() function body of the program in Listing 16.7. As you can see, str is a four-element array of pointers to a set of character strings. I have adopted four sentences of a poem written by Lord Byron and used them as four character strings in the program.

You can get access to a character string by using a corresponding pointer in the array. In fact, there are two functions, StrPrint1() and StrPrint2(), in Listing 16.7. Both of them can be called to gain access to the character strings. From the function declaration in line 4, you can see that the StrPrint1() function is passed with a pointer of pointers—that is, **str1, which is dereferenced inside the StrPrint1() function to represent the four pointers that point to the four character strings. The definition of StrPrint1() is in lines 23–29.

The StrPrint2() function, on the other hand, only takes a pointer variable as its argument, and prints out a character string referenced by the pointer. Lines 31–35 give the definition of the StrPrint2() function.

Now back to the main() function. The StrPrint1() function is called in line 16 with the name of the array of pointers, str, as the argument. StrPrint1() then displays the four sentences of Byron's poem on the screen. The for loop in lines 17 and 18 does the same thing by calling the StrPrint2() function four times. Each time, the start address of a sentence is passed to StrPrint2(). Therefore, you see all the sentences of the poem printed on the screen twice.

Pointing to Functions

Before you finish the course for this hour, there is one more interesting thing you need to learn about: pointers to functions.

As with pointers to arrays, you can declare a pointer that is initialized with the left value of a function. (The left value is the memory address at which the function is located.) Then you can call the function via the pointer.

The program in Listing 16.8 is an example that declares a pointer to a function.

TYPE   **Listing 16.8. Pointing to a function.**

```
1:  /* 16L08.c: Pointing to a function */
2:  #include <stdio.h>
3:  /* function declaration */
4:  int StrPrint(char *str);
5:  /* main() function */
6:  main()
7:  {
8:     char str[24] = "Pointing to a function.";
9:     int (*ptr)(char *str);
10:
11:    ptr = StrPrint;
12:    if (!(*ptr)(str))
13:       printf("Done!\n");
14:
15:    return 0;
16: }
17: /* function definition */
18: int StrPrint(char *str)
19: {
20:    printf("%s\n", str);
21:    return 0;
22: }
```

After the executable, 16L08.exe, of the program in Listing 16.8 is created and executed, the following output is shown on the screen:

OUTPUT
```
C:\app>16L08
Pointing to a function.
Done!
C:\app>
```

ANALYSIS   As usual, a function declaration comes first in Listing 16.8. The StrPrint() function is declared with the int data type specifier and an argument of a char pointer in line 4.

The statement in line 9 gives the declaration of a pointer (ptr) to the StrPrint() function (that is, int (*ptr)(char *str);).

Note that the pointer, ptr, is specified with the int data type and passed with a char pointer. In other words, the format of the pointer declaration in line 9 is quite similar to the declaration of StrPrint() in line 4. Please remember that you have to put the *ptr expression between a pair of parentheses ((and)) so that the compiler won't confuse it with a function name.

In line 11, the left value (that is, the address) of the StrPrint() function is assigned to the ptr pointer. Then, the (*ptr)(str) expression in line 12 calls the StrPrint() function via the dereferenced pointer ptr, and passes the address of the string declared in line 8 to the function.

From the definition of the StrPrint() function in lines 18–22, you can tell that the function prints out the content of a string whose address is passed to the function as the argument. Then, 0 is returned at the end of the function.

In fact, the if statement in lines 12 and 13 checks the value returned by the StrPrint() function. When the value is 0, the printf() function in line 13 displays the string of Done! on the screen.

The output of the program in Listing 16.8 shows that the StrPrint() function has been invoked successfully by using a pointer that holds the address of the function.

Summary

In this lesson you've learned the following:

- [ ] You should always make sure that a pointer is pointing to a legal and valid memory location before you use it.
- [ ] The position of a pointer can be moved by adding or subtracting an integer.
- [ ] The scalar size of a pointer is determined by its data type, which is specified in the pointer declaration.
- [ ] For two pointers of the same type, you can subtract one pointer value from the other.
- [ ] The elements in an array can be accessed via a pointer that holds the start address of the array.
- [ ] You can pass an unsized array as a single argument to a function.
- [ ] Also, you can pass an array to a function through a pointer. The pointer should hold the start address of the array.
- [ ] You can either pass the unsized format of a multidimensional array or a pointer that contains the start address of the multidimensional array to a function.
- [ ] Arrays of pointers are useful in many cases that deal with character strings.
- [ ] You can call a function via a pointer that holds the address of the function.

In the next lesson you'll learn how to allocate memory in C.

Q&A

Q Why do you need pointer arithmetic?

A The beauty of using pointers is that you can move pointers around to get access to valid data that is saved in those memory locations referenced by the pointers. To do so, you can perform the pointer arithmetic to add (or subtract) an integer to (or from) a pointer. For example, if a character pointer, ptr_str, holds the start address of a character string, the ptr_str+1 expression means to move to the next memory location that contains the second character in the string.

Q How does the compiler determine the scalar size of a pointer?

A The compiler determines the scalar size of a pointer by its data type specified in the declaration. When an integer is added to or subtracted from a pointer, the actual value the compiler uses is the multiplication of the integer and the size of the pointer type. For instance, given an int pointer ptr_int, the ptr_int + 1 expression is interpreted by the compiler as ptr_int + 1 * sizeof(int). If the size of the int type is 2 bytes, then the ptr_int + 1 expression really means to move 2 bytes higher from the memory location referenced by the ptr_int pointer.

Q How do you get access to an element in an array by using a pointer?

A For a one-dimensional array, you can assign the start address of an array to a pointer of the same type, and then move the pointer to the memory location that contains the value of an element in which you're interested. Then you dereference the pointer to obtain the value of the element. For multidimensional arrays, the method is similar, but you have to think about the other dimensions at the same time. (See the example shown in Listing 16.6.)

Q Why do you need to use arrays of pointers?

A In many cases, it's helpful to use arrays of pointers. For instance, it's convenient to use an array of pointers to point to a set of character strings so that you can access any one of the strings referenced by a corresponding pointer in the array.

Workshop

To help solidify your understanding of this hour's lesson, you are encouraged to answer the quiz questions and finish the exercises provided in the Workshop before you move to the next lesson. The answers and hints to the questions and exercises are given in Appendix E, "Answers to Quiz Questions and Exercises."

Quiz

1. Given a char pointer, ptr_ch, an int pointer, ptr_int, and a float pointer, ptr_flt, how many bytes will be added, respectively, in the following expressions on your machine?

   ☐ ptr_ch + 4

   ☐ ptr_int + 2

   ☐ ptr_flt + 1

   ☐ ptr_ch + 12

☐ `ptr_int + 6`

☐ `ptr_flt + 3`

2. If the address held by an int pointer, `ptr1`, is `0x100A`, and the address held by another int pointer, `ptr2`, is `0x1006`, what will you get from the subtraction of `ptr1-ptr2`?

3. Given that the size of the `double` data type is 8 bytes long, and the current address held by a `double` pointer variable, `ptr_db`, is `0x0238`, what are the addresses held, respectively, by `ptr_db-1` and `ptr_db+5`?

4. Given the following declarations and assignments:

```
char ch[] = {'a', 'b', 'c', 'd', 'A', 'B', 'C', 'D'};
char *ptr;
ptr = &ch[1];
```

what do these expressions do separately?

☐ `*(ptr + 3)`

☐ `ptr - ch`

☐ `*(ptr - 1)`

☐ `*ptr = 'F'`

Exercises

1. Given a character string, `I like C!`, write a program to pass the string to a function that displays the string on the screen.

2. Rewrite the program of exercise 1. This time, change the string of `I like C!` to `I love C!` by moving a pointer that is initialized with the start address of the string and updating the string with new characters. Then, pass the updated string to the function to display the content of the string on the screen.

3. Given a two-dimensional character array, `str`, that is initialized as

```
char str[2][15] = { "You know what,", "C is powerful." };
```

write a program to pass the start address of `str` to a function that prints out the content of the character array.

4. Rewrite the program in Listing 16.7. This time, the array of pointers is initialized with the following strings:

```
"Sunday", "Monday", "Tuesday", "Wednesday", "Thursday", "Friday", and
"Saturday".
```

Hour 17

Allocating Memory

It's just as unpleasant to get more than you bargain for as to get less.

—*G. B. Shaw*

So far you've learned how to declare and reserve a piece of memory space before it is used in your program. For instance, you have to specify the size of an array in your program (or the compiler has to figure out the size if you declare an unsized array) before you assign any data to it at runtime. In this lesson you'll learn to allocate memory space dynamically when your program is running. The four dynamic memory allocation functions covered in this lesson are

- [ ] The `malloc()` function
- [ ] The `calloc()` function
- [ ] The `realloc()` function
- [ ] The `free()` function

Allocating Memory at Runtime

There are many cases when you do not know the exact sizes of arrays used in your programs, until much later when your programs are actually being executed.

You can specify the sizes of arrays in advance, but the arrays can be too small or too big if the numbers of data items you want to put into the arrays change dramatically at runtime.

Fortunately, C provides you with four dynamic memory allocation functions that you can employ to allocate or reallocate certain memory spaces while your program is running. Also, you can release allocated memory storage as soon as you don't need it. These four C functions, `malloc()`, `calloc()`, `realloc()`, and `free()`, are introduced in the following sections.

The `malloc()` Function

You can use the `malloc()` function to allocate a specified size of memory space.

SYNTAX

The syntax for the `malloc()` function is

```
#include <stdlib.h>
void *malloc(size_t size);
```

Here `size` indicates the number of bytes of storage to allocate. The `malloc()` function returns a `void` pointer.

Note that the header file, `stdlib.h`, has to be included before the `malloc()` function can be called. Because the `malloc()` function returns a `void` pointer, its type is automatically converted to the type of the pointer on the left side of an assignment operator.

If the `malloc()` function fails to allocate a piece of memory space, it returns a null pointer. Normally, this happens when there is not enough memory. Therefore, you should always check the returned pointer from `malloc()` before you use it.

Listing 17.1 demonstrates the use of the `malloc()` function.

TYPE   **Listing 17.1. Using the `malloc()` function.**

```
1:   /* 17L01.c: Using the malloc function */
2:   #include <stdio.h>
3:   #include <stdlib.h>
4:   #include <string.h>
5:   /* function declaration */
6:   void StrCopy(char *str1, char *str2);
7:   /* main() function */
8:   main()
9:   {
10:     char str[] = "Use malloc() to allocate memory.";
11:     char *ptr_str;
12:     int result;
13:     /* call malloc() */
14:     ptr_str = malloc( strlen(str) + 1);
15:     if (ptr_str != NULL){
16:        StrCopy(str, ptr_str);
17:        printf("The string pointed to by ptr_str is:\n%s\n",
```

```
18:                 ptr_str);
19:         result = 0;
20:     }
21:     else{
22:         printf("malloc() function failed.\n");
23:         result = 1;
24:     }
25:     return result;
26: }
27: /* function definition */
28: void StrCopy(char *str1, char *str2)
29: {
30:     int i;
31:
32:     for (i=0; str1[i]; i++)
33:         str2[i] = str1[i];
34:     str2[i] = '\0';
35: }
```

The following output is shown on the screen after the executable, 17L01.exe, of the program in Listing 17.1 is created and executed:

OUTPUT
```
C:\app>17L01
The string pointed to by ptr_str is:
Use malloc() to allocate memory.
C:\app>
```

ANALYSIS The purpose of the program in Listing 17.1 is to use the malloc() function to allocate a piece of memory space that has the same size as a character string. Then, the content of the string is copied to the allocated memory referenced by the pointer returned from the malloc() function. The content of the memory is displayed on the screen to prove that the memory space does contain the content of the string after the allocation and duplication.

Note that two more header files, stdlib.h and string.h, are included in lines 3 and 4, respectively, for the functions malloc() and strlen(), which are called in line 14.

Line 10 declares a char array, str, that is initialized with a character string of "Use malloc() to allocate memory.". A char pointer variable, ptr_str, is declared in line 11.

The statement in line 14 allocates a memory space of strlen(str)+1 bytes by calling the malloc() function. Because the strlen() function does not count the null character at the end of a string, adding 1 to the value returned by strlen(str) gives the total number of bytes that need to be allocated. The value of the returned pointer is assigned to the char pointer variable ptr_str after the malloc() function is called in line 14.

The if-else statement in lines 15–24 checks the returned pointer from the malloc() function. If it's a null pointer, an error message is printed out, and the return value of the main() function is set to 1 in lines 22 and 23. (Remember that a nonzero value returned by the return statement indicates an abnormal termination.)

But if the returned pointer is not a null pointer, the start address of the str array and the pointer ptr_str are passed to a subfunction called StrCopy() in line 16. The StrCopy() function, whose definition is given in lines 28–35, copies the content of the str array to the allocated memory pointed to by ptr_str. Then, the printf() function in lines 17 and 18 prints out the copied content in the allocated memory. Line 19 sets the return value to 0 after the success of the memory allocation and string duplication.

The output on my screen shows that a piece of memory has been allocated and that the string has been copied to the memory.

There is a potential problem if you keep allocating memory, because there is always a limit. You can easily run out of memory when you just allocate memory without releasing it. In the next section, you'll learn how to use the free() function to free up memory spaces allocated for you when you don't need them.

Releasing Allocated Memory with free()

Because memory is a limited resource, you should allocate an exactly sized piece of memory right before you need it, and release it as soon as you don't need it.

The program in Listing 17.2 demonstrates how to release allocated memory by calling the free() function.

Listing 17.2. Using the free() and malloc() functions together.

`TYPE`

```
1:  /* 17L02.c: Using the free() function */
2:  #include <stdio.h>
3:  #include <stdlib.h>
4:  /* function declarations */
5:  void DataMultiply(int max, int *ptr);
6:  void TablePrint(int max, int *ptr);
7:  /* main() function */
8:  main()
9:  {
10:    int *ptr_int, max;
11:    int termination;
12:    char key = 'c';
13:
14:    max = 0;
15:    termination = 0;
16:    while (key != 'x'){
17:       printf("Enter a single digit number:\n");
18:       scanf("%d", &max);
19:
20:       ptr_int = malloc(max * max * sizeof(int));  /* call malloc() */
21:       if (ptr_int != NULL){
22:          DataMultiply(max, ptr_int);
```

17

```
23:             TablePrint(max, ptr_int);
24:             free(ptr_int);
25:         }
26:         else{
27:             printf("malloc() function failed.\n");
28:             termination = 1;
29:             key = 'x';   /* stop while loop */
30:         }
31:         printf("\n\nPress x key to quit; other key to continue.\n");
32:         scanf("%s", &key);
33:     }
34:     printf("\nBye!\n");
35:     return termination;
36: }
37: /* function definition */
38: void DataMultiply(int max, int *ptr)
39: {
40:     int i, j;
41:
42:     for (i=0; i<max; i++)
43:         for (j=0; j<max; j++)
44:             *(ptr + i * max + j) = (i+1) * (j+1);
45: }
46: /* function definition */
47: void TablePrint(int max, int *ptr)
48: {
49:     int i, j;
50:
51:     printf("The multiplication table of %d is:\n",
52:             max);
53:     printf("  ");
54:     for (i=0; i<max; i++)
55:         printf("%4d", i+1);
56:     printf("\n ");
57:     for (i=0; i<max; i++)
58:         printf("----", i+1);
59:     for (i=0; i<max; i++){
60:         printf("\n%d¦", i+1);
61:         for (j=0; j<max; j++)
62:             printf("%3d ", *(ptr + i * max + j));
63:     }
64: }
```

While the executable 17L02.exe is being run, I enter two integers, 4 and 2 (highlighted in the following output), to obtain a multiplication table for each; then I quit running the program by pressing the *x* key:

OUTPUT

```
C:\app>17L02
Enter a single digit number:
4
The multiplication table of 4 is:
     1   2   3   4
   -------------
1¦ 1   2   3   4
2¦ 2   4   6   8
```

```
3¦ 3    6    9   12
4¦ 4    8   12   16
Press x-key to quit; other key to continue.
C
Enter a single digit number:
2
The multiplication table of 2 is:
    1    2
    ......
1¦ 1    2
2¦ 2    4
Press x-key to quit; other key to continue.
x
Bye!
C:\app>
```

ANALYSIS The purpose of the program in Listing 17.2 is to build a multiplication table based on the integer given by the user. The program can continue building multiplication tables until the user presses the *x* key to quit. The program also stops execution if the malloc() function fails.

To show you how to use the free() function, the program allocates a temporary memory storage to hold the items of a multiplication table. As soon as the content of a multiplication table is printed out, the allocated memory is released by calling the free() function.

Lines 5 and 6 declare two functions, DataMultiply() and TablePrint(), respectively. The former is for performing multiplication and building a table, whereas the latter prints out the table on the screen. The definitions of the two functions are given in lines 38–45 and lines 47–64, respectively.

Inside the main() function, there is a while loop in lines 16–33 that keeps asking the user to enter an integer number (see lines 17 and 18) and then building a multiplication table based on the integer.

To hold the result of the multiplication, the statement in line 20 allocates a memory storage that has the size of max*max*sizeof(int), where the int variable max contains the integer value entered by the user. Note that the sizeof(int) expression gives the byte number of the int data type of the computer on which the program is being run.

If the malloc() function returns a null pointer, the return value of the main() function is set to 1 to indicate an abnormal termination (see line 28), and the while loop is stopped by assigning the key variable with 'x' in line 29.

Otherwise, if the malloc() function allocates a memory storage successfully, the DataMultiply() function is called in line 22 to calculate each multiplication. The results are saved into the memory storage pointed to by the ptr_int pointer. Then the multiplication table is printed out by calling the TablePrint() function in line 23.

As soon as I no longer need to keep the multiplication table, I call the free() function in line 24 to release the allocated memory storage pointed to by the ptr_int pointer.

17

If I did not release the memory, the program would take more and more memory as the user keeps entering integer numbers to build more multiplication tables. Eventually, the program would either crash the operating system or be forced to quit. By using the free() and malloc() functions, I am able to keep running the program by taking the exact amount of memory storage I need, no more and no less.

The calloc() Function

Besides the malloc() function, you can also use the calloc() function to allocate a memory storage dynamically. The differences between the two functions are that the latter takes two arguments and that the memory space allocated by calloc() is always initialized to 0. There is no such guarantee that the memory space allocated by malloc() is initialized to 0.

The syntax for the calloc() function is

```
#include <stdlib.h>
void *calloc(size_t nitem, size_t size);
```

Here *nitem* is the number of items you want to save in the allocated memory space. *size* gives the number of bytes that each item takes. The calloc() function returns a void pointer too.

If the calloc() function fails to allocate a piece of memory space, it returns a null pointer.

Listing 17.3 contains an example of using the calloc() function. The initial value of the memory space allocated by calloc() is printed out.

TYPE **Listing 17.3. Using the calloc() function.**

```
1:   /* 17L03.c: Using the calloc() function */
2:   #include <stdio.h>
3:   #include <stdlib.h>
4:   /* main() function */
5:   main()
6:   {
7:       float *ptr1, *ptr2;
8:       int i, n;
9:       int termination = 1;
10:
11:      n = 5;
12:      ptr1 = calloc(n, sizeof(float));
13:      ptr2 = malloc(n * sizeof(float));
14:      if (ptr1 == NULL)
15:          printf("malloc() failed.\n");
16:      else if (ptr2 == NULL)
17:          printf("calloc() failed.\n");
18:      else {
19:          for (i=0; i<n; i++)
20:              printf("ptr1[%d]=%5.2f,  ptr2[%d]=%5.2f\n",
21:                  i, *(ptr1 + i), i, *(ptr2 + i));
```

continues

17

Listing 17.3. continued

```
22:        free(ptr1);
23:        free(ptr2);
24:        termination = 0;
25:    }
26:    return termination;
27: }
```

The following output appears on the screen after running the executable 17L03.exe:

OUTPUT
```
C:\app>17L03
ptr1[0] = 0.00,   ptr2[0] = 7042.23
ptr1[1] = 0.00,   ptr2[1] = 1427.00
ptr1[2] = 0.00,   ptr2[2] = 2787.14
ptr1[3] = 0.00,   ptr2[3] =    0.00
ptr1[4] = 0.00,   ptr2[4] = 5834.73
C:\app>
```

ANALYSIS   The purpose of the program in Listing 17.3 is to use the calloc() function to allocate a piece of memory space. To prove that the calloc() function initializes the allocated memory space to 0, the initial values of the memory are printed out. Also, another piece of memory space is allocated by using the malloc() function, and the initial values of the second memory space is printed out too.

As you see in line 12, the calloc() function is called with two arguments passed to it: the int variable n and the sizeof(float) expression. The float pointer variable ptr1 is assigned the value returned by the calloc() function.

Likewise, the malloc() function is called in line 13. This function only takes one argument that specifies the total number of bytes that the allocated memory should have. The value returned by the malloc() function is then assigned to another float pointer variable, ptr2.

From lines 12 and 13, you can tell that the calloc() and malloc() functions actually plan to allocate two pieces of memory space with the same size.

The if-else-if-else statement in lines 14–25 checks the two values returned from the calloc() and malloc() functions and then prints out the initial values from the two allocated memory spaces if the two return values are not null.

I ran the executable program in Listing 17.3 several times. Each time, the initial value from the memory space allocated by the calloc() function was always 0. But there is no guarantee for the memory space allocated by the malloc() function. The output shown here is one of the results from running the executable program on my machine. You can see that there is some "garbage" in the memory space allocated by the malloc() function. That is, the initial value in the memory is unpredictable. (Sometimes, the initial value in a memory block allocated by the malloc() function is 0. But it is not guaranteed that the initial value is always 0 each time when the malloc() function is called.)

17

The `realloc()` Function

The `realloc()` function gives you a means to change the size of a piece of memory space allocated by the `malloc()` function, the `calloc()` function, or even itself.

The syntax for the `realloc()` function is

```
#include <stdlib.h>
void *realloc(void *block, size_t size);
```

Here *block* is the pointer to the start of a piece of memory space previously allocated. *size* specifies the total byte number you want to change to. The `realloc()` function returns a void pointer.

The `realloc()` function returns a null pointer if it fails to reallocate a piece of memory space.

The `realloc()` function is equivalent to the `malloc()` function if the first argument passed to `realloc()` is NULL. In other words, the following two statements are equivalent:

```
ptr_flt = realloc(NULL, 10 * sizeof(float));
ptr_flt = malloc(10 * sizeof(float));
```

Also, you can use the `realloc()` function as the `free()` function. You do this by passing 0 to `realloc()` as its second argument. For instance, to release a block of memory pointed to by a pointer `ptr`, you can either call the `free()` function like this:

```
free(ptr);
```

or use the `realloc()` function in the following way:

```
realloc(ptr, 0);
```

The program in Listing 17.4 demonstrates the use of the `realloc()` function in memory reallocation.

TYPE   **Listing 17.4. Using the `realloc()` function.**

```
 1:  /* 17L04.c: Using the realloc() function */
 2:  #include <stdio.h>
 3:  #include <stdlib.h>
 4:  #include <string.h>
 5:  /* function declaration */
 6:  void StrCopy(char *str1, char *str2);
 7:  /* main() function */
 8:  main()
 9:  {
10:     char *str[4] = {"There's music in the sighing of a reed;",
11:                     "There's music in the gushing of a rill;",
12:                     "There's music in all things if men had ears;",
13:                     "There earth is but an echo of the spheres.\n"
14:                     };
```

continues

Listing 17.4. continued

```
15:    char *ptr;
16:    int i;
17:
18:    int termination = 0;
19:
20:    ptr = malloc((strlen(str[0]) + 1) * sizeof(char));
21:    if (ptr == NULL){
22:      printf("malloc() failed.\n");
23:      termination = 1;
24:    }
25:    else{
26:      StrCopy(str[0], ptr);
27:      printf("%s\n", ptr);
28:      for (i=1; i<4; i++){
29:        ptr = realloc(ptr, (strlen(str[i]) + 1) * sizeof(char));
30:        if (ptr == NULL){
31:          printf("realloc() failed.\n");
32:          termination = 1;
33:          i = 4;     /* break the fro loop */
34:        }
35:        else{
36:          StrCopy(str[i], ptr);
37:          printf("%s\n", ptr);
38:        }
39:      }
40:    }
41:    free(ptr);
42:    return termination;
43: }
44: /* function definition */
45: void StrCopy(char *str1, char *str2)
46: {
47:    int i;
48:
49:    for (i=0; str1[i]; i++)
50:        str2[i] = str1[i];
51:    str2[i] = '\0';
52: }
```

The following output is obtained by running the executable 17L04.exe:

OUTPUT

```
C:\app>17L04
There's music in the sighing of a reed;
There's music in the gushing of a rill;
There's music in all things if men had ears;
There earth is but an echo of the spheres.
C:\app>
```

ANALYSIS   The purpose of the program in Listing 17.4 is to allocate a block of memory space to hold a character string. There are four strings in this example, and the length of each string may vary. I use the realloc() function to adjust the size of the previously allocated memory so it can hold a new string.

17

As you can see in lines 10–13, there are four character strings containing a lovely poem written by Lord Byron. (You can tell that I love Byron's poems.) Here I use an array of pointers, str, to refer to the strings.

A piece of memory space is first allocated by calling the malloc() function in line 20. The size of the memory space is determined by the (strlen(str[0])+1)*sizeof(char) expression. As mentioned earlier, because the C function strlen() does not count the null character at the end of a string, you have to remember to allocate one more piece of memory to hold the full size of a string. The sizeof(char) expression is used here for portability, although the char data type is 1 byte long on most computers.

Exercise 4 at the end of this lesson asks you to rewrite the program in Listing 17.4 and replace the malloc() and free() functions with their equivalent formats of the realloc() functions.

If the malloc() function doesn't fail, the content of the first string pointed to by the str[0] pointer is copied to the block memory allocated by malloc(). To do this, a function called StrCopy() is called in line 26. Lines 45–52 give the definition of StrCopy().

The for loop, in lines 28–39, copies the remaining three strings, one at a time, to the block of memory pointed to by ptr. Each time, the realloc() function is called in line 29 to reallocate and adjust the previously allocated memory space based on the length of the next string whose content is about to be copied to the memory block.

After the content of a string is copied to the memory block, the content is also printed out (see lines 27 and 37).

In this example, a block of memory space is allocated and adjusted based on the length of each of the four strings. The realloc() function, as well as the malloc() function, does the memory allocation and adjustment dynamically.

Summary

In this lesson you've learned the following:

- [ ] In C, there are four functions that can be used to allocate, reallocate, or release a block of memory space dynamically at runtime.
- [ ] The malloc() function allocates a block of memory whose size is specified by the argument passed to the function.
- [ ] The free() function is used to free up a block of memory space previously allocated by the malloc(), calloc(), or realloc() function.
- [ ] The calloc() function can do the same job as the malloc() function. In addition, the calloc() function can initialize the allocated memory space to 0.

☐ The `realloc()` function is used to reallocate a block of memory that has been allocated by the `malloc()` or `calloc()` function.

☐ If a null pointer is passed to the `realloc()` function as its first argument, the function acts like the `malloc()` function.

☐ If the second argument of the `realloc()` function is set to 0, the `realloc()` function is equivalent to the `free()` function that releases a block of allocated memory.

☐ You have to include the header file `stdlib.h` before you can call the `malloc()`, `calloc()`, `realloc()`, or `free()` function.

☐ You should always check the values returned from the `malloc()`, `calloc()`, or `realloc()` function, before you use the allocated memory made by these functions.

In the next lesson you'll learn more about data types in C.

Q&A

Q Why do you need to allocate memory at runtime?

A Very often, you don't know the exact sizes of arrays until your program is being run. You might be able to estimate the sizes for those arrays, but if you make those arrays too big, you waste the memory. On the other hand, if you make those arrays too small, you're going to lose data. The best way is to allocate blocks of memory dynamically and precisely for those arrays when their sizes are determined at runtime. There are four C library functions, `malloc()`, `calloc()`, `realloc()`, and `free()`, which you can use in memory allocation at runtime.

Q What does it mean if the `malloc()` function returns a null pointer?

A If the `malloc()` function returns a null pointer, it means the function fails to allocate a block of memory whose size is specified by the argument passed to the function. Normally, the failure of the `malloc()` function is caused by the fact that there is not enough memory to allocate. You should always check the value returned by the `malloc()` function to make sure that the function has been successful before you use the block of memory allocated by the function.

Q What are the differences between the `calloc()` and `malloc()` functions?

A Basically, there are two differences between the `calloc()` and `malloc()` functions, although both of them can do the same job. The first difference is that the `calloc()` function takes two arguments, while the `malloc()` function takes only one. The second one is that the `calloc()` function initializes the allocated memory space to 0, whereas there is no such guarantee made by the `malloc()` function.

17

Q Is the `free()` function necessary?

A Yes. The `free()` function is very necessary, and you should use it to free up allocated memory blocks as soon as you don't need them. As you know, memory is a limited resource in a computer. Your program shouldn't take too much memory space when it allocates blocks of memory. One way to reduce the size of memory taken by your program is to use the `free()` function to release the unused allocated memory in time.

Workshop

To help solidify your understanding of this hour's lesson, you are encouraged to answer the quiz questions and finish the exercises provided in the Workshop before you move to the next lesson. The answers and hints to the questions and exercises are given in Appendix E, "Answers to Quiz Questions and Exercises."

Quiz

1. Provided that the `char` data type is 1 byte, the `int` data type is 2 bytes, and the `float` data type is 4 bytes, how many bytes of memory do the following functions try to allocate?

   ☐ `malloc(100 * sizeof(int))`

   ☐ `calloc(200, sizeof(char))`

   ☐ `realloc(NULL, 50 * sizeof(float))`

   ☐ `realloc(ptr, 0)`

2. Given an `int` pointer, `ptr`, that is pointing to a block of memory that can hold 100 integers, if you want to reallocate the memory block to hold up to 150 integers, which of the two following statements do you use?

   ☐ `ptr = realloc(ptr, 50 * sizeof(int));`

   ☐ `ptr = realloc(ptr, 150 * sizeof(int));`

3. After the following statements are executed successfully, what is the final size of the allocated memory block pointed to by the `ptr` pointer?

```
. . .
ptr = malloc(300 * sizeof(int));
. . .
ptr = realloc(ptr, 500 * sizeof(int));
. . .
ptr = realloc(ptr, 60 * sizeof(int));
```

4. What is the final size of the allocated memory block pointed to by the `ptr` pointer, if the following statements are executed successfully?

```
. . .
ptr = calloc(100 * sizeof(char));
. . .
free(ptr);
ptr = realloc(NULL, 200 * sizeof(char));
. . .
ptr = realloc(ptr, 0);
```

Exercises

1. Write a program to ask the user to enter the total number of bytes he or she wants to allocate. Then, initialize the allocated memory with consecutive integers, starting from 1. Add all the integers contained by the memory block and print out the final result on the screen.

2. Write a program that allocates a block of memory space to hold 100 items of the `float` data type by calling the `calloc()` function. Then, reallocate the block of memory in order to hold 50 more items of the `float` data type.

3. Write a program to ask the user to enter the total number of `float` data. Then use the `calloc()` and `malloc()` functions to allocate two memory blocks with the same size specified by the number, and print out the initial values of the two memory blocks.

4. Rewrite the program in Listing 17.4. This time, use the two special cases of the `realloc()` function to replace the `malloc()` and `free()` functions.

Hour **18**

More Data Types and Functions

That's all there is, there isn't any more.

—*E. Barrymore*

In Hour 4, "Data Types and Names in C," you learned about most of the data types, such as char, int, float, and double. In Hour 15, "Functions in C," you learned the basics of using functions in C. In this hour, you'll learn more about data types and functions from the following topics:

- ☐ The enum data type
- ☐ The typedef statement
- ☐ Function recursion
- ☐ Command-line arguments

The enum **Data Type**

The C language provides you with an additional data type—the enum data type. enum is short for *enumerated*. The enumerated data type can be used to declare named integer constants. The enum data type makes the C program more readable and easier to maintain. (Another way to declare a named constant is to use the `#define` directive, which is introduced later in this book.)

Declaring the enum Data Type

The general form of the enum data type declaration is

```
enum tag_name {enumeration_list} variable_list;
```

Here `tag_name` is the name of the enumeration. `variable_list` gives a list of variable names that are of the enum data type. `enumeration_list` contains defined enumerated names that are used to represent integer constants. (Both `tag_name` and `variable_list` are optional.)

For instance, the following declares an enum data type with the tag name of `automobile`:

```
enum automobile {sedan, pick_up, sport_utility};
```

Given this, you can define enum variables like this:

```
enum automobile  domestic, foreign;
```

Here the two enum variables, `domestic` and `foreign`, are defined.

Of course, you can always declare and define a list of enum variables in a single statement, as shown in the general form of the enum declaration. Therefore, you can rewrite the enum declaration of `domestic` and `foreign` like this:

```
enum automobile {sedan, pick_up, sport_utility} domestic, foreign;
```

Assigning Values to enum Names

By default, the integer value associated with the leftmost name in the enumeration list field, surrounded by the braces (`{` and `}`), starts with 0, and the value of each name in the rest of the list increases by one from left to right. Therefore, in the previous example, `sedan`, `pick_up`, and `sport_utility` have the values of 0, 1, and 2, respectively.

In fact, you can assign integer values to enum names. Considering the previous example, you can initialize the enumerated names like this:

```
enum automobile {sedan = 60, pick_up = 30, sport_utility = 10};
```

Now, `sedan` represents the value of 60, `pick_up` has the value of 30, and `sport_utility` assumes the value of 10.

The program shown in Listing 18.1 prints out the values of enum names.

TYPE **Listing 18.1. Defining** enum **data types.**

```
1:  /* 18L01.c: Defining enum data types */
2:  #include <stdio.h>
3:  /* main() function */
4:  main()
5:  {
6:      enum language {human=100,
7:                         animal=50,
8:                         computer};
9:      enum days{SUN,
10:               MON,
11:               TUE,
12:               WED,
13:               THU,
14:               FRI,
15:               SAT};
16:
17:     printf("human: %d,  animal: %d,  computer: %d\n",
18:         human, animal, computer);
19:     printf("SUN: %d\n", SUN);
20:     printf("MON: %d\n", MON);
21:     printf("TUE: %d\n", TUE);
22:     printf("WED: %d\n", WED);
23:     printf("THU: %d\n", THU);
24:     printf("FRI: %d\n", FRI);
25:     printf("SAT: %d\n", SAT);
26:
27:     return 0;
28: }
```

The following output is shown on the screen after the executable, 18L01.exe, of the program in Listing 18.1 is created and executed:

OUTPUT
```
C:\app>18L01
human: 100,  animal: 50,  computer: 51
SUN: 0
MON: 1
TUE: 2
WED: 3
THU: 4
FRI: 5
SAT: 6
C:\app>
```

ANALYSIS The purpose of the program in Listing 18.1 is to show you the default values of the enum names, as well as the values assigned to some enum names by the programmer.

As you can tell, there are two enum declarations, in lines 6–8 and lines 9–15, respectively. Note that the variable lists in the two enum declarations are omitted because there is no need for the variable lists in the program.

The first declaration has a tag name called language and three enumerated names, human, animal, and computer. In addition, human is assigned the value of 100; animal is initialized with 50. According to the enum definition, the default value of computer is the value of animal increased by 1. Therefore, in this case, the default value of computer is 51.

The output made by the statement in line 17 shows that the values of human, animal, and computer are indeed 100, 50, and 51.

The second enum declaration in the program contains seven items with their default values. Then, lines 19–25 print out these default values one at a time. It is not surprising to see that the values represented by the enumerated names, SUN, MON, TUE, WED, THU, FRI, and SAT, are 0, 1, 2, 3, 4, 5, and 6, respectively.

Now, let's look at another example, shown in Listing 18.2, that demonstrates how to use the enum data type.

TYPE   **Listing 18.2. Using the enum data type.**

```
 1:  /* 18L02.c: Using the enum data type */
 2:  #include <stdio.h>
 3:  /* main() function */
 4:  main()
 5:  {
 6:     enum units{penny = 1,
 7:               nickel = 5,
 8:               dime = 10,
 9:               quarter = 25,
10:               dollar = 100};
11:     int money_units[5] = {
12:               dollar,
13:               quarter,
14:               dime,
15:               nickel,
16:               penny};
17:     char *unit_name[5] = {
18:               "dollar(s)",
19:               "quarter(s)",
20:               "dime(s)",
21:               "nickel(s)",
22:               "penny(s)"};
23:     int cent, tmp, i;
24:
25:     printf("Enter a monetary value in cents:\n");
26:     scanf("%d", &cent);  /* get input from the user */
27:     printf("Which is equivalent to:\n");
28:     tmp = 0;
29:     for (i=0; i<5; i++){
30:        tmp = cent / money_units[i];
31:        cent -= tmp * money_units[i];
32:        if (tmp)
33:          printf("%d %s ", tmp, unit_name[i]);
34:     }
```

18

```
35:    printf("\n");
36:    return 0;
37: }
```

While the executable (18L02.exe) is being executed, I enter 141 (for 141 cents) and obtain the following output from the screen:

```
C:\app>18L02
Enter a monetary value in cents:
141
Which is equivalent to:
1 dollar(s) 1 quarter(s) 1 dime(s) 1 nickel(s) 1 penny(s)
C:\app>
```

The purpose of the program in Listing 18.2 is to use the enum data type to represent the value of the amount of money entered by the user.

Inside the main() function, an enum declaration with a tag name of units is made in lines 6–10. The numbers assigned to the enumerated names are based on their ratios to the unit of cent. For instance, one dollar is equal to 100 cents. Therefore, the enum name dollar is assigned the value of 100.

After the enum declaration, an int array, called money_units, is declared, and is initialized with the enumerated names from the enum declaration. According to the definition of the enum data type, the declaration of the money_units array in the program is actually equivalent to the following one:

```
int money_units[5] = {
            100,
            25,
            10,
            5,
            1};
```

So now you see that you can use enumerated names, instead of integer numbers, to make up other expressions or declarations in your program.

In lines 17–22, an array of pointers, unit_name, is declared and initialized. (The usage of arrays of pointers was introduced in Hour 16, "Applying Pointers.")

Then, the statement in line 15 asks the user to enter an integer number in the unit of cent. The scanf() function in line 26 stores the number entered by the user to an int variable called cent.

The for loop in lines 29–34 divides the entered number and represents it in a dollar-quarter-dime-nickel-penny format.

Note that the integer constants represented by the enumerated names are used in lines 30 and 31, through the money_units array. If the value of a unit is not 0, a corresponding string pointed to by the array of pointers, unit_name, is printed out in line 33. Therefore, when I enter 141 (in unit of cent), I see its equivalent in the output: 1 dollar(s) 1 quarter(s) 1 dime(s) 1 nickel(s) 1 penny(s).

Making typedef Definitions

You can create your own names for data types with the help of the typedef keyword in C, and make those name synonyms for the data types. Then, you can use the name synonyms, instead of the data types themselves, in your programs. Often, the name synonyms defined by typedef can make your program more readable.

For instance, you can declare TWO_BYTE as a synonym for the int data type:

```
typedef  int  TWO_BYTE;
```

Then, you can start to use TWO_BYTE to declare integer variables like this:

```
TWO_BYTE i, j;
```

which is equivalent to

```
int i, j;
```

Remember that a typedef definition must be made before the synonym created in the definition is used in any declarations in your program.

Why Use typedef?

There are several advantages to using typedef definitions. First, you can consolidate complex data types into a single word and then use the word in variable declarations in your program. In this way, you don't need to type a complex declaration over and over, which helps to avoid typing errors.

The second advantage is that you just need to update a typedef definition, which fixes every use of that typedef definition if the data type is changed in the future.

typedef is so useful, in fact, that there is a header file called stddef.h included in the ANSI-standard C that contains a dozen typedef definitions. For instance, size_t is a typedef for the value returned by the sizeof operator.

The program shown in Listing 18.3 is an example of using typedef definitions.

TYPE **Listing 18.3. Using typedef definitions.**

```
1:   /* 18L03.c: Using typedef definitions */
2:   #include <stdio.h>
3:   #include <stdlib.h>
4:   #include <string.h>
5:
```

```
6:  enum constants{ITEM_NUM = 3,
7:                  DELT='a'-'A'};
8:  typedef char *STRING[ITEM_NUM];
9:  typedef char *PTR_STR;
10: typedef char BIT8;
11: typedef int BIT16;
12:
13: void Convert2Upper(PTR_STR str1, PTR_STR str2);
14:
15: main()
16: {
17:     STRING str;
18:     STRING moon = {"Whatever we wear",
19:                    "we become beautiful",
20:                    "moon viewing!"};
21:     BIT16 i;
22:     BIT16 term = 0;
23:
24:     for (i=0; i<ITEM_NUM; i++){
25:       str[i] = malloc((strlen(moon[i])+1) * sizeof(BIT8));
26:       if (str[i] == NULL){
27:         printf("malloc() failed.\n");
28:         term = 1;
29:         i = ITEM_NUM;   /* break the for loop */
30:       }
31:       Convert2Upper(moon[i], str[i]);
32:       printf("%s\n", moon[i]);
33:     }
34:     for (i=0; i<ITEM_NUM; i++){
35:       printf("\n%s", str[i]);
36:       free (str[i]);
37:     }
38:
39:     return term;
40: }
41: /* function definition */
42: void Convert2Upper(PTR_STR str1, PTR_STR str2)
43: {
44:     BIT16 i;
45:
46:     for (i=0; str1[i]; i++){
47:       if ((str1[i] >= 'a') &&
48:           (str1[i] <= 'z'))
49:         str2[i] = str1[i] - DELT;
50:       else
51:         str2[i] = str1[i];
52:     }
53:     str2[i] = '\0';   /* add null character */
54: }
```

I have the following output displayed on the screen after running the executable, 18L03.exe, of the program in Listing 18.3:

```
C:\app>18L03
Whatever we wear
we become beautiful
moon viewing!

WHATEVER WE WEAR
WE BECOME BEAUTIFUL
MOON VIEWING!
C:\app>
```

The purpose of the program in Listing 18.3 is to show you how to create your own names for data types such as char and int. The program in Listing 18.3 converts all characters in a Japanese haiku into their uppercase counterparts.

In lines 3 and 4, two more header files, stdlib.h and string.h, are included because the malloc() and strlen() functions are invoked later in the program.

An enum declaration is made in lines 6 and 7 with two enumerated names, ITEM_NUM and DELT. In addition, ITEM_NUM is assigned the value of 3 because there are three strings in the haiku. DELT contains the value of the difference between a lowercase character and its uppercase counterpart in the ASCII code. In line 7, the values of 'a' and 'A' are used to calculate the difference.

In lines 8–11, I define names, STRING, PTR_STR, BIT8, and BIT16, for a char array of pointers with three elements, a char pointer, a char, and an int data type, respectively, so that I can use these names as synonyms to these data types in the program.

For instance, the prototype of the Convert2Upper() function in line 13 contains two arguments that are all char pointers declared with PTR_STR.

In lines 17–20, two arrays of pointers, str and moon, are declared with STRING. moon is initialized to point to the strings of the Japanese haiku. In lines 21 and 22, two int variables, i and term, are declared with BIT16.

The for loop in lines 24–33 allocates enough memory space dynamically based on the size of the haiku. The Conver2Upper() function is then called in line 31 to copy strings referenced by moon to the memory locations pointed to by str and to convert all lowercase characters to their uppercase counterparts as well. Line 32 prints out the strings referenced by moon. The definition of the Conver2Upper() function is shown in lines 42–54.

In lines 34–37, another for loop is made to print out the content from the memory locations referenced by str. There are a total of three strings with uppercase characters in the content. After a string is displayed on the screen, the memory space allocated for the string is released by calling the free() function.

On the screen, you see two copies of the haiku—the original one and the one with all-uppercase characters.

Recursive Functions

You already know that in C a function can be called by another function. But can a function call itself? The answer is yes. A function can call itself from a statement inside the body of the function itself. Such a function is said to be *recursive*.

Listing 18.4 contains an example of calling a recursive function to add integers from 1 to 100.

TYPE   **Listing 18.4. Calling a recursive function.**

```
1:  /* 18L04.c: Calling a recursive function */
2:  #include <stdio.h>
3:
4:  enum con{MIN_NUM = 0,
5:           MAX_NUM = 100};
6:
7:  int fRecur(int n);
8:
9:  main()
10: {
11:    int i, sum1, sum2;
12:
13:    sum1 = sum2 = 0;
14:    for (i=1; i<=MAX_NUM; i++)
15:       sum1 += i;
16:    printf("The value of sum1 is %d.\n", sum1);
17:    sum2 = fRecur(MAX_NUM);
18:    printf("The value returned by fRecur() is %d.\n", sum2);
19:
20:    return 0;
21: }
22: /* function definition */
23: int fRecur(int n)
24: {
25:    if (n == MIN_NUM)
26:       return 0;
27:    return  fRecur(n - 1) + n;
28: }
```

After the executable 18L04.exe is created and executed, the following output is displayed on the screen:

OUTPUT
```
C:\app>18L04
The value of sum1 is 5050.
The value returned by fRecur() is 5050.
C:\app>
```

ANALYSIS   In the program in Listing 18.4, a recursive function, fRecur(), is declared in line 7 and defined in lines 23–28.

You can see from the definition of the fRecur() function that the recursion is stopped in line 26 if the incoming int variable, n, is equal to the value contained by the enum name MIN_NUM. Otherwise, the fRecur() function is called by itself over and over in line 27. Note that each time the fRecur() function is called, the integer argument passed to the function is decreased by one.

Now, let's have a look at the main() function of the program. The for loop, shown in lines 14 and 15, adds integers from 1 to the value represented by another enum name, MAX_NUM. In lines 4 and 5, MIN_NUM and MAX_NUM are respectively assigned 0 and 100 in an enum declaration. The printf() function in line 16 then prints out the sum of the addition made by the for loop.

In line 17, the recursive function, fRecur(), is called and passed with an integer argument starting at the value of MAX_NUM. The value returned by the fRecur() function is then assigned to an int variable, sum2.

Eventually, the value saved by sum2 is printed out in line 18. From the output, you can see that the execution of the recursive function fRecur() actually produces the same result as the for loop inside the main() function.

NOTE

> Recursive functions are useful in making clearer and simpler implementations of algorithms. On the other hand, however, recursive functions may run slower than their iterative equivalents due to the overhead of repeated function calls.
>
> Function arguments and local variables of a program are stored temporarily in a block of memory called the *stack*. Each call to a recursive function makes a new copy of the arguments and local variables. The new copy is then put on the stack. If you see your recursive function behaving strangely, it's probably overwriting other data stored on the stack.

Revisiting the main() Function

As you've learned, each C program should have one and only one main() function. The execution of a program starts and ends at its main() function.

As with other functions in C, you can pass arguments to a main() function. So far, I've been using the void keyword in the definition of the main() function to indicate that there are no arguments passed to the function. Now, the question is how to do it if you want to pass information to the main() function.

Command-Line Arguments

Because each C program starts at its `main()` function, information is usually passed to the `main()` function via command-line arguments.

A *command-line argument* is a parameter that follows a program's name when the program is invoked from the operating system's command line. For instance, given a C program, `test.c`, whose executable file is called `test.exe`, if you run the program from a DOS prompt like this,

```
C:\app>test.exe argument1 argument2 argument3
```

`argument1`, `argument2`, and `argument3` are called command-line arguments to the `main()` function in the `test.c` program.

Of course, you can simply omit an executable file's extension, `.exe`, when you run it from a DOS prompt.

The next subsection teaches you how to receive command-line arguments.

Receiving Command-Line Arguments

There are two built-in arguments in the `main()` function that can be used to receive command-line arguments. Usually, the name of the first argument is `argc`, and it is used to store the number of arguments on the command line. The second argument is called `argv` and is a pointer to an array of `char` pointers. Each element in the array of pointers points to a command-line argument that is treated as a string.

In order to use `argc` and `argv`, you have to declare them in the `main()` function in your program like this:

```
data_type_specifier main(int argc, char *argv[])
{
    . . .
}
```

Here *data_type_specifier* specifies the data type returned by the `main()` function. By default, the data type returned by the `main()` function is `int`. If the `main()` does not return any value, you should put the `void` keyword in front of the `main()` function definition.

Let's continue to use the example shown in the last section. Suppose that the `main()` function defined in the `test.c` program looks like this:

```
void main(int argc, char *argv[])
{
    . . .
}
```

If you run the executable file of the program from a DOS prompt,

```
C:\app>test.exe argument1 argument2 argument3
```

the value received by argc is 4, because the name of the program itself is counted as the first command-line argument. Accordingly, argv[0] holds the string of the path and program name C:\app\test.exe, and argv[1], argv[2], and argv[3] contain the strings of argument1, argument2, and argument3, respectively. (Note that C:\app\ is the path to the executable file on my machine.)

The program in Listing 18.5 is another example of passing command-line arguments to the main() function.

Listing 18.5. Passing command-line arguments to the main() function.

```
1:   /* 18L05.c: Command-line arguments */
2:   #include <stdio.h>
3:
4:   main (int argc, char *argv[])
5:   {
6:       int i;
7:
8:       printf("The value received by argc is %d.\n", argc);
9:       printf("There are %d command-line arguments passed to main().\n",
10:          argc);
11:
12:      printf("The first command-line argument is: %s\n", argv[0]);
13:      printf("The rest of the command-line arguments are:\n");
14:      for (i=1; i<argc; i++)
15:         printf("%s\n", argv[i]);
16:
17:      return 0;
18:  }
```

After the executable, 18L05.exe, is executed and passed with several command-line arguments, the following output is displayed on the screen:

```
C:\app>18L05 Hello, world!
The value received by argc is 3.
There are 3 command-line arguments passed to main().
The first command-line argument is: C:\app\18L05.EXE
The rest of the command-line arguments are:
Hello,
world!
C:\app>
```

ANALYSIS The purpose of the program in Listing 18.5 is to show you how to check the number of command-line arguments and print out the strings that hold the arguments entered by the user.

18

Note that there are two arguments, argc and argv, that are declared in line 4 for the main() function. Then, the statements in lines 8 and 9 print out the value of the total number of arguments held by argc. If there is no command-line argument entered by the user, argc contains the default value of 1 because the name of the program itself is counted as the first argument.

Line 12 prints out the first string saved in the memory location pointed to by argv[0]. As you can see from the output, the content of the first string is the executable file name of the program in Listing 18.5, plus the path to the executable file.

The for loop in lines 14 and 15 displays the rest of the strings that contain the command-line arguments entered by the user. In this example, I enter two command-line argument strings, "Hello," and "world!", which are shown back on the screen after the execution of the for loop.

NOTE

> argc and argv are normally used as the two built-in arguments in the main() function, but you can use other names to replace them in their declarations.
>
> In addition to these two arguments, some compilers may support another argument to the main() function. The third argument is a pointer to an array of pointers that are used to point to memory locations containing the environmental parameters, such as the paths, the Windows boot directory name, the temporary directory name, and so on.

18

Summary

In this lesson you've learned the following:

- ☐ The enum (that is, enumerated) data type can be used to declare named integer constants.
- ☐ By default, the first enum name starts with the value of 0. Each name in the rest of the list increases by one from the value contained by the name on its left side.
- ☐ If needed, you can assign any integer values to enumerated names.
- ☐ You can create your own names for data types with the help of the typedef keyword. Those names can then be used as synonyms for the data types.
- ☐ In ANSI C, there is a header file called stddef.h that contains a dozen typedef definitions.
- ☐ A function in C can be made to call itself. Such a function is said to be recursive.
- ☐ You can use command-line arguments to pass information to the main() function in your program.

☐ There are two built-in arguments to the `main()` function. The executable filename you entered from the operating system's command line is counted as the first command-line argument.

☐ The first built-in argument receives the number of command-line arguments entered by the user. The second built-in argument is a pointer to an array of pointers that refers to the strings of command-line arguments.

In the next lesson you'll learn about collecting variables of different types with structures.

Q&A

Q What can you do with the `enum` data type?

A The `enum` data type can be used to declare names that represent integer constants. You can use the default values held by `enum` names, or you can assign values to `enum` names and use them later in the program. The `enum` data type makes the C program more readable and easier to maintain, because you can use words which you understand as the names of `enum`, and you will only have to go to one place to update the values when needed.

Q Why do you need to use the `typedef` keyword?

A By using the `typedef` keyword, you can define your own names to represent the data types in C. You can represent complex data types in a single word and then use that word in subsequent variable declarations. In this way, you can avoid typing errors when writing a complex declaration over and over. Also, if a data type is changed in the future, you just need to update the `typedef` definition of the data type, which fixes every use of the `typedef` definition.

Q Does a recursive function help to improve the performance of a program?

A Not really. Normally, a recursive function only makes the implementations of some algorithms clearer and simpler. A recursive function may slow down the speed of a program because of the overhead of repeated function calls.

Q What is the first command-line argument passed to a `main()` function?

A The first command-line argument passed to a `main()` function is the executable filename entered by the user, plus the path to the executable file. The executable file is created from the program that contains the `main()` function. The first command-line argument is stored in the memory location referenced by the first element in the array of pointers that is declared as the second argument to the `main()` function.

Workshop

To help solidify your understanding of this hour's lesson, you are encouraged to answer the quiz questions and finish the exercises provided in the Workshop before you move to the next lesson. The answers and hints to the questions and exercises are given in Appendix E, "Answers to Quiz Questions and Exercises."

Quiz

1. What are the values represented by the following enum names?

```
enum months { Jan, Feb, Mar, Apr,
              May, Jun, Jul, Aug,
              Sep, Oct, Nov, Dec };
```

2. What are the values represented by the following enum names?

```
enum tag { name1,
           name2 = 10,
           name3,
           name4 };
```

3. Which statements in the following are equivalent in the variable declaration?

   ☐ typedef long int BYTE32; BYTE32 x, y, z;

   ☐ typedef char *STRING[16]; STRING str1, str2, str3;

   ☐ long int x, y, z;

   ☐ char *str1[16], *str2[16], *str3[16];

4. Can you pass some command-line arguments to a main() function that has the following definition?

```
int main(void)
{
   . . .
}
```

Exercises

1. Write a program to print out the values represented by the enumerated names declared in Quiz question 2.

2. Given the following declarations:

```
typedef char WORD;
typedef int SHORT;
typedef long LONG;
typedef float FLOAT;
typedef double DFLOAT;
```

   write a program to measure the sizes of the synonyms to the data types.

18

3. Rewrite the program in Listing 18.4. This time, add integers starting at the value of MIN_NUM instead of the value of MAX_NUM.

4. Write a program that accepts command-line arguments. If the number of command-line arguments, not including the name of the executable itself, is less than two, print out the usage format of the program and ask the user to reenter the command-line arguments. Otherwise, display all command-line arguments entered by the user.

Part V

V

Structure, Union, File I/O, and More

Hour

PART
V

Hour 19

Collecting Data Items of Different Types

The art of programming is the art of organizing complexity.

—*W. W. Dijkstra*

In Hour 12, "Storing Similar Data Items," you learned how to store data of the same type into arrays. In this hour, you'll learn to use structures to collect data items that have different data types. The following topics are covered in this lesson:

☐ Declaring and defining structures
☐ Referencing structure members
☐ Structures and pointers
☐ Structures and functions
☐ Arrays of structures

What Is a Structure?

As you've learned, arrays can be used to collect groups of variables of the same type. The question now is how to aggregate pieces of data that are not identically typed.

The answer is that you can group variables of different types with a data type called a *structure*. In C, a structure collects different data items in such a way that they can be referenced as a single unit.

There are several major differences between an array and a structure. Besides the fact that data items in a structure can have different types, each data item has its own name instead of a subscript value. In fact, data items in a structure are called *fields* or *members* of the structure.

The next two subsections teach you how to declare structures and define structure variables.

Declaring Structures

The general form to declare a structure is

```
struct struct_tag {
    data_type1 variable1;
    data_type2 variable2;
    data_type3 variable3;
    .
    .
    .
    };
```

Here struct is the keyword used in C to start a structure declaration. struct_tag is the tag name of the structure. variable1, variable2, and variable3 are the members of the structure. Their data types are specified respectively by data_type1, data_type2, and data_type3. As you can see, the declarations of the members have to be enclosed within the opening and closing braces ({ and }) in the structure declaration, and a semicolon (;) has to be included at the end of the declaration.

The following is an example of a structure declaration:

```
struct automobile {
    int year;
    char model[8];
    int engine_power;
    float weight;
    };
```

Here struct is used to start a structure declaration. automobile is the tag name of the structure. In this example, there are three types of variables, char, int, and float. The variables have their own names, such as year, model, engine_power, and weight.

Note that a structure tag name, like automobile, is a label to a structure. The compiler uses the tag name to identify the structure labeled by that tag name.

Defining Structure Variables

After declaring a structure, you can define the structure variables. For instance, the following structure variables are defined with the structure data type of `automobile` from the previous section:

```
struct automobile sedan, pick_up, sport_utility;
```

Here three structure variables, `sedan`, `pick_up`, and `sport_utility`, are defined by the structure of `automobile`. All three structure variables contain the four members of the structure data type of `automobile`.

Also, you can combine the structure declaration and definition into one statement like this:

```
struct automobile {
    int year;
    char model[8];
    int engine_power;
    float weight;
    } sedan, pick_up, sport_utility;
```

Here three structure variables, `sedan`, `pick_up`, and `sport_utility`, are defined with the structure data type of `automobile` in the single statement.

Referencing Structure Members with the Dot Operator

Now, let's see how to reference a structure member. Given the structure data type of `automobile` and the structure of `sedan`, for instance, I can access its member, `year`, and assign an integer to it in the following way:

```
sedan.year = 1997;
```

Here the structure name and its member's name are separated by the dot (.) operator so that the compiler knows that the integer value of 1997 is assigned to the variable called `year`, which is a member of the structure `sedan`.

Likewise, the following statement assigns the start address of the character array of `model`, which is another member of the structure `sedan`, to a `char` pointer, `ptr`:

```
ptr = sedan.model;
```

The program in Listing 19.1 gives another example to reference the members of a structure.

19

TYPE   **Listing 19.1. Referencing the members of a structure.**

```c
1:  /* 19L01.c Access to structure members */
2:  #include <stdio.h>
3:
4:  main(void)
5:  {
6:      struct computer {
7:          float cost;
8:          int year;
9:          int cpu_speed;
10:         char cpu_type[16];
11:         } model;
12:
13:     printf("The type of the CPU inside your computer?\n");
14:         gets(model.cpu_type);
15:     printf("The speed(MHz) of the CPU?\n");
16:         scanf("%d", &model.cpu_speed);
17:     printf("The year your computer was made?\n");
18:         scanf("%d", &model.year);
19:     printf("How much you paid for the computer?\n");
20:         scanf("%f", &model.cost);
21:
22:     printf("Here are what you entered:\n");
23:     printf("Year: %d\n", model.year);
24:     printf("Cost: $%6.2f\n", model.cost);
25:     printf("CPU type: %s\n", model.cpu_type);
26:     printf("CPU speed: %d MHz\n", model.cpu_speed);
27:
28:     return 0;
29: }
```

I have the following output shown on the screen after I run the executable (19L01.exe) of the program in Listing 19.1 and enter my answers to the questions (in the output, the bold characters or numbers are the answers entered from my keyboard):

OUTPUT
```
C:\app>19L01
The type of the CPU inside your computer?
Pentium
The speed(MHz) of the CPU?
100
The year your computer was made?
1996
How much you paid for the computer?
1234.56
Here are what you entered:
Year: 1996
Cost: $1234.56
CPU type: Pentium
CPU speed: 100 MHz
C:\app>
```

19

ANALYSIS   The purpose of the program in Listing 19.1 is to show you how to reference members of a structure. As you can see from the program, there is a structure called model that is defined with a structure data type of computer in lines 6–11. The structure has one float variable, two int variables, and one char array.

The statement in line 13 asks the user to enter the type of CPU (central processing unit) used inside his or her computer. Then, line 14 receives the string of the CPU type entered by the user and saves the string into the char array called cpu_type. Because cpu_type is a member of the model structure, the model.cpu_type expression is used in line 14 to reference the member of the structure. Note that the dot operator (.) is used to separate the two names in the expression.

Lines 15 and 16 ask for the CPU speed and store the value of an integer entered by the user to another member of the model structure—the int variable cpu_speed. Note that in line 16, the address-of operator (&)is prefixed to the model.cpu_speed expression inside the scanf() function because the argument should be an int pointer.

Likewise, lines 17 and 18 receive the value of the year in which the user's computer was made, and lines 19 and 20 get the number for the cost of the computer. After the execution, the int variable year and the float variable cost in the model structure contain the corresponding values entered by the user.

Then, lines 23–26 print out all values held by the members of the model structure. From the output, you can tell that each member of the structure has been accessed and assigned a number or string correctly.

Initializing Structures

A structure can be initialized by a list of data called *initializers*. Commas are used to separate data items in a list of data.

Listing 19.2 contains an example of initializing a structure before it's updated by the user.

TYPE   **Listing 19.2. Initializing a structure.**

```
1:   /* 19L02.c Initializing a structure */
2:   #include <stdio.h>
3:
4:   main(void)
5:   {
6:       struct employee {
7:           int id;
8:           char name[32];
9:           };
10:      /* structure initialization */
11:      struct employee info = {
12:          1,
```

continues

Listing 19.2. continued

```
13:        "B. Smith"
14:        };
15:
16:    printf("Here is a sample:\n");
17:    printf("Employee Name: %s\n", info.name);
18:    printf("Employee ID #: %04d\n\n", info.id);
19:
20:    printf("What's your name?\n");
21:        gets(info.name);
22:    printf("What's your ID number?\n");
23:        scanf("%d", &info.id);
24:
25:    printf("\nHere are what you entered:\n");
26:    printf("Name: %s\n", info.name);
27:    printf("ID #: %04d\n", info.id);
28:
29:    return 0;
30: }
```

When the executable 19L02.exe is being run, the initial content saved in a structure is displayed. Then, I enter my answers to the questions and get the updated information shown on the screen:

OUTPUT

```
C:\app>19L02
Here is a sample:
Employee Name: B. Smith
Employee ID #: 0001

What's your name?
T. Zhang
What's your ID number?
1234

Here are what you entered:
Name: T. Zhang
ID #: 1234
C:\app>
```

ANALYSIS The purpose of the program in Listing 19.2 is to initialize a structure and then ask the user to update the content held by the structure.

The structure data type, labeled as employee, is declared in lines 6–9. Then, the variable, info, is defined with the structure data type and initialized with the integer 1 and the string "B. Smith" in lines 11–14.

You can also combine the declaration, definition, and initialization of a structure into a single statement. Here's an example:

```
struct employee {
        int id;
        char name[32];
```

```
      } info = {
      1,
      "B. Smith"
      };
```

The statements in lines 17 and 18 display the initial contents stored by the two members of the info structure on the screen. Then, lines 20–23 ask the user to enter his or her name and employee ID number and save them into the two structure members, name and id, respectively.

Before the end of the program, the updated contents contained by the two members are printed out by the statements in lines 26 and 27.

Again, the dot operator (.) is used in the program to reference the structure members.

Structures and Function Calls

The C language allows you to pass an entire structure to a function. In addition, a function can return a structure back to its caller.

To show you how to pass a structure to a function, I rewrite the program in Listing 19.1 and create a function called DataReceive() in the program. The upgraded program is shown in Listing 19.3.

TYPE   **Listing 19.3. Passing a structure to a function.**

```
 1:  /* 19L03.c Passing a structure to a function */
 2:  #include <stdio.h>
 3:
 4:  struct computer {
 5:     float cost;
 6:     int year;
 7:     int cpu_speed;
 8:     char cpu_type[16];
 9:  };
10:  /* create synonym */
11:  typedef struct computer SC;
12:  /* function declaration */
13:  SC DataReceive(SC s);
14:
15:  main(void)
16:  {
17:     SC model;
18:
19:     model = DataReceive(model);
20:     printf("Here are what you entered:\n");
21:     printf("Year: %d\n", model.year);
22:     printf("Cost: $%6.2f\n", model.cost);
23:     printf("CPU type: %s\n", model.cpu_type);
```

19

continues

Listing 19.3. continued

```
24:      printf("CPU speed: %d MHz\n", model.cpu_speed);
25:
26:      return 0;
27: }
28: /* function definition */
29: SC DataReceive(SC s)
30: {
31:      printf("The type of the CPU inside your computer?\n");
32:          gets(s.cpu_type);
33:      printf("The speed(MHz) of the CPU?\n");
34:          scanf("%d", &s.cpu_speed);
35:      printf("The year your computer was made?\n");
36:          scanf("%d", &s.year);
37:      printf("How much you paid for the computer?\n");
38:          scanf("%f", &s.cost);
39:      return s;
40: }
```

After I run the executable, 19L03.exe, and enter my answers to the questions, I get the following output, which is the same as the output from the executable program of Listing 19.1:

```
C:\app>19L03
The type of the CPU inside your computer?
Pentium
The speed(MHz) of the CPU?
100
The year your computer was made?
1996
How much you paid for the computer?
1234.56
Here are what you entered:
Year: 1996
Cost: $1234.56
CPU type: Pentium
CPU speed: 100 MHz
C:\app>
```

ANALYSIS The purpose of the program in Listing 19.3 is to show you how to pass a structure to a function. The structure in Listing 19.3, with the tag name of computer, is declared in lines 4–9.

Note that in line 11 the typedef keyword is used to define a synonym, SC, for structure computer. Then SC is used in the sequential declarations.

The DataReceive() function is declared in line 13, with the structure of computer as its argument (that is, the synonym SC and the variable name s), so that a copy of the structure can be passed to the function.

In addition, the DataReceive() function returns the copy of the structure back to the caller after the content of the structure is updated. To do this, sc is prefixed to the function in line 13 to indicate the data type of the value returned by the function.

The statement in line 17 defines the structure model with SC. The DataReceive() function is passed with the name of the model structure in line 19, and then the value returned by the function is assigned back to model as well. Note that if the DataReceive() function return value is not assigned to model, the changes made to s in the function will not be evident in model.

The definition of the DataReceive() function is shown in lines 29–40, from which you can see that the new data values entered by the user are saved into the corresponding members of the structure that is passed to the function. At the end of the function, the copy of the updated structure is returned in line 39.

Then, back to the main() function of the program, lines 21–24 print out the updated contents held by the members of the structure. Because the program in Listing 19.3 is basically the same as the one in Listing 19.1, I see the same output on my screen after running the executable file, 19L03.exe.

Pointing to Structures

As you can pass a function with a pointer that refers to an array, you can also pass a function with a pointer that points to a structure.

However, unlike passing a structure to a function, which sends an entire copy of the structure to the function, passing a pointer of a structure to a function is simply passing the address that associates the structure to the function. The function can then use the address to access the structure members without duplicating the structure. Therefore, it's more efficient to pass a pointer of a structure, rather than the structure itself, to a function.

Accordingly, the program in Listing 19.3 can be rewritten to pass the DataReceive() function with a pointer that points to the structure. The rewritten program is shown in Listing 19.4.

19

Listing 19.4. Passing a function with a pointer that points to a structure.

TYPE

```
1:  /* 19L04.c Pointing to a structure */
2:  #include <stdio.h>
3:
4:  struct computer {
5:     float cost;
6:     int year;
7:     int cpu_speed;
8:     char cpu_type[16];
9:  };
```

continues

Listing 19.4. continued

```
10:
11: typedef struct computer SC;
12:
13: void DataReceive(SC *ptr_s);
14:
15: main(void)
16: {
17:    SC model;
18:
19:    DataReceive(&model);
20:    printf("Here are what you entered:\n");
21:    printf("Year: %d\n", model.year);
22:    printf("Cost: $%6.2f\n", model.cost);
23:    printf("CPU type: %s\n", model.cpu_type);
24:    printf("CPU speed: %d MHz\n", model.cpu_speed);
25:
26:    return 0;
27: }
28: /* function definition */
29: void DataReceive(SC *ptr_s)
30: {
31:    printf("The type of the CPU inside your computer?\n");
32:        gets((*ptr_s).cpu_type);
33:    printf("The speed(MHz) of the CPU?\n");
34:        scanf("%d", &(*ptr_s).cpu_speed);
35:    printf("The year your computer was made?\n");
36:        scanf("%d", &(*ptr_s).year);
37:    printf("How much you paid for the computer?\n");
38:        scanf("%f", &(*ptr_s).cost);
39: }
```

Similarly, I obtain output that is the same as the one from the program in Listing 19.3 after I run the executable (19L04.exe) of the program in Listing 19.4:

OUTPUT

```
C:\app>19L04
The type of the CPU inside your computer?
Pentium
The speed(MHz) of the CPU?
100
The year your computer was made?
1996
How much you paid for the computer?
1234.56
Here are what you entered:
Year: 1996
Cost: $1234.56
CPU type: Pentium
CPU speed: 100 MHz
C:\app>
```

ANALYSIS The program in Listing 19.4 is almost identical to the one in Listing 19.3, except that the argument passed to the DataReceive() function is a pointer defined with SC— that is, structure computer. (Refer to lines 11 and 13.) Also, the DataReceive()

function does not need to return a copy of the structure because the function can access all members of the original structure, not the copy, via the pointer passed to it. That's why the void keyword is prefixed to the function name in line 13.

The statement in line 17 defines the structure model. And in line 19, the address of the model structure is passed to the DataReceive function by applying the address-of operator (&).

When you look at the definition of the DataReceive() function in lines 29–39, you see that the dereferenced pointer *ptr_s is used to reference the members of the model structure. For instance, to access the char array of cpu_type, (*ptr_s) is used in the (*ptr_s).cpu_type expression to indicate to the compiler that cpu_type is a member in the structure pointed to by the pointer ptr_s. Note that the dereferenced pointer *ptr_s has to be enclosed within the parentheses ((and)).

Another example is the &(*ptr_s).cpu_speed expression in line 34, which leads to the address of the cpu_speed variable that is a member of the structure pointed to by the pointer ptr_s. Again, the dereferenced pointer *ptr_s is surrounded by the parentheses ((and)).

The next subsection shows you how to use the arrow operator (->) to refer to a structure member with a pointer.

Referencing a Structure Member with ->

You can use the arrow operator -> to refer to a structure member with a pointer that points to the structure.

For instance, you can rewrite the (*ptr_s).cpu_type expression in Listing 19.4 with this:

```
ptr_s -> cpu_type
```

or you could replace the &(*ptr_s).cpu_speed expression with this:

```
&(ptr_s->cpu_speed)
```

Because of its clearness, the -> operator is more frequently used in programs than the dot operator. Exercise 3, later in this hour, gives you a chance to rewrite the entire program in Listing 19.4 using the -> operator.

Arrays of Structures

In C, you can declare an array of a structure by preceding the array name with the structure name. For instance, given a structure with the tag name of x, the following statement

```
struct x array_of_structure[8];
```

declares an array, called array_of_structure, with the structure data type of x. The array has eight elements.

19

The program shown in Listing 19.5 demonstrates how to use an array of a structure by printing out two pieces of Japanese haiku and their authors' names.

TYPE   **Listing 19.5. Using arrays of structures.**

```
1:  /* 19L05.c Arrays of structures */
2:  #include <stdio.h>
3:
4:  struct haiku {
5:      int start_year;
6:      int end_year;
7:      char author[16];
8:      char str1[32];
9:      char str2[32];
10:     char str3[32];
11: };
12:
13: typedef struct haiku HK;
14:
15: void DataDisplay(HK *ptr_s);
16:
17: main(void)
18: {
19:     HK poem[2] = {
20:        { 1641,
21:          1716,
22:          "Sodo",
23:          "Leading me along",
24:          "my shadow goes back home",
25:          "from looking at the moon."
26:        },
27:        { 1729,
28:          1781,
29:          "Chora",
30:          "A storm wind blows",
31:          "out from among the grasses",
32:          "the full moon grows."
33:        }
34:     };
35:     int i;
36:
37:     for (i=0; i<2; i++)
38:        DataDisplay(&poem[i]);
39:
40:     return 0;
41: }
42: /* function definition */
43: void DataDisplay(HK *ptr_s)
44: {
45:     printf("%s\n", ptr_s->str1);
46:     printf("%s\n", ptr_s->str2);
47:     printf("%s\n", ptr_s->str3);
48:     printf("--- %s\n", ptr_s->author);
49:     printf("   (%d-%d)\n\n", ptr_s->start_year, ptr_s->end_year);
50: }
```

19

After running the executable (19L05.exe) of the program in Listing 19.5, I see the two pieces of Japanese haiku printed on the screen:

```
C:\app>19L05
Leading me along
my shadow goes back home
from looking at the moon.
--- Sodo
    (1641-1716)

A storm wind blows
out from among the grasses
the full moon grows.
--- Chora
    (1729-1781)
C:\app>
```

ANALYSIS In Listing 19.5, a structure data type, with the tag name of haiku, is declared in lines 4–11. The structure data type contains two int variables and four char arrays as its members. The statement in line 13 creates a synonym, HK, for the struct haiku data type.

Then, in lines 19–34, an array of two elements, poem, is declared and initialized with two pieces of haiku written by Sodo and Chora, respectively. The following is a copy of the two pieces of haiku from poem:

```
"Leading me along",
"my shadow goes back home",
"from looking at the moon."
```

and

```
"A storm wind blows",
"out from among the grasses",
"the full moon grows."
```

The initializer also includes the authors' names and the years of their births and deaths (refers to lines 20–22 and lines 27–29). Note that the poem array, declared with HK, is indeed an array of the haiku structure.

The DataDisplay() function is called twice in a for loop in lines 37 and 38. Each time, the address of an element of poem is passed to the DataDisplay() function. According to the definition of the function in lines 43–50, DataDisplay() prints out three strings of a haiku, the author's name, and the period of time in which he lived.

From the output, you can see that the contents stored in the poem array of the haiku structure are displayed on the screen properly.

Nested Structures

A structure is called a *nested structure* when one of the members of the structure is itself a structure. For instance, given a structure data type of x, the following statement

```
struct y {
   int i;
   char ch[8];
   struct x nested;
};
```

declares a nested structure with a tag name of y, because one of the members of the y structure is a structure with the variable name of nested that is defined by the structure data type of x.

Listing 19.6 contains an example of using a nested structure to receive and print out information about an employee.

TYPE Listing 19.6. Using nested structures.

```
1:  /* 19L06.c Using nested structures */
2:  #include <stdio.h>
3:
4:  struct department {
5:      int  code;
6:      char name[32];
7:      char position[16];
8:  };
9:
10: typedef struct department DPT;
11:
12: struct employee {
13:     DPT d;
14:     int id;
15:     char name[32];
16: };
17:
18: typedef struct employee EMPLY;
19:
20: void InfoDisplay(EMPLY *ptr);
21: void InfoEnter(EMPLY *ptr);
22:
23: main(void)
24: {
25:     EMPLY info = {
26:         { 1,
27:           "Marketing",
28:           "Manager"
29:         },
30:         1,
31:         "B. Smith"
32:     };
33:
34:     printf("Here is a sample:\n");
35:     InfoDisplay(&info);
36:
37:     InfoEnter(&info);
38:
39:     printf("\nHere are what you entered:\n");
40:     InfoDisplay(&info);
41:
42:     return 0;
```

19

```
43: }
44: /* function definition */
45: void InfoDisplay(EMPLY *ptr)
46: {
47:    printf("Name: %s\n", ptr->name);
48:    printf("ID #: %04d\n", ptr->id);
49:    printf("Dept. name: %s\n", ptr->d.name);
50:    printf("Dept. code: %02d\n", ptr->d.code);
51:    printf("Your position: %s\n", ptr->d.position);
52: }
53: /* function definition */
54: void InfoEnter(EMPLY *ptr)
55: {
56:    printf("\nPlease enter your information:\n");
57:    printf("Your name:\n");
58:       gets(ptr->name);
59:    printf("Your position:\n");
60:       gets(ptr->d.position);
61:    printf("Dept. name:\n");
62:       gets(ptr->d.name);
63:    printf("Dept. code:\n");
64:       scanf("%d", &(ptr->d.code));
65:    printf("Your employee ID #:\n");
66:       scanf("%d", &(ptr->id));
67: }
```

When the executable, 19L06.exe, is running, the initial content of the nested structure is printed out first. Then, I enter my employment information, which is in bold in the following output and displayed back on the screen, too:

OUTPUT

```
C:\app>19L06
Here is a sample:
Name: B. Smith
ID #: 0001
Dept. name: Marketing
Dept. code: 01
Your position: Manager

Please enter your information:\n");
Your name:
T. Zhang
Your position:\n");
Engineer
Dept. name:
R&D
Dept. code:
3
Your employee ID #:
1234

Here are what you entered:
Name: T. Zhang
ID #: 1234
Dept. name: R&D
Dept. code: 03
Your position: Engineer
C:\app>
```

19

ANALYSIS There are two structure data types in Listing 19.6. The first one, called department, is declared in lines 4–8. The second one, employee, declared in lines 12–16, contains a member of the department structure data type. Therefore, the employee structure data type is a nested structure data type.

Two synonyms, DPT for the struct department data type, and EMPLY for the struct employee data type, are created in two typedef statements, respectively, in lines 10 and 18. In the program, there are two functions, InfoDisplay() and InfoEnter(), whose prototypes are declared with a pointer of EMPLY as the argument (see lines 20 and 21).

The statement in 25–32 initializes a nested structure, which is called info and defined with EMPLY. Note that the nested braces ({ and }) in lines 26 and 29 enclose the initializers for the d structure of DPT that is nested inside the info structure.

Then, the statement in line 35 displays the initial contents held by the nested info structure by calling the InfoDisplay() function. Line 37 calls the InfoEnter() function to ask the user to enter his or her employment information and then save it into the info structure. The InfoDisplay() function is called again in line 40 to display the information that the user entered and is now stored in the nested structure.

The definitions for the two functions, InfoDisplay() and InfoEnter(), are listed in lines 45–52 and lines 54–67, respectively.

Forward-Referencing Structures

If one of the members of a structure is a pointer pointing to another structure that has not been declared yet, the structure is called a *forward-referencing structure*.

For example, the following statement declares a forward-referencing structure:

```
struct x {
   int i;
   char ch[8];
   struct y *ptr;
};
```

It is presumed that the structure y has not been declared yet.

If the pointer in a structure points to the structure itself, the structure is called a *self-referencing structure*. The following declaration is an example of a self-referencing structure:

```
struct x {
   int i;
   char ch[8];
   struct x *ptr;
};
```

Now, let's move to the program in Listing 19.7, which provides you with another example of declaring a forward-referencing structure.

19

Listing 19.7. Using forward-referencing structures.

```
 1: /* 19L07.c Forward-referencing structures */
 2: #include <stdio.h>
 3: /* forward-referencing structure */
 4: struct resume {
 5:     char name[16];
 6:     struct date *u;
 7:     struct date *g;
 8: };
 9: /* referenced structure */
10: struct date {
11:     int year;
12:     char school[32];
13:     char degree[8];
14: };
15:
16: typedef struct resume RSM;
17: typedef struct date DATE;
18:
19: void InfoDisplay(RSM *ptr);
20:
21: main(void)
22: {
23:     DATE under = {
24:         1985,
25:         "Rice University",
26:         "B.S."
27:         };
28:     DATE graduate = {
29:         1987,
30:         "UT Austin",
31:         "M.S."
32:         };
33:     RSM new_employee = {
34:         "Tony",
35:         &under,
36:         &graduate
37:         };
38:
39:     printf("Here is the new employee's resume:\n");
40:     InfoDisplay(&new_employee);
41:
42:     return 0;
43: }
44: /* function definition */
45: void InfoDisplay(RSM *ptr)
46: {
47:     printf("Name: %s\n", ptr->name);
48:     /* undergraduate */
49:     printf("School name: %s\n", ptr->u->school);
50:     printf("Graduation year: %d\n", ptr->u->year);
51:     printf("Degree: %s\n", ptr->u->degree);
52:     /* graduate */
53:     printf("School name: %s\n", ptr->g->school);
54:     printf("Graduation year: %d\n", ptr->g->year);
55:     printf("Degree: %s\n", ptr->g->degree);
56: }
```

19

I have the following output displayed on the screen after I run the executable, 19L07.exe, of the program in Listing 19.7:

```
C:\app>19L07
Here is the new employee's resume:
Name: Tony
School name: Rice University
Graduation year: 1985
Degree: B.S.
School name: UT Austin
Graduation year: 1987
Degree: M.S.
C:\app>
```

The purpose of the program in Listing 19.7 is to show you how to declare and initialize a forward-referencing structure. As you can see, the forward-referencing structure data type, labeled with resume, is declared in lines 4–8. This structure data type has two members, u and g, which are pointers defined with the date structure data type. However, the date structure data type has not yet been declared at this moment. The structure data type of resume is thus called a forward-referencing structure data type.

The referenced date structure data type is declared in lines 10–14. Then, I make two synonyms, RSM and DATE, to represent struct resume and struct date, respectively, in lines 16 and 17.

Because there are two pointers inside the resume structure data type that reference the date structure data type, I define and initialize two structures with DATE in lines 23–32. under and graduate are the names of the two structures.

Then, in lines 33–37, a structure, called new_employee, is defined with RSM and initialized with the addresses of the two structures, under and graduate (see lines 35 and 36). In this way, the forward-referencing structure new_employee is assigned with access to the contents of the two referenced structures, under and graduate.

The statement in line 40, which calls the InfoDisplay() function, prints out all the contents held by the new_employee structure, as well as that of the under and graduate structures.

Lines 45–56 give the definition of the InfoDisplay() function, from which you can see that the expressions, such as ptr->u->school and ptr->g->school, are used to reference the members in the under and graduate structures. Since ptr, u, and g are all pointers, two arrows (->) are used in the expressions.

In exercise 5, later in this hour, you'll be asked to rewrite the program in Listing 19.7 with an array of pointers to replace the two pointers defined inside the forward-referencing structure of resume.

WARNING

> Don't include forward references in a typedef statement. It's not legal in C.

Summary

In this lesson you've learned the following:

- [ ] You can group variables of different types with a data type called a structure.
- [ ] The data items in a structure are called fields or members of the structure.
- [ ] The struct keyword is used to start a structure declaration or a structure variable definition.
- [ ] The dot operator (.) is used to separate a structure name and a member name in referencing the structure member.
- [ ] The arrow operator (->) is commonly used to reference a structure member with a pointer.
- [ ] A structure can be passed to a function, and a function can return a structure back to the caller.
- [ ] Passing a function with a pointer that points to a structure is more efficient than passing the function with the entire structure.
- [ ] Arrays of structures are permitted in C.
- [ ] You can enclose a structure within another structure. The latter is called a nested structure.
- [ ] It's legal to put a pointer into a structure even though the pointer may point to another structure that has not been declared yet.

In the next lesson you'll learn to use unions to collect dissimilar data items in C.

Q&A

Q Why do you need structures?

A In practice, you need to collect and group data items that are relevant but of different types. The structure data type provides a convenient way to aggregate those differently typed data items.

19

Q **Can you declare a structure and define a structure variable in a single statement?**

A Yes. You can put the struct keyword, a tag name, a list of declarations of structure members, and a variable name into a single statement to declare a structure and define a structure variable. Then, the structure can be identified by the tag name; the variable is of the struct data type of the tag name.

Q **How do you reference a structure member?**

A You can reference a structure member by prefixing the structure member's name with the structure variable name and a dot operator (.). If the structure is pointed to by a pointer, you can use the arrow operator (->), followed by the pointer name, to reference the structure member.

Q **Why is it more efficient to pass a pointer that refers to a structure to a function?**

A When an entire structure is passed to a function, a copy of the structure is made and saved in a temporary block of memory called the stack. After the copy is modified by the function, it has to be returned and written back to the storage that holds the original content of the structure. Passing a function with a pointer that points to a structure, on the other hand, simply passes the address of the structure to the function, not the entire copy of the structure. The function can then access the original memory location of the structure and modify the content held by the structure without duplicating the structure on the stack. Therefore, it's more efficient to pass a pointer of a structure than to pass the structure itself to a function.

Workshop

To help solidify your understanding of this hour's lesson, you are encouraged to answer the quiz questions and finish the exercises provided in the Workshop before you move to the next lesson. The answers and hints to the questions and exercises are given in Appendix E, "Answers to Quiz Questions and Exercises."

Quiz

1. What's wrong with the following structure declaration?

```
struct automobile {
    int year;
    char model[8];
    int engine_power;
    float weight;
    }
```

2. How many structure variables are defined in the following statement?

```
struct x {int y; char z} u, v, w;
```

3. Given a structure declaration

```
struct automobile {
     int year;
     char model[8]};
```

   and two car models, Taurus and Accord, which are made in 1997, initialize an array of two elements, car, that is defined with the automobile structure data type.

4. In the following structure declarations, which one is a forward-referencing structure, and which one is a self-referencing structure? (Assume that the structures, employment and education, have not been declared yet.)

```
struct member {
     char name[32];
     struct employment *emp;
     struct education *edu;};

struct list {
     int x, y;
     float z;
     struct list *ptr_list;};
```

Exercises

1. Given the following declaration and definition of a structure

```
struct automobile {
     int year;
     char model[10];
     int engine_power;
     double weight;
     } sedan = {
     1997,
     "New Model",
     200,
     2345.67};
```

   write a program to display the initial values held by the structure on the screen.

2. Rewrite the program in Listing 19.2. This time, create a function that can display the content in the employee structure. Then, make calls to the function by passing the structure to it.

3. Rewrite the program in Listing 19.4. This time, use the arrow operator (->) with the pointers to structures.

4. Rewrite the program in Listing 19.5. This time, add an array of pointers that is declared with HK. Then pass each element in the array of pointers to the DataDisplay() function.

5. Rewrite the program in Listing 19.7. This time, declare an array of pointers to forward-reference the date structure and rewrite the InfoDisplay() function in the program.

19

Hour 20

Unions: Another Way to Collect Dissimilar Data

Coming together is a beginning;
keeping together is progress;
working together is success.

—T. Roosevelt

In the previous hour's lesson you learned how to store data of different types into structures. In this hour you'll learn another way to collect differently typed data items by using unions. You'll learn about the following topics in this lesson:

- ☐ How to declare and define unions
- ☐ How to initialize unions
- ☐ The differences between unions and structures
- ☐ Nested unions with structures
- ☐ Manipulating the bit field with `struct`

What Is a Union?

A *union* is a block of memory that is used to hold data items of different types. In C, a union is similar to a structure, except that data items saved in the union are overlaid in order to share the same memory location. More details on the differences between unions and structures are discussed in the following sections.

Declaring Unions

The syntax for declaring a union is similar to the syntax for a structure. The following is an example of a union declaration:

```
union automobile {
    int year;
    char model[8];
    int engine_power;
    float weight;
};
```

Here union is the keyword that specifies the union data type. automobile is the tag name of the union. The variables, such as year, model, engine_power, and weight, are members of the union, and are declared within the braces ({ and }). The union declaration ends with a semicolon (;).

Like a structure tag name, a union tag name is a label to a union, which is used by the compiler to identify the union.

Defining Union Variables

You can define union variables after declaring a union. For instance, the following union variables are defined with the union labeled with automobile from the previous section:

```
union automobile sedan, pick_up, sport_utility;
```

Here the three variables, sedan, pick_up, and sport_utility, are defined as the union variables.

Of course, you can declare a union and define variables of the union in a single statement. For instance, you can rewrite the previous union declaration and definition like this:

```
union automobile {
    int year;
    char model[8];
    int engine_power;
    float weight;
} sedan, pick_up, sport_utility;
```

Here three union variables, sedan, pick_up, and sport_utility, are defined by the union of automobile in which there are four members of different data types. If you declare a union and define variables of the union in a single statement, and there is no more union variable definition made with the union, you can omit the tag name of the union. For instance, the tag name automobile can be omitted in the union definition like this:

```
union {
     int year;
     char model[8];
     int engine_power;
     float weight;
} sedan, pick_up, sport_utility;
```

Referring a Union with . or ->

As well as being used to reference structure members, the dot operator (.) can be used in referencing union members. For example, the following statement assigns the value of 1997 to one of the members of the sedan union:

```
sedan.year = 1997;
```

Here the dot operator is used to separate the union name sedan and the member name year.

In addition, if you define a pointer ptr like this:

```
union automobile *ptr;
```

then you can reference one of the union members in the following way:

```
ptr->year = 1997;
```

Here the arrow operator (->)is used to reference the union member year with the pointer ptr.

The program in Listing 20.1 gives another example of how to reference and assign values to the members of a union.

TYPE **Listing 20.1. Referencing the members of a union.**

20

```
1:  /* 20L01.c Referencing a union */
2:  #include <stdio.h>
3:  #include <string.h>
4:
5:  main(void)
6:  {
7:     union menu {
8:        char name[23];
9:        double price;
10:    } dish;
11:
```

continues

Listing 20.1. continued

```
12:     printf("The content assigned to the union separately:\n");
13:     /* reference name */
14:     strcpy(dish.name, "Sweet and Sour Chicken");
15:     printf("Dish Name: %s\n", dish.name);
16:     /* reference price */
17:     dish.price = 9.95;
18:     printf("Dish Price: %5.2f\n", dish.price);
19:
20:     return 0;
21: }
```

After running the executable 20L01.exe of the program in Listing 20.1, I have the following output shown on my screen:

OUTPUT
```
C:\app>20L01
The content assigned to the union separately:
Dish Name: Sweet and Sour Chicken
Dish Price: 9.95
C:\app>
```

ANALYSIS The purpose of the program in Listing 20.1 is to show you how to reference union members with the dot operator.

Inside the main() function, a union, called dish, is first defined with the union data type of menu in lines 7–10. There are two members, name and price, in the union.

Then the statement in line 14 assigns the string "Sweet and Sour Chicken" to the character array name that is one of the union members. Note that the dish.name expression is used as the first argument to the strcpy() function in line 14. When the compiler sees the expression, it knows that we want to reference the memory location of name that is a member of the dish union.

The strcpy() function is a C function that copies the contents of a string pointed to by the function's second argument to the memory storage pointed to by the function's first argument. I included the header file string.h in the program before calling the strcpy() function. (See line 3.)

Line 15 prints out the contents copied to the name array by using the dish.name expression one more time.

The statement in line 17 assigns the value 9.95 to the double variable price, which is another member for the dish union. Note that the dish.price expression is used to reference the union member. Then line 18 displays the value assigned to price by calling the printf() function and passing the dish.price expression as an argument to the function.

According to the results shown in the output, the two members of the `dish` union, `name` and `price`, have been successfully referenced and assigned corresponding values.

Unions Versus Structures

You might notice that in Listing 20.1, I assigned a value to one member of the `dish` union, and then immediately printed out the assigned value before I moved to the next union member. In other words, I didn't assign values to all the union members together before I printed out each assigned value from each member in the union.

I did this purposely because of the reason that is explained in the following section. So keep reading. (In exercise 1 at the end of this lesson, you'll see a different output when you rewrite the program in Listing 20.1 by exchanging the orders between the statements in lines 15 and 17.)

Initializing a Union

As mentioned earlier in this lesson, data items in a union are overlaid at the same memory location. In other words, the memory location of a union is shared by different members of the union at different times. The size of a union is equal to the size of the largest data item in the list of the union members, which is large enough to hold any members of the union, one at a time. Therefore, it does not make sense to initialize all members of a union together because the value of the latest initialized member overwrites the value of the preceding member. You initialize a member of a union only when you are ready to use it. The value contained by a union is the value that is latest assigned to a member of the union.

For instance, if we declare and define a union on a 16-bit machine (that is, the `int` data type is 2 bytes long) like this:

```
union u {
    char ch;
    int x;
} a_union;
```

then the following statement initializes the `char` variable `ch` with the character constant `'H'`:

```
a_union.ch = 'H';
```

and the value contained by the `a_union` union is the character constant `'H'`. However, if the `int` variable `x` is initialized by the following statement:

```
 a_union.x = 365;
```

then the value contained by the `a_union` union becomes the value of `365`. Figure 20.1 demonstrates the content change of the union during the two initializations.

20

Figure 20.1.

The content of the
a_union *union is the*
same as the content
assigned to one of its
members.

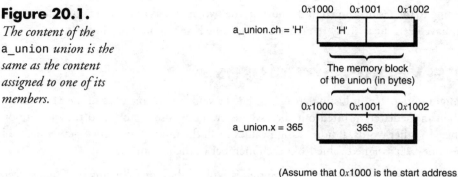

(Assume that 0x1000 is the start address
of the union.)

According to the ANSI C standard, a union can be initialized by assigning the first union member with a value. For instance, in the following statement:

```
union u {
    char ch;
    int x;
} a_union = {'H'};
```

the a_union union is said to be initialized because the character constant 'H' is assigned to the first union member, ch.

If the first member of a union is a structure, the entire structure has to be initialized with a list of values before the union can be said to have been initialized.

Let's see what will happen if we try to assign values to all members of a union together. Listing 20.2 gives such an example.

TYPE **Listing 20.2. The members of a union share the same memory location.**

```
1:  /* 20L02.c:  Memory sharing in unions */
2:  #include <stdio.h>
3:
4:  main(void)
5:  {
6:      union employee {
7:          int start_year;
8:          int dpt_code;
9:          int id_number;
10:     } info;
11:
12:     /* initialize start_year */
13:     info.start_year = 1997;
14:     /* initialize dpt_code */
```

```
15:      info.dpt_code = 8;
16:      /* initialize id */
17:      info.id_number = 1234;
18:
19:      /* display content of union */
20:      printf("Start Year:  %d\n", info.start_year);
21:      printf("Dpt. Code:   %d\n", info.dpt_code);
22:      printf("ID Number:   %d\n", info.id_number);
23:
24:      return 0;
25: }
```

After the executable 20L02.exe is created and executed, the following output is displayed on the screen:

OUTPUT
```
C:\app>20L02
Start Year:  1234
Dpt. Code:   1234
ID Number:   1234
C:\app>
```

ANALYSIS As you can see in Listing 20.2, a union called info has three int variable members, start_year, dpt_code, and id_number. (See lines 6–10.) Then, these three union members are assigned with different values consecutively in lines 13, 15, and 17. And in lines 20–22, we try to print out the values assigned to the three members. However, the output shows that every member in the info union has the same value, 1234, which is the integer assigned to the third member of the union, id_number. Note that id_number is the member that is assigned with 1234 last; the info union does hold the latest value assigned to its members.

The Size of a Union

You've been told that the members of a union share the same memory location. The size of a union is the same as the size of the largest member in the union.

In contrast with a union, all members of a structure can be initialized together without any overwriting. This is because each member in a structure has its own memory storage. The size of a structure is equal to the sum of sizes of its members instead of the size of the largest member.

How do I know whether all these are true? Well, I can prove it by measuring the size of a union or a structure. Listing 20.3 contains a program that measures the size of a union as well as the size of a structure. The structure has exactly the same members as the union.

20

TYPE   **Listing 20.3. Measuring the size of a union.**

```
1:   /* 20L03.c The size of a union */
2:   #include <stdio.h>
3:   #include <string.h>
4:
5:   main(void)
6:   {
7:      union u {
8:          double x;
9:          int y;
10:     } a_union;
11:
12:     struct s {
13:         double x;
14:         int y;
15:     } a_struct;
16:
17:     printf("The size of double: %d-byte\n",
18:             sizeof(double));
19:     printf("The size of int:    %d-byte\n",
20:             sizeof(int));
21:
22:     printf("The size of a_union:  %d-byte\n",
23:             sizeof(a_union));
24:     printf("The size of a_struct: %d-byte\n",
25:             sizeof(a_struct));
26:
27:     return 0;
28:  }
```

The compiler on your machine may generate several warning messages, something like "unreferenced local variables." This is because the a_union union and the a_struct structure are not initialized in the program. You can ignore the warning messages. The following output is displayed on the screen after the executable 20L03.exe is created and executed:

OUTPUT
```
C:\app>20L03
The size of double: 8-byte
The size of int:    2-byte
The size of a_union:  8-byte
The size of a_struct: 10-byte
C:\app>
```

ANALYSIS   The purpose of the program in Listing 20.3 is to show the difference between a union memory allocation and a structure memory allocation, although both the union and the structure consist of the same members.

A union, called a_union, is defined in lines 7–10; it has two members, a double variable x and an int variable y. In addition, a structure, called a_structure and defined in lines 12–15, also consists of two members, a double variable x and an int variable y.

20

The statements in lines 17–20 first measure the sizes of the double and int data types on the host machine. For instance, on my machine, the size of the double data type is 8 bytes long and the int data type is 2 bytes long.

Then lines 22–25 measure the sizes of the a_union union and the a_structure structure, respectively. From the output, we see that the size of a_union is 8 bytes long. In other words, the size of the union is the same as the size of the largest member, x, in the union.

The size of the structure, on the other hand, is the sum of the sizes of two members, x and y, in the structure (10 bytes in total).

Using Unions

Now let's focus on the applications of unions. Basically, there are two kinds of union applications, which are introduced in the following two sections.

Referencing the Same Memory Location Differently

The first application of unions is to reference the same memory location with different union members.

To get a better idea about referencing the same memory with different union members, let's have a look at the program in Listing 20.4, which uses the two members of a union to reference the same memory location. (We assume that the char data type is 1 byte long, and the int data type is 2 bytes long, which are true on many machines.)

TYPE   Listing 20.4. Referencing the same memory location with different union members.

```
1:   /* 20L04.c: Referencing the same memory in different ways */
2:   #include <stdio.h>
3:
4:   union u{
5:       char ch[2];
6:       int num;
7:   };
8:
9:   int UnionInitialize(union u val);
10:
11:  main(void)
12:  {
13:      union u val;
14:      int x;
15:
16:      x = UnionInitialize(val);
17:
```

20

continues

Listing 20.4. continued

```
18:     printf("The two character constants held by the union:\n");
19:     printf("%c\n", x & 0x00FF);
20:     printf("%c\n", x >> 8);
21:
22:     return 0;
23: }
24: /* function definition */
25: int UnionInitialize(union u val)
26: {
27:     val.ch[0] = 'H';
28:     val.ch[1] = 'i';
29:
30:     return val.num;
31: }
```

The following output is printed on the screen after the executable 20L04.exe is created and executed:

OUTPUT

```
C:\app>20L04
The two character constants held by the union:
H
i
C:\app>
```

ANALYSIS   As you see from the program in Listing 20.4, a union called val is defined in line 13. It contains two members; one is a char array ch and the other is an int variable num. If a char data type is 1 byte long and an int data type is 2 bytes long, the ch array and the integer variable num have the same length of memory storage on those machines.

A function named UnionInitialize() is called and passed with the union name val in line 16. The definition of the UnionInitialize() function is shown in lines 25–31.

From the function definition, you can see that the two elements of the char array ch are initialized with two character constants, 'H' and 'i' (in lines 27 and 28). Because the char array ch and the int variable num share the same memory location, we can return the value of num that contains the same content as the ch array. (See line 30.) Here we've used the two members, ch and num, in the val union to reference the same memory location and the same contents of the union.

The value returned by the UnionInitialize() function is assigned to an int variable x in line 16 inside the main() function. The statements in lines 19 and 20 print out the 2 bytes of the int variable num. Each byte of num corresponds to a character that is used to initialize the ch array because num and ch are all in the same union and have the same content of the union. Line 19 displays the low byte of num returned by the x & 0x00FF expression. In line 20, the

20

high byte of num is obtained by shifting the x variable to the right by 8 bits. That is, by using the shift-right operator in the x >> 8 expression. (The bitwise operator (&) and the shift operator (>>) are introduced in Hour 8, "More Operators.")

From the output, you can see that the content of the val union is shown on the screen correctly.

Figure 20.2 shows the locations of the two character constants in memory.

Figure 20.2.

The memory locations of the two character constants.

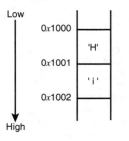

(Assume that 0x1000 is the start address.)

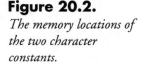

There are two formats to store a multiple-byte quantity, such as the int variable num in Listing 20.4. One of the formats is called the *little-endian* format; the other is the *big-endian* format.

For the little-endian format, the high bytes of a multiple-byte quantity are stored at higher memory addresses and the low bytes are saved at lower addresses. The little-endian format is used by Intel's 80x86 microprocessors. My computer's CPU is a Pentium microprocessor, which is one of the members in the 80x86 family. Therefore, in Listing 20.4, the character constant 'H', which is a low byte, is stored at the lower address. 'i' is stored at the higher address because it's a high byte.

The big-endian format is just opposite. That is, the high bytes are stored at lower addresses; the low bytes are stored at higher addresses. Motorola's 68000 microprocessor family uses the big-endian format.

Making Structures Flexible

The second application of unions is to nest a union inside a structure so that the structure can hold different types of values.

For example, suppose we want to write a program that asks the user about the name of a cable company or a satellite dish company that provides service to the user. Assume that the user either uses a cable or a satellite dish at home, but not both. Then, if we define two character arrays to store the cable company and satellite dish company names respectively, one of the arrays will be empty due to the assumption. In this case, we can declare a union with the two character arrays as its members so that the union can hold either a cable company name or a satellite dish company name, depending on the user's input. Listing 20.5 demonstrates how to write a program with such a union.

TYPE **Listing 20.5. Making a structure flexible.**

```
1:  /* 20L05.c: Using unions */
2:  #include <stdio.h>
3:  #include <string.h>
4:
5:  struct survey {
6:     char name[20];
7:     char c_d_p;
8:     int age;
9:     int hour_per_week;
10:    union {
11:       char cable_company[16];
12:       char dish_company[16];
13:    } provider;
14: };
15:
16: void DataEnter(struct survey *s);
17: void DataDisplay(struct survey *s);
18:
19: main(void)
20: {
21:    struct survey tv;
22:
23:    DataEnter(&tv);
24:    DataDisplay(&tv);
25:
26:    return 0;
27: }
28: /* function definition */
29: void DataEnter(struct survey *ptr)
30: {
31:    char is_yes[4];
32:
33:    printf("Are you using cable at home? (Yes or No)\n");
34:       gets(is_yes);
35:    if ((is_yes[0] == 'Y') ||
36:       (is_yes[0] == 'y')){
37:       printf("Enter the cable company name:\n");
38:       gets(ptr->provider.cable_company);
39:       ptr->c_d_p = 'c';
40:    } else {
41:       printf("Are you using a satellite dish? (Yes or No)\n");
42:          gets(is_yes);
43:       if ((is_yes[0] == 'Y') ||
44:          (is_yes[0] == 'y')){
45:          printf("Enter the satellite dish company name:\n");
46:          gets(ptr->provider.dish_company);
47:          ptr->c_d_p = 'd';
```

```
48:        } else {
49:            ptr->c_d_p = 'p';
50:        }
51:    }
52:    printf("Please enter your name:\n");
53:        gets(ptr->name);
54:    printf("Your age:\n");
55:        scanf("%d", &ptr->age);
56:    printf("How many hours you spend on watching TV per week:\n");
57:        scanf("%d", &ptr->hour_per_week);
58: }
59: /* function definition */
60: void DataDisplay(struct survey *ptr)
61: {
62:    printf("\nHere's what you've entered:\n");
63:    printf("Name: %s\n", ptr->name);
64:    printf("Age:  %d\n", ptr->age);
65:    printf("Hour per week: %d\n", ptr->hour_per_week);
66:    if (ptr->c_d_p == 'c')
67:       printf("Your cable company is: %s\n",
68:           ptr->provider.cable_company);
69:    else if (ptr->c_d_p == 'd')
70:       printf("Your satellite dish company is: %s\n",
71:           ptr->provider.dish_company);
72:    else
73:       printf("You don't have cable or a satellite dish.\n");
74:    printf("\nThanks and Bye!\n");
75: }
```

When the executable program 20L05.exe is being run, I enter my answers to the survey and have the following output displayed on the screen (my answers are shown in **bold monospace** type in the output):

OUTPUT

```
C:\app>20L05
Are you using cable at home? (Yes or No)
No
Are you using a satellite dish? (Yes or No)
Yes
Enter the satellite dish company name:
ABCD company
Please enter your name:
Tony Zhang
Your age:
30
How many hours you spend on watching TV per week:
8

Here's what you've entered:
Name: Tony Zhang
Age: 30
Hour per week: 8
Your satellite dish company is: ABCD company

Thanks and Bye!
C:\app>
```

20

ANALYSIS As you can see in lines 5–14, a structure data type with the tag name survey is declared, and in it a nested union called provider has two members, the cable_company array and the dish_company array. The two members of the union are used to hold the names of cable or satellite dish companies, depending on the user's input.

The statements in lines 16 and 17 declare two functions, DataEnter() and DataDisplay(), in which a pointer with struct survey is passed to the two functions as the argument.

A structure called tv is defined in line 21 inside the main() function. Then in lines 23 and 24, the DataEnter() and DataDisplay() functions are invoked with the address of the tv structure as their argument.

Lines 29–58 contain the definition of the DataEnter() function, which asks the user to enter proper information based on the survey questions. Under the assumption we made earlier, the user can use either cable or a satellite dish, but not both. If the user does use cable, then line 38 receives the cable company name entered by the user and saves it into the memory storage referenced by one of the members in the provider union, cable_company.

If the user uses a satellite dish, then line 46 stores the satellite dish company name entered by the user into the same location of the provider union. But this time the name of another union member, dish_company, is used to reference the memory location. Now you see how to save the memory by putting two exclusive data items into a union.

In fact, the program supports another situation in which the user has neither cable nor a satellite dish. In this case, the char variable c_d_p, which is a member of the structure, is assigned with the character constant 'p'.

Lines 60–75 give the definition of the DataDisplay() function that prints out the information entered by the user back to the screen. The output shown here is a sample I made by running the executable program of Listing 20.5 on my machine.

Defining Bit Fields with struct

In this section, we'll revisit our old friend the struct keyword to declare a very small object. Then we'll use the object with unions.

As you know, char is the smallest data type in C. On many machines, the char data type is 8 bits long. However, with the help of the struct keyword, we can declare a smaller object—a *bit field*—which allows you to access a single bit. A bit is able to hold one of the two values, 1 or 0.

The general form to declare and define bit fields is

```
struct tag_name {
   data_type name1: length1;
   data_type name2: lenght2;
   . . .
   data_type nameN: lengthN;
} variable_list;
```

Here the struct keyword is used to start the declaration. *tag_name* is the tag name of the struct data type. *data_type*, which must be either int, unsigned, or signed, specifies the data type of bit fields. *names1*, *name2*, and *nameN* are names of bit fields. *length1*, *length2*, and *lengthN* indicate the lengths of bit fields, which may not exceed the length of the int data type. *variable_list* contains the variable names of the bit field.

For instance, the following statement defines a variable called jumpers with three bit fields:

```
struct bf {
    int jumper1: 1;
    int jumper2: 2;
    int jumper3: 3;
} jumpers;
```

Here jumper1, jumper2, and jumper3 are the three bit fields with lengths of 1 bit, 2 bits, and 3 bits, respectively. Figure 20.3 demonstrates the memory allocations of the three bit fields.

Figure 20.3.

The memory allocations of jumper1, jumper2, *and* jumper3.

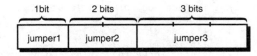

The program in Listing 20.6 is an example of using the bit fields defined with struct. In fact, the program in Listing 20.6 is a modified version of the program in Listing 20.5.

TYPE   **Listing 20.6. Applying bit fields.**

```
1:  /* 20L06.c: Applying bit fields */
2:  #include <stdio.h>
3:  #include <string.h>
4:
5:  struct bit_field {
6:     int cable: 1;
7:     int dish: 1;
8:  };
9:
10: struct survey {
11:    char name[20];
12:    struct bit_field c_d;
13:    int age;
14:    int hour_per_week;
15:    union {
16:        char cable_company[16];
17:        char dish_company[16];
18:    } provider;
19: };
20:
```

continues

Listing 20.6. continued

```
21: void DataEnter(struct survey *s);
22: void DataDisplay(struct survey *s);
23:
24: main(void)
25: {
26:    struct survey tv;
27:
28:    DataEnter(&tv);
29:    DataDisplay(&tv);
30:
31:    return 0;
32: }
33: /* function definition */
34: void DataEnter(struct survey *ptr)
35: {
36:    char is_yes[4];
37:
38:    printf("Are you using cable at home? (Yes or No)\n");
39:       gets(is_yes);
40:    if ((is_yes[0] == 'Y') ||
41:       (is_yes[0] == 'y')){
42:       printf("Enter the cable company name:\n");
43:       gets(ptr->provider.cable_company);
44:       ptr->c_d.cable = 1;
45:       ptr->c_d.dish = 0;
46:    } else {
47:       printf("Are you using a satellite dish? (Yes or No)\n");
48:          gets(is_yes);
49:       if ((is_yes[0] == 'Y') ||
50:          (is_yes[0] == 'y')){
51:          printf("Enter the satellite dish company name:\n");
52:          gets(ptr->provider.dish_company);
53:          ptr->c_d.cable = 0;
54:          ptr->c_d.dish = 1;
55:       } else {
56:          ptr->c_d.cable = 0;
57:          ptr->c_d.dish = 0;
58:       }
59:    }
60:    printf("Please enter your name:\n");
61:       gets(ptr->name);
62:    printf("Your age:\n");
63:       scanf("%d", &ptr->age);
64:    printf("How many hours you spend on watching TV per week:\n");
65:       scanf("%d", &ptr->hour_per_week);
66: }
67: /* function definition */
68: void DataDisplay(struct survey *ptr)
69: {
70:    printf("\nHere's what you've entered:\n");
71:    printf("Name: %s\n", ptr->name);
```

20

```
72:    printf("Age:  %d\n", ptr->age);
73:    printf("Hour per week: %d\n", ptr->hour_per_week);
74:    if (ptr->c_d.cable && !ptr->c_d.dish)
75:       printf("Your cable company is: %s\n",
76:          ptr->provider.cable_company);
77:    else if (!ptr->c_d.cable && ptr->c_d.dish)
78:       printf("Your satellite dish company is: %s\n",
79:          ptr->provider.dish_company);
80:    else
81:       printf("You don't have cable or a satellite dish.\n");
82:    printf("\nThanks and Bye!\n");
83: }
```

Because the program in Listing 20.6 is basically the same as the one in Listing 20.5, I have the same output shown on the screen after I run the executable 20L06.exe and enter the same answers to the survey:

OUTPUT
```
C:\app>20L06
Are you using cable at home? (Yes or No)
No
Are you using a satellite dish? (Yes or No)
Yes
Enter the satellite dish company name:
ABCD company
Please enter your name:
Tony Zhang
Your age:
30
How many hours you spend on watching TV per week:
8

Here's what you've entered:
Name: Tony Zhang
Age: 30
Hour per week: 8
Your satellite dish company is: ABCD company

Thanks and Bye!
C:\app>
```

ANALYSIS The purpose of the program in Listing 20.6 is to show you how to declare bit fields and how to use them. As you can see in lines 5–8, two bit fields, cable and dish, are declared with the struct data type. Each of the bit fields is 1 bit long. Then a structure called c_d is defined with the two bit fields in line 12, which is within another structure declaration from line 10 to line 19.

The bit fields cable and dish are used as flags to indicate whether the user is using cable or a satellite dish based on the answers made by the user. If the user has cable, then the cable bit field is set to 1 and the dish bit field is set to 0. (See lines 44 and 45.) On the other hand, if the user has a satellite dish, then dish is set to 1 and cable is set to 0, as shown in lines 53

20

and 54. If, however, the user has neither cable nor a satellite dish, both `cable` and `dish` are set to `0` in lines 56 and 57.

So you see, we've used the combinations of the two bit fields, `cable` and `dish`, to represent the three situations: having cable, having a satellite dish, or having neither cable nor a satellite dish.

Since the program in Listing 20.6 is basically the same as the one in Listing 20.5, I get the same output after I run the executable program of Listing 20.6 and enter the same information as I did to the executable `20L05.exe`.

Summary

In this hour you've learned the following:

- [ ] A union is a block of memory that is used to hold data items of different types.
- [ ] A union is similar to a structure, except that data items saved in the union are overlaid in order to share the same memory location.
- [ ] The size of a union is the same as the size of the largest member in the union.
- [ ] The `union` keyword has to be used to specify the union data type in a union declaration or a union variable definition.
- [ ] To reference a union member, you can use either a dot operator (`.`) to separate the union name and the union member name or an arrow operator (`->`) to separate the name of a pointer that points to the union and the union member name.
- [ ] The ANSI C standard allows you to initialize a union by assigning the first union member a value.
- [ ] You can access the same memory location with different union members.
- [ ] To make a structure flexible, you can nest a union inside a structure so that the structure can hold different types of values.
- [ ] You can define the bit fields, which can be a single bit or any number of bits up to the number of bits in an integer, by using the `struct` data type.

In the next hour you'll learn how to read from or write to disk files.

Q&A

Q What are the differences between a union and a structure?

A Basically, the difference between a union and a structure is that the members in a union are overlaid and they share the same memory location, whereas the members in a structure have their own memory locations. A union can be referenced by using one of its member names.

Q **What will happen if you initialize all members of a union together?**

A The value that is assigned to a union member last will be the value that stays in the memory storage of the union until the next assignment to the union. In ANSI C, you can initialize a union by initializing its first member.

Q **How do you reference a union member?**

A If the name of a union is used to reference the union members, then the dot operator (.) can be used to separate the union name and the name of a union member. If a pointer, which points to a union, is used to reference the union members, then the arrow operator (->) can be used between the pointer name and the name of a union member.

Q **Can you access the same memory location with different union members?**

A Yes. Since all union members in a union share the same memory location, you can access the memory location with different union members. For example, in the program in Listing 20.4, two character constants are assigned to a union memory storage through one of the union members. The two characters saved at the memory location of the union are printed out with the help from another union member.

Workshop

To help solidify your understanding of this hour's lesson, you are encouraged to answer the quiz questions and finish the exercises provided in the Workshop before you move to the next lesson. The answers and hints to the questions and exercises are given in Appendix E, "Answers to Quiz Questions and Exercises."

Quiz

1. Of the following two statements, which one is the declaration of a union and which one is the definition of union variables?

```
union a_union {
    int x;
    char y;
    };

union a_union x, y;
```

2. What's wrong with the following union declaration?

```
union automobile {
    int year;
    char model[8]
    float weight;
    }
```

20

3. In the following statement, what are the values contained by the two union members?

```
union u {
     int date;
     char year;
} a_union = {1997};
```

4. Given a structure and a union, what are the sizes of the structure and the union? (Assume that the char data type is 1 byte long and the int data type is 2 bytes long.)

```
struct s {
     int x;
     char ch[4];
} a_structure;

union u {
     int x;
     char ch[4];
} a_union;
```

Exercises

1. Rewrite the program in Listing 20.1 by switching the order between the statement in line 15 and the statement in line 17. What do you get after running the rewritten program?

2. Rewrite the program in Listing 20.2. This time, print out values held by all the members in the info union each time one of the members is assigned an integer.

3. Write a program to ask the user to enter his or her name. Then ask the user whether he or she is a U.S. citizen. If the answer is Yes, ask the user to enter the name of the state where he or she comes from. Otherwise, ask the user to enter the name of the country he or she comes from. (You're required to use a union in your program.)

4. Modify the program you wrote in exercise 3. Add a bit field and use it as a flag. If the user is a U.S. citizen, set the bit field to 1. Otherwise, set the bit field to 0. Print out the user's name and the name of country or state by checking the value of the bit field.

Hour 21

Disk File Input and Output: Part I

I can only assume that a "Do Not File" document is filed in a "Do Not File" file.

—*F. Church*

In Hour 5, "Reading from and Writing to Standard I/O," you learned how to read or write characters through standard input or output. In this lesson you'll learn to read data from or write data to disk files. The following topics are discussed in this lesson:

☐ Files and streams
☐ Opening a file with `fopen()`
☐ Closing a file with `fclose()`
☐ The `fgetc()` and `fputc()` functions
☐ The `fgets()` and `fputs()` functions
☐ The `fread()` and `fwrite()` functions
☐ The `feof()` function

Files Versus Streams

The C language provides a set of rich library functions to perform input and output (I/O) operation. Those functions can read or write any type of data to files. Before we go any further in discussing the C I/O functions, let's first understand the definitions of files and streams in C.

What Is a File?

In C, a *file* can refer to a disk file, a terminal, a printer, or a tape drive. In other words, a file represents a concrete device with which you want to exchange information. Before you perform any communication to a file, you have to open the file. Then you need to close the opened file after you finish exchanging information with it.

What Is a Stream?

The data flow you transfer from your program to a file, or vice versa, is called a *stream*, which is a series of bytes. Not like a file, a stream is device-independent. All streams have the same behavior. To perform I/O operations, you can read from or write to any type of files by simply associating a stream to the file.

There are two formats of streams. The first one is called the *text stream*, which consists of a sequence of characters (that is, ASCII data). Depending on the compilers, each character line in a text stream may be terminated by a newline character. Text streams are used for textual data, which has a consistent appearance from one environment to another, or from one machine to another.

The second format of streams is called the *binary stream*, which is a series of bytes. The content of an .exe file would be one example. Binary streams are primarily used for nontextual data, which is required to keep the exact contents of the file.

Buffered I/O

In C, a memory area, which is temporarily used to store data before it is sent to its destination, is called a *buffer*. With the help of buffers, the operating system can improve efficiency by reducing the number of accesses to I/O devices (that is, files).

By default, all I/O streams are buffered. The buffered I/O is also called the high-level I/O. Accordingly, the low-level I/O refers to the unbuffered I/O.

The Basics of Disk File I/O

Now let's focus on how to open and close a disk data file and how to interpret error messages returned by I/O functions.

Pointers of FILE

The FILE structure is the file control structure defined in the header file stdio.h. A pointer of type FILE is called a file pointer, which references a disk file. A file pointer is used by a stream to conduct the operation of the I/O functions. For instance, the following defines a file pointer called fptr:

```
FILE *fptr;
```

In the FILE structure there is a member, called the *file position indicator*, that points to the position in a file where data will be read from or written to. You'll learn how to move the file position indicator in the next lesson.

Opening a File

The C I/O function fopen() gives you the ability to open a file and associate a stream to the opened file. You need to specify the way to open a file and the filename with the fopen() function.

The syntax for the fopen() function is

```
#include <stdio.h>
FILE *fopen(const char *filename, const char *mode);
```

Here *filename* is a char pointer that references a string of a filename. The filename is given to the file that is about to be opened by the fopen() function. *mode* points to another string that specifies the way to open the file. The fopen() function returns a pointer of type FILE. If an error occurs during the procedure to open a file, the fopen() function returns a null pointer.

The following list shows the possible ways to open a file by various strings of modes:

- [ ] "r" opens an existing text file for reading.
- [ ] "w" creates a text file for writing.
- [ ] "a" opens an existing text file for appending.
- [ ] "r+" opens an existing text file for reading or writing.
- [ ] "w+" creates a text file for reading or writing.
- [ ] "a+" opens or creates a text file for appending.
- [ ] "rb" opens an existing binary file for reading.
- [ ] "wb" creates a binary file for writing.
- [ ] "ab" opens an existing binary file for appending.
- [ ] "r+b" opens an existing binary file for reading or writing.
- [ ] "w+b" creates a binary file for reading or writing.
- [ ] "a+b" opens or creates a binary file for appending.

Note that you might see people use the mode "rb+" instead of "r+b". These two strings are equivalent. Similarly, "wb+" is the same as "w+b"; "ab+" is equivalent to "a+b".

The following statements try to open a file called test.txt:

```
FILE *fptr;
if ((fptr = fopen("test.txt", "r")) == NULL){
   printf("Cannot open test.txt file.\n");
   exit(1);
}
```

Here "r" is used to indicate that a text file is about to be opened for reading only. If an error occurs when the fopen() function tries to open the file, the function returns a null pointer. Then an error message is printed out by the printf() function and the program is aborted by calling the exit() function with a nonzero value.

Closing a File

After a disk file is read, written, or appended with some new data, you have to disassociate the file from a specified stream by calling the fclose() function.

The syntax for the fclose() function is

```
#include <stdio.h>
int fclose(FILE *stream);
```

Here *stream* is a file pointer that is associated with a stream to the opened file. If fclose() closes a file successfully, it returns 0. Otherwise, the function returns EOF. Normally, the fclose() function fails only when the disk is removed before the function is called or there is no more space left on the disk.

Since all high-level I/O operations are buffered, the fclose() function flushes data left in the buffer to ensure that no data will be lost before it disassociates a specified stream with the opened file.

Note that a file that is opened and associated with a stream has to be closed after the I/O operation. Otherwise, the data saved in the file may be lost; some unpredictable errors might occur during the execution of your program.

The program in listing 21.1 shows you how to open and close a text file and how to check the returned file pointer value as well.

TYPE **Listing 21.1. Opening and closing a text file.**

```
1:  /* 21L01.c: Opening and closing a file */
2:  #include <stdio.h>
3:
4:  enum {SUCCESS, FAIL};
5:
6:  main(void)
```

```
7:  {
8:     FILE *fptr;
9:     char filename[]= "haiku.txt";
10:    int reval = SUCCESS;
11:
12:    if ((fptr = fopen(filename, "r")) == NULL){
13:       printf("Cannot open %s.\n", filename);
14:       reval = FAIL;
15:    } else {
16:       printf("The value of fptr: 0x%p\n", fptr);
17:       printf("Ready to close the file.");
18:       fclose(fptr);
19:    }
20:
21:    return reval;
22: }
```

The following output shows on my screen after running the executable 21L01.exe of the program in Listing 21.1. (Note that the value of the fptr is likely to be different on your machine. That's okay.)

OUTPUT
```
C:\app>21L01
The value of fptr: 0x013E
Ready to close the file.
C:\app>
```

ANALYSIS The purpose of the program in Listing 21.1 is to show you how to open a text file. From the expression in line 12, you can see that the fopen() function tries to open a text file with the name contained by the character array filename for reading. The filename array is defined and initialized with the name haiku.txt in line 9.

If an error occurs when you try to open the text file, the fopen() function returns a null pointer. Line 13 then prints a warning message, and line 14 assigns the value represented by the enum name FAIL to the int variable reval. From the declaration of the enum data type in line 4, we know that the value of FAIL is 1.

If, however, the fopen() function opens the text file successfully, the statement in line 16 prints the value contained by the file pointer fptr. Line 17 tells the user that the program is about to close the file, and line 18 then closes the file by calling the fclose() file.

In line 21, the return statement returns the value of reval that contains 0 if the text file has been opened successfully, or 1 otherwise.

From the output shown on my screen, I see that the value held by the file pointer fptr is 0x013E after the text file is opened.

Reading and Writing Disk Files

The program in Listing 21.1 does not do anything with the text file, haiku.txt, except open and close it. In fact, there are two pieces of Japanese haiku, written by Sodo and Chora, saved in the haiku.txt file. So how can you read them from the file?

In C, you can perform I/O operations in the following ways:

☐ Read or write one character at a time.

☐ Read or write one line of text (that is, one character line) at a time.

☐ Read or write one block of characters at a time.

The following three sections explain the three ways to read and write to disk files.

One Character at a Time

Among the C I/O functions, there is a pair of functions, fgetc() and fputc(), that can be used to read from or write to a disk file one character at a time.

The syntax for the fgetc() function is

```
#include <stdio.h>
int fgetc(FILE *stream);
```

Here stream is the file pointer that is associated with a stream. The fgetc() function fetches the next character from the stream specified by stream. The function then returns the value of an int that is converted from the character.

The syntax for the fputc() function is

```
#include <stdio.h>
int fputc(int c , FILE *stream);
```

Here c is an int value that represents a character. In fact, the int value is converted to an unsigned char before being outputted. stream is the file pointer that is associated with a stream. The fputc() function returns the character written if the function is successful; otherwise, it returns EOF. After a character is written, the fputc() function advances the associated file pointer.

To learn how to use the fgetc() and fputc() functions, let's have a look at Listing 21.2, which contains a program that opens a text file, and then reads and writes one character at a time.

TYPE Listing 21.2. Reading and writing one character at a time.

```
1:   /* 21L02.c: Reading and writing one character at a time */
2:   #include <stdio.h>
3:
4:   enum {SUCCESS, FAIL};
5:
```

21

```
6:  void CharReadWrite(FILE *fin, FILE *fout);
7:
8:  main(void)
9:  {
10:    FILE *fptr1, *fptr2;
11:    char filename1[]= "outhaiku.txt";
12:    char filename2[]= "haiku.txt";
13:    int reval = SUCCESS;
14:
15:    if ((fptr1 = fopen(filename1, "w")) == NULL){
16:       printf("Cannot open %s.\n", filename1);
17:       reval = FAIL;
18:    } else if ((fptr2 = fopen(filename2, "r")) == NULL){
19:       printf("Cannot open %s.\n", filename2);
20:       reval = FAIL;
21:    } else {
22:       CharReadWrite(fptr2, fptr1);
23:       fclose(fptr1);
24:       fclose(fptr2);
25:    }
26:
27:    return reval;
28: }
29: /* function definition */
30: void CharReadWrite(FILE *fin, FILE *fout)
31: {
32:    int c;
33:
34:    while ((c=fgetc(fin)) != EOF){
35:       fputc(c, fout);    /* write to a file */
36:       putchar(c);        /* put the character on the screen */
37:    }
38: }
```

After running the executable 21L02.exe, I get the following output:

OUTPUT

```
C:\app>21L02
Leading me along
my shadow goes back home
from looking at the moon.
--- Sodo
   (1641-1716)

A storm wind blows
out from among the grasses
the full moon grows.
--- Chora
   (1729-1781)
C:\app>
```

21

ANALYSIS The purpose of the program in Listing 21.2 is to read one character from a file, write the character to another file, and then display the character on the screen. (You need to copy the file, haiku.txt, from the CD-ROM in the book, and put it in the same directory where you save the executable file 21L02.exe. haiku.txt is the text file that is going to be read by 21L02.exe.)

In Listing 21.2 there is a function called CharReadWrite(), which has two file pointers as its arguments. (See the declaration of the CharReadWrite() function in line 6.)

The statement in line 10 defines two file pointers, fptr1 and fptr2, which are used later in the program. Lines 11 and 12 define two character arrays, filename1 and filename2, and initialize the two arrays with two strings containing filenames, outhaiku.txt and haiku.txt.

In line 15, a text file with the name outhaiku.txt is opened for writing. outhaiku.txt is contained by the filename1 array. The file pointer fptr1 is associated with the file. If the fopen() function returns NULL, which means an error occurs, a warning message is printed out in line 16. Also, in line 17, the reval variable is assigned 1 and is represented by the enum name FAIL.

If the file outhaiku.txt is opened successfully, another text file, called haiku.txt, is opened for reading in line 18. The file pointer fptr2 is associated with the opened text file.

If no error occurs, the CharReadWrite() function is invoked in line 22 with two file pointers, fptr1 and fptr2, passed to the function as arguments. From the definition of the CharReadWrite() function in lines 30 and 38, we see that there is a while loop that keeps calling the fgetc() function to read the next character from the haiku.txt text file until the function reaches the end of the file. (See line 34.)

Within the while loop, the fputc() function in line 35 writes each character read from the haiku.txt file to another text file, outhaiku.txt, which is pointed to by fout. In addition, putchar() is called in line 36 in order to put the character returned by the fgetc() function on the screen.

After the CharReadWrite() function finishes its job, the two opened files, which are associated with fptr1 and fptr2, are closed with a call to the fclose() function respectively in lines 23 and 24.

As mentioned earlier, the haiku.txt file contains two pieces of Japanese haiku written by Sodo and Chora. If the program in Listing 21.2 is run successfully, we see the two pieces of haiku shown on the screen, and they are written into the outhaiku.txt file as well. You can view outhaiku.txt in a text editor to confirm that the content of haiku.txt has been correctly copied to outhaiku.txt.

One Line at a Time

Besides reading or writing one character at a time, you can also read or write one character line at time. There is a pair of C I/O functions, fgets() and fputs(), that allows you to do so.

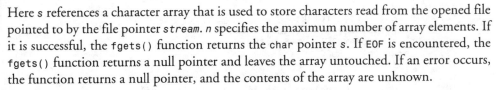

SYNTAX

The syntax for the `fgets()` function is

```
#include <stdio.h>
char *fgets(char *s, int n, FILE *stream);
```

Here *s* references a character array that is used to store characters read from the opened file pointed to by the file pointer *stream*. *n* specifies the maximum number of array elements. If it is successful, the `fgets()` function returns the char pointer *s*. If EOF is encountered, the `fgets()` function returns a null pointer and leaves the array untouched. If an error occurs, the function returns a null pointer, and the contents of the array are unknown.

The `fgets()` function can read up to *n*-1 characters, and can append a null character after the last character fetched, until a newline or an EOF is encountered. Note that if a newline is encountered during the reading, the `fgets()` function includes the newline in the array. This is different from what the `gets()` function does. The `gets()` function just replaces the newline character with a null character. (The `gets()` function was introduced in Hour 13, "Manipulating Strings.")

The syntax for the `fputs()` function is

```
#include <stdio.h>
int fputs(const char *s, FILE *stream);
```

Here *s* points to the array that contains the characters to be written to a file associated with the file pointer *stream*. The *const* modifier indicates that the content of the array pointed to by *s* cannot be changed. (You learned about the *const* modifier in Hour 14, "Scope and Storage Classes in C.") If it fails, the `fputs()` function returns a nonzero value; otherwise, it returns zero.

Note that the character array must include a null character at the end as the terminator to the `fputs()` function. Also, unlike the `puts()` function, the `fputs()` function does not insert a newline character to the string written to a file. (The `puts()` function was introduced in Hour 13.)

We can modify the program in Listing 21.2 to read or write one character line at a time by calling the `fgets()` and `fputs()` functions. The modified version is shown in Listing 21.3.

Listing 21.3. Reading and writing one character line at a time.

TYPE

```
1:  /* 21L03.c: Reading and writing one line at a time */
2:  #include <stdio.h>
3:
4:  enum {SUCCESS, FAIL, MAX_LEN = 81};
5:
6:  void LineReadWrite(FILE *fin, FILE *fout);
```

continues

21

Listing 21.3. continued

```
7:
8:  main(void)
9:  {
10:     FILE *fptr1, *fptr2;
11:     char filename1[]= "outhaiku.txt";
12:     char filename2[]= "haiku.txt";
13:     int reval = SUCCESS;
14:
15:     if ((fptr1 = fopen(filename1, "w")) == NULL){
16:        printf("Cannot open %s for writing.\n", filename1);
17:        reval = FAIL;
18:     } else if ((fptr2 = fopen(filename2, "r")) == NULL){
19:        printf("Cannot open %s for reading.\n", filename2);
20:        reval = FAIL;
21:     } else {
22:        LineReadWrite(fptr2, fptr1);
23:        fclose(fptr1);
24:        fclose(fptr2);
25:     }
26:
27:     return reval;
28: }
29: /* function definition */
30: void LineReadWrite(FILE *fin, FILE *fout)
31: {
32:     char buff[MAX_LEN];
33:
34:     while (fgets(buff, MAX_LEN, fin) != NULL){
35:        fputs(buff, fout);
36:        printf("%s", buff);
37:     }
38: }
```

Because the program in Listing 21.3 reads the same text file, haiku.txt, as the program in Listing 21.2 did, I get the same output on the screen:

OUTPUT

```
C:\app>21L03
Leading me along
my shadow goes back home
from looking at the moon.
--- Sodo
    (1641-1716)

A storm wind blows
out from among the grasses
the full moon grows.
--- Chora
    (1729-1781)
C:\app>
```

ANALYSIS From the program in Listing 21.3, you can see that a function called LineReadWrite() has replaced the CharReadWrite() function.

21

The definition of the LineReadWrite() function is shown in lines 30–38. The fgets() function is called repeatedly in a while loop to read one character line at a time from the haiku.txt text file, until it reaches the end of the text file. In line 34, the array name buff and the maximum number of the array elements MAX_LEN are passed to the fgets() function, along with the file pointer fin that is associated with the opened haiku.txt file.

Meanwhile, each line read by the fgets() function is written to another opened text file called outhaiku.txt that is associated with the file pointer fout. This is done by invoking the fputs() function in line 35.

The statement in line 36 prints the contents of each string on the screen so that you see the two pieces of Japanese verse after running the program in Listing 21.3. Also, you can view the outhaiku.txt file in a text editor to make sure that the contents of the haiku.txt file have been copied to the outhaiku.txt file.

One Block at a Time

If you like, you can also read or write a block of data at a time. In C, there are two I/O functions, fread() and fwrite(), that can be used to perform block I/O operations. The fread() and fwrite() functions are mirror images of each other.

The syntax for the fread() function is

```
#include <stdio.h>
size_t fread(void *ptr, size_t size, size_t n, FILE *stream);
```

Here *ptr* is a pointer to an array in which the data is stored. *size* indicates the size of each array element. *n* specifies the number of elements to read. *stream* is a file pointer that is associated with the opened file for reading. *size_t* is an integral type defined in the header file stdio.h. The fread() function returns the number of elements actually read.

The number of elements read by the fread() function should be equal to the value specified by the third argument to the function, unless an error occurs or an EOF (end-of-file) is encountered. The fread() function returns the number of elements that are actually read, if an error occurs or an EOF is encountered.

The syntax for the fwrite() function is

```
#include <stdio.h>
size_t fwrite(const void *ptr, size_t size, size_t n, FILE *stream);
```

Here *ptr* references the array that contains the data to be written to an opened file pointed to by the file pointer *stream*. *size* indicates the size of each element in the array. *n* specifies the number of elements to be written. The fwrite() function returns the number of elements actually written.

21

If there is no error occurring, the number returned by fwrite() should be the same as the third argument in the function. The return value may be less than the specified value if an error occurs.

Note that it's the programmer's responsibility to ensure that the array is large enough to hold data for either the fread() function or the fwrite() function.

In C, a function called feof() can be used to determine when the end of a file is encountered. This function is more useful when you're reading a binary file because the values of some bytes may be equal to the value of EOF. If you determine the end of a binary file by checking the value returned by fread(), you may end up at the wrong position. Using the feof() function helps you to avoid mistakes in determining the end of a file.

SYNTAX

The syntax for the feof() function is

```
#include <stdio.h>
int feof(FILE *stream);
```

Here *stream* is the file pointer that is associated with an opened file. The feof() function returns 0 if the end of the file has not been reached; otherwise, it returns a nonzero integer.

The program in Listing 21.4 demonstrates how to read and write one block of characters at a time by calling the fread() and fwrite() functions. In fact, the program in Listing 21.4 is another modified version of the program from Listing 21.2.

TYPE

Listing 21.4. Reading and writing one block of characters at a time.

```
1:  /* 21L04.c: Reading and writing one block at a time */
2:  #include <stdio.h>
3:
4:  enum {SUCCESS, FAIL, MAX_LEN = 80};
5:
6:  void BlockReadWrite(FILE *fin, FILE *fout);
7:  int ErrorMsg(char *str);
8:
9:  main(void)
10: {
11:     FILE *fptr1, *fptr2;
12:     char filename1[]= "outhaiku.txt";
13:     char filename2[]= "haiku.txt";
14:     int reval = SUCCESS;
15:
16:     if ((fptr1 = fopen(filename1, "w")) == NULL){
17:         reval = ErrorMsg(filename1);
18:     } else if ((fptr2 = fopen(filename2, "r")) == NULL){
19:         reval = ErrorMsg(filename2);
20:     } else {
21:         BlockReadWrite(fptr2, fptr1);
22:         fclose(fptr1);
```

21

```
23:        fclose(fptr2);
24:    }
25:
26:    return reval;
27: }
28: /* function definition */
29: void BlockReadWrite(FILE *fin, FILE *fout)
30: {
31:    int num;
32:    char buff[MAX_LEN + 1];
33:
34:    while (!feof(fin)){
35:        num = fread(buff, sizeof(char), MAX_LEN, fin);
36:        buff[num * sizeof(char)] = '\0';  /* append a null character */
37:        printf("%s", buff);
38:        fwrite(buff, sizeof(char), num, fout);
39:    }
40: }
41: /* function definition */
42: int ErrorMsg(char *str)
43: {
44:    printf("Cannot open %s.\n", str);
45:    return FAIL;
46: }
```

Again, I get the same output on the screen because the program in Listing 21.4 also reads the same text file, haiku.txt:

OUTPUT
```
C:\app>21L04
Leading me along
my shadow goes back home
from looking at the moon.
--- Sodo
   (1641-1716)

A storm wind blows
out from among the grasses
the full moon grows.
--- Chora
   (1729-1781)
C:\app>
```

ANALYSIS   The purpose of the program in Listing 21.4 is to show you how to invoke the fread() and fwrite() functions in your program to perform block I/O operations. In Listing 21.4, the haiku.txt file is read by the fread() function, and then the fwrite() function is used to write the contents read from haiku.txt to another file called outhaiku.txt. We call the two C I/O functions from our own function, BlockReadWrite().

From the definition of the BlockReadWrite() function in lines 29–40, you can see that a character array called buff is defined with the number of elements of MAX_LEN + 1 in line 32, although we only read MAX_LEN number of characters by calling the fread() function in line 35. The reason is that we append a null character in line 36 after the last character read so

21

that we ensure the block of characters saved in buff is treated as a string and can be printed out on the screen properly by the printf() function in line 37.

The while loop, shown in lines 34–39, keeps calling the fread() function to read a character block with MAX_LEN elements, until the feof() function in line 34 returns 0, which means that the end of the text file has been reached. As shown in lines 35 and 38, we use the sizof operator to measure the size of the char data type because the elements in the buff array are all characters.

If everything goes smoothly, you should see the Japanese verses again on the screen or in the outhaiku.txt file after running the program in Listing 21.4.

Summary

In this lesson you've learned the following:

- ☐ In C, a file can refer to a disk file, a terminal, a printer, or a tape drive.
- ☐ The data flow you transfer from your program to a file, or vice versa, is called a stream.
- ☐ A stream is a series of ordered bytes.
- ☐ Not like a file, a stream is device-independent.
- ☐ There are two stream formats: text stream and binary stream.
- ☐ The file position indicator in the FILE structure points to the position in a file where data will be read from or written to.
- ☐ The fopen() function is used to open a file and associate a stream to the opened file.
- ☐ You can specify different modes for opening a file.
- ☐ The fclose() function is responsible for closing an opened file and disassociating a stream with the file.
- ☐ The fgetc() and fputc() functions read or write one character at a time.
- ☐ The fgets() and fputs() functions read or write one line at a time.
- ☐ The fread() and fwrite() functions read or write one block of data at a time.
- ☐ The feof() function can determine when the end of a file has been reached.
- ☐ In a binary file, the feof() function should be used to detect EOF.

In the next lesson you'll learn more about disk file I/O in C.

Q&A

Q **What are the differences between a text stream and a binary stream?**

A A text stream is a sequence of characters that may not have a one-to-one relationship with the data on the device. Text streams are normally used for textual data, which have a consistent appearance from one environment to another, or from one machine to another. A binary stream, on the other hand, is a sequence of bytes that has a one-to-one correspondence to those on the device. Binary streams are primarily used for nontextual data that is needed to keep the exact contents on the device.

Q **Why do you need a file pointer?**

A A file pointer is used to associate a stream with an opened file for reading or writing purposes. A pointer of the type FILE is called a file pointer. FILE is a typedef for a structure that contains overhead information about a disk file. A file pointer plays an important role in the communication between programs and disk files.

Q **What does the fclose() function do before it closes an opened file?**

A As you know, all high-level I/O operations are buffered. One of the jobs of the fclose() function is to flush data left in the buffer to ensure that no data is lost. For instance, when you finish writing several blocks of characters to an opened text file, you call the fclose() function to disassociate a specified stream and close the text file. The fclose() function will first flush all characters left in the buffer and write them into the text file before it closes the file. In this way, all characters you write to the file will be saved properly.

Q **What is the difference between fgets() and gets()?**

A The major difference between the fgets() and gets() functions is that the fgets() function includes a newline character in the array if the newline is encountered during the reading, whereas the gets() function just replaces the newline character with a null character.

Workshop

To help solidify your understanding of this lesson, you are encouraged to answer the quiz questions and finish the exercises provided in the Workshop before you move to the next lesson. The answers and hints to the questions and exercises are given in Appendix E, "Answers to Quiz Questions and Exercises."

21

Quiz

1. What do the following expressions do?

```
fopen("test.bin", "r+b")
fopen("test.txt" "a")
fopen("test.ini", "w+")
```

2. What's wrong with the following code segment?

```
FILE *fptr;
int c;
if ((fptr = fopen("test1.txt", "r")) == NULL){
    while ((c=fgetc(fptr)) != EOF){
        putchar(c);
    }
}
fclose(fptr);
```

3. What's wrong with the following code segment?

```
FILE *fptr;
int c;
if ((fptr = fopen("test2.txt", "r")) != NULL){
    while ((c=fgetc(fptr)) != EOF){
        fputc(c, fptr);
    }
    fclose(fptr);
}
```

4. What's wrong with the following code segment?

```
FILE *fptr1, *fptr2;
int c;
if ((fptr1 = fopen("test1.txt", "r")) != NULL){
    while ((c=fgetc(fptr1)) != EOF){
        putchar(c);
    }
}
fclose(fptr1);
if ((fptr2 = fopen("test2.txt", "w")) != NULL){
    while ((c=fgetc(fptr1)) != EOF){
        fputc(c, fptr2);
    }
}
fclose(fptr2);
```

21

Exercises

1. Write a program to read the text file haiku.txt and count the number of characters in the file. Also, print out the contents of the file and the total character number on the screen.

2. Write a program to receive a string entered by the user, and then save the string into a file with the name also given by the user.

3. Given the string "Disk file I/O is tricky.", write a program to write the string into a file called test_21.txt by writing one character at a time. Meanwhile, print out the string on the screen.

4. Rewrite exercise 3. This time, try to write one block of characters (that is, one string) at a time.

21

Hour **22**

Disk File Input and Output: Part II

Disk space: the final frontier.

—*Captain Kirk's younger brother*

In last hour's lesson you learned the basics of reading and writing disk data files. In this lesson you'll learn more about communication with disk data files. The main topics discussed in this hour are

☐ Random access to files

☐ Reading or writing binary data

☐ Redirecting the standard streams

In addition, the following C I/O functions are introduced in this lesson:

☐ The `fseek()`, `ftell()`, and `rewind()` functions

☐ The `fscanf()` and `fprintf()` functions

☐ The `freopen()` function

Random Access to Disk Files

So far you've learned how to read or write data sequentially to an opened disk file, known as *sequential access*. In other words, you start with the first byte and keep reading or writing each successive byte in order. In many cases, however, you need to access particular data somewhere in the middle of a disk file. One way to do this is to keep reading data from the file until the particular data is fetched. Obviously, this is not an efficient way, especially when the file contains many data items.

Random access is another way to read or write data to disk files. In random access, specific file elements can be accessed in random order (that is, without reading through all the preceding data).

In C there are two I/O functions, `fseek()` and `ftell()`, that are designed to deal with random access.

The `fseek()` and `ftell()` Functions

As just mentioned, we need functions that enable us to access files randomly. The `fseek()` and `ftell()` functions provide us with such a capability.

In the previous lesson you learned that one of the members in the FILE structure is called the *file position indicator*. The file position indicator has to point to the desired position in a file before data can be read from or written to there. You can use the `fseek()` function to move the file position indicator to the spot you want to access in a file.

SYNTAX

The syntax for the `fseek()` function is

```
#include <stdio.h>
int fseek(FILE *stream, long offset, int whence);
```

Here `stream` is the file pointer associated with an opened file. `offset` indicates the number of bytes from a fixed position, specified by `whence`, that can have one of the following integral values represented by SEEK_SET, SEEK_CUR, and SEEK_END. If it is successful, the `fseek()` function returns 0; otherwise, the function returns a nonzero value.

You can find the values represented by SEEK_SET, SEEK_CUR, and SEEK_END in the header file `stdio.h`.

If SEEK_SET is chosen as the third argument to the `fseek()` function, the offset is counted from the beginning of the file and the value of the offset is greater than or equal to zero. If, however, SEEK_END is picked up, then the offset starts from the end of the file; the value of the offset should be negative. When SEEK_CUR is passed to the `fseek()` function, the offset is calculated from the current value of the file position indicator.

You can obtain the value of the current file position indicator by calling the `ftell()` function.

SYNTAX

The syntax for the `ftell()` function is

```
#include <stdio.h>
long ftell(FILE *stream);
```

Here *stream* is the file pointer associated with an opened file. The `ftell()` function returns the current value of the file position indicator.

The value returned by the `ftell()` function represents the number of bytes from the beginning of the file to the current position pointed to by the file position indicator.

If the `ftell()` function fails, it returns `-1L` (that is, a `long` value of minus 1). One thing that can cause the failure of the `ftell()` function is the file being a terminal or some other type for which the file position indicator becomes meaningless.

The program in Listing 22.1 shows how to randomly access a disk file by using the `fseek()` and `ftell()` functions.

TYPE ## Listing 22.1. Random access to a file.

```
 1:  /* 22L01.c: Random access to a file */
 2:  #include <stdio.h>
 3:
 4:  enum {SUCCESS, FAIL, MAX_LEN = 80};
 5:
 6:  void PtrSeek(FILE *fptr);
 7:  long PtrTell(FILE *fptr);
 8:  void DataRead(FILE *fptr);
 9:  int ErrorMsg(char *str);
10:
11:  main(void)
12:  {
13:     FILE *fptr;
14:     char filename[]= "haiku.txt";
15:     int reval = SUCCESS;
16:
17:     if ((fptr = fopen(filename, "r")) == NULL){
18:        reval = ErrorMsg(filename);
19:     } else {
20:        PtrSeek(fptr);
21:        fclose(fptr);
22:     }
23:
24:     return reval;
25:  }
26:  /* function definition */
27:  void PtrSeek(FILE *fptr)
28:  {
29:     long offset1, offset2, offset3;
30:
31:     offset1 = PtrTell(fptr);
```

continues

Listing 22.1. continued

```
32:    DataRead(fptr);
33:    offset2 = PtrTell(fptr);
34:    DataRead(fptr);
35:    offset3 = PtrTell(fptr);
36:    DataRead(fptr);
37:
38:    printf("\nRe-read the haiku:\n");
39:    /* re-read the third verse of the haiku */
40:    fseek(fptr, offset3, SEEK_SET);
41:    DataRead(fptr);
42:    /* re-read the second verse of the haiku */
43:    fseek(fptr, offset2, SEEK_SET);
44:    DataRead(fptr);
45:    /* re-read the first verse of the haiku */
46:    fseek(fptr, offset1, SEEK_SET);
47:    DataRead(fptr);
48: }
49: /* function definition */
50: long PtrTell(FILE *fptr)
51: {
52:    long reval;
53:
54:    reval = ftell(fptr);
55:    printf("The fptr is at %ld\n", reval);
56:
57:    return reval;
58: }
59: /* function definition */
60: void DataRead(FILE *fptr)
61: {
62:    char buff[MAX_LEN];
63:
64:    fgets(buff, MAX_LEN, fptr);
65:    printf("---%s", buff);
66: }
67: /* function definition */
68: int ErrorMsg(char *str)
69: {
70:    printf("Cannot open %s.\n", str);
71:    return FAIL;
72: }
```

I have the following output shown on my screen after running the executable 22L01.exe of the program in Listing 22.1:

OUTPUT

```
C:\app>22L01
The fptr is at 0
---Leading me along
The fptr is at 18
---my shadow goes back home
The fptr is at 44
---from looking at the moon.
```

22

```
Re-read the haiku:
---from looking at the moon.
---my shadow goes back home
---Leading me along
C:\app>
```

ANALYSIS The purpose of the program in Listing 22.1 is to move the file position indicator around in order to read different verses from the `haiku.txt` file.

Inside the `main()` function, a file pointer `fptr` is defined in line 13, and the name of the `haiku.txt` file is assigned to the array called `filename` in line 14. Then, in line 17, we try to open the `haiku.txt` file for reading by calling the `fopen()` function. If successful, we invoke the `PtrSeek()` function with the `fptr` file pointer as the argument in line 20.

The definition of our first function `PtrSeek()` is shown in lines 27–48. The statement in line 31 obtains the original value of the `fptr` file pointer by calling another function, `PtrTell()`, which is defined in lines 50–58. The `PtrTell()` function can find and print out the value of the file position indicator with the help of the C `ftell()` function. The original value of the file position indicator contained by `fptr` is assigned to the `long` variable `offset1` in line 31.

In line 32, the third function, `DataRead()`, is called to read one line of characters from the opened file and print out the line of characters on the screen. Line 33 gets the value of the `fptr` file position indicator right after the reading and assigns the value to another `long` variable, `offset2`.

Then the `DataRead()` function in line 34 reads the second line of characters from the opened file. Line 35 obtains the value of the file position indicator that points to the first byte of the third verse and assigns the value to the third `long` variable `offset3`. Line 36 calls the `DataRead()` function to read the third verse and print it out on the screen.

Therefore, from the first portion of the output, you can see the three different values of the file position indicator at three different positions, and the three verses of the haiku written by Sodo. The three values of the file position indicator are saved respectively by `offset1`, `offset2`, and `offset3`.

Now, starting from line 40 to line 47, we read Sodo's haiku backward, one verse at a time. That is, we read the third verse first, then the second verse, and finally the first verse. To do so, we first call the `fseek()` function to move the file position indicator to the beginning of the third verse by passing the value contained by `offset3` to the function. Then we call `fseek()` again and pass the value of `offset2` to the function so that the file position indicator is set to point to the first byte of the second verse. Finally, we move the file position indicator to the beginning of the first verse by passing the value of `offset1` to the `fseek()` function. Therefore, in the second portion of the output, you see the three verses of the haiku in reverse order.

The `rewind()` Function

Sometimes you might want to reset the file position indicator and put it at the beginning of a file. There is a handy C function, called `rewind()`, that can be used to rewind the file position indicator.

The syntax for the `rewind()` function is

```
#include <stdio.h>
void rewind(FILE *stream);
```

Here `stream` is the file pointer associated with an opened file. No value is returned by the `rewind()` function.

In fact, the following statement of the `rewind()` function

```
rewind(fptr);
```

is equivalent to this:

```
(void)fseek(fptr, 0L, SEEK_SET);
```

Here the `void` data type is cast to the `fseek()` function because the `rewind()` function does not return a value. Listing 22.2 contains an example that calls the `rewind()` function to move the file position indicator to the beginning of an opened file.

More Examples of Disk File I/O

The following sections show several more examples of disk file I/O, such as reading and writing binary data and redirecting the standard streams. Three more I/O functions, `fscanf()`, `fprintf()`, and `freopen()`, are introduced, too.

Reading and Writing Binary Data

As you learned in Hour 21, "Disk File Input and Output: Part I," you can indicate to the compiler that you're going to open a binary file by setting a proper mode when calling the `fopen()` function. For instance, the following statement tries to open an existing binary file for reading:

```
fptr = fopen("test.bin", "rb");
```

Note that the `"rb"` mode is used to indicate that the file we're going to open for reading is a binary file.

Listing 22.2 contains an example of reading and writing binary data.

22

TYPE **Listing 22.2. Reading and writing binary data.**

```
1:  /* 22L02.c: Reading and writing binary data */
2:  #include <stdio.h>
3:
4:  enum {SUCCESS, FAIL, MAX_NUM = 3};
5:
6:  void DataWrite(FILE *fout);
7:  void DataRead(FILE *fin);
8:  int ErrorMsg(char *str);
9:
10: main(void)
11: {
12:     FILE *fptr;
13:     char filename[]= "double.bin";
14:     int reval = SUCCESS;
15:
16:     if ((fptr = fopen(filename, "wb+")) == NULL){
17:         reval = ErrorMsg(filename);
18:     } else {
19:         DataWrite(fptr);
20:         rewind(fptr);   /* reset fptr */
21:         DataRead(fptr);
22:         fclose(fptr);
23:     }
24:
25:     return reval;
26: }
27: /* function definition */
28: void DataWrite(FILE *fout)
29: {
30:     int i;
31:     double buff[MAX_NUM] = {
32:                 123.45,
33:                 567.89,
34:                 100.11};
35:
36:     printf("The size of buff: %d-byte\n", sizeof(buff));
37:     for (i=0; i<MAX_NUM; i++){
38:         printf("%5.2f\n", buff[i]);
39:         fwrite(&buff[i], sizeof(double), 1, fout);
40:     }
41: }
42: /* function definition */
43: void DataRead(FILE *fin)
44: {
45:     int i;
46:     double x;
47:
48:     printf("\nRead back from the binary file:\n");
49:     for (i=0; i<MAX_NUM; i++){
50:         fread(&x, sizeof(double), (size_t)1, fin);
51:         printf("%5.2f\n", x);
52:     }
53: }
```

continues

Listing 22.2. continued

```
54: /* function definition */
55: int ErrorMsg(char *str)
56: {
57:    printf("Cannot open %s.\n", str);
58:    return FAIL;
59: }
```

After running the executable 22L02.exe, I have the following output on the screen:

```
C:\app>22L02
The size of buff: 24-byte
123.45
567.89
100.11

Read back from the binary file:
123.45
567.89
100.11
C:\app>
```

ANALYSIS The purpose of the program in Listing 22.2 is to write three values of the double data type into a binary file and then rewind the file position indicator and read back the three double values from the binary file. The two functions, DataWrite() and DataRead(), that perform the writing and reading, are declared in lines 6 and 7.

The enum names, SUCCESS, FAIL, and MAX_NUM, are defined in line 4 with values of 0, 1, and 3, respectively.

Inside the main() function, the statement in line 16 tries to create and open a binary file called double.bin for both reading and writing. Note that the "wb+" mode is used in the fopen() function in line 16.

If the fopen() function is successful, the DataWrite() function is called in line 19 to write three double data items, 123.45, 567.89, and 100.11, into the opened binary file, according to the definition of the DataWrite() function in lines 28–41. The fwrite() function in line 39 does the writing. Because the three double data items are saved in an array named buff, we also measure and print out the size of the buff array in line 36. On my machine, the size of the buff array is 24 bytes because each double data item is 8 bytes.

Right after the execution of the DataWrite() function, the file position indicator is reset to the beginning of the binary file by calling the rewind() function in line 20 because we want to read back all three double data items written to the file.

Then in line 21, the DataRead() function reads the three double data items from the opened binary file double.bin. From the definition of the DataRead() function in lines 43–53, you can see that the fread() function is used to perform the reading operation (see line 50).

The output from running the program in Listing 22.2 shows the three `double` data items before the writing and after the reading as well.

The `fscanf()` and `fprintf()` Functions

As you learned, the two C library functions `scanf()` and `printf()` can be used to read or write formatted data through the standard I/O (that is, `stdin` and `stdout`). Among the C disk file I/O functions, there are two equivalent functions, `fscanf()` and `fprintf()`, that can do the same jobs as the `scanf()` and `printf()` functions. In addition, the `fscanf()` and `fprintf()` functions allow the programmer to specify I/O streams.

The syntax for the `fscanf()` function is

```
#include <stdio.h>
int fscanf(FILE *stream, const char *format, …);
```

Here *stream* is the file pointer associated with an opened file. *format*, whose usage is the same as in the `scanf()` function, is a `char` pointer pointing to a string that contains the format specifiers. If successful, the `fscanf()` function returns the number of data items read. Otherwise, the function returns `EOF`.

The syntax for the `fprintf()` function is

```
#include <stdio.h>
int fprintf(FILE *stream, const char *format, …);
```

Here *stream* is the file pointer associated with an opened file. *format*, whose usage is the same as in the `printf()` function, is a `char` pointer pointing to a string that contains the format specifiers. If successful, the `fprintf()` function returns the number of formatted expressions. Otherwise, the function returns a negative value.

To know more about the `fprintf()` and `fscanf()` functions, you can review the explanations on the `printf()` and `scanf()` functions in Hour 5, "Reading from and Writing to Standard I/O," and Hour 13, "Manipulating Strings."

The program in Listing 22.3 demonstrates how to use the `fscanf()` and `fprintf()` functions to read and write differently typed data items.

TYPE **Listing 22.3. Using the `fscanf()` and `fprintf()` functions.**

```
1:  /* 22L03.c: Using the fscanf() and fprintf() functions */
2:  #include <stdio.h>
3:
4:  enum {SUCCESS, FAIL,
5:        MAX_NUM = 3,
6:        STR_LEN = 23};
7:
8:  void DataWrite(FILE *fout);
9:  void DataRead(FILE *fin);
10: int ErrorMsg(char *str);
```

continues

Listing 22.3. continued

```
11:
12: main(void)
13: {
14:     FILE *fptr;
15:     char filename[]= "strnum.mix";
16:     int reval = SUCCESS;
17:
18:     if ((fptr = fopen(filename, "w+")) == NULL){
19:         reval = ErrorMsg(filename);
20:     } else {
21:         DataWrite(fptr);
22:         rewind(fptr);
23:         DataRead(fptr);
24:         fclose(fptr);
25:     }
26:
27:     return reval;
28: }
29: /* function definition */
30: void DataWrite(FILE *fout)
31: {
32:     int i;
33:     char cities[MAX_NUM][STR_LEN] = {
34:                 "St.Louis->Houston:",
35:                 "Houston->Dallas:",
36:                 "Dallas->Philadelphia:"};
37:     int miles[MAX_NUM] = {
38:                 845,
39:                 243,
40:                 1459};
41:
42:     printf("The data written:\n");
43:     for (i=0; i<MAX_NUM; i++){
44:         printf("%-23s  %d miles\n", cities[i], miles[i]);
45:         fprintf(fout, "%s  %d", cities[i], miles[i]);
46:     }
47: }
48: /* function definition */
49: void DataRead(FILE *fin)
50: {
51:     int i;
52:     int miles;
53:     char cities[STR_LEN];
54:
55:     printf("\nThe data read:\n");
56:     for (i=0; i<MAX_NUM; i++){
57:         fscanf(fin, "%s%d", cities, &miles);
58:         printf("%-23s  %d miles\n", cities, miles);
59:     }
60: }
61: /* function definition */
62: int ErrorMsg(char *str)
63: {
64:     printf("Cannot open %s.\n", str);
65:     return FAIL;
66: }
```

22

The following output is shown on the screen after the executable 22L03.exe is created and run:

OUTPUT

```
C:\app>22L03
The data written:
St.Louis->Houston:      845 miles
Houston->Dallas:        243 miles
Dallas->Philadelphia:  1459 miles

The data read:
St.Louis->Houston:      845 miles
Houston->Dallas:        243 miles
Dallas->Philadelphia:  1459 miles
C:\app>
```

ANALYSIS The purpose of the program in Listing 22.3 is to write data items of different types into a file with the help of the fprintf() function and read back the data items in the same format by calling the fscanf() functions. The two functions declared in lines 8 and 9, DataWrite() and DataRead(), actually perform the writing and reading.

The statement of the main() function in line 18 tries to create and open a text file called strnum.mix for both reading and writing by specifying the second argument to the fopen() function as "w+". If fopen() does not return a null pointer, the DataWrite() function is called in line 21 to write strings and int data items into the strnum.mix file. Note that the fprintf() function is invoked inside the DataWrite() function in line 45 to write the formatted data into the text file.

From the definition of the DataWrite() function in lines 30–47, you can see that there are two arrays, cities and miles. The cities array contains three strings that indicate three pairs of cities, and the miles array has three int values representing the corresponding distances between the cities shown in the cities array. For instance, 845 in the miles array is the distance (in miles) between the two cities expressed by the string St.Louis->Houston: in the cities array.

In line 22, the rewind() function is called to rewind the file position indicator and reset it to the beginning of the strnum.mix file. Then the DataRead() function in line 23 reads back what has been saved in strnum.mix with the help of the fscanf() function. The definition of the DataRead() function is shown in lines 49–60.

From this example, you see that it is convenient to use the fprintf() and fscanf() functions together to perform formatted disk file I/O operations.

Redirecting the Standard Streams with freopen()

In Hour 5 you learned how to read from or write to standard I/O. Also, you were told that the C functions, such as getc(), gets(), putc, and printf(), direct their I/O operations automatically to either stdin or stdout.

In this section you're going to learn how to redirect the standard streams, such as stdin and stdout, to disk files. A new C function you're going to use is called freopen(), which can associate a standard stream with a disk file.

The syntax for the freopen() function is

```
#include <stdio.h>
FILE *freopen(const char *filename, const char *mode, FILE *stream);
```

Here *filename* is a char pointer referencing the name of a file that you want to associate with the standard stream represented by *stream*. *mode* is another char pointer pointing to a string that defines the way to open a file. The values that *mode* can have in freopen() are the same as the mode values in the fopen() function. (The definition of all mode values is given in Hour 21.)

The freopen() function returns a null pointer if an error occurs. Otherwise, the function returns the standard stream that has been associated with a disk file identified by *filename*.

Listing 22.4 demonstrates an example of redirecting the standard output, stdout, with the help of the freopen() function.

TYPE   **Listing 22.4. Redirecting the standard stream stdout.**

```
1:  /* 22L04.c: Redirecting a standard stream */
2:  #include <stdio.h>
3:
4:  enum {SUCCESS, FAIL,
5:        STR_NUM = 4};
6:
7:  void StrPrint(char **str);
8:  int ErrorMsg(char *str);
9:
10: main(void)
11: {
12:    char *str[STR_NUM] = {
13:           "Be bent, and you will remain straight.",
14:           "Be vacant, and you will remain full.",
15:           "Be worn, and you will remain new.",
16:           "---- by Lao Tzu"};
17:    char filename[]= "LaoTzu.txt";
18:    int reval = SUCCESS;
19:
20:    StrPrint(str);
21:    if (freopen(filename, "w", stdout) == NULL){
22:        reval = ErrorMsg(filename);
23:    } else {
24:       StrPrint(str);
25:       fclose(stdout);
26:    }
27:    return reval;
28: }
```

22

```
29: /* function definition */
30: void StrPrint(char **str)
31: {
32:     int i;
33:
34:     for (i=0; i<STR_NUM; i++)
35:         printf("%s\n", str[i]);
36: }
37: /* function definition */
38: int ErrorMsg(char *str)
39: {
40:     printf("Cannot open %s.\n", str);
41:     return FAIL;
42: }
```

Note that if you're using Microsoft Visual C++ on your machine, you need to make sure the project type is set to MS-DOS application (.EXE). Don't set the project type to QickWin application (.EXE) or other Windows application types, because there might be some conflicts between a Windows environment and the freopen() function. After the executable 22L04.exe is created and run, the following output is printed on the screen:

OUTPUT
```
C:\app>22L04
Be bent, and you will remain straight.
Be vacant, and you will remain full.
Be worn, and you will remain new.
---- by Lao Tzu

C:\app>
```

ANALYSIS The purpose of the program in Listing 22.4 is to save a paragraph of *Tao Te Ching* written by a Chinese philosopher, Lao Tzu, into a text file, LaoTzu.txt. To do so, we call the printf() function instead of the fprintf() function or other disk I/O functions after we redirect the default stream, stdout, of the printf() function to point to the text file.

The function that actually does the writing is called StrPrint(), which invokes the C function printf() to send out formatted character strings to the output stream. (See the definition of the StrPrint() function in lines 30–36.)

Inside the main() function, we call the StrPrint() function in line 20 before we redirect stdout to the LaoTzu.txt file. It's not surprising to see that the paragraph adopted from *Tao Te Ching* is printed on the screen because the printf() function automatically sends out the paragraph to stdout that directs to the screen by default.

Then, in line 21, we redirect stdout to the LaoTzu.txt text file by calling the freopen() function. There the "w" is used as the mode that indicates to open the text file for writing. If freopen() is successful, we then call the StrPrint() function in line 24. However, this time, the StrPrint() function writes the paragraph into the opened text file, LaoTzu.txt. The reason is that stdout is now associated with the text file, not the screen, so that strings sent out by the printf() function inside StrPrint() are directed to the text file.

After the execution of the program in Listing 22.4, you can open the LaoTzu.txt file in a text editor and see that the paragraph of *Tao Te Ching* has been saved in the file.

> **NOTE**
>
> As mentioned previously, the I/O streams are buffered by default. Occasionally, you may want to turn off the buffering so that you can process the input immediately. In C there are two functions, setbuf() and setvbuf(), that can be used to turn off the buffering. Appendix B contains the syntax of the two functions, although unbuffering I/O is beyond the scope of this book.
>
> Also, there is a set of low-level I/O functions, such as open(), create(), close(), read(), write(), lseek(), and tell(), which are not supported by the ANSI C standard. You may still see them in some platform-dependent C programs. To use them, you need to read your C compiler's reference manual to make sure they're available.

Summary

In this lesson you've learned the following:

☐ The file position indicator can be reset by the fseek() function.

☐ The ftell() function can tell you the value of the current file position indicator.

☐ The rewind() function can set the file position indicator to the beginning of a file.

☐ After you specify the mode of the fopen() function for the binary file, you can use the fread() or fwrite() functions to perform I/O operations on binary data.

☐ Besides the fact that the fscanf() and fprintf() functions can do the same jobs as the scanf() and printf() functions, the fscanf() and fprintf() functions also allow the programmer to specify I/O streams.

☐ You can redirect the standard streams, such as stdin and stdout, to a disk file with the help of the freopen() function.

In the next lesson you'll learn about the C preprocessor.

Q&A

Q Why is random access to a disk file necessary?

A When you want to fetch a piece of information from a large file that contains a huge amount of data, random access to the file is a more efficient way than sequential access at the file. The functions that perform random access can put the file position

22

indicator directly at the right place in the file, and then you can simply start to fetch the required information from there. In C, the `fseek()` and `ftell()` functions are two handy functions that help you to carry out the random access operation.

Q How do you specify the format of a new disk file you're going to create by calling `fopen()`?

A We have to add b to the mode argument to the `fopen()` function to specify that the file we're going to create is a binary file. We can use `"wb"` to create a new file for writing and `"wb+"` to create a new file for writing and reading. If, however, the file to be created is a text file, no b is needed in the mode argument.

Q What is the difference between the `printf()` and `fprintf()` functions?

A Basically, the `printf()` and `fprintf()` functions can do a similar job: send the formatted data items to the output streams. However, the `printf()` function automatically sends formatted data to `stdout`, whereas the `fprintf()` function can be assigned a file pointer that is associated with a specified output stream.

Q Can you redirect a standard stream to a disk file?

A Yes. With the help of the `freopen()` function, you can redirect a standard stream and associate the stream with a disk file.

Workshop

To help solidify your understanding of this hour's lesson, you are encouraged to answer the quiz questions and finish the exercises provided in the Workshop before you move to the next lesson. The answers and hints to the questions and exercises are given in Appendix E, "Answers to Quiz Questions and Exercises."

Quiz

1. Are the following two statements equivalent?

```
rewind(fptr);
(void)fseek(fptr, 0L, SEEK_SET);
```

2. Are the following two statements equivalent?

```
rewind(fptr);
(void)fseek(fptr, 0L, SEEK_CUR);
```

3. After the statement

```
freopen("test.txt", "r", stdin);
```

is executed successfully, where does the `scanf()` function in the following statement read from?

```
scanf("%s%d", str, &num);
```

4. Given that the size of the `double` data type is 8 bytes long and includes four `double` data items, if you write the four `double` data items into a binary file, how many bytes do the four data items take in the file?

Exercises

1. Assume that the following paragraph of *Tao Te Ching* is saved in a text file called `LaoTzu.txt`:

```
Be bent, and you will remain straight.
Be vacant, and you will remain full.
Be worn, and you will remain new.
```

Write a program to use `ftell()` to find the positions of the three strings in the file, and then call `fseek()` to set the file position indicator in such a way that the three strings are printed out in reverse order.

2. Rewrite the program you made in exercise 1 by calling the `rewind()` function to reset the file position indicator at the beginning of the `LaoTzu.txt` file.

3. Given a `double` value of `123.45` and an `int` value of `10000`, write a program to save them into a binary file, called `data.bin`, and then read them back from the binary file. Also, print out what you're writing or reading. What do you think the size of the binary file will be?

4. Read the text file `strnum.mix`, which is created by the program in Listing 22.3. Redirect the input stream so that you can use the `scanf()` function to perform the reading operation. (Note that if you're using Microsoft Visual C++ on your machine, make sure the project type is set to MS-DOS application (.EXE).)

Hour 23

The C Preprocessor

Intelligence is the faculty of making artificial objects, especially tools to make tools.

—*H. Bergson*

In Hour 2, "Writing Your First C Program," you learned how to use the #include preprocessor directive to include C header files. Since then, the #include directive has been used in every program in this book. In this lesson you'll learn more about the C preprocessor and making macro definitions with the preprocessor directives. The following topics are discussed in this hour:

☐ What the C preprocessor can do

☐ Macro definitions and macro substitutions

☐ The #define and #undef directives

☐ How to define function-like macros with #define

☐ The #ifdef, #ifndef, and #endif directives

☐ The #if, #elif, and #else directives

☐ How to nest #if and #elif directives

What Is the C Preprocessor?

If there is a constant appearing in several places in your program, it's a good idea to associate a symbolic name to the constant, and then use the symbolic name to replace the constant throughout the program. There are two advantages to doing so. First, your program will be more readable. Second, it's easier to maintain your program. For instance, if the value of the constant needs to be changed, find the statement that associates the constant with the symbolic name and replace the constant with the new one. Without using the symbolic name, you have to look everywhere in your program to replace the constant. Sounds great, but can we do this in C?

Well, C has a special program called the C preprocessor that allows you to define and associate symbolic names with constants. In fact, the C preprocessor uses the terminology *macro names* and *macro body* to refer to the symbolic names and the constants. The C preprocessor runs before the compiler. During preprocessing, the operation to replace a macro name with its associated macro body is called *macro substitution* or *macro expansion.*

You can put a macro definition anywhere in your program. However, a macro name has to be defined before it can be used in your program.

In addition, the C preprocessor gives you the ability to include other source files. For instance, we've been using the preprocessor directive `#include` to include C header files, such as `stdio.h`, `stdlib.h`, and `string.h`, in the programs throughout this book. Also, the C preprocessor enables you to compile different sections of your program under specified conditions.

The C Preprocessor Versus the Compiler

One important thing you need to remember is that the C preprocessor is not part of the C compiler.

The C preprocessor uses a different syntax. All directives in the C preprocessor begin with a pound sign (#). In other words, the pound sign denotes the beginning of a preprocessor directive, and it must be the first nonspace character on the line.

The C preprocessor is line oriented. Each macro statement ends with a newline character, not a semicolon. (Only C statements end with semicolons.) One of the most common mistakes made by the programmer is to place a semicolon at the end of a macro statement. Fortunately, many C compilers can catch such errors.

The following sections describe some of the most frequently used directives, such as `#define`, `#undef`, `#if`, `#elif`, `#else`, `#ifdef`, `#ifndef`, and `#endif`.

> **TIP**
> Macro names, especially those that will be substituted with constants, are normally represented with uppercase letters so that they can be distinguished from other variable names in the program.

The #define and #undef **Directives**

The #define directive is the most common preprocessor directive, which tells the preprocessor to replace every occurrence of a particular character string (that is, a macro name) with a specified value (that is, a macro body).

The syntax for the #define directive is

```
#define macro_name   macro_body
```

Here *macro_name* is an identifier that can contain letters, numerals, or underscores. *macro_body* may be a string or a data item, which is used to substitute each *macro_name* found in the program.

As mentioned earlier, the operation to replace occurrences of *macro_name* with the value specified by *macro_body* is known as macro substitution or macro expansion.

The value of the macro body specified by a #define directive can be any character string or number. For example, the following definition associates STATE_NAME with the string "Texas" (including the quotation marks):

```
#define STATE_NAME    "Texas"
```

Then, during preprocessing, all occurrences of STATE_NAME will be replaced by "Texas".

Likewise, the following statement tells the C preprocessor to replace SUM with the string (12 + 8):

```
#define SUM  (12 + 8)
```

On the other hand, you can use the #undef directive to remove the definition of a macro name that has been previously defined.

The syntax for the #undef directive is

```
#undef macro_name
```

Here *macro_name* is an identifier that has been previously defined by a #define directive.

The #undef directive "undefines" a macro name. For instance, the following segment of code:

```
#define STATE_NAME "Texas"
   printf("I am moving out of %s.\n", STATE_NAME);
#undef STATE_NAME
```

defines the macro name STATE_NAME first, and uses the macro name in the printf() function; then it removes the macro name.

Defining Function-Like Macros with #define

You can specify one or more arguments to a macro name defined by the #define directive, so that the macro name can be treated like a simple function that accepts arguments.

For instance, the following macro name, MULTIPLY, takes two arguments:

```
#define MULTIPLY(val1, val2)  ((val1) * (val2))
```

When the following statement:

```
result = MULTIPLY(2, 3) + 10;
```

is preprocessed, the preprocessor substitutes the expression 2 for val1 and 3 for val2, and then produces the following equivalent:

```
result = ((2) * (3)) + 10;
```

The program in Listing 23.1 is an example of using the #define directive to perform macro substitution.

TYPE **Listing 23.1. Using the #define directive.**

```
1:  /* 23L01.c:  Using #define */
2:  #include <stdio.h>
3:
4:  #define METHOD        "ABS"
5:  #define ABS(val)      ((val) < 0 ? -(val) : (val))
6:  #define MAX_LEN       8
7:  #define NEGATIVE_NUM -10
8:
9:  main(void)
10: {
11:    char *str = METHOD;
12:    int array[MAX_LEN];
13:    int i;
14:
15:    printf("The orignal values in array:\n");
16:    for (i=0; i<MAX_LEN; i++){
17:       array[i] = (i + 1) * NEGATIVE_NUM;
18:       printf("array[%d]: %d\n", i, array[i]);
19:    }
```

23

```
20:
21:     printf("\nApplying the %s macro:\n", str);
22:     for (i=0; i<MAX_LEN; i++){
23:         printf("ABS(%d): %3d\n", array[i], ABS(array[i]));
24:     }
25:
26:     return 0;
27: }
```

The following output appears on the screen after you run the executable 23L01.exe of the program in Listing 23.1:

OUTPUT

```
C:\app>23L01
The orignal values in array:
array[0]: -10
array[1]: -20
array[2]: -30
array[3]: -40
array[4]: -50
array[5]: -60
array[6]: -70
array[7]: -80

Applying the ABS macro:
ABS(-10):  10
ABS(-20):  20
ABS(-30):  30
ABS(-40):  40
ABS(-50):  50
ABS(-60):  60
ABS(-70):  70
ABS(-80):  80
C:\app>
```

ANALYSIS The purpose of the program in Listing 23.1 is to define different macro names, including a function-like macro, and use them in the program.

In lines 4–7, four macro names, METHOD, ABS, MAX_LEN, and NEGATIVE_NUM are defined with the #define directive. Among them, ABS can accept one argument. The definition of ABS in line 5 checks the value of the argument and returns the absolute value of the argument. Note that the conditional operator ?: is used to find the absolute value for the incoming argument. (The ?: operator was introduced in Hour 8, "More Operators.")

Then, inside the main() function, the char pointer str is defined and assigned with METHOD in line 11. As you can see, METHOD is associated with the string "ABS". In line 12, an int array called array is defined with the element number specified by MAX_LEN.

In lines 16–19, each element of array is initialized with the value represented by the (i + 1) * NEGATIVE_NUM expression that produces a series of negative integer numbers.

The for loop in lines 22–24 applies the function-like macro ABS to each element of array and obtains the absolute value for each element. Also, all absolute values are printed on the screen. The output from the program in Listing 23.1 proves that each macro defined in the program works very well.

Nested Macro Definitions

A previously defined macro can be used as the value in another #define statement. The following is an example:

```
#define ONE        1
#define TWO        (ONE + ONE)
#define THREE      (ONE + TWO)
result = TWO * THREE;
```

Here the macro ONE is defined to be equivalent to the value 1, and TWO is defined to be equivalent to (ONE + ONE), where ONE is defined in the previous macro definition. Likewise, THREE is defined to be equivalent to (ONE + TWO), where both ONE and TWO are previously defined.

Therefore, the assignment statement following the macro definitions is equivalent to the following statement:

```
result = (1 + 1) * (1 + (1 + 1));
```

WARNING

When you are using the #define directive with a macro body that is an expression, you need to enclose the macro body in parentheses. For example, if the macro definition is

```
#define SUM  12 + 8
```

then the following statement:

```
result = SUM * 10;
```

becomes this:

```
result = 12 + 8 * 10;
```

which assigns 92 to result.

However, if you enclose the macro body in parentheses like this:

```
#define SUM   (12 + 8)
```

then the assignment statement becomes this:

```
result = (12 + 8) * 10;
```

and produces the result 200, which is likely what you want.

Compiling Your Code Under Conditions

You can select portions of your C program that you want to compile by using a set of preprocessor directives. This is useful, especially when you're testing a piece of new code or debugging a portion of code.

The #ifdef and #endif Directives

The #ifdef and #endif directives control whether a given group of statements is to be included as part of your program.

The general form to use the #ifdef and #endif directives is

```
#ifdef macro_name
    statement1
    statement2
    . . .
    statementN
#endif
```

Here macro_name is any character string that can be defined by a #define directive. statement1, statement2, and statementN are statements that are included in the program if macro_name has been defined. If macro_name has not been defined, statement1, statement2, and statementN are skipped.

Because the statements under the control of the #ifdef directive are not enclosed in braces, the #endif directive must be used to mark the end of the #ifdef block.

For instance, the #ifdef directive in the following code segment:

```
. . .
#ifdef DEBUG
    printf("The contents of the string pointed to by str: %s\n", str);
#endif
. . .
```

indicates that if the macro name DEBUG is defined, the printf() function in the statement following the #ifdef directive is included in the program. The compiler will compile the statement so that the contents of a string pointed to by str can be printed out after the statement is executed.

The #ifndef Directive

The #ifndef directive enables you to define code that is to be executed when a particular macro name is not defined.

The general format to use #ifndef is the same as for #ifdef:

```
#ifndef macro_name
    statement1
    statement2
```

```
    . . .
    statementN
#endif
```

Here *macro_name*, *statement1*, *statement2*, and *statementN* have the same meanings as those
in the form of #ifdef introduced in the previous section. Again, the #endif directive is needed
to mark the end of the #ifndef block.

Listing 23.2 contains a program that demonstrates how to use the #ifdef, #ifndef, and
#endif directives together.

TYPE | **Listing 23.2. Using the #ifdef, #ifndef, and #endif directives.**

```
1:  /* 23L02.c:  Using #ifdef, #ifndef, and #endif */
2:  #include <stdio.h>
3:
4:  #define UPPER_CASE  0
5:  #define NO_ERROR    0
6:
7:  main(void)
8:  {
9:     #ifdef UPPER_CASE
10:       printf("THIS LINE IS PRINTED OUT,\n");
11:       printf("BECAUSE UPPER_CASE IS DEFINED.\n");
12:    #endif
13:    #ifndef LOWER_CASE
14:       printf("\nThis line is printed out,\n");
15:       printf("because LOWER_CASE is not defined.\n");
16:    #endif
17:
18:    return NO_ERROR;
19: }
```

The following output is shown on the screen after the executable 23L02.exe is created
and run:

OUTPUT
```
C:\app>23L02
THIS LINE IS PRINTED OUT,
BECAUSE UPPER_CASE IS DEFINED.

This line is printed out,
because LOWER_CASE is not defined.
C:\app>
```

ANALYSIS The purpose of the program in Listing 23.2 is to use #ifdef and #ifndef directives
to control whether a piece of message needs to be printed out.

Two macro names, UPPER_CASE and NO_ERROR, are defined in lines 4 and 5.

The #ifdef directive in line 9 checks whether the UPPER_CASE macro name has been defined.
Because the macro name has been defined in line 4, the two statements in lines 10 and 11
are executed before the #endif directive in line 12 marks the end of the #ifdef block.

In line 13, the #ifndef directive tells the preprocessor to include the two statements in lines 14 and 15 in the program if the LOWER_CASE macro name has not been defined. As you can see, LOWER_CASE is not defined in the program at all. Therefore, the two statement in lines 14 and 15 are counted as part of the program.

The output from running the program in Listing 23.2 shows that the printf() functions in lines 10, 11, 14, and 15 are executed accordingly, under the control of the #ifdef and #ifndef directives.

The #if, #elif, and #else Directives

The #if directive specifies that certain statements are to be included only if the value represented by the conditional expression is nonzero. The conditional expression can be an arithmetic expression.

The general form to use the #if directive is

```
#if expression
    statement1
    statement2
    . . .
    statementN
#endif
```

Here expression is the conditional expression to be evaluated. statement1, statement2, and statementN represent the code to be included if expression is nonzero.

Note that the #endif directive is included at the end of the definition to mark the end of the #if block, as it does for an #ifdef or #ifndef block.

In addition, the #else directive provides an alternative to choose. The following general form uses the #else directive to put statement_1, statement_2, and statement_N into the program if expression is zero:

```
#if expression
    statement1
    statement2
    . . .
    statementN
#else
    statement_1
    statement_2
    . . .
    statement_N
#endif
```

Again, the #endif directive is used to mark the end of the #if block.

Also, a macro definition can be used as part of the conditional expression evaluated by the #if directive. If the macro is defined, it has a nonzero value in the expression; otherwise, it has the value 0.

For example, look at the following portion of code:

```
#ifdef DEBUG
   printf("The value of the debug version: %d\n", debug);
#else
   printf("The value of the release version: %d\n", release);
#endif
```

If DEBUG has been defined by a #define directive, the value of the debug version is printed out by the printf() function in the following statement:

```
printf("The value of the debug version: %d\n", debug);
```

Otherwise, if DEBUG has not been defined, the following statement is executed:

```
printf("The value of the release version: %d\n", release);
```

Now consider another example:

```
#if 1
 printf("The line is always printed out.\n");
#endif
```

The printf() function is always executed because the expression 1 evaluated by the #if directive never returns 0.

In the following example:

```
#if MACRO_NAME1 || MACRO_NAME2
   printf("MACRO_NAME1 or MACRO_NAME2 is defined.\n");
#else
   printf("MACRO_NAME1 and MACRO_NAME2 are not defined.\n");
#endif
```

the logical operator || is used, along with MACRO_NAME1 and MACRO_NAME2 in the expression evaluated by the #if directive. If one of the macro names, MACRO_NAME1 or MACRO_NAME2, has been defined, the expression returns a nonzero value; otherwise, the expression returns 0.

The C preprocessor has another directive, #elif, which stands for "else if." You can use #if and #elif together to build an if-else-if chain for multiple conditional compilation.

The program shown in Listing 23.3 is an example of using the #if, #elif, and #else directives.

TYPE Listing 23.3. Using the #if, #elif, and #else directives.

```
1:  /* 23L03.c:  Using #if, #elif, and #else */
2:  #include <stdio.h>
3:
4:  #define C_LANG    'C'
5:  #define B_LANG    'B'
6:  #define NO_ERROR  0
```

```
7:
8:    main(void)
9:    {
10:      #if C_LANG == 'C' && B_LANG == 'B'
11:        #undef C_LANG
12:        #define C_LANG "I know the C language.\n"
13:        #undef B_LANG
14:        #define B_LANG "I know BASIC.\n"
15:        printf("%s%s", C_LANG, B_LANG);
16:      #elif C_LANG == 'C'
17:        #undef C_LANG
18:        #define C_LANG "I only know C language.\n"
19:        printf("%s", C_LANG);
20:      #elif B_LANG == 'B'
21:        #undef B_LANG
22:        #define B_LANG "I only know BASIC.\n"
23:        printf("%s", B_LANG);
24:      #else
25:        printf("I don't know C or BASIC.\n");
26:      #endif
27:
28:      return NO_ERROR;
29:   }
```

After the executable 23L03.exe is created and run, the following output is displayed on the screen:

OUTPUT

```
C:\app>23L03
I know C language.
I know BASIC.
C:\app>
```

ANALYSIS The purpose of the program in Listing 23.3 is to use the #if, #elif, and #else directives to select portions of code that are going to be compiled.

Inside the main() function, the #if directive in line 10 evaluates the conditional expression C_LANG == 'C' && B_LANG == 'B'. If the expression returns nonzero, then statements in lines 11–15 are selected to be compiled.

In line 11 the #undef directive is used to remove the C_LANG macro name. Line 12 then redefines C_LANG with the string "I know the C language.\n". Likewise, line 13 removes the B_LANG macro name and line 14 redefines B_LANG with another character string. The printf() function in line 15 prints the two newly assigned strings associated with C_LANG and B_LANG.

The #elif directive in line 16 starts to evaluate the expression C_LANG == 'C' if the expression in line 10 fails to return a nonzero value. If the C_LANG == 'C' expression returns nonzero, the statements in lines 17–19 are compiled.

If, however, the expression in line 16 also fails to return a nonzero value, the B_LANG == 'B' expression in line 20 is evaluated by another #elif directive. The statements in lines 21–23 are skipped, and the statement in line 25 is compiled finally if the B_LANG == 'B' expression returns 0.

In line 26 the #endif directive marks the end of the #if block that starts on line 10.

From the program in Listing 23.3 you can tell that C_LANG and B_LANG have been properly defined in lines 4 and 5. Therefore, the statements in lines 11–15 are selected as part of the program and compiled by the C compiled. The two character strings assigned to C_LANG and B_LANG during the redefinition are printed out after the program in Listing 23.3 is executed.

You're advised to change the value of the macros C_LANG and B_LANG to test the other executions in the program.

Nested Conditional Compilation

According to the ANSI C standard, the #if and #elif directives can be nested at least eight levels.

For example, the #if directive is nested in the following code segment:

```
#if MACRO_NAME1
   #if MACRO_NAME2
      #if MACRO_NAME3
         printf("MACRO_NAME1, MACRO_NAME2, and MACRO_NAME3\n");
      #else
         printf("MACRO_NAME1 and MACRO_NAME2\n");
      #endif
   #else
      printf("MACRO_NAME1\n");
   #endif
#else
   printf("No macro name defined.\n");
#endif
```

Here the #if directive is nested to three levels. Note that each #else or #endif is associated with the nearest #if.

Now let's have a look at another example in Listing 23.4, in which the #if directives are nested.

TYPE   **Listing 23.4. Nesting the #if directive.**

```
 1:  /* 23L04.c: Nesting #if   */
 2:  #include <stdio.h>
 3:
 4:  /* macro definitions */
 5:  #define ZERO      0
 6:  #define ONE       1
 7:  #define TWO       (ONE + ONE)
 8:  #define THREE     (ONE + TWO)
 9:  #define TEST_1    ONE
10:  #define TEST_2    TWO
11:  #define TEST_3    THREE
12:  #define MAX_NUM   THREE
13:  #define NO_ERROR  ZERO
```

```
14: /* function declaration */
15: void StrPrint(char **ptr_s, int max);
16: /* the main() function */
17: main(void)
18: {
19:     char *str[MAX_NUM] = {"The choice of a point of view",
20:                           "is the initial act of culture.",
21:                           "--- by O. Gasset"};
22:
23:     #if TEST_1 == 1
24:        #if TEST_2 == 2
25:           #if TEST_3 == 3
26:              StrPrint(str, MAX_NUM);
27:           #else
28:              StrPrint(str, MAX_NUM - ONE);
29:           #endif
30:        #else
31:           StrPrint(str, MAX_NUM - TWO);
32:        #endif
33:     #else
34:        printf("No TEST macro has been set.\n");
35:     #endif
36:
37:     return NO_ERROR;
38: }
39: /* function definition */
40: void StrPrint(char **ptr_s, int max)
41: {
42:     int i;
43:
44:     for (i=0; i<max; i++)
45:        printf("Content: %s\n",
46:                ptr_s[i]);
47: }
```

The following output is shown on the screen after the executable 23L04.exe is created and run on my machine:

OUTPUT

```
C:\app>23L04
Content: The choice of a point of view
Content: is the initial act of culture.
Content: --- by O. Gasset
C:\app>
```

ANALYSIS   The purpose of the program in Listing 23.4 is to print the content of character strings controlled by the nested #if directives.

At the beginning of the program, nine macro names are defined in lines 5–13. The prototype of a function, StrPrint(), is given in line 15. Lines 19–21 define and initialize an array of char pointers called str.

The #if directives in lines 23–25 evaluate macro names, TEST_1, TEST_2, and TEST_3, respectively. If the three macro names all return nonzero values, then in line 26, StrPrint() is invoked to print the content of all character strings pointed to by the pointers in the str array.

If, however, only TEST_1 and TEST_2 are nonzero, the statement in line 28 prints out the content of the MAX_NUM-ONE strings. Likewise, if only TEST_1 returns a nonzero value, the StrPrint() function is called in line 31 to print out the content of the MAX_NUM-TWO strings.

The last case is that TEST_1, TEST_2, and TEST_3 all return zero. Then the printf() function in line 34 is executed to display the message No TEST macro has been set. onscreen.

As you can tell from the program in Listing 23.4, TEST_1, TEST_2, and TEST_3 are all defined with nonzero constants; the content of all character strings referenced by the pointers of the str array are printed out as the output from the program.

You're advised to change the value of the macros TEST_1, TEST_2, and TEST_3 to test the other executions in the program.

Summary

In this lesson you've learned the following:

- ☐ The C preprocessor runs before the compiler. During preprocessing, all occurrences of a macro name are replaced by the macro body associated with the macro name.
- ☐ The C preprocessor also enables you to include additional source files to the program or compile sections of C code conditionally.
- ☐ The C preprocessor is not part of the C compiler.
- ☐ A macro statement ends with a newline character, not a semicolon.
- ☐ The #define directive tells the preprocessor to replace every occurrence of a macro name defined by the directive with a macro body that is associated with the macro name.
- ☐ The #undef directive is used to remove the definition of a macro name that has been previously defined.
- ☐ You can specify one or more arguments to a macro name defined by the #define directive.
- ☐ The #ifdef directive enables you to define code that is to be included when a particular macro name is defined.
- ☐ The #ifndef directive is a mirror directive to the #ifdef directive. The former enables you to define code that is to be included when a particular macro name is not defined.
- ☐ The #endif is used to mark the end of an #ifdef, an #ifndef, or an #if block.
- ☐ The #if, #elif, and #else directives enable you to select portions of code to compile.

In the next lesson you'll see a summary of what you've learned and what you can do after studying this book.

Q&A

Q Is the C preprocessor part of the C compiler?

A No. The C preprocessor is not part of the C compiler. With its own line-oriented grammar and syntax, the C preprocessor runs before the compiler in order to handle named constants, macros, and inclusion of files.

Q How do you remove a macro name?

A By putting a macro name after the #undef directive, the macro name can be removed. According to the ANSI C standard, a macro name has to be removed before it can be redefined.

Q Why do you need the #endif directive?

A The #endif directive is used with an #if, #ifdef, or #ifndef directive because statements under the control of a conditional preprocessor directive are not enclosed in braces ({ and }). Therefore, #endif must be employed to mark the end of the block of statements.

Q Can the conditional expression following the #if directive be an arithmetic expression?

A Yes. The conditional expression evaluated by the #if directive can be an arithmetic expression. If the expression returns a nonzero value, the code between the #if directive and the next nearest directive are included for compilation. Otherwise, the code is skipped.

Workshop

To help solidify your understanding of this hour's lesson, you are encouraged to answer the quiz questions and finish the exercises provided in the Workshop before you move to the next lesson. The answers and hints to the questions and exercises are given in Appendix E, "Answers to Quiz Questions and Exercises."

Quiz

1. What's wrong with the following macro definition?

   ```
   #define  ONE   1;
   ```

2. What is the final value assigned to result after the assignment statement is executed?

   ```
   #define ONE       1
   #define NINE       9
   #define EXPRESS    ONE + NINE
   result = EXPRESS * NINE;
   ```

3. What message will be printed out from the following code segment?

```
#define MACRO_NAME  0
#if MACRO_NAME
    printf("Under #if.\n");
#else
    printf("Under #else.\n");
#endif
```

4. What message will be printed out from the following code segment?

```
#define MACRO_NAME  0
#ifdef MACRO_NAME
    printf("Under #ifdef.\n");
#endif
#ifndef MACRO_NAME
    printf("Under #ifndef.\n");
#endif
```

Exercises

1. In Hour 18, "More Data Types and Functions," you learned how to define enum data. Rewrite the program in Listing 18.1 with the #define directive.

2. Define a macro name that can multiply two arguments. Write a program to calculate the multiplication of 2 and 3 with the help of the macro. Print out the result of the program.

3. Rewrite the program in Listing 23.2 with the #if, #elif, and #else directives.

4. Rewrite the program in Listing 23.3 with nested #if directives.

23

Hour 24

What You Can Do Now

It's not what you know, but what you can.

—*A. Alekhine*

Congratulations! You're now in the last chapter of this book. You just need to spend one more hour to complete your 24-hour journey. In this lesson you'll learn more about the C language from the following topics:

☐ Programming style

☐ Modular programming

☐ Debugging

Also, a brief review of what you've learned from this book is included in this lesson. Before we start to cover these topics, let's have a look at the last example in this book.

Creating a Linked List

In this section, I'm going to build functions that can create a linked list, and add items to or delete items from that linked list. I save those functions into a source file (that is, a module; refer to the section "Modular Programming" in this lesson). In addition, I will set up an interface between the module file and the user. In other words, the user can call one of the functions saved in the module via the interface. The interface is invoked in the main() function that is saved in another source file. I will put data declarations and function prototypes in a separate header file.

A *linked list* is a chain of nodes (or elements). Each node consists of data items and a pointer that points to the next node in the list. A linked list with N nodes is shown in Figure 24.1.

As you can see from Figure 24.1, the first node in the list is pointed to by another pointer that is a start pointer for the list. The pointer in the last (*N*th) node is a null pointer.

Figure 24.1.

A linked list with N nodes.

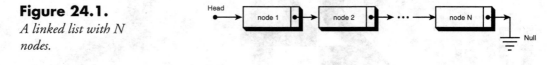

The linked list I'm going to build is a very simple one, in which each element contains only two items: student name and ID number. Listing 24.1 contains the module program, which is saved in the source file named 24L01.c.

Listing 24.1. Putting cohesive functions in the module program.

TYPE

```
1:   /* 24L01.c: A module file */
2:   #include "24L02.h"
3:
4:   static NODE *head_ptr = NULL;
5:
6:   /**
7:    ** main_interface()
8:    **/
9:   void main_interface(int ch)
10:  {
11:     switch (ch){
12:       case 'a':
13:          list_node_add();
14:          break;
15:       case 'd':
16:          if (!list_node_delete())
17:             list_node_print();
18:          break;
19:       case 'p':
20:          list_node_print();
21:          break;
22:       default:
23:          break;
24:     }
25:  }
26:  /**
```

24

```
27:   ** list_node_create()
28:   **/
29: NODE *list_node_create(void)
30: {
31:    NODE *ptr;
32:
33:    if ((ptr=(NODE *)malloc(sizeof(NODE))) == NULL)
34:       ErrorExit("malloc() failed.\n");
35:
36:    ptr->next_ptr = NULL;  /* set the next pointer to NULL */
37:    ptr->id = 0; /* initialization */
38:    return ptr;
39: }
40:
41: /**
42:   ** list_node_add()
43:   **/
44: void list_node_add(void)
45: {
46:    NODE *new_ptr, *ptr;
47:
48:    new_ptr = list_node_create();
49:    printf("Enter the student name and ID: ");
50:    scanf("%s%ld", new_ptr->name, &new_ptr->id);
51:
52:    if (head_ptr == NULL){
53:       head_ptr = new_ptr;
54:    } else {
55:       /* find the last node in the list */
56:       for (ptr=head_ptr;
57:            ptr->next_ptr != NULL;
58:            ptr=ptr->next_ptr)
59:          ; /* doing nothing here */
60:       /* link to the last node */
61:       ptr->next_ptr = new_ptr;
62:    }
63: }
64: /**
65:   ** list_node_delete()
66:   **/
67: int list_node_delete(void)
68: {
69:    NODE *ptr, *ptr_saved;
70:    unsigned long id;
71:    int deleted = 0;
72:    int reval = 0;
73:
74:    if (head_ptr == NULL){
75:       printf("Sorry, nothing to delete.\n");
76:       reval = 1;
77:    } else {
78:       printf("Enter the student ID: ");
79:       scanf("%ld", &id);
80:
81:       if (head_ptr->id == id){
82:          ptr_saved = head_ptr->next_ptr;
```

continues

Listing 24.1. continued

```
83:              free(head_ptr);
84:              head_ptr = ptr_saved;
85:              if (head_ptr == NULL){
86:                  printf("All nodes have been deleted.\n");
87:                  reval = 1;
88:              }
89:          } else {
90:              for (ptr=head_ptr;
91:                   ptr->next_ptr != NULL;
92:                   ptr=ptr->next_ptr){
93:                  if (ptr->next_ptr->id == id){
94:                      ptr_saved = ptr->next_ptr->next_ptr;
95:                      free(ptr->next_ptr);
96:                      ptr->next_ptr = ptr_saved;
97:                      deleted = 1;
98:                      break;
99:                  }
100:             }
101:             if (!deleted){
102:                 printf("Can not find the student ID.\n");
103:             }
104:         }
105:     }
106:     return reval;
107: }
108: /**
109:  ** list_node_print()
110:  **/
111: void list_node_print(void)
112: {
113:     NODE *ptr;
114:
115:     if (head_ptr == NULL){
116:         printf("Nothing to display.\n");
117:     } else {
118:         printf("The content of the linked list:\n");
119:         for (ptr = head_ptr;
120:              ptr->next_ptr != NULL;
121:              ptr = ptr->next_ptr){
122:             printf("%s:%d -> ",
123:                 ptr->name,
124:                 ptr->id);
125:         }
126:         printf("%s:%d ->¦",
127:             ptr->name,
128:             ptr->id);
129:         printf("\n");
130:     }
131: }
132: /**
133:  ** list_node_free()
134:  **/
135: void list_node_free()
136: {
```

```
137:     NODE *ptr, *ptr_saved;
138:
139:     for (ptr=head_ptr; ptr != NULL; ){
140:        ptr_saved = ptr->next_ptr;
141:        free(ptr);
142:        ptr = ptr_saved;
143:     }
144:     free(ptr);
145: }
146: /**
147:  ** ErrorExit()
148:  **/
149: void ErrorExit(char *str)
150: {
151:     printf("%s\n", str);
152:     exit(ERR_FLAG);
153: }
```

There is no direct output from the module program in Listing 24.1.

ANALYSIS The purpose of the program in Listing 24.1 is to provide a module program that contains all cohesive functions for linked list creation, node addition, and node reduction. Figure 24.2 demonstrates the tasks performed by functions, such as list_node_create(), list_node_add(), and list_node_delete(), from the program.

Figure 24.2.

Use functions defined in 24L01.c *(refer to the following paragraphs for explanation).*

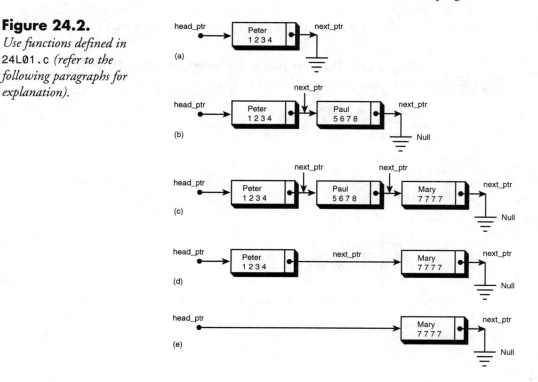

As you can see in Figure 24.2 (a), the first linked list node is created by calling the list_node_create() function, and the data items are added with the help of the list_node_add() function. Also, the node is pointed to by the head_ptr pointer. Here Peter is the student name; 1234 is his ID number. Because there are no more nodes linked, the next_ptr pointer of the first node is set to be null.

In Figure 24.2 (b), another node is added to the linked list, with Paul as the student name and 5678 as the ID number. Note that the next_ptr pointer of the first node is reset to point to the second node, while the next_ptr pointer of the second node is set to be null.

Likewise, in Figure 24.2 (c), the third node is added to the linked list. The next_ptr pointer of the third node is a null pointer. The pointer in the second node is reset to point to the third node.

If I want to delete one of the nodes, I can call the list_node_delete() function. As shown in Figure 24.2 (d), the second node is deleted, so the pointer of the first node has to be reset to point to the former third node that contains the student name Mary and her ID number, 7777.

In Figure 24.2 (e), the first node is deleted by applying the list_node_delete() function again. There is only one node left in the linked list. The head_ptr pointer has to be reset to point to the last node.

The header file, 24L02.h, included in the module program 24L01.c, is shown in Listing 24.2. (The header file is also included by the driver program in Listing 24.3.)

TYPE Listing 24.2. Putting data declarations and function prototypes into the header file.

```
1:  /* lnk_list.h: the header file */
2:  #include <stdio.h>
3:  #include <stdlib.h>
4:
5:  #ifndef LNK_LIST_H
6:  #define LNK_LIST_H
7:  #define ERR_FLAG  1
8:  #define MAX_LEN   16
9:
10: struct lnk_list_struct
11: {
12:     char name[MAX_LEN];
13:     unsigned long id;
14:     struct lnk_list_struct *next_ptr;
15: };
16:
17: typedef struct lnk_list_struct NODE;
18:
19: NODE *list_node_create(void);
20: void list_node_add(void);
```

24

```
21:  int list_node_delete(void);
22:  void list_node_print(void);
23:  void list_node_free(void);
24:  void ErrorExit(char *);
25:  void main_interface(int);
26:
27:  #endif /* for LNK_LIST_H */
```

There is no direct output from the program in Listing 24.2.

ANALYSIS   The purpose of the program in Listing 24.2 is to declare a structure with the tag name of lnk_list_struct in lines 10–15, and define a new variable name, of the structure NODE, in line 17.

The prototypes of the functions defined in the module program in Listing 24.1, such as list_node_create(), list_node_add(), and list_node_delete(), are listed in lines 19–25.

Note that the #ifndef and #endif preprocessor directives are used in lines 5 and 27. The declarations and definitions located between the two directives are compiled only if the macro name LNK_LIST_H has not been defined. Also, line 6 defines the macro name if it's not been defined. It's a good idea to put the #ifndef and #endif directives in a header file so as to avoid cross-inclusions when the header file is included by more than one source file. In this case, the declarations and definitions in the 24L02.h header file will not be included more than one time.

The module program in Listing 24.3 provides an interface that the user can use to call the functions saved in the source file (24L01.c).

TYPE   **Listing 24.3. Calling functions saved in the module file.**

```
1:  /* 24L03.c:  The driver file */
2:  #include "24L02.h"     /* include header file */
3:
4:  main(void)
5:  {
6:     int ch;
7:
8:     printf("Enter a for adding, d for deleting,\n");
9:     printf("p for displaying, and q for exit:\n");
10:    while ((ch=getchar()) != 'q'){
11:       main_interface(ch);   /* process input from the user */
12:    }
13:
14:    list_node_free();
15:    printf("\nBye!\n");
16:
17:    return 0;
18: }
```

I compile the source files, 24L01.c and 24L03.c, separately with Microsoft Visual C++, and then link their object files and C library functions together to produce a single executable program called 24L03.exe. I have the following output shown on the screen after I run the executable 24L03.exe, and enter or delete several student names and their ID numbers (the bold characters or numbers in the output section are what I entered from the keyboard):

```
C:\app>24L03
Enter a for adding, d for deleting,
p for displaying, and q for exit:
a
Enter the student name and ID: Peter 1234
a
Enter the student name and ID: Paul 5678
a
Enter the student name and ID: Mary 7777
p
The content of the linked list:
Peter:1234 -> Paul:5678 -> Mary:7777 ->¦
d
Enter the student ID: 1234
The content of the linked list:
Paul:5678 -> Mary:7777 ->¦
d
Enter the student ID: 5678
The content of the linked list:
Mary:7777 ->¦
d
Enter the student ID: 7777
All nodes have been deleted.
q

Bye!
C:\app>
```

ANALYSIS   The purpose of the program in Listing 24.3 is to provide the user with an interface. The functions, such as list_node_create(), list_node_add(), and list_node_delete(), can be invoked through the interface. Also, the main() function is located inside the program of Listing 24.3.

The content of a linked list node can be printed out in the format of

name:id ->

The following is an example:

Peter:1234 -> Paul:5678 -> Mary:7777 ->¦

Here the sign ¦ is used to indicate that the pointer of the last node is a null pointer.

Figure 24.3 shows the relationship among the 24L01.c, 24L02.h, and 24L03.c files.

To learn to compile separate source files and link their object files together to make a single executable program, you need to check the technical reference from your C compiler vendor.

Figure 24.3.

The relationship among the `24L01.c`, `24L02.h`, *and* `24L03.c` *files.*

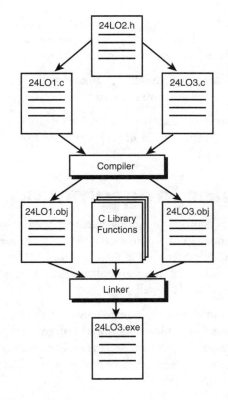

Programming Style

In this section, I'd like to briefly highlight some points that will help you write clean programs that can easily be read, understood, and maintained.

First, make sure the variable or function names in your program describe the meanings of the variables or tasks of the functions precisely and concisely.

Put comments into your code so that you or the other readers can have clues as to what your code is doing, or at least what the code intends to do, but might do incorrectly.

Whenever possible, keep using local variables, not global variables. Try to avoid sharing global data among functions; instead, pass the shared data as arguments to functions.

You should be careful when using C operators, especially the assignment operator (=) and the conditional operator (==), because misuse of these two operators can lead to an unexpected result and make the debugging very difficult.

Avoid using the goto statement; instead, use other control flow statements whenever needed.

Use named constants in your program, instead of numeric constants, because named constants can make your program more readable, and you will have to go to only one place to update the values of constants.

You should put parentheses around each constant expression or argument defined by a preprocessor directive to avoid side effects.

Also, you should set up a reasonable rule for spacing and indentation so that you can follow the rule consistently in all the programs you write. The rule should help make your programs easy to read.

Modular Programming

It's not a good programming practice to try to solve a complex problem with a single function. The proper way to approach it is to break the problem into several smaller and simpler pieces that can be understood in more details, and then start to define and build functions to solve those smaller and simpler problems. Keep in mind that each of your functions should do only one task, but do it well.

As your program continues to grow, you should consider breaking it into several source files, with each source file containing a small group of cohesive functions. Such source files are also called *modules*. Put data declarations and function prototypes into header files so that any changes to the declarations or prototypes can be automatically signified to all source files that include the header file.

For instance, in the section "Creating a Linked List," all functions that can be used to create a linked list and add or delete a node are put into the same module (24L01.c). Data structure and variable declarations, and function prototypes are saved into a header file (24L02.h). The main() function and the interface are saved into another module (24L03.c).

You can use a software-engineering technique known as *information hiding* to reduce the complexity of programming. Simply speaking, information hiding requires a module to withhold information from other modules unless it's necessary.

The C compiler enables you to compile and debug different source files separately. In this way, you can focus on one source file at a time, and complete the compiling before you move to the next one. With the separate compilation, you can compile only those source files that have been changed and leave the source files that have already been compiled and debugged unattached.

If you're interested in knowing more about software engineering, study Ian Sommerville's classic book, *Software Engineering*, which is on the list of recommended books at the end of this lesson.

Debugging

I've mentioned debugging several times in this lesson. What is a bug, anyway?

A *bug* in this context refers to any erroneous behavior of a computer system or a software program. *Debugging* means finding bugs and fixing them. Please be aware that no computer system or software program is immune to bugs. Programmers, like you and I, make bugs, because we're human beings.

When you're debugging your program, learn how to isolate the erroneous behavior performed by your program. Many C compilers provide built-in debuggers that you can use. Also, there are quite a few debugging tools available from third-party software vendors.

As has been said, debugging requires patience, ingenuity, and experience. I recommend that you read a good book that will teach you all the techniques of debugging; in fact, I recommend one in the list of the books in the next section.

A Brief Review

The following subsections provide you with a brief review of the basics of the C language. The review is a summary that you will find useful to brush up on what you've learned in the previous hours.

C Keywords

In C, certain words have been reserved. These reserved words, called C *keywords*, have special meaning in the C language. The following are the C keywords:

auto	int
break	long
case	register
char	return
const	short
continue	signed
default	sizeof
do	static
double	struct
else	switch
enum	typedef
extern	union
float	unsigned
for	void
goto	volatile
if	while

Operators

Operators can help you manipulate data. C provides you with a rich set of operators. Table 24.1 contains a list of the operators used in C.

Table 24.1. The operators in C.

Operator	Description
=	Assignment operator
+=	Addition assignment operator
-=	Subtraction assignment operator
*=	Multiplication assignment operator
/=	Division assignment operator
%=	Remainder assignment operator
-	Unary minus operator
++	Increment operator
--	Decrement operator
==	Equal to
!=	Not equal to
>	Greater than
<	Less than
>=	Greater or equal to
<=	Less or equal to
sizeof	Size-of operator
&&	Logical AND operator
¦¦	Logical OR operator
!	Logical negation operator
&	Bitwise AND operator
¦	Bitwise OR operator
^	Bitwise exclusive OR (XOR) operator
~	Bitwise complement operator
>>	Right shift operator
<<	Left shift operator
?:	Conditional operator

Constants

Constants are elements whose values in the program do not change. In C, there are several different types of constants.

Integer Constants

Integer constants are decimal numbers. You can suffix an integer constant with u or U to specify that the constant is of the unsigned data type. An integer constant suffixed with l or L is a long int constant.

An integer constant is prefixed with a 0 (zero) to indicate that the constant is in the octal format. If an integer constant is prefixed with 0X or 0x, the constant is a hexadecimal number.

Character Constants

A character constant is a character enclosed by single quotes. For instance, 'C' is a character constant.

In C, there are several character constants that represent certain special characters. (See Table 24.2.)

Table 24.2. Special characters in C.

Character	Meaning
\a	Audible alert
\b	Backspace
\f	Form feed
\n	New line
\r	Carriage return
\t	Horizontal tab
\v	Vertical tab
\"	Double quote
\'	Single quote
\0	Null
\\	Backslash
\N	Octal constant (Here N is an octal constant.)
\xN	Hexadecimal constant (Here N is a hexadecimal constant.)

Floating-Point Constants

Floating-point constants are decimal numbers that can be suffixed with f, F, l, or L to specify float or long double. A floating-point constant without a suffix is of the double data type by default. For instance, the following statements declare and initialize a `float` variable (`flt_num`) and a `double` variable (`db_num`):

```
float   flt_num = 1234.56f;
double  db_num = 1234.56;
```

A floating-point can also be represented in scientific notation.

String Constants

A *string constant* is a sequence of characters enclosed by double quotes. For instance, `"This is a string constant."` is a string constant. Note that the double quotes are not part of the content of the string. Also, the C compiler automatically adds a null character (`\0`) at the end of a string constant to indicate the end of the string.

Data Types

The basic *data types* provided by the C language are `char`, `int`, `float`, and `double`. In addition, there are array, `enum`, `struct`, and `union` data types which you can declare and use in your C programs.

The general form to define a list of variables with a specified data type is

```
data_type    variable_name_list;
```

Here `data_type` can be one of the keywords of the data types. `variable_name_list` represents a list of variable names separated by commas.

The Array Data Type

An *array* is a collection of variables that are of the same data type. The following is the general form to declare an array:

```
data-type   array-name[array-size];
```

Here `data-type` is the type specifier that indicates the data type of the array elements. `array-name` is the name of the declared array. `array-size` defines how many elements the array can contain. Note that the brackets (`[` and `]`) are required in declaring an array. The pair of `[` and `]` is also called the *array subscript operator*.

In addition, C supports multidimensional arrays.

The `enum` Data Type

`enum` is a short name for *enumerated*. The enumerated data type is used to declare named integer constants. The general form of the `enum` data type declaration is

```
enum tag_name {enumeration_list} variable_list;
```

Here `tag_name` is the name of the enumeration. `variable_list` gives a list of variable names that are of the enum data type. Both `tag_name` and `variable_list` are optional. `enumeration_list` contains defined enumerated names that are used to represent integer constants. Names represented by `variable_list` or `enumeration_list` are separated by commas.

The `struct` Data Type

In C, a structure collects different data items in such a way that they can be referenced as a single unit. The general form to declare a structure is

```
struct struct_tag {
    data_type1 variable1;
    data_type2 variable2;
    data_type3 variable3;
    .
    .
    .
    };
```

Here `struct` is the keyword used in C to start a structure declaration. `struct_tag` is the tag name of the structure. `variable1` , `variable2`, and `variable3` are the members of the structure. Their data types are specified respectively by `data_type1`, `data_type2`, and `data_type3`. The declarations of the members have to be enclosed within the opening and closing braces (`{` and `}`) in the structure declaration, and a semicolon (`;`) has to be included at the end of the declaration.

The following is an example of a structure declaration:

```
struct automobile {
    int year;
    char model[8];
    int engine_power;
    float weight;
    };
```

Here `struct` is used to start a structure declaration. `automobile` is the tag name of the structure. In the example here, there are three types of variables: `char`, `int`, and `float`. The variables have their own names, such as `year`, `model`, `engine_power`, and `weight`. They are all members of the structure, and are declared within the braces (`{` and `}`).

The `union` Data Type

A *union* is a block of memory that is used to hold data items of different types. In C, a union is similar to a structure, except that data items saved in the union are overlaid in order to share the same memory location. The syntax for declaring a union is similar to the syntax for a structure. The general form to declare a union is

```
union union_tag {
    data_type1 variable1;
    data_type2 variable2;
    data_type3 variable3;
    .
    .
    .
    };
```

Here `union` is the keyword used in C to start a union declaration. `union_tag` is the tag name of the union. `variable1` , `variable2`, and `variable3` are the members of the union. Their data types are specified respectively by *data_type1*, *data_type2*, and *data_type3*. The union declaration is ended with a semicolon (;).

The following is an example of a union declaration:

```
union automobile {
    int year;
    char model[8];
    int engine_power;
    float weight;
};
```

Here union specifies the union data type. automobile is the tag name of the union. The variables, such as year, model, engine_power, and weight, are the members of the union and are declared within the braces ({ and }).

Defining New Type Names with typedef

You can create your own names for data types with the help of the typedef keyword in C, and use those names as synonyms for the data types. For instance, you can declare TWO_BYTE as a synonym for the int data type:

```
typedef  int  TWO_BYTE;
```

Then, you can use TWO_BYTE to declare integer variables like this,

```
TWO_BYTE i, j;
```

which is equivalent to

```
int i, j;
```

Remember that a typedef definition must be made before the synonym made in the definition is used in any declarations in your program.

Expressions and Statements

An *expression* is a combination of constants or variables that is used to denote computations.

For instance,

```
(2 + 3) * 10
```

is an expression that adds 2 and 3 first, and then multiplies the sum by 10.

In the C language, a *statement* is a complete instruction, ended with a semicolon. In many cases, you can turn an expression into a statement by simply adding a semicolon at the end of the expression.

A null statement is represented by an isolated semicolon.

A group of statements can form a *statement block* that starts with an opening brace ({) and ends with a closing brace (}). The C compiler treats a statement block as a single statement.

Control Flow Statements

In C, there is a set of control flow statements that can be divided into two categories: looping and conditional branching.

The `for`, `while`, **and** `do-while` **Loops**

The general form of the `for` statement is

```
for (expression1; expression2; expression3) {
   statement1;
   statement2;
      .
      .
      .
}
```

The `for` statement first evaluates *expression1*, which is usually an expression that initializes one or more variables. The second expression, *expression2*, is the conditional part that is evaluated and tested by the `for` statement for each looping. If *expression2* returns a nonzero value, the statements within the braces, such as *statement1* and *statement2*, are executed. Usually, the nonzero value is 1 (one). If *expression2* returns 0 (zero), the looping is stopped and the execution of the `for` statement is finished. The third expression in the `for` statement, *expression3*, is evaluated after each looping before the statement goes back to test *expression2* again.

The following `for` statement makes an infinite loop:

```
for ( ; ; ){
   /* statement block */
}
```

The general form of the `while` statement is

```
while (expression) {
   statement1;
   statement2;
      .
      .
      .
}
```

Here *expression* is the field of the expression in the `while` statement. The expression is evaluated first. If it returns a nonzero value, the looping continues; that is, the statements inside the statement block, such as *statement1* and *statement2*, are executed. After the execution, the expression is evaluated again. Then the statements are executed one more time if the expression still returns a nonzero value. The process is repeated over and over until the expression returns zero.

You can also make a `while` loop infinite by putting 1 (one) in the expression field like this:

```
while (1) {
   /* statement block */
}
```

The general form for the `do-while` statement is

```
do {
    statement1;
    statement2;
         .
         .
         .
} while (expression);
```

Here *expression* is the field for the expression that is evaluated in order to determine whether the statements inside the statement block are executed one more time. If the expression returns a nonzero value, the `do-while` loop continues; otherwise, the looping stops. Note that the `do-while` statement ends with a semicolon, which is an important distinction. The statements controlled by the `do-while` statement are executed at least once before the expression is evaluated. Note that a `do-while` loop ends with a semicolon (;).

Conditional Branching

The `if`, `if-else`, `switch`, `break`, `continue`, and `goto` statements fall into the conditional branching category.

The general form of the `if` statement is

```
if (expression) {
    statement1;
    statement2;
         .
         .
         .
}
```

Here *expression* is the conditional criterion. If *expression* is logical TRUE (that is, nonzero), the statements inside the braces ({ and }), such as *statement1* and *statement2*, are executed. If *expression* is logical FALSE (0), the statements are skipped.

As an expansion of the `if` statement, the `if-else` statement has the following form:

```
if (expression) {
    statement1;
    statement2;
         .
         .
         .
}
else {
    statement_A;
    statement_B;
         .
         .
         .
}
```

Here if *expression* is logical TRUE, the statements controlled by if, including *statement1* and *statement2*, are executed. Otherwise, the statements, such as *statement_A* and *statement_B*, inside the statement block following the else keyword are executed, if *expression* is logical FALSE.

The general form of the switch statement is

```
switch (expression) {
   case expression1:
       statement1;
   case expression2:
       statement2;
   .
   .
   .
   default:
       statement-default;
}
```

Here the conditional expression, *expression*, is evaluated first. If the return value of *expression* is equal to the constant expression *expression1*, then execution begins at the statement *statement1*. If the value of *expression* is the same as the value of *expression2*, execution then begins at *statement2*. If, however, the value of *expression* is not equal to any values of the constant expressions labeled by the case keyword, the statement, *statement-default*, following the default keyword is executed.

You can add a break statement at the end of the statement list following each case label if you want to exit the switch construct after the statements within a selected case have been executed.

Also, the break statement can be used to break an infinite loop.

There are times when you want to stay in a loop but skip over some of the statements within the loop. To do this, you can use the continue statement provided by C.

The following gives the general form of the goto statement:

```
label-name:
   statement1;
   statement2;
   .
   .
   .
   goto  label-name;
```

Here *label-name* is a label name that tells the goto statement where to jump. You have to place *label-name* in two places: at the place where the goto statement is going to jump and at the place following the goto keyword. Also, the place for the goto statement to jump to can appear either before or after the statement. Note that a colon (:) must follow the label name at the place where the goto statement will jump to.

Pointers

A *pointer* is a variable whose value is used to point to another variable. The general form of a pointer declaration is

```
data-type   *pointer-name;
```

Here `data-type` specifies the type of data to which the pointer points. `pointer-name` is the name of the pointer variable, which can be any valid variable name in C. When the compiler sees the asterisk (*) prefixed to the variable name in the declaration, it makes a note in its symbol table so that the variable can be used as a pointer.

Usually, the address associated with a variable name is called the *left value* of the variable. When a variable is assigned with a value, the value is stored in the reserved memory location of the variable as the content. The content is also called the *right value* of the variable.

A pointer is said to be a *null pointer* when its right value is 0. Remember that a null pointer can never point to valid data.

The dereference operator (*) is a unary operator that requires only one operand. For instance, the `*ptr_name` expression returns the value pointed to by the pointer variable `ptr_name`, where `ptr_name` can be any valid variable name in C.

The `&` operator is called the *address-of operator* because it can return the address (that is, left value) of a variable.

Several pointers can point to the same location of a variable in the memory. In C, you can move the position of a pointer by adding or subtracting integers to or from the pointer.

Note that for pointers of different data types, the integers added to or subtracted from the pointers have different scalar sizes.

Pointing to Objects

You can access an element in an array by using a pointer. For instance, given an array, `an_array`, and a pointer, `ptr_array`, if `an_array` and `ptr_array` are of the same data type, and `ptr_array` is assigned with the start address of the array like this:

```
ptr_array = an_array;
```

the expression

```
an_array[n]
```

is equivalent to the expression

```
*(ptr_array + n)
```

Here `n` is a subscript number in the array.

24

In many cases, it's useful to declare an array of pointers and access the contents pointed to by the array through dereferencing each pointer. For instance, the following declaration declares an int array of pointers:

```
int *ptr_int[3];
```

In other words, the variable ptr_int is a three-element array of pointers with the int type.

Also, you can define a pointer of struct and refer to an item in the structure via the pointer. For example, given the following structure declaration:

```
struct computer {
   float cost;
   int year;
   int cpu_speed;
   char cpu_type[16];
};
```

a pointer can be defined like this:

```
struct computer *ptr_s;
```

Then, the items in the structure can be accessed by dereferencing the pointer. For instance, to assign the value of 1997 to the int variable year in the computer structure, you can have the following assignment statement:

```
(*ptr_s).year = 1997;
```

Or, you can use the arrow operator (->) for the assignment, like this:

```
ptr_s->year = 1997;
```

Note that the arrow operator (->) is commonly used to reference a structure member with a pointer.

Functions

Functions are the building blocks of C programs. Besides the standard C library functions, you can also use some other functions made by you or by another programmer in your C program. The opening brace ({) signifies the start of a function body, while (}), the closing brace, marks the end of the function body.

According to the ANSI standard, the *declaration* of a variable or function specifies the interpretation and attributes of a set of identifiers. The *definition*, on the other hand, requires the C compiler to reserve storage for a variable or function named by an identifier.

In fact, a variable declaration is a definition. But the same is not true for functions. A *function declaration* alludes to a function that is defined elsewhere, and specifies what kind of value returned by the function. A *function definition* defines what the function does, as well as the number and type of arguments passed to the function.

With the ANSI standard, the number and types of arguments passed to a function are allowed to be added into the function declaration. The number and types of argument are called the *function prototype*.

The general form of a function declaration, including its prototype, is as follows:

```
data_type_specifier  function_name(
      data_type_specifier argument_name1,
      data_type_specifier argument_name2,
      data_type_specifier argument_name3,
      .
      .
      .
      data_type_specifier argument_nameN,
);
```

Here `data_type_specifier` determines the type of the return value made by the function or specifies the data types of arguments, such as `argument_name1`, `argument_name2`, `argument_name3`, and `argument_nameN`, passed to the function with the name of `function_name`.

The purpose of using a function prototype is to help the compiler to check whether the data types of arguments passed to a function match what the function expects. The compiler issues an error message if the data types do not match. The `void` data type is needed in the declaration of a function that takes no argument.

To declare a function that takes a variable number of arguments, you have to specify at least the first argument and use the ellipsis (. . .) to represent the rest of the arguments passed to the function.

A function call is an expression that can be used as a single statement or within other expressions or statements.

It's more efficient to pass the address of an argument, instead of its copy, to a function so that the function can access and manipulate the original value of the argument. Therefore, it's a good idea to pass the name of a pointer, which points to an array, as an argument to a function, instead of the array elements themselves.

You can also call a function via a pointer that holds the address of the function.

Input and Output (I/O)

In C, a *file* refers to a disk file, a terminal, a printer, or a tape drive. In other words, a file represents a concrete device with which you want to exchange information. A *stream*, on the other hand, is a series of bytes through which you read or write data to a file. Unlike a file, a stream is device-independent. All streams have the same behavior.

In addition, there are three file streams that are pre-opened for you:

- ☐ `stdin`—The standard input for reading.
- ☐ `stdout`—The standard output for writing.

24

☐ stderr—The standard error for writing error message.

Usually, the standard input stdin links to the keyboard, while the standard output stdout and the standard error stderr point to the screen. Also, many operating systems allow you to redirect these file streams.

By default, all I/O streams are buffered. The buffered I/O is also called the *high-level I/O.*

The FILE structure is the file control structure defined in the header file stdio.h. A pointer of type FILE is called a *file pointer* and references a disk file. A file pointer is used by a stream to conduct the operation of the I/O functions. For instance, the following defines a file pointer called fptr:

FILE *fptr;

In the FILE structure, there is a member, called the *file position indicator*, that points to the position in a file where data will be read from or written to.

The C language provides a set of rich library functions to perform I/O operations. Those functions can read or write any types of data to files. Among them, fopen(), fclose(), fgetc(), fputc(), fgets(), fputs(), fread(), fwrite(), feof(), fscanf(), fprintf(), fseek(), ftell(), rewind(), and freopen() have been introduced in this book.

The C Preprocessor

The *C preprocessor* is not part of the C compiler. The C preprocessor runs before the compiler. During preprocessing, all occurrences of a macro name are replaced by the macro body that is associated with the macro name. Note that a macro statement ends with a newline character, not a semicolon.

The C preprocessor also enables you to include additional source files to the program or compile sections of C code conditionally.

The #define directive tells the preprocessor to replace every occurrence of a macro name defined by the directive with a macro body that is associated with the macro name. You can specify one or more arguments to a macro name defined by the #define directive.

The #undef directive is used to remove the definition of a macro name that has been previously defined.

The #ifdef directive controls whether a given group of statements is to be included as part of the program. The #ifndef directive is a mirror directive to the #ifdef directive; it enables you to define code that is to be included when a particular macro name is not defined.

The #if, #elif, and #else directives enable you to filter out portions of code to compile. #endif is used to mark the end of an #ifdef, #ifndef, or #if block because the statements under the control of these preprocessor directives are not enclosed in braces.

24

The Road Ahead...

I believe that you can start to run now after you learn to walk in the world of the C language through this book. Although you're on your own, you're not alone. You can revisit this book whenever you feel like it. Besides, the following books, which I recommend to you, can send you in the right direction to continue your journey in the C world:

The C Programming Language
by Brian Kernighan and Dennis Ritchie, published by Prentice Hall

C Interfaces and Implementations
by David Hanson, published by Addison-Wesley

Practical C Programming
by Steve Oualline, published by O'Reilly & Associates, Inc.

No Bugs!—Delivering Error-Free Code in C and C++
by David Thielen, published by Addison-Wesley

Software Engineering
by Ian Sommerville, published by Addison-Wesley

The Mythical Man-Month: Essays on Software Engineering
by F. P. Brooks, Jr., published by Addison-Wesley

Summary

Before you close this book, I'd like to thank you for your patience and the effort you have put into learning the basics of the C language in the past 24 hours. Now, it's your turn to apply what you've learned from this book to solving the problems in the real world. Good luck!

INDEX*

Symbols

---

*Due to printing constraints, the appendixes appear on the CD-ROM rather than in the printed book. This index does encompass the material covered in the appendixes as indicated when you see *(CD-ROM)* following an entry's page number. Please see the CD for information on that topic.

MACMILLAN COMPUTER PUBLISHING USA

A VIACOM COMPANY

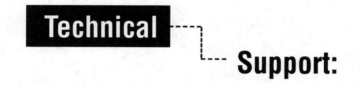

Technical ---- Support:

Teach Yourself C++ in 24 Hours

Jesse Liberty

Teach Yourself C++ in 24 Hours follows the step-by-step approach of the *Teach Yourself* series to show readers C++ basics in a quick, easy-to-learn format. Because this book doesn't focus on any one compiler, readers learn to program in C++ using the compiler of their choice.

Price: $24.99 USA/$35.95 CDN   User level: Beginning—Intermediate

ISBN: 0-672-31067-8   480 pages

UPC: 7-52063-10678-5

Teach Yourself C++ in 21 Days, Second Edition

Jesse Liberty

The proven, best-selling elements of the *Teach Yourself* series and the immense popularity of the C++ programming language make *Teach Yourself C++ in 21 Days, Second Edition* the most efficient way to learn programming with C++. And because it doesn't focus on any one particular compiler, it allows the reader to jump from one compiler to another.

Price: $29.99 USA/$42.95 CDN   User level: Beginning—Intermediate

ISBN: 0-672-31070-8   756 pages

UPC: 7-52063-10708-9

Visual C++ 5 Unleashed, Second Edition

Viktor Toth

This is the perfect book for advanced Visual C++ programmers. Its 1,100 pages explore the most advanced topics while its enclosed CD-ROM allows the user to quickly learn by working through the programs in the book. It not only covers Visual C++ 5 and its capabilities but also teaches LAN programming, OLE, DLLs, OLE automation, and how to update old programs to the new version of Visual C++.

Price: $49.99 USA/$70.95 CDN   User level: Accomplished—Expert

ISBN: 0-672-31013-9   1,100 pages

UPC: 7-52063-10139-1

Teach Yourself Visual Basic 5 in 21 Days, Fourth Edition

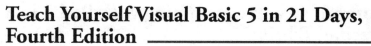

Nathan Gurewich & Ori Gurewich

Using a logical, easy-to-follow approach, this international best-seller teaches readers the fundamentals of developing programs. It starts with the basics of writing a program and then moves on to adding voice, music, sound, and graphics.

Price: $29.99 USA/$42.95 CDN   User level: New—Casual

ISBN: 0-672-30978-5   800 pages

UPC: 7-52063-09785-4

Visual Basic 5 Developer's Guide

Anthony T. Mann

Visual Basic 5 Developer's Guide takes the programmer with a basic knowledge of Visual Basic programming to a higher skill level. Readers learn how to exploit the new features of the latest version of Visual Basic, in addition to implementing Visual Basic in a network setting and in conjunction with other technologies and software.

Price: *$49.99 USA/$70.95 CDN*   User level: *Accomplished—Expert*

ISBN: *0-672-31048-1*   *1,000 pages*

UPC: *7-52063-10481-1*

Teach Yourself Visual Basic for Applications 5 in 21 Days, Third Edition

Matthew Harris

This book covers all fundamental aspects of this programming language and teaches novice programmers how to design, create, and debug macro programs written in the VBA programming language.

Price: *$39.99 USA/$56.95 CDN*   User level: *New—Casual*

ISBN: *0-672-31016-3*   *1,000 pages*

UPC: *7-52063-10163-6*

CGI Programming Unleashed

Dan Berlin, et al.

Readers of this book will learn to master CGI, a popular scripting language used to develop professional Web content. Unlike other titles on the subject, this book is devoted entirely to CGI and covers every aspect of this poular tool. It guides programmers through creating dynamic Web pages, designing shared workgroup applications, and implementing CGI-based commercial applications.

Price: *$49.99 USA/$70.95 CDN*   User level: *Advanced—Expert*

ISBN: *1-57521-151-3*   *620 pages*

UPC: *7-52063-11513-8*

Teach Yourself CGI Programming with Perl 5 in a Week, Second Edition

Eric Herrmann

Teach Yourself CGI Programming with Perl 5 in a Week, Second Edition is the follow-up to the best-seller, completely revised and updated to cover Perl 5 in greater detail. It includes complete coverage of Windows CGI and Perl QuickStart to bring the beginning programmer quickly up to speed.

Price: *$39.99 USA/$56.95 CDN*   User level: *Beginning—Intermediate*

ISBN: *1-57521-196-3*   *625 pages*

UPC: *7-52063-11963-1*

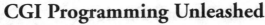

Add to Your Sams Library Today with the Best Books for Programming, Operating Systems, and New Technologies

The easiest way to order is to pick up the phone and call

1-800-428-5331

between 9:00 a.m. and 5:00 p.m. EST.

For faster service please have your credit card available.

ISBN	Quantity	Description of Item	Unit Cost	Total Cost
0-672-31067-8		Teach Yourself C++ in 24 Hours (book/CD-ROM)	$24.99	
0-672-31070-8		Teach Yourself C++ in 21 Days, Second Edition	$29.99	
0-672-31013-9		Visual C++ 5 Unleashed, Second Edition (book/CD-ROM)	$49.99	
0-672-30978-5		Teach Yourself Visual Basic 5 in 21 Days, Fourth Edition	$29.99	
0-672-31048-1		Visual Basic 5 Developer's Guide (book/CD-ROM)	$49.99	
0-672-31016-3		Teach Yourself Visual Basic for Applications in 21 Days, Third Edition	$39.99	
1-57521-151-3		CGI Programming Unleashed	$49.99	
1-57521-196-3		Teach Yourself CGI Programming with Perl 5 in a Week, Second Edition (book/CD-ROM)	$39.99	
		Shipping and Handling: See information below.		
		TOTAL		

Shipping and Handling: $4.00 for the first book, and $1.75 for each additional book. Floppy disk: add $1.75 for shipping and handling. If you need to have it now, we can ship product to you in 24 hours for an additional charge of approximately $18.00, and you will receive your item overnight or in two days. Overseas shipping and handling adds $2.00 per book and $8.00 for up to three disks. Prices subject to change. Call for availability and pricing information on latest editions.

201 W. 103rd Street, Indianapolis, Indiana 46290

1-800-428-5331 — Orders   1-800-835-3202 — Fax   1-800-858-7674 — Customer Service

Book ISBN 0-672-31068-6